BRIAN LANE was an expert in the field of true crime. He came to writing via fine art, theatre and experimental music and also spent a number of years with the United Nations in Geneva and Vienna. He founded The Murder Club in 1987 and compiled the formidable six-volume series of *Murder Club Guides to Great Britain*. He sadly died in 1999.

The Encyclopedia of Women Killers

Brian Lane

Magpie Books, London

Constable & Robinson Ltd
3 The Lanchesters
162 Fulham Palace Road
London W6 9ER

This edition published by Magpie Books,
an imprint of Constable & Robinson Ltd 2004

First published in the UK by Headline Book Publishing in 1994.

A copy of the British Library Cataloguing in
Publication Data is available from the British Library

ISBN 1-84119-850-1

Printed and bound in the EU

Contents

Introduction

There are few truly 'encyclopedic' works, and inevitably a book on the subject of women who kill can never claim to contain the records of *all* the women who have ever killed. To a great extent the selection is purely subjective, and emphasis has been placed on as wide a range of different *types* of crime as possible. For this reason method and motive have frequently proved a greater incentive to include a story than mere notoriety.

It is my considered conclusion that there are two broad compartments into which most women who kill can be placed. Those who *want* to kill and those who *do not*.

The celebrated writer on matters of true crime Miss F. Tennyson Jesse was the first to put forward the theory that all murders could be divided between just six fundamental motives. These were Gain, Jealousy, Revenge, Elimination, Lust and Conviction. In a recent study of twentieth-century homicide I was inclined to propose that a seventh category be added, that of Thrill. This was a response to certain modern-day, mostly American, killers who, though in some aspects resembling Lust killers, were not *motivated* by sexual gratification; or murders where, if sexual abuse does occur, it is secondary to the experience, or 'thrill'. Quite simply the *act* of killing is its own reward.

It is certainly true that in each of these seven categories we will encounter the female of the species, though their distribution by comparison with men is very different. Few of either gender have rivalled the Gain killings of Mary Ann Cotton, who through a long and successful career as a poisoner in the second half of the nineteenth century, is thought to have been responsible for as many as fifteen murders, mostly members of her own family; and although her body count was considerably lower, Mrs Jean Daddow's contract killing of her husband in 1991 was for an identical motive – money. However, this line of exploration has also emphasized one of the main differences in victim trait; for while the majority of homicides committed by men are directed at comparative strangers, women on the whole choose victims with whom they have an 'intimate' contact – husbands, lovers, children, sexual rivals, their charges if they are nurses our baby-minders. Women are rarely associated with fatal incidents resulting from drunken fights, sports rivalry, muggings and burglaries, so-called 'spontaneous killings'. When women *do* kill, it is commonly as a last resort, and the acts themselves are characterized by a desperate intensity of emotion. Which brings us to the second of our classic motives – Jealousy.

Even when it has some rational basis, jealousy can be the most destructive of forces, and though it most frequently rears its head in a marital or sexual context, rivalries can also occur within families, such as that between Mrs Styllou Christofi and her daughter-in-law Hella which led to the younger woman's untimely and savage death in 1954. But imagine the havoc wreaked by irrational, unfounded jealousy aimed towards a partner whose loyalty and fidelity are not in question. Charles Bolton put up with his wife Mildred's ceaseless accusations, fierce rows and physical violence for years with docile patience; it made no difference, in 1936 she killed him anyway, still convinced he was seeing other women. It is 'the woman scorned' though, who accounts for the largest number of homicides in the crime of passion category. Sad individuals like Betty Broderick who, after finally losing her home, her family and her husband to another woman shot them both dead in their beds. Or women like Jeanne Favre-Bulle, who left her family for a younger lover who then announced that he expected her to share his favours with another mistress. It was the type of *crime passionel* for which the French, with some justification, have become famous. Although Jeanne was found guilty of murder when she shot Léon Merle in 1930, the court decided that there were 'extenuating circumstances'. In passing, I would like to mention that although the staid English would never dream of using the word 'passion' any more often than absolutely necessary, the Homicide Act does allow the plea of diminished responsibility which, like the French *crime passionnel,* effectively turns a charge of murder into one of manslaughter on the grounds that the balance of the mind was disturbed at the time of the crime.

Revenge, too, plays its part in the crime of passion, adding another powerful motive to murder, and leading women like Henriette Caillaux to commit one of the most scandalous crimes of the century when in 1914 she shot dead the editor of France's leading newspaper *Le Figaro;* or sixteen-year-old Brenda Wiley, who in 1990 carried out a manic knife attack on her mother and brother in a fit of pique over a boyfriend.

The motive of Elimination is deceptively simple, because in a sense it is at the basis of most killings, the disposal of an unwanted spouse when the fatal triangle tightens its grip (as in the cases of Noeleen Hendley in England, Pamela Smart, America's 'Ice Princess', or Scotland's Sheila Garvie); or the disposal of a person for the purpose of inheritance or insurance, or simply to steal from them. These are motives which seem to be fairly evenly distributed between the genders throughout crime's history.

Women tend as a rule not to engage in Lust killings, partly because of physical restrictions and cultural expectations, and partly because men are a great deal more difficult to rape than women. Female Thrill killers are also very rare, though the case of the Australian Caroline Grills presents a woman who clearly enjoyed the power over life and death which poisoning gave her.

Killers by Conviction are represented by the psychotics, the ones who hear voices – almost totally a male preserve. An exception was the series of killings carried out by Suzan Bear and her husband for the alleged purpose of 'ridding the world of witches'. The Austrian 'Angel of Death', nurse Waltraud Wagner, claimed that she was sending her elderly patients 'to heaven', though it is clear that she too enjoyed the act of killing.

However, there are other sub-groupings of motive that do indeed attract almost exclusively women, and there are generally sociological reasons for it. For example, the female poisoner of the Victorian age has become a stereotype of Grand Guignol, but she owes her origin to very real problems. It was a time when arsenic was more easy to obtain than a legal separation, and the ruin and destitution which were the inevitable consequences of divorce for women were often worth the risk of the penalty for murder. Of course, women still kill husbands, but the kitchen knife is more common than rat poison and the killing more likely to be a response to extremes of violence than to a desperation at the endless repression of Victorian domestic expectations. Another recurrent problem of an earlier age was the lack of adequate methods of birth control, leading the lower classes to indulge, alarmingly frequently, in infanticide, and the wealthier classes to use the services of 'baby farmers' – which also often ended in death for the unlucky infant. The dreadful Mrs Dyer killed so many she lost count.

There are other categories of mainly female endeavour when it comes to murder; there are the servants who kill, such as Mrs Merrifield and Kate Webster in England and the Papin sisters in France. By her very description, the *femme fatale* is a lethal predator, in cases such as those of Gabrielle Bompard, Jean Lee and the notorious Russian Countess Tarnowska, leaving behind a trail of broken hearts, suicides and murders.

But no serious study of women who kill would be complete without discussion of what has become a serious social and legal problem by the late twentieth century; the so-called 'Battered Woman Syndrome', the woman who does not *want* to kill. It occurs at the stage where inter-personal violence, often over many years and escalating in frequency and severity, has reached a point where for some women the only way out of the nightmare is to remove the object of fear permanently. This is not to trivialize each individual's story – many are told in the book – but to lay the foundation for a unified legal viewpoint that takes account of a *history* of domestic violence, and that does not rely on the defence of Provocation or Self-Defence. The wide variation of treatment meted out to these female victims has ranged in recent years from suspended sentences to life imprisonment.

At present, in the instance of murder (unlike other crimes), Provocation is a legal defence that will result in a verdict of 'voluntary homicide' – where the defendant had intended to kill or 'otherwise had the mental element for murder'. A life sentence is never given for a provoked killing. There is, moreover, an implicit requirement to distinguish between homicide committed in 'hot blood', where there is no calculation before the act, and a killing in 'cold blood', where a deliberate decision is involved (called 'malice aforethought').

The problem in many cases that have recently come before the courts is that although a defendant has been 'provoked' in the moral sense of having suffered years of abuse, in legal terms they have calculatedly waited until a violent partner is asleep before killing (as in the case of Pam Sainsbury) or had made such preparations to kill that a deliberate decision could be proved (as in the case of Kiranjit Ahluwalia). For the same

technical reason ('deliberate decision') a plea of self-defence
would not be permissible.

As things stand at the moment, many forward-looking and
compassionate legal representatives are looking to the United
States, where some progress is being made in effecting just
such changes in the law as would permit a defence of 'battered
woman syndrome'. On 22 December 1990, twenty-five
inmates of Ohio's state prison received an early Christmas
present. Governor Richard F. Celeste granted clemency to the
twenty-five women who had been convicted of murdering the
men they said physically abused them. It was a move
guaranteed to arouse strong emotions. Not surprisingly
women's rights activists throughout the nation were highly
optimistic; equally unsurprisingly many members of the
judiciary were less enchanted.

In the first review since a historic decision was taken by the
state's Supreme Court earlier in the year (that a defence of
'battered woman syndrome' was legally valid), Governor
Celeste examined the records of more than one hundred cases
before deciding to commute the sentences of the twenty-five.
He explained: 'These women were entrapped physically and
emotionally. They were the victims of violence, repeated
violence. They loved these men even though they beat them
and frightened them. They were so emotionally entangled they
were incapable of walking away; if I thought they would be a
threat I wouldn't have commuted their sentences.'

Prosecutors were more apprehensive, fearing that the
Governor's action would encourage women to take murder as
the escape route from domestic abuse; in effect offering the
defence that being battered validated doing the battering. As
the President of the Ohio Prosecuting Attorneys' Association
expressed it: 'Now instead of going to the courts or getting a
divorce, these women will think "Maybe I'll kill him"; taking a
human life is not something we want to promote.' Others
feared that while some women would be able to substantiate a

defence of 'battered woman syndrome', there would always be: 'Some of these women making it up.' Governor Celeste, however, saw no such problems: 'I don't believe anyone in their right mind should take this as any licence to kill. Being battered is no guarantee of acquittal.' A sentiment no doubt endorsed by women's rights workers everywhere: 'This is a signal to the rest of the country that women will no longer permit themselves to be battered and abused by men . . . Women don't kill men unless they've been pushed to a point of desperation.'

And indeed it was taken as a signal by other parts of the country. Within days of the Ohio decision, the King County Coalition Against Domestic Violence based in Seattle asked the Governor of Washington to take similar action. Governor Gardner had already used his power of clemency to commute the sentence of a woman who had been physically abused, and he undertook to look at the cases of sixty-five women currently serving sentences in the state prison.

And so it can be seen that there is a very sharp distinction between those women who want to kill and those who are driven to it. In the case of the former, in Great Britain at least, the clear-up rate for homicide is a credit to the nation's police forces. In the case of the latter we still have a long way to go in extending our understanding to women who find themselves terrorised by brutal partners. Ironically, the reverse seems to be true in the United States where the rate of solution for homicide is depressingly low, though the slow but sure changes in the law of 'battered woman syndrome' are being effected.

Brian Lane

A

ADAMS, Millicent Axel Schmidt had no idea that Millie was pregnant when he ditched her; mind you, he was such a thoroughly bad lot that it probably wouldn't have made much difference if he had. Schmidt, you see, was on his way to the top of society's ladder, and nothing and nobody was going to stop him.

Millicent Adams was a student at Bryn Mawr at the time she met Axel Schmidt, and had all the benefits that came with being born into the affluent society around Philadelphia's Chestnut Hill; in fact, it was at one of those lavish charity functions so beloved of the upper classes that they met. Axel was also decidedly from the right side of the tracks, and despite showing a tendency to ruthless greed, was a promising post-graduate engineering student. To make a long courting story brief, they fell in love and Millicent fell pregnant. Then along came a more seductive offer from another young socialite somewhat better placed and rather wealthier than Miss Adams, and Axel's head was turned.

Now if Axel Schmidt had shown callousness in his treatment of Millie Adams, she was to prove equally single-minded. In short, she bought herself a .22 calibre Smith and Wesson. At the same time she purchased a large St Bernard dog, which she coaxed to an unused room in the house and shot dead. The object of the target practice was apparently to make sure the gun worked. It is unclear whether, at the time, she intended to use the gun on herself or Axel Schmidt, because she claimed the former and carried out the latter.

It was October 1962, and Millie had been to bed with Schmidt for the last time. Actually it was the last time Axel Schmidt would go to bed with anybody; his was to be the long sleep. All it required was one bullet from Millie's .22.

Despite the fact that, on the face of it, Millicent Adams had coldly calculated this killing, her defence attorney entered a plea of temporary insanity and the court accepted a reduced charge of manslaughter. Indeed, all the fates must have been smiling on Millie that afternoon, because she was sentenced to ten years' probation; the only condition being that she attend as a voluntary patient at a mental health centre. After just three years she was discharged as 'rehabilitated', and moved to the West Coast to take up again her life of luxury. It is not, perhaps, for authors to question the wisdom of court decisions, or to criticize judgements; however, one cannot help wondering whether, without the undoubted wealth and influence of her family, Millicent Adams might not have suffered a somewhat harsher fate.

AHLUWALIA, Kiranjit   On the night of 9 May 1989, neighbours in Coombe Close, Crawley, in West Sussex, heard an agonized scream pierce the dark from the direction of the house that Deepak Ahluwalia shared with his wife Kiranjit and their children. Looking out to see what the commotion might be they saw an Asian woman carrying a child, barefoot and apparently in distress, climbing from a downstairs window and fleeing from a house that was rapidly becoming engulfed in flames. At just before 3.00 a.m. the police and fire brigade reached the house, and within a very short time the investigators became convinced that they did not have a fire with a 'natural' origin. In other words, somebody had set fire to the house. Nor did it take long to establish who that somebody was. When Mrs Ahluwalia was picked up and taken to Crawley police station for questioning she gave every cooperation and during her recorded interview admitted setting fire to her own home and, along with it, her husband.

Like many of the dozen or so women every year who kill their partners, Mrs Ahluwalia had endured years of the most intense physical and mental abuse – ten of them in all. Trapped by her religion and her culture into a life of silent suffering, she could finally take no more.

Kiranjit Ahluwalia never denied killing her husband, and in court she pleaded guilty to manslaughter. The plea, however, was rejected on legal grounds, and the defendant was charged with, and eventually convicted of, murder. When she appeared before Lewes Crown Court in December 1989, Mrs Ahluwalia did not feel confident enough to give evidence on her own behalf (and in Britain at least, it is the unassailable right of the accused not to be put in the witness box – and to have no inference of guilt result from it). Had she done so, the jury would have heard from her own lips the catalogue of appalling domestic violence from which Deepak's death represented the only available means of escape.

There is, of course, an alarming number of women the world over who could tell much the same story – an increasing number of women's refuges and the divorce courts are filled with these victims of male violence. But for Asian women there is a far greater cultural pressure to remain with a husband no matter how intolerable the marriage may be. The wife is simply told, as Kiranjit was, to 'try harder'. The custom is called *izzat*. Despite the fact that she told her family about her husband's violence, which was well known to his own, nothing was done to help or protect Kiranjit Ahluwalia. Eventually she made an unsuccessful attempt to take her own life.

Kiranjit's attorney tried to advance a defence of Provocation at her trial. At present, in the instance of murder, Provocation is a legal defence that will result in a verdict of 'voluntary manslaughter' – where the defendant had intended to kill or 'otherwise had the mental element for murder'. A life sentence is never given for a provoked killing. There is, moreover, an implicit requirement to distinguish between homicide committed in 'hot blood', where there is no calculation before the act, and a killing in 'cold blood', where a deliberate decision is involved (also called in legal terms 'malice afore-thought'). The problem faced by Mrs Ahluwalia's defence counsel was that although his client had been 'provoked' in the moral sense of having suffered years of beatings, in the legal sense she had calculatedly waited for her husband to fall asleep, collected various paraphernalia from around the house – petrol, candles, matches – and then set fire to him. For the same technical reason a plea of self-defence would fail against the fact that Deepak Ahluwalia was asleep at the time he was set alight.

Meanwhile, in a taped message from prison, Kiranjit Ahluwalia posed this question: 'Nobody asked why all this had happened, and why, though I had two little children and worked without rest for fifty or sixty hours a week in order to build up my home I should set fire to that house . . . why did everyone use me as they chose? This is the essence of my culture, society and religion, where a woman is a toy, a plaything. She can be stuck together at will, broken at will. For ten years I lived a life of beatings and degradation and no one noticed. Now the law has decreed that I should serve a sentence for life. Why?'

It is a question that deserves urgent and careful study. Not because there is any doubt that Mrs Ahluwalia was correctly convicted – it is clear that she was convicted and sentenced correctly *according to the law*. What is in question is whether that law should be qualified to take account of such cases of exceptional suffering.

As for Kiranjit Ahluwalia, she served three years of her

prison sentence before being released in the autumn of 1992 by the Court of Appeal after it accepted fresh evidence on the state of her mental health at the time she killed her husband. In a rather touching postscript, Mrs Ahluwalia met the Princess of Wales at the Chiswick Family Rescue, a centre for battered women, in March 1993. The eminent royal told her she was 'very brave', and should write a book about her experience of domestic violence and imprisonment.

ALDRETE, Sara Maria, and CONSTANZO, Adolfo de Jesus Mark Kilroy, a twenty-one-year-old student at the University of Texas was on spring vacation with three class-mates when they decided to take in the Mexican town of Motomoros. They arrived on 14 March 1987, and during a tour of the town's bars, Mark disappeared. Investigations instigated by the Kilroy family seemed to have reached a dead end when drug-squad officers informed the parents that during a recent raid on the remote Rancho Santa Elena they had detained several men, one of whom said that he had seen a 'blond Gringo' bound and gagged in the back of a van parked at the ranch.

As the search of the Santa Elena progressed, large quantities of marijuana and cocaine were found in a shed. The shed itself was dominated by a makeshift altar, and around the building were an alarming number of bloodstains, scraps of human hair and a substance only later identified as human brain pulp. In view of this, the least of the horrors was a prominently displayed severed goat's head. Those detained in the drug raid claimed allegiance to a Satanist cult loosely based on Santeria, and said that Mark Kilroy had been kidnapped and later 'sacrificed' on the orders of the cult's leaders – the man they referred to reverentially as 'the Godfather', born Adolfo de Jesus Constanzo, and Sara Maria Aldrete, the cult's High Priestess. The primary object of the slaughter appears to have been to appease Satan in return for inviolability from police arrest and so that they would not be harmed by bullets in the event of a shoot-out. Whenever a major drug deal was about to take place, a human sacrifice was offered and the victim's heart and brains were ripped out to be boiled up in a cauldron as a 'cannibal feast'. Later, the detainees led officers to the graves of fifteen men and boys, including Mark Kilroy. Many of the bodies had been decapitated and all of them had been extensively mutilated.

Needless to say, by this time Constanzo and Aldrete were on the run. On 5 May 1989, they were traced to an apartment in Mexico City. Following a siege, Sara Aldrete fled the building screaming: 'He's dead! He's dead!' Police entering the apartment found three of the cult's members alive, but Constanzo and his homosexual lover had been shot dead, locked in a final embrace in a walk-in wardrobe; they had been killed on their own orders, rather than be taken into custody. Sara Aldrete, not surprisingly, denied any involvement in the killings, but was indicted along with the other survivors of the cult on multiple charges including murder and drug offences.

In August 1990, Sara Maria Aldrete was acquitted of involvement in Constanzo's murder, but was sentenced to six years for criminal association. Her claim to have been quite innocent of the Rancho Santa Elena atrocities was rejected by a jury in 1994, and she was sentenced to 64 years' imprisonment. There she is perhaps haunted by the final words of her monstrous cult leader – Constanzo reassured the man he had just ordered to kill him with the words: "Don't worry. I won't be dead for long."

ALLEN, Margaret   Margaret Allen was born in Rawtenstall, Lancashire, the twentieth of her mother's twenty-two children, in 1909. For most of her childhood and youth she was a lonely, unhappy girl, increasingly aware of a latent homosexuality which in adulthood was to manifest itself in an aggressive masculine personality serving only to push her even further from any hope of normal social relations. Margaret began to dress her short, stocky body in men's clothing, and to wear her hair cut short; she preferred to be called 'Bill', and boasted variously of working as a building labourer and of having had a sex-change operation.

In 1942, in her thirty-third year, 'Bill' Allen started work as a bus conductor with Rawtenstall Corporation; the job seemed to suit her temperament and she might well have continued to find some satisfaction in her life had her mother not died suddenly a year later. Margaret was very badly affected by her bereavement, and her isolation prevented any normal expression of grief with which others could identify and offer comfort. Instead she became a virtual recluse, her appearance shabby and unkempt, her mind subject to acute depression; finally, after bouts of dizziness, she was forced to give up her work on the buses. The last tie with civilized society severed, Margaret Allen took to wandering the streets of Rawtenstall aimlessly by day and by night. It was probably on one of these rambles amid the grey houses that she made the acquaintance of sixty-eight-year-old Nancy Ellen Chadwick, an eccentric old lady well known in the district as a fortune-teller and (less affectionately) as a miser – a reputation that seemed amply justified by her frequent visits to the park, where she was seen to sit and count her money.

In the early morning of Sunday 29 August 1948, a passing bus driver found Nancy Chadwick lying dead in the roadway almost outside Margaret Allen's run-down stone cottage at 137 Bacup Road, just by the turning into Fallbarn Close. Thoughts that she might have been the victim of a hit-and-run driver were quickly dispelled by the police pathologist, who thought it more likely that old Nancy had met her death on the receiving end of a rain of blows to her head with a blunt instrument. Margaret Allen was routinely questioned later that morning and understandably denied all knowledge of what was now clearly a murder. But as 'Bill' Allen she showed a distinctly unhealthy preoccupation with Nancy Chadwick's passing, offering theories and judgements to anybody who cared to listen – including policemen, to whom the obsession seemed to require further consideration.

When representatives of Scotland Yard visited Margaret Allen's house on Wednesday 1 September they could hardly miss the blood which liberally stained the walls and back door. There was no need to coax Margaret now: 'Come on,' she volunteered, 'I'll tell you about it.' And, pointing to the cellar door: 'That's where I put her!' Margaret's subsequent statement to the police reads, in part:

> I was coming out of the house on Saturday morning about 9.20 and Mrs Chadwick came round the corner. She asked me if this was where I lived and could she come in? I told her I was going out. I was in a nervy mood and she just seemed to get on my nerves, although she had not said anything. I told her to go and she could see me sometime else. But she seemed to insist on coming in. I happened to look round and saw a hammer in the kitchen. At this time we were talking just inside the kitchen with the front door shut. On the spur of the moment I hit her with the hammer. She gave a shout and that seemed to start me off more. I hit her a few times, but I don't know how many. I pulled the body in my coal house.

Margaret had intended to dispose of the body finally under cover of night in the river Irwell, but finding the burden too heavy, she simply abandoned it in the street, scant yards from the scene of the crime.

Of the trial at Manchester Assizes in December there is little to say. Margaret appeared as 'Bill' with close-cropped hair and wearing a man's suit; her counsel Mr W.A. Gorman KC (subsequently Mr Justice Gorman) made a brave plea of insanity, but could never have hoped to fit 'this purposeless, fatuous, and mad murder' into the rigid requirements of the McNaghten Rules. For the Crown it was advanced that Margaret Allen knew quite well what she was doing when she bludgeoned poor old Nancy – she was robbing her. The jury agreed, and after a trial lasting only five hours took only fifteen minutes to bring in a verdict of guilty with no recommendation to mercy.

Margaret Allen made no appeal, and the petition for her reprieve organized by Mrs Annie Cook was signed by only 152 of Rawtenstall's population of 26,000. Behind the bleak facade of Strangeways prison Margaret Allen was hanged on 12 January 1949, unloved, unmourned. If the report that she told Mrs Cook: 'It would help if I could cry, but my manhood holds back my tears' is true then Margaret had at last understood the lifelong tragedy of 'Bill' Allen.

ALLITT, Beverley   Beverley Allitt began work as a student nurse at the Grantham and Kesteven General Hospital in December 1990. She had passed her SEN exams, but had been unable to register until she had made up time lost through ill health. Rather a lot of time, to be honest – 126 days in all, surrendered to a bewildering assortment of accidents, injuries, symptoms and sufferings. Frankly, none of the adult wards had wanted this accident-prone liability on their staff, so Beverley Allitt was passed on to Ward Four; the children's ward. Then, for fifty-eight days in the spring of 1991, carnage erupted on Ward Four. No fewer than twenty-six attacks were carried out on the young boys and girls entrusted to the care of the ward. They were crushed, asphyxiated, poisoned with insulin or potassium chloride. Four children died, nine others were injured. Of those who survived, some will never fully recover.

The first incident occurred on 21 February. Eight-week-old Liam Taylor had been admitted with congested lungs; nothing that a couple of nights in hospital couldn't sort out. Liam's parents left him with a staff nurse and a young SEN, Bev, who was going to feed him. When Chris and Joanne Taylor returned they were shocked to find Liam cold and white, scarcely breathing. Even so, after a day in the Treatment Room Liam was getting back to normal, and his parents were allowed to sleep on the ward and keep a check on Liam's monitors, which would sound an alarm if breathing problems developed. Liam Taylor had his second attack at five o'clock on the morning of the twenty-third, when the other two nurses on duty were out of sight. When they returned Liam was chalk-white with red blotches. A cardiac arrest. He had stopped breathing for a while, and was having convulsions, which indicated brain damage. After a two-hour struggle to revive him, the consultant ordered that the mechanical support should be switched off. A post-mortem examination revealed all the organs to be in a healthy state except the heart, whose left ventricle was massively damaged. Myocardial infarction: a heart attack.

It was a pattern which, with a few variations, was to become terribly familiar to the staff at Grantham. Particularly to the Crash Team – a pool of staff drawn from the duty roster with responsibility for emergency resuscitation. It was rare enough for the Team to be called to the children's ward at all; they were alerted five times in a single month. Ward Four was developing a reputation that it could do very well without. Parents were talking, nurses were talking. What was wrong with the place? Was there some sort of virus, Legionnaire's perhaps? Was one of the staff transmitting a disease? Was it just bad luck, or coincidence? Surely the authorities would *do* something. On the ward itself, Night Sister Jean Savill was so worried that she went first to the union for help and then wrote to the ward manager, detailing the problems of inadequate staffing, the resuscitation equipment which 'did not comply with minimum recommended standards', and begging for investment in the ward 'before a tragedy occurs'.

But tragedies *had* occurred. And they continued to occur. For example, on the afternoon of 9 April Dr Karen Bradshaw was starting to inject young Michael Davidson with antibiotics when the child went rigid and stopped breathing, his back arched and his face turned dark blue. Another cardiac arrest on Ward Four. Consultant Dr Nanayakkara diagnosed chronic fear of the hypodermic needle; Dr Bradshaw disagreed. Dr Porter disagreed with both of them. In fact, relations between the consultants were not good, though, it must be said, no worse than between any professionals.

It was Dr Porter who took the call from the Department of Medical Biochemistry at the University of Cardiff; it was the afternoon of Friday 12 April, and it was in connection with a sample of blood taken from Paul Crampton, the five-month-old who in the previous month had survived three attacks of hypoglycaemia – blood sugar starvation. The lab had tested for the presence of insulin and the needle had swung off the edge of the dial; the sample contained more insulin than the apparatus was capable of measuring. The only plausible explanation was that Paul had been poisoned with insulin.

With hindsight, it is easy to say that at this stage there should have been an inquiry; the ward should have been closed; the medical records of all the victims of inexplicable deaths and illnesses should have been scrutinized until an answer was found. It is easy to wonder whether the police should have been informed now. The fact was, *any* other explanation seemed preferable to the one confronting Grantham's medical staff now – *that a murderer was loose* on *Ward Four*.

Over the next three days there were a further five attacks involving two fundamentally fit children. The pattern was becoming so plain now that it was shouting. But how could it possibly be that a nurse who was devoting her working life to the care of sick children was systematically destroying their lives in this casual, almost random manner? But the pattern was there. On every occasion when the patient was on an intravenous drip, the ward was quiet, and few staff were on duty, Bev Allitt made an excuse to her colleagues so that she might be alone for a few minutes. It would be Bev who raised the alarm, sometimes before much seemed to be wrong; often she would diagnose the type of attack before the symptoms were even showing clearly. Then, when the Crash Team arrived, Beverley would melt into the background, arms folded across her chest, and a strange, remote smile on her face. Slowly, however, the truth was beginning to emerge. Dr Porter had recently been away at a medical conference in Warwick, where a paper on a little-known condition called Munchausen Syndrome by Proxy had started to ring all sorts of bells. Finally he drew up a list of thirteen suspected victims and started to demand action – blood tests for insulin, video cameras to monitor activity on Ward Four, the intervention of the police . . .

It fell to Detective Superintendent Stuart Clifton to make some legal sense out of the chaos of medical reports, biological samples, X-rays, facts, figures and fears. But one thing was quite clear: of all the possible culprits, one name recurred again and again, one name on the duty roster every time there had been an incident – Beverley Allitt. Bev was taken into custody on the morning of 21 May 1991; she was accused of the murder of Paul Crampton and denied it. In the end she had to be released, but as a wise precaution she was sent on home leave while the investigation proceeded. At this point, Stuart Clifton began talking to Leeds-based paediatrician Roy Meadows. Meadows is an expert on the condition which had so intrigued Dr Porter at Warwick – Munchausen Syndrome by Proxy. The syndrome in its initial stages was characterized by a lust for attention. Sufferers made up stories, pretended to be ill, became virtually addicted to medical treatment. In its advanced stages, mercifully much less common, they inflicted illness on others. Most often a mother would harm her own child, but there had been a few reported cases where nurses with Munchausen Syndrome by Proxy began to murder their patients.

In November 1991 Beverley Allitt was formally charged

with four counts of murder, eight attempted murders, and eight counts of causing grievous bodily harm. In February of the following year she was charged with three further attempted murders.

When the trial opened at Nottingham Crown Court on 15 February 1993, Bev Allitt's appearance had changed dramatically. She had lost five of her twelve stones in weight through a form of anorexia. Since August 1992 she had been confined to Rampton for specialist treatment. During this time, besides refusing to eat or drink, Beverley Allitt had deliberately scalded herself and put broken glass in her mouth. A few weeks into the trial she collapsed at Rampton and the court was obliged to continue in her absence. The jury retired on 11 May 1993, and after a gruelling sixteen-hour deliberation the first verdicts were recorded: guilty on two counts of murder. Over the next four days every news bulletin, every headline brought the verdicts home. Guilty of two further murders, guilty on three counts of attempted murder, guilty on each of six charges of causing grievous bodily harm. On 28 May Mr Justice Latham gave Beverley Allitt life sentences on each of the convictions, thirteen in all. He told her: 'You are cunning and manipulative and have shown no remorse for the trail of destruction you have left behind you . . . There is no real prospect that the time will come when you can safely be released.'

In the decade since, the undoubtedly guilty Beverley Allitt was sent first to jail then back to the Rampton high security mental unit. Professor Roy Meadows has received many plaudits for his discovery of Munchausen Syndrome by Proxy, including a knighthood. He has also served as a respected expert witness in many trials involving the suspicious deaths of infants. However, in recent years, his reputation has come under attack.

Some leading paediatricians question the so-called 'Meadows' Law' concerning cot death – "unless proven otherwise, one cot death is a tragedy, two is suspicious and three is murder" – insisting that it is too glib to be safely used as the basis of clinical or legal judgements. The general public were also angered at revelations made during the acquittal, on appeal, of Sally Clark in 2003. At her original trial, Sir Roy Meadows described the possibility that Clark's two baby sons had died of natural causes as "one in 73 million"; a figure that undoubtedly convinced the jury that she was guilty of infanticide, but later proved to have been vastly overestimated by Sir Roy.

A number of British mothers, convicted of killing their children, now plan to apply to the Appeals Court to question the validity of evidence given by expert witnesses like Professor Meadows. And many people now believe that Munchausen Syndrome by Proxy has been disastrously over diagnosed – with tragic consequences for bereaved mothers whose only crime was to innocently fall foul of 'Meadows' Law.'

ANARGEROS, Sophie   It didn't take Sophie long to go to the bad; in fact, by the time she was fifteen she had already driven her mother to such distraction that the unhappy woman was obliged to have Sophie confined to a school for juvenile delinquents. Having spent most of her time there causing disruption, Sophie Anargeros was released on to the good citizens of Reno, Nevada. Actually it proved just the place for Sophie – or Sandra as she was calling herself now. She found work around the gambling halls and bars, mostly in the field of what one might loosely call 'customer liaison'. On a trip to southern California she was married to a man named Peterson, but the marriage did not last long and by 1950 she was in Texas hitching rides and robbing the drivers. Sometimes she worked a twosome with a fourteen-year-old girl – or a threesome if you count the gun. Things went badly wrong when Lewis Patterson decided not to part with his money. Sandra (or was it Sophie again?) thought she would try a little unfriendly persuasion; Patterson died of his bullet wounds. The Rangers caught up with the two modern-day highway robbers in San Angelo, and while Sophie was prepared to admit the shooting, she insisted it was self-defence when Patterson tried to rape her. Unfortunately, Sophie hadn't told this version to her young friend, and the girl gave an entirely different version of things.

On 20 January 1951, under the name of Sophie Peterson, the former Sophie Anargeros was found guilty of murder with malice and sentenced to life. She was released on 19 December 1961.

ANGEL MAKERS OF NAGYREV   The small village of Nagyrev is situated some sixty miles to the south-east of Budapest on the river Tisza. At the time of the 'Angel Makers', the village possessed no hospital, nor even a doctor, which left the medical care of the inhabitants pretty much in the hands of the midwife and her assistants. The midwife was Mrs Julius Fazekas.

All manner of ills, rightly or wrongly, are blamed on the Great War, but it would certainly be true to say that without the First World War the phenomenon that occurred at Nagyrev could never have happened. For one thing, all the menfolk were away at the front; for another, the outskirts of the village were playing host to camps full of prisoners of war. In no time husbands and fiancés were relegated to memory in the face of this new influx of captive males, and it seemed the whole village was about to set up in direct competition with Sodom and Gomorrah. Women of all ages began to consider themselves very badly off if they could not attract at least two or three casual lovers from the camps. In fact, the average housewife was having such a good time of it that when husbands did eventually trickle back from the blighted battle-fields of Europe demanding their rightful place at the head of the family, they received a very cool reception. In short, they were superfluous to requirements.

What madness their own promiscuity had wrought on these

previously virtuous wives and sweethearts we shall never understand. What we know for a fact is that they were forming queues at the door of the midwife Fazekas, who had temporarily taken on the duties of a dispensing chemist and was distributing a steady supply of the arsenic that she boiled off mountains of flypapers. Poisoning became the village's most popular pastime, and the area acquired a new name – 'The Murder District'. What had started as the disposal of a few unwanted spouses had become the accepted means of getting *what*ever you wanted or removing *who*ever you wanted – parents, children, neighbours, anybody who was in the way. And if these murderesses should quarrel among themselves, then was it not justice that they settle their differences with poison? In all there were about fifty women involved in the 'Magyar Murder Incorporated', and they became known as the 'Angel Makers of Nagyrev'. Whenever officialdom got uncomfortably close to examining the uncommonly high death rate in the region, those investigators were referred to the impeccably filed death certificates authorized by none other than the midwife's cousin!

And so the deaths continued, hundreds of them; from the first – the murder of Peter Hegedus in 1914, to the last in 1929. It was in July of this latter year that an accusation was made against a Mrs Ladislaus Szabo by a man who claimed she had poisoned his wine. Taken into custody, Mrs Szabo was clearly reluctant to face the music alone and implicated her friend Mrs Bukenoveski. Mrs Bukenoveski made no secret of having poisoned her aged mother, or of throwing her into the river Tisza; in fact, she was rather proud of this last deception, because when the old lady was pulled from the water she was certified 'drowned'. Wishing perhaps to share her new-found notoriety, Mrs Bukenoveski in her turn pointed the finger in Mrs Fazekas' direction, and the midwife was taken in for questioning. Wiser than her accuser, Mrs Fazekas denied everything, and short of any more concrete evidence than hearsay she was released from custody; and she did exactly as the police had predicted. Officers tailed the midwife while she went about the village warning her customers that the game was up, following behind making the arrests. As a result, thirty-eight women were arrested, twenty-six of whom were later tried at Szolnok – eight were sentenced to death, seven to life imprisonment, and the rest to varying terms in gaol.

Among those sentenced to death was the midwife's accomplice, who distributed the poisons for her. Susannah Olah – apparently called 'Auntie Susi' by her regular customers – also had the general reputation of being a witch, and stories abounded of the menagerie of poisonous reptiles which she had taught to creep into people's beds and kill them.

Aunt Susi's sister, a septuagenarian hag named Lydia, was also given the death penalty, as was forty-five-year-old Marie Kardos who had notched up an impressive record of familicide even by Nagyrev standards, including her husband, her lover and her frail son; she had persuaded her son on his deathbed to sing for her. Mrs Kardos told the court: 'I said "Sing, my boy, sing my favourite song!" He sang with his lovely clear voice, then suddenly he cried out, gripped his stomach, gasped and was dead.'

Rosalie Sebestyen and Rosa Hoyba poisoned their 'boring' husbands, as did Mrs Julius Csaba, though she was treated rather more leniently when it was established that she had been married to a violent drunk. Maria Varga was convicted of killing her blind war-hero husband and her lover – though she denied it to her dying day. Juliane Lipka, described as 'squat and shapeless, with the most evil expression', was responsible for at least seven murders which included her stepmother, aunt, sister-in-law, brother, and by way of a novel Christmas present to herself, her husband. Having disposed of most of her own family, Mrs Lipka then offered her wide experience to her neighbour Maria Koteles: 'I was sorry for the wretched woman, so I gave her a bottle of poison and told her that if nothing else helped her marriage to try that.'

Mrs Lipka joined seven others on the gallows, and their bodies were left hanging till they rotted, a reminder of the madness that had gripped the village for almost sixteen years.

As for the ringleader, Mrs Fazekas, she had escaped earthly justice by taking poison just as the police arrived to arrest her. If any evidence had been needed, the squalid rooms were filled with pots of soaking flypapers.

ANGELS OF DEATH *see* **WAGNER, Waltraud, et al.**

ANSELL, Mary It was a sad fact of nature that poor Caroline Ansell had been born mentally less well-equipped than most, so that for the greater part of her adult life she had been confined to the Leavesden Asylum in Watford; and there she might have ended her days in childlike ignorance of the world outside. However, Caroline had a sister in domestic service, Mary Ansell, who was not terribly bright either, but canny enough to remain on the outside of Leavesden's high walls. Mary was just about to introduce her sister to a whiff of that cruel world outside. Not that there was any animosity between the two women – in fact, Caroline treated her younger sister with a pathetic, almost dog-like devotion. The problem was that Mary had taken out a modest insurance policy on her sister's life, and was anxious to collect. As it was a life insurance policy it was clear that Caroline would have to die; and Mary knew exactly how.

On 9 March 1899 a cake was delivered to Caroline Ansell with very best wishes from Mary. Overwhelmed by this gesture of sisterly affection, Caroline shared her good fortune with the other patients. All of them suffered excruciating abdominal pains, and Caroline, who had eaten the lion's share, died in unimaginable agony. Meanwhile, Mary was dashing off a couple of virtually illiterate letters. One was to the director of Leavesden Asylum forbidding them to conduct an autopsy on Caroline's body, and was signed as if by their mother. The second letter, in her own name, was to the insurance company demanding the £20 on Caroline's policy. The asylum authorities ignored the letter from 'Mrs Ansell', and carried out a post-mortem which revealed that Caroline had died from phosphorus poisoning. The insurance company had no time to pay up before Mary Ansell was arrested and charged with murder. To which Mary replied: 'I am as innocent a girl as ever was born.'

The evidence at her trial in June 1899 did not confirm this opinion, and Mary's explanation that she had bought phosphorus 'for my own protection against them, as I was frightened of them' (she meant rats), was not believed. The jury convicted Mary Ansell of the capital charge, though it is fair to say that their spokesman afterwards claimed they did not think she would be hanged. The fact is that, right up to the time of Britain's abolition of capital punishment in the 1960s, their crime was held in such loathing that poisoners were rarely reprieved. Sentencing Mary to the gallows, Mr Justice Matthew expressed this view when he told her: 'You deliberately took the life of your sister, an afflicted woman, who had never been a burden to you, and who had a peculiar claim on your affection. You were moved to this terrible crime for the sake of a small sum of money which you would receive on the policy of insurance. Never in my experience has so terrible a crime been committed for a motive so utterly inadequate.'

Mary Ansell went to her death within the walls of St Albans Prison on 19 July 1899; she was twenty-two years old.

ARCHER-GILLIGAN, Amy   Amy Archer opened her Home for the Elderly and Infirm at Windsor, Connecticut, in 1907. She called herself 'Sister Amy', which was quite reassuring if you didn't know she had no qualifications to be a nurse let alone a sister. In 1913, having lost one husband rather unexpectedly, Amy became Mrs Archer-Gilligan, and when Michael Gilligan suddenly died twelve months later, she became the respectable, if tragic, widow Archer-Gilligan. But there were other problems, for it had not gone entirely unnoticed in the small local community that the residents of the Archer Home were dropping like flies – in fact, there had been forty-eight deaths in the space of five years. The latest victim had been Franklin R. Andrews, who had enjoyed apparently sturdy health until 30 May 1914, when he quite suddenly expired during the night.

Local tongues were beginning to wag, and gossip is never a good thing because that kind of talk inevitably attracts the attention of the press and the police. Thus, between them, the representatives of the pen and the 'sword' amassed sufficient incriminating evidence to secure exhumation orders on a selection of the victims of the Archer Home. Post-mortem examinations established that very little of the prodigious quantity of arsenic shown to have been purchased by Mrs Archer-Gilligan to rid the Home of rats was ever put to that use.

During the months of June and July 1917, Amy Archer-Gilligan stood trial at Hartford court-house, Connecticut, initially on a multiple indictment containing five charges of murder, though it was finally reduced to one – the killing of Franklin R. Andrews. Amy denied the charge of course, claiming that her dedication, in equal proportion, to the welfare of her residents and to following the teachings of the Christian Church automatically precluded such activities as murder. It was not a view shared by the judge and jury. The latter convicted Mrs Archer-Gilligan of murder and the former passed sentence of death upon her. But in the end Amy did not hang; following an appeal a new trial was ordered at which she pleaded guilty and was sentenced to life imprisonment. She was later certified insane and spent the rest of her days in an asylum, dying in 1928 at the age of fifty-nine.

ARDEN, Alice   The conversion of real-life drama into a literary or theatrical drama ensures its elevation to immortality. Where would William Corder and Maria Marten have been relegated if not for the rash of melodramatic theatricals celebrating The Murder in the Red Barn; or Eugene Aram without his illustrious biographer Edward George Bulwer-Lytton? And will John Reginald Christie's body be forever surmounted by Richard Attenborough's head?

One of the earliest English dramatisations of true-crime was the Elizabethan play *The Lamentable and True Tragedie of Master Arden of Feversham*. The fact that the drama has endured is in a great part due to the way in which the unknown author* departed from the prevailing tendency of Elizabethan theatre to take as its subject matter the royal court and 'diplomatic service' to deal with more fundamental social and domestic preoccupations, painting as it does a realistic, if sordid, picture of low-life and base passions; passions and intrigues that result in the foul murder, in 1550, of Thomas Arden (or Ardern, or Arderne) in his own front parlour.

Arden was a Kentish gentleman and former mayor of the town of Faversham. He had made a good and profitable marriage to Alice Misfin, stepdaughter of Sir Edward North, and his civic responsibilities included Commissionership of the Customs of the Port of Faversham. He was subsequently granted some of the Abbey lands by Sir Thomas Cheney, in the process of which he is said to have defrauded a man named Greene – an accusation voiced especially loudly by the victim and which was to play a seminal role in Arden's death.

Alice's dowry having been secured, and her family connections established, Thomas transferred his attention to the relentless pursuit of money. Alice, meanwhile, transferred her attention to the relentless pursuit of a man named Thomas Mosbie (or Mosby, or Morsby, or Mosbye), formerly a tailor, now her stepfather's steward.

*It has been advanced, not too seriously, that William Shakespeare had a finger in the development of the text as a result of his visit to Faversham as a member of Lord Leicester's Players in 1590. The Bard is said to have played the part of Shaghag and in consequence 'adapted' the play to give his character more prominence.

The earliest factual account of the case – Raphael Holinshed's *Chronicles* (1577) – informs us that Arden was 'contented to winke at her filthie disorder, and both permitted and also invited Mosbye verie often to lodge in his house'. Inevitably, the master becomes an unnecessary burden to the adulterous pair and Alice and Mosbie plot to murder him. It is quite clear who is the stronger personality, and evident that Mosbie finds himself less and less enthusiastic about the scheme. Indeed, after the extraordinary device of the poisoned crucifix fails . . .

> A crucifix impoysoned
> That who so looke upon it should wax blinde
> And with the sent be stifeled that ere long
> He should dye poysoned that did view it wel.

. . . he resorts to employing two characters with the unlikely names of Black Will and Shagbag (or Shakebag) whose incompetence borders on the burlesque, and the man Greene, who is still smarting from the former real or imagined injustice. The conspirators rendezvous frequently over ale at the *Fleur de Luce* to cement their plans.

There follow some of the most ludicrous assassination attempts in the history of crime, and it is a wonder that *The Lamentable and True Tragedie* . . . does not veer into concentrated farce. In one plan Will and Shagbag lie in wait for Arden in the shadows of a shop; as Arden approaches the shopkeeper happens to swing open his shutters, which catch Black Will such a crack on the head that he falls unconscious to the ground and has to be helped back to the *Fleur de Luce* by his accomplice.

Finally it is decided that Arden shall be 'sent to everlasting night' in his own home, and to this end Black Will and Shakebag are secreted in the parlour, while Alice encourages her husband to play a game of tables (a sort of backgammon) with her lover Mosbie:

ARDEN: Come Alice, is our supper ready yet?

ALICE: Ay! when you have a game at tables played.

ARDEN: Come, Master Mosbie, what shall we play for?

MOSBIE: Three games for a French crown, sir, and please
you. ARDEN: Content.

*[They go to a small table on the left of the stage and play
tables on a draught-board with counters and dice. Mosbie
is in the aimchair and Arden sits on a stool. Will and
Shakebag appear at the back. Will has a towel in his
hand]*

WILL: Can he not take him yet? what a spite is that?

ALICE: Not yet, Will; take heed he see thee not.

WILL: I fear he will spy me as I am coming.

SHAKEBAG: To prevent that, creep betwixt my legs.

MOSBIE: One ace, or else I lose the game.

ARDEN: Marry, sir, there's two for failing.

MOSBIE: Ah, Master Arden, 'now I can take you'.

*[Will, by means of the towel held in both hands, like a
noose, pulls Arden off the stool]*

ARDEN: Mosbie! Michael! Alice! what will you do?

WILL: Nothing but take you up, sir, nothing else.

MOSBIE: There's for the pressing iron you told me of.
[Stabs him]

SHAKEBAG: And there's for the ten pound in my sleeve.
[Stabs him]

ALICE: What! groans thou? nay, then give me the weapon!
Take this for hindering Mosbie's love and mine. *[Stabs
him]*

MICHAEL: O, mistress!

WILL: Ah, that villain will betray us all.

MOSBIE: Tush, fear him not; he will be secret.

MICHAEL: Why, dost thou think I will betray myself?

WILL: Shift for yourselves; we two will leave you now.

ALICE: But first convey the body to the fields, and throw
the knife and towel down the well.

SHAKEBAG: We have our gold; Mistress Alice, adieu;
Mosbie, farewell, and Michael, farewell too.
[*The body is carried down the passage by Will, Shakebag
and Michael; Alice and Susan tidy the room. Knocking is
heard at the porch door . . .*]

But true to their natures, the buffoons Will and Shakebag in
carrying the body to the meadow not only lift up a handful of
rushes from the floor thus sowing a trail of debris to the corpse,
but seem oblivious of the fact that they are leaving behind them
a track of perfect footprints in the newly fallen snow.

Vengeance was both swift and violent. The punishment for
husband killing (a category of *petit treason)* was to be burnt
alive at the stake, a fate Alice Arden shared with her maid-
servant Susan. The executions took place at Canterbury on 14
March.

Mosbie was hanged in London, at Smithfield; Michael, the
treacherous servant, was hung in chains at Faversham; and
Black Will was burnt on a scaffold at Flushing. Greene and
Shagbag escaped, though the latter is said to have been
subsequently murdered in London.

ARMISTEAD, Norma Jean   Norma Jean was forty-four
years old, a nurse at Los Angeles' Kaiser Hospital, and
desperately unhappy to have reached middle-age childless.
Now, desperate people frequently resort to desperate measures,
but few could have been as bizarre as the measures taken by
Nurse Armistead in her quest for a baby.

In October 1974 she let herself into the hospital records
office, checked that she was alone, and made a single entry in
the maternity ledger – her own name. Having thus established
the medical existence of her baby, Norma Jean could do
nothing but wait. If colleagues at the hospital were surprised
they were on the whole too polite to say; and if they felt she was
taking a long time to 'fill out' then they never mentioned it in

her company. The wait must have seemed like an eternity to Nurse Armistead, but at last a believable time for her to give birth arrived. On 15 May 1975 she visited twenty-eight-year-old Kathryn Viramontes, who was about to give birth to her own baby; Kathryn would never see that child. Quite suddenly, Norma Jean drew a knife from her handbag and cut through the woman's throat. As quickly and carefully as she could, to avoid damage to the foetus, Nurse Armistead performed an *ad hoc* Caesarean section and removed the child from its dead mother's womb. That evening Norma Jean admitted herself to the Kaiser, claiming that she had given birth prematurely at home.

Desperate the crime certainly was, and bizarre it certainly was; but it was far from clever. The discovery of the mutilated body of Kathryn Viramontes and the disappearance of her unborn baby inevitably led police to the Kaiser Hospital where Kathryn was registered in the maternity unit; the same place in which Norma Jean Armistead now lay with her own 'premature' baby.

In many ways it would have been perfectly understandable if Norma Jean Armistead had been judged as suffering from diminished responsibility; the jury, however, decided that she was sane when she killed Kathryn Viramontes, and found her guilty of first-degree murder.

ARRINGTON, Marie Dean   On 28 April 1968 the shotgun-blasted remains of thirty-seven-year-old Vivian Ritter were found, ending a six-day search for the missing woman around the Leesburg, Florida, area. Vivian Ritter had for some years been private secretary to the town's public defender, Robert Pierce, and a reconstruction of her disappearance had already established that she had left Pierce's office at what looked like gunpoint on the afternoon of 22 April. Her abductor, from witness descriptions, could only have been Marie Dean Arrington, an old enemy of the public defender. Some time before, Pierce had represented Mrs Arrington's two sons on armed robbery charges and they had been convicted; blaming Pierce for their imprisonment Marie Arrington had been threatening revenge ever since. That she was quite capable of carrying out such a threat was obvious from the fact that at the time she abducted Vivian Ritter, Arrington was on bail awaiting sentencing for killing her husband.

Within hours of the discovery of the body of Vivian Ritter, Florida police had Mrs Arrington in custody. She had originally gone gunning for Robert Pierce, but finding him out of the office, thought the secretary would do for the time being, and drove her out to the swamps where she tortured and killed her. Marie Arrington was in big trouble; killing her own husband was worth twenty years, but the murder of Vivian Ritter earned Arrington an appointment with the electric chair, and she was put on the guest list at Lowell's Death Row. On 1 March 1969, Marie Arrington escaped from the women's prison and was on the run for almost four years before she was picked up by FBI agents in New Orleans and returned to Florida.

B

BANISZEWSKI, Gertrude Wright   Rarely has a more truly wicked killer emerged from the black book of twentieth-century crime than thirty-seven-year-old Gertrude Baniszewski; indeed, if one were to give credence to the concept of evil, then she would be its human embodiment.

In 1965 sixteen-year-old Sylvia Likens and her fifteen-year-old handicapped sister Jenny were placed in the hands of the Indianapolis divorcée while their parents travelled with the circus. It was agreed the children's board should be $20 a week. Their treatment was never far from harsh, and the two girls were kept permanently hungry, cold and comfortless. But as time went on these privations gave way to more severe punishments, savage beatings administered first by Mrs Baniszewski alone, then assisted by her own three awful children and some of the local roughs – young degenerates for the most part, who shared Gertrude's taste for sadism. The tormentors felt some sort of brute sympathy with Jenny's infirmity which meant she was spared the worst excesses, but her sister was tortured mercilessly, and as in all cases of obsessive cruelty, the savagery escalated. It began with punches and slaps, then kicks; then two local louts were invited in to practise their karate throws on the wretched girl. They in turn brought along other friends to join in the beatings and sexual degradation. This appalling mistreatment reached its peak when Mrs Baniszewski burned the message 'I am a prostitute and proud of it' across Sylvia's stomach with a red-hot needle. It was inevitable that Sylvia Likens would die if this abuse continued; and so she did, in October, after a particularly severe beating.

As it was obvious the police were going to be involved at some stage, Mrs Baniszewski cunningly took the initiative and reported Sylvia's death herself. The girl, she told them, had always been wayward, always running with a gang of ne'er-do-well local boys who had finally raped and beaten her to death. Well at least it was partly true, and Gertrude Baniszewski might even have got away with it had young Jenny Likens not found the courage to tell the whole truth.

At her trial Mrs Baniszewski made no attempt to defend herself or to offer any explanation for her awful crime, other than that 'the girl needed to be taught a lesson'; what lesson that was we will never know. The motley rabble of poor Sylvia's tormentors received various short terms of imprisonment, and the ogress herself was sentenced to life.

BARBER, Susan   It happened to Susan and Michael Barber in exactly the same way that it happens to scores of other couples. They had been married long enough to have produced three children, and the relationship had long since soured. Susan had worked her way through a succession of lovers and had left home twice, only to return for the sake of the children.

And so things might have dragged self-destructively on for many more years; but then, in May 1981, Michael Barber returned home early from a fishing trip and found his wife in bed with his best friend. Understandably peeved, Barber beat his wife and threw her bed-partner out of the house. Next day Susan made her husband one of his favourite meals, steak and kidney pie; only this time it had an extra ingredient – a dose of weed-killer containing paraquat. Now paraquat is as lethal to human beings as it is to weeds, producing fibrosis of the lungs with symptoms identical to pneumonia and kidney disorder. On 27 June 1981 Barber died in London's Hammersmith Hospital. Fortunately for justice, an observant pathologist named David Evans suspected some form of poisoning and removed samples from Barber's internal organs for analysis. The results from the National Poisons Unit confirmed that Michael Barber had been poisoned with paraquat.

In April 1982 Susan Barber was arrested and charged with murder, and at Chelmsford Crown Court in November of the same year she was joined in the dock by her former lover – she received a life sentence for murder, he collected two years for conspiracy. But by this time Susan Barber had a new amour, and in July 1983 she was briefly released from Holloway Prison in order to marry him.

BARFIELD, Velma Velma married her first husband, Thomas Burke, while she was still at high school, and the couple settled in Parkton, South Carolina, where she reared two children – a boy and a girl. Burke began to drink heavily in the mid-1960s, though whether this was the result of a deterioration in the marriage or whether it caused the deterioration will never be known for certain. Velma, though, suffered a mental breakdown, and as a direct result of the medical treatment she became a registered drug addict. In April 1969, a mysterious fire swept through the Burkes' house leaving Thomas dead.

Velma married for the second time, a man named Jennings L. Barfield. Having suffered ill-health for many years there was little surprise when shortly after the marriage Barfield died suddenly of what was certified as a 'heart attack'. There was certainly no shortage of praise for Mrs Barfield who had, despite her own battle against drugs, appeared to spare no effort or personal sacrifice in nursing the ailing man. Locally anyway, Velma was a saint.

Following Barfield's death, Velma moved into her parents'

house, which she set about ridding of vermin with liberal supplies of arsenic bait. First her father died – old age; later her mother, Lillie MacMillan Bullard, died after enduring violent stomach upsets. Then Velma suffered the indignity of a spell in jail for forging her mother's signature in order to secure a loan.

Loosed on the Carolinas once more, Velma Barfield was taken into service as housekeeper to an elderly couple named Edwards. Shortly afterwards the old man suffered an apparently natural death, following which disputes between Dollie Edwards and her housekeeper escalated. In March 1977, Velma made a small purchase of rat poison and Dollie joined her husband. This left Velma with the Edwards' nephew Stuart Taylor, a fifty-three-year-old tobacco farmer who would prove to be her Nemesis.

John Henry Lee and his wife Record were the next to benefit from Velma's unique style of housekeeping, with John Henry's hard-earned cash being spent on, among more personal frivolities, the very rodent exterminator that would soon claim his life. Velma had also been plundering Stuart Taylor's modest inheritance, and to prevent any acrimonious scenes if he discovered her deceit, Velma gave him the proverbial arsenic sandwich. Taylor sickened, seemed to recover, grew worse, was admitted to hospital, and died. This time the authorities demanded an autopsy which established death as due to arsenical poisoning. Under interrogation, Velma admitted poisoning Dollie Edwards, John Henry Lee and her own mother. She categorically denied responsibility for the deaths of her husbands, though the exhumed corpse of Jennings Barfield revealed traces of arsenic.

Velma Barfield was tried only for the murder of Stuart Taylor, though this single charge was enough to earn her the death sentence. North Carolina legislation offered its prisoners the choice between lethal injection and the gas chamber, and Velma opted for the former. Despite the customary lengthy appeal process which occupied her six years on Death Row,

Velma Barfield was executed at North Carolina's Central Prison, Raleigh, on 2 November 1984. She wore pink pyjamas for the occasion.

BARNEY, Elvira Dolores   Mrs Elvira Dolores Barney, whose case was so soon to become a *cause célèbre,* was twenty-seven at the time she shot to prominence, but due to the ravages wrought by the gin bottle looked some years older. She had been born into a wealthy family of good breeding, and her father, Sir John Mullins, was a Government Broker. Elvira had married an American cabaret singer, but the couple soon tired of each other and Mr Barney returned to the United States and was never seen or heard from again. Mrs Barney was what used to be described as a 'socialite', though in the worst possible interpretation of that word – in short, she was rich, spoilt and hopelessly addicted to alcohol and men. Michael Scott Stephen was one of those men. Twenty-four-year-old Stephen was described in court by Sir Patrick Hastings, Mrs Barney's attorney, as being 'as worthless as she herself had become; he had no money and no occupation, although it is said that he was once engaged to a dress designer, and he was apparently quite content to exist upon such funds as Mrs Barney was prepared to provide for him'. It was an uneasy kind of partnership, and inflamed by drink the couple frequently fell to loud quarrelling.

   On the night of 30 May 1932 Elvira had given a party at her home, which was attended by the usual rag-bag of idlers, ne'er-do-wells and hangers-on, and when this gathering broke up she and Michael transferred their drinking first to the bar of the Café de Paris, and then to the Blue Angel Club in London's Soho. The couple left the Blue Angel at around midnight while they were still just able to stand, and returned to Williams Mews where, according to custom, they continued drinking and squabbling loudly. Neighbours subsequently recalled hearing the quarrel, and a woman's voice screaming: 'I will shoot you.' One might have thought that the fact that this was followed by a couple of shots would have prompted neighbours to call the police; but they had heard it all before – too many times. The shouting, the abuse, the threats. Mrs Barney had taken pot-shots at Stephen from the window on one occasion. So what really happened that morning? One thing was certain, Michael Stephen was never going to give his version of the events, and on 3 June Elvira Barney was arrested and charged with his murder.

Quite how things would have turned out for Mrs Barney had she not secured the services of Sir Patrick Hastings to present her defence it is difficult to say; certainly he was the strongest card in her hand. According to her own story, Mrs Barney had told the police that Stephen had, during their 'disagreement', threatened to leave her; she then, in a histrionic gesture, threatened to kill herself with the revolver she kept beside the bed. There followed a brief struggle during which Stephen tried to wrestle the gun from his lover's hand, and it suddenly went off with tragic results.

The trial of Elvira Barney opened at the Old Bailey in July and was presided over by Mr Justice Humphreys. Patrick Hastings was opposed by Sir Percival Clarke acting for the Crown. The prosecution had no shortage of ammunition in its armoury – not least did they have the medical brilliance of Bernard Spilsbury and the ballistics expertise of gunsmith Robert Churchill. Churchill's evidence was that the gun in question was one of the safest types manufactured, and due to the fact that it could not be cocked by hand and required an especially long pull on the trigger to activate the internal hammer, it was unlikely to be fired by mistake. Spilsbury built on this by adding that the direction of the wound (horizontal) and the lack of scorch marks on Stephen's clothes around the entry point of the bullet suggested that the gun had been fired from a greater distance than would have been the case in an intimate struggle for possession of the weapon.

However, despite this seemingly overwhelming scientific

evidence, one piece of courtroom drama (some might say trickery) turned the tide in Elvira Barney's favour. Cross-examining Robert Churchill, Patrick Hastings asked if it was true that the weapon in question was particularly difficult to fire. Churchill replied that, needing a 14lb pull on the trigger to release the firing hammer, the Smith and Wesson .32 pistol was one of the least accident-prone guns available.

'Is that so?' Hastings asked conversationally and, taking the empty gun from the evidence table, pointed it at the ceiling and proceeded to pull and release the trigger in very fast succession. The loud clicking of the firing hammer filled the courtroom and seriously undermined Churchill's testimony.

In fact, as Hastings admitted privately after the trial, it had been very difficult to pull the trigger, and his cowboy performance had badly bruised his index finger.

From the witness box, Mrs Barney first related incidents from her unsatisfactory life with a brutal husband which helped create an atmosphere of sympathy for her. Mrs Barney went on to describe her deep love for Stephen, and the cruel and careless way in which he treated her: 'I was so unhappy I thought I would make him think I was going to commit suicide. So when he was outside I fired the pistol at random in the [bed]room. I thought that if he really believed I'd killed myself he'd go and fetch people . . .'

In his closing speech to the jury, Patrick Hastings concluded: 'I claim that on evidence that has been put before you Mrs Barney is entitled – as a right – to a verdict in her favour. I ask you, as a matter of justice, that you should set her free.'

After a retirement of one hour and fifty minutes, the jury did exactly that, and as she left the court, a large crowd of well-wishers cheered Mrs Barney in the street. She went to France shortly afterwards, and following four more years abusing her body with alcohol, she died in Paris.

BARTLETT, Adelaide Adelaide Blanche de la Tremoille was born in Orléans in 1856, the daughter of a wealthy

Englishman then living in France, and was brought to England as a child. In 1875 she was lodging in Kingston, in the same house as a young man named Frank Bartlett. There she met Frank's elder brother, Edwin, a grocer who owned a chain of six shops in South London. Within a very short time a marriage had been arranged by Adelaide's father between herself and Edwin, who was ten years her senior and, in the beginning at least, looked upon himself as a second father to Adelaide, dispatching her first to a school in Stoke Newington, and thence to a convent in Belgium for twelve months; she undertook the duties of a wife during her holidays.

To all outward appearances, the Bartletts seemed a happy couple, with Edwin an indulgent, even doting, husband. From the evidence that later came out in court, it appears that Edwin held rather eccentric views on marriage. He believed, for example, that a man should have two wives, one for intellectual companionship and the other for what he termed 'use'. Adelaide seems to have fulfilled the former function, and later claimed that she only had sexual contact with her husband on one occasion. This led to an uncomfortable pregnancy and miscarriage in 1881, and she was not encouraged to try the experiment again.

In 1883 the couple moved to a house in Phipps Bridge Road, Merton. There they met the young minister of the local Wesleyan Chapel, the Reverend Mr George Dyson. All three seemed to get on famously and it was quickly decided that Dyson should visit the house to give Adelaide some further tutoring. Adelaide and Dyson were thus thrown together alone for large parts of the day, with the predictable result that an inappropriate degree of affection soon grew between the two of them. For his part, Edwin Bartlett seemed positively to encourage the relationship, going so far as to write to thank Dyson for sending his wife a love letter.

In October the Bartletts decided to move again, this time back into the centre of London, taking rooms at 85 Claverton

Street, Pimlico. Dyson moved his ministry to a Methodist church in Putney, a far more convenient location, and Edwin paid for his season ticket up to Pimlico.

Bartlett had always been blessed with the most robust health, but on 8 December 1885, he was taken ill and the local medic, Dr Alfred Leach, was summoned. The symptoms were perplexing; he had a pain in his side, intermittent diarrhoea and intestinal haemorrhaging and, most curiously, a blue line round the edge of his gums. He was also very exhausted and depressed.

During this period Adelaide had been nursing her husband with the utmost devotion, staying by his bedside, sleeping in a chair next to him at night and holding his toe, a curious comfort which seemed to calm Mr Bartlett. The Rev. Dyson continued to call regularly, and on one visit Mrs Bartlett made the unusual request that he should obtain some chloroform for her, which she said she used to relieve her husband's pains. This Dyson agreed to, obtaining the drug in small quantities from three separate chemists in Putney and Wimbledon, decanting the supply into one large bottle to give to Adelaide.

On Thursday 31 December Edwin Bartlett seemed generally to be in better spirits. Four o'clock the next morning, however, found Adelaide knocking wildly on the door of her landlord, Mr Dogget – explaining that she thought her husband had expired. The doctor was called and the fact confirmed. Edwin Bartlett had been dead for more than two hours. Edwin's father was sent for, and took an understandably suspicious view of developments, demanding that a post-mortem be carried out. The results left little doubt as to the cause of death. Edwin Bartlett had been murdered; he had been poisoned with a large dose of chloroform.

Chloroform is a strong poison, but it has rarely been the cause of death, and certainly not of murder, because it inflames and burns the internal organs and would be excruciatingly painful, not to say impossible, to drink. The inexplicable fact about Edwin Bartlett's death was that while his stomach reeked of chloroform, his throat and digestive passages were not in the least inflamed.

In fact any competent doctor could have offered at least two explanations to the mystery. The chloroform, having first been used to render Edwin unconscious, could have either been fed down his throat with a funnel and a flexible, orogastric tube – similar to those used to pump out the stomachs of poisoning victims – or, more probably, a large injection needle might have been used to introduce the caustic liquid directly into his stomach. Both procedures were perfectly possible in 1885, even for a non-medico, and would have overcome the problem of Edwin automatically spitting the caustic fluid out if it had been introduced directly into his mouth. So the real mystery was why the prosecution did not think of these obvious explanations and call in experts to examine the corpse for telltale signs.

At the inquest into Bartlett's death the coroner's jury, no doubt scandalized by what they would have seen as the immoral goings-on within the Bartlett household, were predisposed to take a stern view of events, and returned a verdict that Bartlett had died of chloroform administered by his wife, and that George Dyson had been an accessory.

The trial of Adelaide Bartlett opened at the Old Bailey on 12 April 1886, before Mr Justice Wills. The Crown had decided to offer no evidence against George Dyson and he was formally acquitted.

The trial created considerable interest, mainly due to the curious relationship that had existed between Edwin Bartlett and his wife, to say nothing of her unconventional relationship with the Reverend Mr Dyson, over which the judge seemed particularly outraged.

Nevertheless, there were many inconsistencies in the Crown's case, in particular they could not explain how the poison could have been administered. Edward Clarke made a memorable six-hour speech in Adelaide Bartlett's defence which seemed to seal the matter. When the jury returned the foreman did not answer yea or nay to the clerk's traditional inquiry, but read a statement:

> Although we think that there is the gravest suspicion attaching to the prisoner, we do not think there is sufficient evidence to show how or by whom the chloroform was administered.

Adelaide Bartlett had been found not guilty.

In popular fiction Adelaide would no doubt have married George Dyson; but she did not. She changed her name, and was heard of no more. The final epitaph to the case has to be left to the famous surgeon Sir James Paget, who attended the trial. 'Mrs Bartlett,' he declared, 'was no doubt properly acquitted. But now it is to be hoped that, in the interests of science, she will tell us how she did it!'

BATEMAN, Mary Until her marriage to John Bateman, Mary had been in service to a number of wealthy families in the area around Leeds and York, and had been summarily dismissed by each of them as soon as the family silver started to disappear.

Bateman, a wheelwright by trade, joined the army in around 1804, and with Mary by his side moved to several bases located around the British Isles. Mary, who had now begun to supplement her stealing with fortune-telling, pursued her own career.

In 1806 she met the Perigo family, William and his wife Rebecca. Poor superstitious Rebecca, frightened out of her wits by the belief that a curse, or 'evil wish' had been laid upon her, readily accepted the services of 'Miss Blythe', a non-existent wise-woman who, through Mary Bateman, promised to lift the curse. Having swindled the Perigos out of most of their money and possessions in return for this bogus occult protection service, Mary prepared for them, in the name of Miss Blythe, a special pudding, after eating which William Perigo became very ill, and Rebecca died.

Mary Bateman, known as the 'Yorkshire Witch', was put on trial at York Castle on 17 March 1809. She was convicted and sentenced to death, and in a final irony, when Mary was cut down from the gallows her skin was flayed from her body and sold as good-luck charms.

BAXTER, Jeannie   That pre-eminent defender Mr Edward Marshall Hall, never at a loss for an elegant turn of phrase, introduced the Jeannie Baxter case as one which would require 'the pen of a Zola and the brush of a Hogarth' to do full justice to it. A lot to live up to, perhaps, but in retrospect one can certainly see his point.

At the time Zola (or Hogarth) would have been interested in Jeannie Baxter she was in her early twenties. She had been comfortably 'looked after' by a wealthy middle-aged northerner, and would no doubt have continued to enjoy this mutually convenient relationship but for the intrusion into her life of Mr Julian Bernard Hall – a far different kettle of fish. A younger, wholly more glamorous man than Jeannie was accustomed to, Hall was not only rich, but adventurous, being a pioneer of the aircraft and a patron of the art of boxing; less attractive was his serious drink problem. Nevertheless, Jeannie consented to be his mistress, and while Hall lived in luxury in a flat just behind London's Piccadilly, he installed Jeannie in a comfortable apartment just across town at Carlton Mansions, Maida Vale.

There was just one obstacle – Jeannie's former lover, whom we will call, to preserve his blameless name, 'Jennings'. Though Mr Jennings was conveniently far away at the other end of England, he was, nevertheless, making increasingly persistent demands for Jeannie to return to him and the country cottage which he had provided for her use. In December 1912

Mr Jennings journeyed to London in order to visit Jeannie at Carlton Mansions. Unhappily for all concerned (though presumably luckily for the Zolas and Hogarths), Julian Hall had arrived ahead of him. Hall opened the proceedings by swigging down a magnum of champagne and loosing off a few random shots around the room from a revolver he was wielding. By the time a now very apprehensive Jeannie opened the front door to her former lover, Hall was best part down a second bottle of bubbly, and in pugnacious mood. Jennings, sober as always, found himself confronted by the gun-toting Hall who challenged him to a duel. Hall produced another revolver from his pocket and proposed that he and Jennings should each light a cigarette. Jeannie would turn the light out, and they would shoot at each other using only the glowing tips of the cigarettes for guidance. Wisely, Jennings declined to participate and Hall, lurching around and muttering oaths, shot at a framed photograph of Jennings instead. 'Are you in love with this girl?' slurred Hall, gesturing menacingly at Jeannie. 'I am,' replied the older man (with a lot more courage than sense, if you ask me). Hall grunted again, turned the lights out anyway, and shot a few more wild slugs into the sitting-room walls; this time, quite by chance, he hit a photograph of Jeannie. As a last gesture of defiance, Julian Hall swore that if Jeannie would ditch her former lover, then they could be married. He then stumbled out of the door firing a parting shot over his shoulder.

One might have thought that this display would have given Jeannie Baxter pause to think of the wisdom of any permanent relationship with the crazy drunk who had just shot up her flat; but this sort of behaviour clearly appealed to the girl, for she promptly dismissed the nice Mr Jennings and announced to Hall that she wished to get married the following spring – on the fifteenth of April. She left it up to him to make the arrangements.

April the fourteenth; the day before the wedding. Jeannie, who had hardly been able to think about anything else for days, arrived at Hall's Denman Street apartment to go over the final preparations. She was irritated, though by no means surprised, to find her fiancé propped up in bed guzzling brandy. The irritation turned to fury when Jeannie learned that no arrangements had been made for the wedding at all – just this gibbering alcoholic moaning 'The drink is killing me.' How prophetic those words proved to be!

Minutes later a friend of Hall's who had been staying at the flat heard the loud report of shots coming from behind the bedroom door, followed by a woman's voice pleading: 'Come here; come and look. I have shot Jack.' And when the bewildered guest leaped up and into the bedroom, sure enough there lay Julian Hall, bullet wounds in his arm and chest. 'Oh Jack!', Jeannie was crying, then: 'He made me do it!'

By the time her trial for murder came up at the Old Bailey in June 1913, Jeannie Baxter had expanded her story into the defence which her learned counsel, Edward Marshall Hall, was to present to the jury. Jeannie, he explained, had arrived at the flat late in the morning and found 'Jack' drinking; she also found that he had done nothing about organizing the impending wedding. Angry and frustrated, she had yelled: 'Jack, I think you are a coward to treat me like this!' He seems to have taken exception to the tone of Jeannie's voice and punched her in the face; then he pulled a revolver out of the bedside cupboard and laid it on the bed. After pouring himself another tumbler of brandy Hall shouted: 'You and I will never be married, I cannot keep my promise; it is better to finish it.' He then picked up the gun and began to wave it in the air. Jeannie, fearing for her safety, told him to put it down. 'Do you think you could take it from me?' Hall sneered, and turned the gun to point at his own chest, asking Jeannie to pull the trigger. By now she clearly felt that enough was enough and tried to take the weapon away before Hall got any more drunk and any more dangerous. According to her story, that is when the gun went *off*. A tragic accident, Marshall Hall told a spellbound Court – a tragic accident.

Well, the jury didn't go all the way with him on that. They may have wondered why, if the fatal shot had been accidental, Jack Hall also came to be shot in the arm; they may also have been puzzled as to why, on her own adinission, Jeannie Baxter had picked up the gun and fired a couple of shots into the bedroom ceiling. However, they did meet Marshall Hall half-way; they convicted Jeannie on the lesser charge of manslaughter. She was sentenced to three years' imprisonment.

BEAR, Suzan and Michael *see* **CARSON, Susan and James**

BECK, Martha, and **FERNANDEZ, Raymond** Martha Seabrook was born in 1920, and had already grown prodigiously fat by the age of thirteen when she was raped by her brother. It may or may not have been this unpleasant experience which left her with a great appetite for the bizarre in sex, and the longing for a life of romance. It may also have contributed to an increasingly callous view of her fellow human beings. Martha trained as a nurse and worked as an undertaker's assistant before being appointed superintendent of a home for crippled children at Pensacola, Florida. Her marriage to Alfred Beck in 1944 quickly ended in divorce, as had two previous marriages.

Raymond Fernandez, six years Martha's senior, was born in Hawaii of Spanish parents, brought up in Connecticut, and had lived for some time in Spain where he married and fathered four children, all of whom he had long since abandoned. During the Second World War Fernandez had served – briefly but apparently with some distinction – with the British Intelligence Service, though a head injury sustained in 1945 seems to have unhinged an already none too stable personality. For a start, he embarked on a study of black magic, and he claimed to have an irresistible power over women. Whatever the reason, Raymond Fernandez is thought to have enveigled his way into more than one huudred women's hearts, homes and bank accounts over the next couple of years and swindled them all.

Each of the victims had been selected from notices in newspaper 'Lonely Hearts Clubs'. Which is how, towards the end of 1947, Ray met Martha Beck, and together they added murder to fraud and deceit.

Their problem arose from Martha's fanatical demands on Raymond's fidelity, going to extreme and often burlesque lengths to ensure that he did not consummate any of the lonely-hearts liaisons into which he entered. On one occasion Martha insisted on sleeping with one of the victims herself to make sure there were no nocturnal fun and games. A born philanderer, Fernandez proved a difficult consort to control and, following his frequent falls from grace, became the focus of Martha's considerably violent temper.

In December 1948, Raymond Fernandez made the acquaintance of a sixty-six-year-old widow from New York named Janet Fay. Having plundered her savings via promises of marriage, Raymond invited Mrs Fay to the Long Island apartment which he shared with his 'sister', and strangled and bludgeoned her to death. The body was later buried.

Mrs Delphine Downing, a young widow with a two-year-old daughter, was the next victim, only weeks after the disposal of Mrs Fay. Delphine Downing took Fernandez as her lover – much to Martha's annoyance – and both of them moved into the Downing home in Michigan. After robbing her of what money and possessions they could, Beck and Fernandez forced sleeping pills down Mrs Downing's throat and shot the unconscious woman through the head; to stop the child crying, Beck drowned her in the bath. Despite careful burial of the bodies in the cellar under a new covering of cement, suspicious neighbours reported Delphine and little Rainelle Downing's disappearance to the police.

Arrested for the Michigan murders, Beck and Fernandez were extradited to New York when it was realized that

Michigan could not implement the death penalty. Both prisoners confessed to the Fay and Downing murders, but stubbornly denied the string of seventeen other deaths of which they were suspected. The trial became a *cause célèbre* not so much on account of the murders themselves, but because of Martha Beck's regular dispatches from gaol to the press detailing her and Raymond's far from prosaic sexual exploits. Despite serious doubts as to Raymond Fernandez' state of mind, the 'Lonely Hearts Killers' were judged sane, and guilty. Still expressing undying love for each other, Beck and Fernandez were executed in the electric chair at Sing Sing prison on 8 March 1951.

BECKER, Marie Alexandrine In many respects, Marie Becker's discontent was no different from that of many of her peers – not only in her native Liège, but the civilized world over. The years had passed over her in a drab succession, offering an excess neither of joy nor excitement, and the grey vista of mediocrity stretched as far ahead as she dared look. After fifty-three years, twenty of them spent chained by wedlock to an honest but unromantic and unimaginative cabinet-maker, Madame Becker was desperate for change. In a word, Marie was looking for the *frisson* of romance; which happened to be what Monsieur Lambert Bayer was also seeking. The passionate affair that followed wrought a change in Marie Becker as dangerous as it was unexpected.

The first casualty, in the autumn of 1932, was Charles Becker who, though previously of stout constitution, could not have been expected to withstand the massive dose of digitalis that his wife administered. In November 1934, Becker was followed into the grave by Bayer, and for the time being at least the widow Becker had a little money and a lot of freedom. It seemed almost as though she had recaptured some of the lost years of youth – she began to dress in gaudy clothes and extravagant make-up, and friends and neighbours were more than a little scandalized by this elderly lady's late-night revelling, and the endless string of lovers half her age, for whose 'services' Marie Becker was obliged to pay. And herein lay the problem – Madame Becker still had the freedom, but was rapidly running out of money with which to buy what passed for romance.

Then in July 1935 a friend, Marie Castadot, was seized with attacks of nausea; she was nursed by Madame Becker, but on the twenty-third she died. And so in fairly rapid succession did a number of others among the merry widow's circle of friends and acquaintances. It was not until October 1936, when the police began to receive anonymous letters accusing Marie Becker of poisoning two elderly widows named Lange and Weiss, that investigations uncovered a whole series of similar cases – Julia Bossy, Jeanne Perot, Aline-Louise Damorette, Yvonne Martin, Anne Stevart, Mathilde Bulte and more. All had been nursed in their final days by Madame Becker. A search of her apartment yielded a storehouse of women's clothing and jewellery.

Marie Becker was taken into custody, and when she was searched, a small green flask was found in her handbag, its contents later identified by a chemist as digitalis. The drug was customarily administered in small doses to patients suffering from heart complaints, though in large doses it is a poison as deadly as any. It was to be Madame Becker's consistent claim that she carried the digitalis because she had heart trouble. The problem was that, when exhumed, all the dead women that she had nursed were found to contain fatal residues of the drug.

At her trial, which at times bordered on pantomime, Marie Becker indignantly denied the eleven charges of murder brought against her, though she nevertheless seems greatly to have amused the court with descriptions of her 'patients' as they approached the day of their celestial judgement. One, she thought, 'looked like an angel choked with sauerkraut'. Madame Becker was, predictably, found guilty of murder and routinely sentenced to death. However, in accordance with the established practice in Belgium, the sentence was commuted to life imprisonment.* Marie Becker died some years later in prison.

BELL, Mary Flora Mary first saw the light of day on 26 May 1957, the illegitimate daughter of an emotionally unstable seventeen-year-old Scottish girl. Her parents married after the birth of Mary, though this was little compensation for a childhood characterized by instability and poverty. Indeed, Mary spent much of her early years being shuttled around various relatives and foster homes. Although she was a withdrawn child, Mary developed an outward exhibitionism and boisterousness that at times amounted to aggression; school friends seemed to get 'hurt' more frequently when they played with Mary than they did playing with other children. Playmates complained to their parents that Mary would squeeze their necks until they squealed.

Nobody took much notice of these childish scraps which were attributed to nothing more than naughtiness, until 25 May 1968, when the body of four-year-old Martin Brown was found in a derelict house in the Scotswood area of Newcastle. There were no apparent signs of violence, and at first it was thought that Martin had died after eating the contents of a bottle of pills he found in the house. At the inquest an open verdict was returned.

On the following day a local nursery school was found broken into and a small amount of vandalism committed. When the police looked into the case they discovered a number of scribbled notes, obviously written by a child, one of which read: 'We did murder Martain brown Fuckof you bastard.' Five days later the new alarm installed at the school rang at the police station, and when a patrol car arrived at the building they

*Since 1863 Belgium has only once – in 1918 – used the death penalty for civilian crimes.

found Mary Bell inside with Norma Joyce Bell (she was not a relative, but a close friend and neighbour). The girls denied the previous break-in, but they were charged, and their cases were due to be heard by the juvenile court when they were arrested for murder.

On 31 July Brian Howe, three and a half years old, disappeared; his body was later found on a patch of waste ground. Brian had been strangled and his body pierced and scratched with a broken pair of scissors found beside him. Police conducted their questioning of the local schoolchildren by the novel means of a questionnaire, asking whether they had seen Brian Howe on the day of his disappearance, whether they had seen anything unusual or suspicions, and so on. Mary and her friend both made statements that seemed odd, and on fuller questioning they began to contradict themselves and each other. Then Norma insisted that she had seen Mary strangle Brian Howe, and Mary insisted it had been Norma who had killed the child. Norma Joyce and Mary Bell were taken into custody and charged with the murders of Brian Howe and Martin Brown, whose cause of death had now been certified as strangulation.

The trial opened at Newcastle on 3 December 1968, and lasted for two weeks. Predictably a great deal of the court's time was occupied with the reports of psychiatrists called as expert witnesses. Although he found no indication of mental abnormality, one forensic psychiatrist stated that Mary possessed 'an unsocialized manipulative personality'. To another doctor she had seemed at times to display a complete lack of feeling for other human beings; 'Brian Howe had no mother,' Mary had said, 'so he won't be missed.' Later she added: 'If you're dead, you're dead. It doesn't matter then.'

Norma, although she was the elder by two years, had far less to say for herself, and the general impression was that it was upon her friend that Mary had exercised her 'manipulative personality'. Norma Joyce Bell was acquitted of the charges altogether, and Mary was found guilty only of the manslaughter of Brian Howe and Martin Brown on account of diminished responsibility. Before being sentenced, Mary Bell told a police-woman looking after her: 'Murder isn't that bad. We all die sometime . . .'

Finding Mary guilty was the simple part of the proceedings; deciding what to do with her next proved a lot more difficult. Although there was no shortage of adequate hospital facilities for maladjusted children, none was willing to take the risk of accepting such a potentially dangerous patient as Mary Bell. Mary was instead sentenced to be detained in a maximum security unit of an approved school.

In September 1977, at the age of twenty, Mary Bell escaped from Moor Court open prison to which she had been transferred. She claimed she wanted an opportunity to prove that she could look after herself in the outside world. Mary was recaptured three days later and finally released in 1980.

BESNARD, Marie   Marie Davaillaud was born in France in 1896, and even at the convent school where she spent her early years she was notorious as a liar and a thief. In 1920 she married Auguste Antigny, a cousin. Seven years later he died, but because he was known to suffer from tuberculosis his untimely death aroused no suspicion. The widow Antigny took another husband, Léon Besnard, in 1929, and he became a partner in more than just marriage.

When two of Léon's aunts passed over in 1938 and 1940, their not inconsiderable wealth passed by inheritance to Léon's parents. By November 1940 Marie's father had died of what was diagnosed as a 'cerebral haemorrhage', and her mother had taken up residence with her daughter and son-in-law. Then Léon's father died from eating 'poison mushrooms', followed by his mother who died of 'pneumonia'. The inheritance was then divided between Léon and his sister Lucie, though when poor Lucie inexplicably 'committed suicide' Léon and Marie got the lot.

The Besnards started taking in lodgers. First there was Monsieur and Madame Rivet, who expressed their gratitude by making Marie heir to their estate. It was the worst thing they could have done, because almost before the ink was dry on the document the Rivets had gone to meet their maker – he from 'pneumonia', she from a 'chest infection'. Pauline and Virginie Lalleron, two elderly cousins, took up residence with the Besnards in the mid-1940s, and they too felt constrained to reward Léon and Marie's little attentions by making them beneficiaries. Pauline was the first to go, apparently mistaking a bowl of lye for a bowl of gruel; and when one week later Virginie made exactly the same fatal error nobody even thought to comment on the coincidence.

In 1947 Marie ditched her husband in favour of a German prisoner-of-war who had been put to work in Loudun. In October of the same year Léon died; but before he made his agonized exit, he was able to complain to a friend that Marie had poisoned him. Marie's own mother, last survivor of the immediate Davaillaud/Besnard families, died in 1949, and by now rumours of Léon's suspicious death had begun to circulate around the town. Worse still, some people started to associate the rumour with the other fatal illnesses which had so beset the Besnard household over the previous decade. Marie tried to stop the gossip spreading by sending death-threats to the principal scandalmongers, and even went so far as to burn someone's house down. But in the end the stories reached the ears of the local police. Léon's body was the first to be exhumed, and was found to contain traces of arsenic; then other members of the family were dug up, and the Rivets and Lallerons, and finally Marie's first husband, Auguste Antigny – without exception they had been fed large doses of arsenic before they died.

Although Marie did on one occasion confess her guilt to the

police, by the time she was due to come to trial in February 1952, she had engaged some top Parisian attorneys to defend her. These lawyers demanded a second, independent forensic examination of the alleged victims. Unfortunately the internal organs, which are the most reliable indicators of poisoning, had been destroyed in seven of the thirteen cases. So when Marie Besnard finally stood before the court in March 1954, she was facing only six counts of murder. On this occasion the jury failed to reach a decision and another trial was hastily convened at which, for good measure, the prosecutor decided to reinstate the original thirteen charges. Despite her earlier confession, despite clear scientific evidence of arsenical poisoning, and despite Marie's clumsy attempts to intimidate her accusers, the jury this time acquitted her. And so the woman who had become known throughout France as the 'Queen of Poisoners' walked free from the court.

BESSARABO, Hera *see* **MYRTEL, Hera**

BLANDY, Mary Love, requited or otherwise, must rank equal with money as the root of all kinds of evil – especially the evil of murder. The case of Miss Mary Blandy stands representative of the powerful influence of love in the lives and deaths of humankind.

The Blandys were a family of some considerable means and substance residing at Henley-on-Thames; Mr Francis Blandy was an attorney, and also served as town clerk in that place. Of his daughter Mary, we are told 'her manners were sprightly and affable, and her appearance engaging'. It would seem that the engaging Miss Blandy's hand in marriage was also much sought after 'by many persons whose rank and wealth rendered them fitting to become her partner for life'. The family, however, had an inclination towards gentlemen holding commissions in the Army, and their company at the Blandys' frequent dinner parties and balls was always welcome – not least to Mary.

Enter the Honourable William Henry Cranstoun, a captain with the recruitment service, at the time engaged in recruiting for a foot regiment. William was the son of Lord Cranstoun, a Scottish peer of excellent pedigree, and the nephew of Lord Mark Ker who had obtained his commission for him.

At the time, Cranstoun was forty-six years old and 'devoid of all personal attractions'; Mary was twenty years his junior. Nevertheless, a passion arose between them the strength of which seems quite to have caused the Captain to forget the young lady to whom he had been married since 1745. In the same state of blissful amnesia the rather less than Honourable William Henry proposed marriage to Mary and was enfolded in the bosom of the Blandy family.

It was at this stage that Lord Ker blew the whistle on his errant nephew and informed Mr Blandy of William's present matrimonial status. With no appearance of contrition, Cranstoun compounded his naughtiness:

He felt that some steps were necessary to get his first marriage anulled [not least in view of the anticipated £1,000 dowry that came with Mary's hand]. At length he wrote to his wife requesting her to disown him for a husband. The substance of this letter was that, having no other way of rising to preferment but in the army, he had but little ground to expect advancement there while it was known he was encumbered with a wife and family; but could he once pass for a single man he had not the least doubt of being quickly promoted, which would procure him a sufficiency to maintain her as well as himself in a more genteel manner than he was now able to do. Mrs Cranstoun, ill as she had been treated by her husband, and little hope as she had of more generous usage, was, after repeated letters had passed, induced to give up her claim, and at length wrote a letter disowning him. On this an attempt was made by him to annul the marriage, this letter being produced in evidence; but the artifice being discovered, the suit was dismissed, with costs.

Unsurprisingly, Francis Blandy was less than enchanted by the activities of his prospective son-in-law, and manifested his disapproval by throwing William out of the house. Not so Mary, who was still very enchanted by her future husband – bigamist or no. On his departure for Scotland Cranstoun promised to send Mary some powders which, she subsequently claimed he told her, would have the effect of sweetening her father up. To avoid suspicion, the substances would be labelled 'Powders to clean Scotch pebbles'.

Accordingly, Mary took delivery of the powders and via some water gruel made by a servant administered a hefty dose to her father, repeating the 'cure' on the following day. Despite the physicians' best efforts, Francis Blandy slipped rapidly towards the abyss, and when all hope of recovery was past his contrite daughter rushed to the death-bed in an agony of tears and lamentations and confessed to her wickedness.

At the ensuing Oxford Assizes Mary Blandy was indicted for the wilful murder of her father, and upon her own confession was found guilty. At nine o'clock on the morning of 6 April 1752 Mary, dressed in black bombasine with her arms wound round with black ribbons, stepped up to the foot of the gallows. With a last gesture of maidenly modesty, she begged not to be hanged too high 'for the sake of decency', and on being asked to ascend a little farther expressed a fear that she might fall and hurt herself!

The rope having been put round her neck, she pulled her handkerchief over her face and was turned off on the prearranged signal of holding out the book of devotions that she had been reading.

An interesting postscript is that while she was in prison in Oxford Castle, Mary heard about Elizabeth Jeffries who, with John Swan, had murdered her uncle and was herself awaiting execution. The two ladies entered into a friendly correspondence, though it is recorded that Mary was very shocked by Elizabeth Jeffries' confession to her crime and wrote her a reproachful letter.

But what of the real villain of the piece? Captain the Honourable William Henry Cranstoun was never put on trial for his complicity in the death of Francis Blandy, though he suffered some public vilification. Six months after Mary's execution in Oxford, Cranstoun sought refuge in the town of Furnes in Flanders, where he died shortly afterwards. However, he left certain documents seeming to exonerate himself from blame, and these were published posthumously as *Captain Cranstoun's Account of the Poisoning of the Late Mr Francis Blandy*.

BOLTON, Mildred   The 'battered husband syndrome' rarely receives much publicity, though it certainly exists, and to a far greater extent than one might imagine. One of the prototype henpecked husbands was Charles Bolton. Bolton was a mildmannered, bespectacled businessman from Chicago, industrious at work, helpful in the home. In 1922 he married a vivacious Michigan girl named Mildred. What he did not know until it was too late was that Mildred was insanely and incurably jealous; she was also vicious and quick-tempered, all of which spelled 'lethal combination'. Although he never gave her the slightest cause for concern over his devotion and fidelity to her, Mildred Bolton accused her husband of having affairs with every woman who crossed his path. When he protested his innocence, she got mad; and when she got mad she beat him up a bit. More times than they could remember, neighbours were constrained to call in the police to break up a noisy brawl. On one occasion, poor Charlie had been so badly gashed on his arm that he needed hospital treatment; meanwhile, back at the house Mildred was blithely explaining to the officer that her husband had cut himself shaving – it was three o'clock in the morning.

For years the violence escalated until, in 1936, Mildred went ape. On 15 June she took the elevator to her husband's office on Chicago's West Jackson Street, walked through the door and emptied the six chambers of a revolver into his body. As Charlie floundered and groaned in agony on the floor, Mildred is reported to have turned to horrified onlookers and to have said: 'Don't pay him any mind, he's putting on an act.' When Charles Bolton died some hours later Mildred was charged with his murder, and at her trial was sentenced to 199 years without possibility of parole. Mildred still had 192 to go when, in August 1943, she slashed her own wrists in the penitentiary at Dwight, Illinois.

BOMPARD, Gabrielle, and EYRAUD, Michel It was on 27 July 1889 that forty-nine-year-old Toussaint-Augustin Gouffe, a Paris court bailiff, was reported missing by his brother-in-law. Although Monsieur Gouffe had disappeared on odd occasions before – usually in connection with his fondness for drink and the company of women – after several days the Sûreté's senior officer, Marie-François Goron, decided to investigate. In Gouffe's office on the rue Montmartre, Goron recovered eighteen spent matches from the floor around the safe. The concierge remembered a man – not Gouffe – letting himself into the offices on the night of 26 July and leaving shortly afterwards. The fact that there was no sign of a forced entry indicated that the man must have obtained the bailiff's keys, and the signs of activity around the safe suggested that he was attempting to commit robbery. But where was bailiff Gouffe?

Millery is a village on the river Rhone; not far from Lyons, but a long way from Paris. On 13 August the locals found the body of an unidentified man – or rather, decomposing as it was, the corpse's smell found them. Close by were the broken remains of a wooden trunk, which by the look of it had once contained the body. News of the find reached the Sûreté eventually, and

Gouffe's brother-in-law hastened to Millery to view the remains. Although the corpse had decomposed to such an extent that the local physician had estimated time of death at around one year earlier, it was possible for the brother-in-law to be sure about one thing – unlike the dead man, Gouffe did not have black hair. Chief Goron was less certain – call it an old policeman's 'nose' if you like – and he had the Lyons police send up details of the trunk which had been found near the body. Here, at last, there was a break. The labels attached to the box showed that it had been dispatched by rail from Paris's Gare de Lyon on 27 July – the day Gouffe was reported missing.

It happened that at that time the celebrated scientist Professor Alexandre Lacassagne was head of the forensic department at the University of Lyons, and he was invited to re-examine the still unidentified human remains. The result of Lacassagne's post-mortem was a belief that the body was, after all, that of Toussaint-Augustin Gouffe. The hair had become artificially discoloured while confined in the box, and when the professor washed samples of the hair and beard they were restored to Gouffe's natural brown. Bailiff Gouffe had been found, and he had been strangled. The next question was, who killed him?

Renewed investigations in Paris revealed that during the last days before he disappeared, Gouffe had been seen about town with a notorious prostitute named Gabrielle Bompard and her equally disreputable companion, a crook named Michel Eyraud. However, it was not until the first weeks of the following year that the Sûreté had further word of their suspects. In the months since they were last seen in Paris, Bompard and Eyraud had been on quite an adventure. Having borrowed money they fled France calling in at London and New York, then on to Vancouver, finally coming to rest in San Francisco. Here Gabrielle Bompard ditched Eyraud in favour of a young American businessman, and on the pretence that her former partner was planning to kill her, Gabrielle persuaded her new love to whisk her back to Paris.

Once home the couple walked into the offices of the Sûreté on 26 January where Gabrielle Bompard confessed that Michel Eyraud had killed bailiff Gouffe – claiming no part in the crime herself, of course. Meanwhile, Eyraud had been busy as well. From his self-imposed exile in New York, he penned a lengthy letter in response to the reports he had seen of Gabrielle Bompard's accusation. It took no fewer than twenty pages to make a counterclaim that it had been Bompard who committed the murder and was now trying to frame him for it. By the time Michel Eyraud was arrested in a Cuban brothel on 20 May, his former partner had already succumbed to police persuasion and spilled the beans about Gouffe's death. On 26 July 1889 the bailiff, who had enjoyed Gabrielle Bompard's intimate company on several occasions before, was lured to her apartment on rue Tronson-Ducoudray for a quite different and entirely more sinister purpose. Gabrielle sat the unfortunate man down on a chair in front of an alcove covered by a curtain, behind which lurked Michel Eyraud. Gabrielle then seductively removed the belt from her silk wrap and playfully put it round Gouffe's neck, passing the end to her accomplice who attached it to an elaborate pulley system which was meant to haul the victim upwards and so hang him. In the event the device failed and Eyraud was obliged to strangle the man with his bare hands. Bitterly disappointed not to find the bailiff's wallet bulging with cash, Eyraud had taken Gouffe's keys and let himself into the office where he suffered another humiliating failure – this time he couldn't open the safe. The couple packed Monsieur Gouffe in a trunk and accompanied it to Lyons near where they dumped it. The rest of the story we know.

In December 1890 Bompard and Eyraud were convicted of murder at the Seine Assize Court. Michel Eyraud was beheaded on the guillotine in February of the following year, and Gabrielle Bompard began a sentence of twenty years' hard labour; she was still only twenty-one years of age.

BORDEN, Lizzie The Fall River Murders are as celebrated to the American people as the Whitechapel Murders are to the British; and the name of Lizzie Borden is as ingrained in that country's folklore as Jack the Ripper is in our own. Like Jack's, Lizzie's story has been told countless times over the decades, in books, plays, films – even in musicals. The obvious difference, of course, is that Lizzie Borden was acquitted of the murders of her father and stepmother, and although the verdict was always a controversial one, we cannot overturn the court's decision. However, a study such as this would be incomplete without at least an outline of Lizzie's ordeal.

It was at about eleven o'clock on the morning of 4 August 1892 that Lizzie Borden, a spinster of thirty-two, summoned the local doctor with the news that her father had been killed. At this point there was no reference to Mrs Borden. When the medic arrived he found sixty-nine-year-old Andrew J. Borden, who had obviously settled down in his study for a rest, lying brutally bludgeoned to death, having sustained no fewer than ten direct blows. One of the neighbours who had been attracted by the commotion now asked where Mrs Borden was. 'I'm sure I don't know,' Lizzie replied, adding cryptically, 'but I don't know perhaps she isn't killed also, for I thought I heard her coming in.' A search of the house revealed sixty-five-year-old Mrs Abby Borden lying where she too had been cut down with a bludgeon while cleaning a spare bedroom; a subsequent post-mortem detailed nineteen separate wounds.

According to the evidence, the two crimes had been separated by about ninety minutes, suggesting that the killer was a member of the household. Lizzie's elder sister Emma had an alibi for the time of the killings, which left Lizzie and the servant. Soon the tongues were wagging and the fingers pointing in Lizzie Borden's direction, not only because she was a 'member of the household' but because it was known there was ill-feeling between herself and her stepmother, and that she resented her father's parsimony which forced them to live in a poor neighbourhood of town. But there was other evidence. Before the murders, Lizzie tried to buy prussic acid, and in the same week everybody in the house except Lizzie had suffered what was diagnosed as 'food poisoning'. A search of the cellar had turned up an axe head which had recently been cleaned, and was a strong candidate for the murder weapon – further proof, if it were needed, of a 'member of the household' being guilty.

The inquest was held in private, and afterwards Lizzie was charged with the two murders. By the time the case got to trial at New Bedford in June 1893, Lizzie had become a household name across the nation. Feelings were mixed as to her guilt, and swung precariously back and forth between 'she must have done it' and 'she couldn't have done it'. Lizzie did everything that a defence attorney could have wanted of her: she looked demure and refined, kept her eyes lowered, but not so as to look shifty, and when she fainted in the middle of the proceedings it was simply seen as proof of an innocent soul in torment. At the end of a ten-day trial Lizzie Borden was acquitted.

Defiantly, Lizzie moved back into the small Fall River community where she bought a large, elegant house. At first she shared it with her sister, but after she and Emma quarrelled, Lizzie lived alone until her death in 1927 at the age of sixty-six. She left an estate totalling around one million dollars, a third of which was willed to animal charities. Although the case remains officially unsolved, there are many who believe firmly in Lizzie Borden's guilt, attributing the killings to some temporary mental aberration such as epilepsy.

BOUVIER, Léone   The village of Saint-Macaire-en-Mauges nestles near the town of Cholet in the Marne-et-Loire region of Western France. It was in the village of Saint-Macaire, in 1930, that Léone Bouvier was born to a peasant couple, both of whom were confirmed alcoholics. Léone endured a loveless, joyless childhood, handicapped by none too beautiful looks and low intelligence. At this time Léone's only close companion was her elder sister Georgette, a quick-witted and attractive girl who at the age of eighteen escaped the domestic nightmare of the Bouvier household and entered a convent at Angers. Left to her own devices, Léone abandoned her meagre schooling and began work in the local shoe factory, her weekly wages helping to keep old Monsieur and Madame Bouvier in strong cider.

One night in 1951, Léone met a young garage mechanic named Emile Clenet at a dance in Cholet; feeling wanted for the first time, Léone embraced the relationship with open arms, and readily consented to a regular Sunday meeting with Emile which consisted mainly of hours spent in a cheap hotel room. Inevitably Léone Bouvier became pregnant. Despite the abortion she underwent at Clenet's insistence, the whole village had become aware of Léone's 'condition'. Shunned by her own parents, who threw her out of the house, and dismissed from her job, now Léone was rejected even by her lover; after a tearful meeting, Emile told her the affair was over.

Desperate, Léone Bouvier travelled to Nantes, where she spent the bitterly cold weeks of January 1952 wandering the streets, picking up what little money she could from prostitution. With what was left of her scant earnings, Léone bought a small .22 calibre automatic pistol. Quite what she was planning we cannot be sure; perhaps suicide seemed an attractive alternative to the misery she was now enduring, or perhaps she had revenge on her mind. What we do know is that the gun was in her purse when, on 15 February 1952 – her twenty-third birthday – Léone summoned all her courage and visited Emile at the garage where he worked. He had not remembered her birthday, and he was not exactly overjoyed to see her, but he did agree to a rendezvous on the following Sunday. Which may be what, temporarily at least, earned him a reprieve.

On their next Sunday meeting Léone and Emile joined the Mardi Gras merrymaking at Cholet, and in many ways it was just like old times. Emile picked her up from their rendezvous point on his motor cycle and they rode into town. They walked hand-in-hand, drinking in the excitement of the carnival atmosphere, paused for an occasional embrace . . . Then Emile dropped the bombshell that cost him his life; he announced that he was leaving France to look for work in North Africa. When Léone reminded him that they had once planned to marry, Emile gave an embarrassed shrug. One thing was clear – he had no intention of marrying her now. He said as much. It was a very deflated Léone Bouvier who took up her position on the pillion of Emile's motor cycle as they left Cholet. When they reached the place where Léone had left her bicycle she asked for just one last kiss. It was certainly that. As Emile bent down to meet her lips, Léone raised her shiny little automatic and shot him once through the neck. Then she mounted her bicycle and pedalled furiously to the only place of safety she knew – the convent at Angers, and the tender, comforting embrace of her sister. And that is where, on the following afternoon, the police arrested her.

It was not until almost two years later, in December 1953, that Léone Bouvier stood before a presiding magistrate at the Maine-et-Loire Assizes. Now, for reasons of custom and culture, the French courts traditionally treat a *crime passionnel* with compassion and leniency. But poor Léone Bouvier was to receive none of that compassion, none of that leniency. The presiding magistrate, in this case Maître Diousidon, plays a much more adversarial role in the French courts than an English judge; and from the very beginning of the trial M. Diousidon made it perfectly clear that he did not like Léone. Things became a whole lot worse when he learned that the prisoner's sister was a nun: 'You see,' he roared from the bench, 'there was no need for you to go wrong.' In his examination, presiding magistrate Diousidon told Léone: 'You kissed him; you kissed Emile Clenet, and at the same time you drew a pistol from beneath your coat, placed it beside his head – rested it on his collar! Then you pulled the trigger. Atrocious!

It was atrocious!' Barely able to speak for rage, Diousidon demanded: 'Why did you kill him?'

With a smail voice that seemed to come from far away, Léone said simply: 'I loved him.'

There was little chance of Léone Bouvier being sentenced to death – the French have rarely executed women, whatever their crime – but she did receive the harshest penalty the court could impose; despite the best efforts of her lawyer, Léone was sentenced to life imprisonment, which meant at least twenty years.

BRADY, Phoebe and Verren and HARMSWORTH, Michael   The body was found on a desolate, treeless moor on the road from Cork to Dublin, buried in a shallow grave. So shallow that one foot protruded above ground, which is what had caught the attention of passing motorist Thomas Gilligan, on the morning of 23 December 1979. The Homicide Squad was alerted, and the body taken down to the morgue where the extent of the injuries became apparent. The man had been gagged and bound, beaten with a dog whip on the back and buttocks, and with iron bars on the chest and head, fracturing his skull, smashing his face and rib cage, rupturing several of the vital organs; his testicles were bruised. He was thirty-six years old, and his name was Eric Willmot.

Willmot had been a tinker who etched a living at the fairs and markets, which is where he had come under the spell of Phoebe Brady in 1973. He had gone to her caravan to have his fortune told, fell for her stunning good looks, and ended up in her bed. A bit of casual fun for a tinker, perhaps, but not for the High Priestess of the Devil Worshippers, the title Phoebe Brady had inherited on the death of her mother. She ruled a sect of twenty or thirty members, who put into practice the laws she ordained. And one of those laws was that having slept with her, Eric Willmot had to wed her.

He did so unwillingly, 'with the sanction of the Devil and

beneath an arch of crossed clubs', and received a wedding ring from Phoebe for his troubles. The honeymoon was an extended sojourn in Phoebe's bed, an exhausting effort to satisfy her lusty appetite.

Over the years Willmot tried to run away a number of times – as had his several predecessors – only to be returned to the fold with a good beating for his pains. On the last occasion, six months before the murder, he had sustained a broken arm and three cracked ribs.

Wisely, Willmot planned to make good his escape. Unwisely, he spread it around the bars in Cork that he was saving his money, was emigrating to Canada, and had sold the wedding ring. That last indiscretion was a heinous offence against the sanctity of the Devil Worshippers, and Phoebe Brady was compelled to take appropriate action. For this she enlisted the aid of a bland petty criminal by the name of Michael Harmsworth, a thirty-five-year-old with the strength of a bull. Four hundred pounds up front, another four hundred for delivering Willmot, bound and gagged, to the moors on the night of the winter solstice. And no, it was nothing illegal, more of a joke really, to teach the man a lesson.

Harmsworth coshed Willmot in an alley in the city, half dragged and half carried 'my drunken friend' out to the moors, took his money and ran. Phoebe and her daughter Verren, Assistant High Priestess, did the rest, carrying out with iron bars the sentence of the court of the sect, which had condemned the man to death for stealing the ring.

The court of law handed out a rather more lenient sentence, on 25 July 1980, of life imprisonment for all three defendants: Michael Harmsworth and the two Priestesses of the Devil Worshippers.

BRANCH, Elizabeth and Mary These wicked women were born at Philips Norton, in Somerset. The mother was famed since childhood for the cruelty of her disposition. She married a farmer named Branch, but he quickly found out what an unfortunate choice he had made; for Elizabeth no sooner came into possession of her matrimonial power than she began to exercise her tyranny on her servants, whom she treated with undeserved and unaccountable cruelty, frequently denying them the common necessities of life, and sometimes turning them out of doors at night in the middle of winter. On these occasions their wages were always sent on to them by Mr Branch, who was as remarkable for his humanity and justice as his wife was for the opposite qualities. Mary Branch, the daughter, was an exact replica of her mother in every part of her diabolical temper.

In time Mr Branch died and left an estate of about three hundred pounds a year; but no sooner was he buried than all the servants quitted the family, determined not to live under so tyrannical a mistress. Indeed, Elizabeth's reputation became so notorious that she could obtain as servants only the poor creatures who were put out by the parish, or casual vagrants who strolled the country.

It would be time-consuming to relate the particulars of all the iniquities perpetrated by this inhuman mother and daughter on their staff, at whom they would hurl plates, knives and forks at any real or imagined offence. But to proceed to an account of their trial and execution for the murder of Jane Buttersworth, a poor girl who had been placed with them by the parish officers.

At the Assizes held at Taunton in March 1740, Elizabeth Branch and Mary, her daughter, were indicted for the wilful murder of Jane Buttersworth; and the evidence against them was as follows: Ann Somers, the dairymaid, deposed that Jane had been sent on an errand for some yeast and, having taken longer than was necessary, excused herself to her old mistress by telling an untruth. Hearing this the daughter struck the unfortunate girl on the head with her fist and pinched her ears. Then both of them, mother and daughter, threw her to the ground and Mary knelt on her neck while the mother whipped her with twigs till the blood ran on the ground; the daughter, taking off one of the girl's shoes, beat her with it in a most cruel manner. Poor Jane now cried out for mercy, and after some struggling ran into the parlour, where the vicious pair followed her and beat her with broomsticks till she fell down senseless. After this Mary Branch threw a pail of water over her and proceeded with other kinds of cruelty too gross to mention.

The dairymaid then went off to milk her cows, but on her return half an hour later, she found her mistress, Elizabeth, sitting by the fire, and the girl Jane lying dead upon the floor. Ann noticed that a clean cap had been put on Jane's head while Ann had been out milking, but that blood had seeped through it. At night the body was secretly buried. This nocturnal activity, added to the character of the Branches, aroused suspicion in the neighbourhood, and a warrant was issued by the coroner to exhume the body. At the subsequent inquest Mr Salmon, the surgeon, declared that the victim had received several wounds, any one of which would have proved fatal.

The verdict of the trial jury was that the prisoners were both guilty and they were sentenced to die.

As the country people were violently enraged against them, Elizabeth and Mary Branch were conducted to the place of execution between three and four o'clock in the morning, attended only by the gaoler and about half a dozen people, lest the felons should be torn to pieces by a mob.

When the party arrived at the spot, it was found that the gibbet had been cut down; upon which the carpenter was sent for who immediately erected another. In the end, mother and daughter were hanged before the hour of six – which proved a great disappointment to the thousands of people from all parts of the country who arrived too late to witness the execution of two such unworthy wretches.

BRANCH, Mary *see* **BRANCH, Elizabeth and Mary**

BRENNAN, Inez It is surprising how many killer couples met through lonely-hearts clubs and magazine columns, and alarming how many killers meet their victims in the same way. George Dether met Inez Brennan through a newspaper advertisement, and they married in Pennsylvania in 1928, when Inez was twenty-five. Inez brought two children to the marriage, Gertrude and Raymond, the products of her former marriage to William Pibram. Although Inez and George were frequently at war with each other, often resulting in fisticuffs, they still managed to find some quiet moments in which to add George Junior and Robert to the family. The battles continued to rage until some time around the mid-1940s when George, who swore his wife was trying to poison him, decamped with the children. Then, in 1947, Inez bought a small place in Laurel Springs and Raymond, George Junior and Robert went to live with her; by this time Gertrude was married.

Not long after the ménage had settled in New Jersey, Inez embarked on her lonely-hearts scam. It had been practised often enough before, by women as well as men, and perhaps the great success of Inez's fellow countrywoman, Belle Gunness (see page 148) inspired her own endeavours. Inez would respond to a newspaper ad, and by the softly-softly approach relieve her prospective partners of their hard-earned savings and anything else worth having. Such a dupe was Fred Schub, poultry farmer of Maryland. He parted with nearly one thousand dollars so that Inez could buy a smallholding where they would live happily ever after as man and wife. Mr Schub subsequently disappeared and was never heard from again. Inez, however, did buy a new property, the bleak Horsepond Road Farm in Delaware.

One of Inez's first visitors at the farm was sixty-seven-year-old Wade Wooldridge. They had corresponded through a lonely-hearts club, and Wooldridge had been invited to lunch. Several months later he sold his home, packed his trunks, took the train to Dover, Delaware and telephoned Inez at Horsepond

Road Farm. By her son Robert's account, Inez was not at all pleased at the prospect of her suitor's imminent arrival, but the family politely made him welcome. Quite why Bobby Brennan decided there and then to kill their visitor is not quite clear, but after supper he took Wooldridge on a tour of the farm and at a safe distance from the house put a bullet in his head. Unfortunately it was Bobby's only bullet, and it failed to deprive Wooldridge of his life. As the boy ran back to the house in a panic, his victim lay on the barn floor yelling fit to wake the dead. Inez immediately dispatched the still shaken Bobby back to finish the job; he achieved this by smashing the old man's skull with the rifle butt. After emptying his pockets, the Brennans buried Wooldridge in the pigsty. Then they plundered the trunks he had brought with him before burning all other traces of their guest's visit.

That had been in the second week of October 1948. By the middle of December Wade Wooldridge's daughter was getting concerned; it was most unlike her normally fastidious father not to have sent notification of his arrival at Dover. Anyway, she was worried enough to alert the sheriff's office. But by now another lamb was being prepared for the slaughter.

In January 1949 Hugo Schulz, another farmer, another of Inez Brennan's pen-pals, made his contribution to the Brennan coffers. Inez and Bobby had journeyed to Schulz's property in New Hampshire where Inez shot him dead. Having sold his farm, Bobby and brother Raymond who had joined them, loaded all the portable possessions along with Hugo Schulz's body wrapped up in a tarpaulin into the pick-up and headed back to Horsepond Road. Schulz joined the late Wade Wooldridge beneath the pig-pen.

In early 1949 Inez decided to sell the farm, a plan which necessitated disposing of the bodies lest a new owner should discover them. Loyal Bobby dug the corpses up and burned them. By now Schulz's friends had begun to get a bit suspicious about not hearing from him, especially as the last time they had spoken he had been so gleeful about his forthcoming marriage to the widow Brennan of Dover. Officers did pay a visit to Horsepond Road Farm, but that was all; Inez hadn't seen Schulz, so she said, since she visited him at his farm. It wasn't long after this that Wooldridge's daughter started making a fuss again, and this time the Dover police put some enthusiasm into the inquiry. They managed to track down one Dolly Dear, who at the time of Wooldridge's disappearance had been nursing Inez Brennan through a minor convalescence. In fact, Dolly had been there when the unfortunate farmer had succumbed not to Cupid's arrow as he had hoped, but to the blunt end of Bobby Brennan's rifle. Terrified though she was of reprisals, Dolly told all, and the long and the short of it was that the Brennans were taken into custody. Property was found on the farm belonging to Wade Wooldridge, and there were still enough traces of the incinerated bodies to identify the remains as human. Besides which, Bobby and Raymond confessed to their part in the murders. So, in the end, did Inez Brennan.

The trial of Robert and Inez Brennan occupied two weeks in the middle of September 1949, and when the jury returned after their five-hour retirement it was to bring guilty verdicts against the two defendants. Both were sentenced to life imprisonment, but the judge made it quite plain that if the State of Delaware had allowed it, he would have been more than happy to send Bobby Brennan to the gallows.

BRINVILLIERS, Marie Marguerite Marie Marguerite was born in the year 1630, eldest of five children of the noble French family of d'Aubray. An attractive and precocious girl, Marie was inducted into the joys of sex at a tender age – it is said in company with her brothers. She was married at twenty-one to the Marquis Antoine de Brinvilliers, though the Marquis made no secret of his preference for the gaming table over the boudoir, and Marie, relieved perhaps to have wealth *and* freedom, took a lover in the person of Gaudin de Sainte-Croix.

Sainte-Croix was a friend of the Marquis, though if he knew of the amour at all, Brinvilliers seemed not to care. Which was far from the case with Marie's straitlaced father, one of the Lieutenants-Civil, or Councillors of State, of France; he was so furious that he had Sainte-Croix thrown into the Bastille. Understandably piqued, Gaudin made good use of his incarceration to learn the rudiments of poisoning from an acknowledged master of the science, a fellow-prisoner named Exili. On his release Sainte-Croix found Marie short of money – having decimated her husband's fortune – and between them they plotted to poison her father that she might inherit.

It became clear that Marie Marguerite was a dutiful daughter in many respects, and rather than cause her father the unneces- sary pain that an ill-considered concoction might induce – not to mention one that could be detected by the physicians – she and Sainte-Croix experimented with various potions. Marie then tried them out on the patients of the Hotel Dieu, Paris's public hospital, where she had so charitably volunteered her occasional services. At least fifty of the unlucky inmates died in the cause of 'science' before Dreux d'Aubray was finally dispatched in 1666.

The following is a contemporary translation of the post- mortem report on d'Aubray's death: 'That for the three last days which Monsieur the Lieutenant-Civil lived, he grew lean, very dry, lost his appetite, vomited often, and had a burning in his stomach. And having been opened . . . they found his stomach all black, the liver gangreen'd and burnt, etc., which must have been occasioned by poison, or a humour which sometimes is so corrupted as to have the same effects as poison.'

Having squandered the resulting fortune, the Marchioness turned her greedy gaze on the estates of her two brothers, and Sainte-Croix was once again put to work with the box of poisons.

But lest it be thought that Madame confined her motives simply to those of financial advancement, it should be explained that Marie was equally happy to poison people who simply annoyed or disagreed with her – and given an inborn arrogance and shortness of temper it may be imagined how great was her scope for victims. In fact, Gaudin de Sainte-Croix is said to have spent so much time mixing poisons that he eventually succumbed to the fumes and died. When officials investigated his sudden death they discovered in his chamber a small cabinet, about a foot square, which contained a number of incriminating documents as well as the whole motley apparatus of his and Madame's 'poison factory'.

Marie Marguerite de Brinvilliers was arraigned in 1676. She was found guilty and sentenced 'to be beheaded on a scaffold which shall be erected for that purpose; her body shall be burnt and her ashes thrown in the air. But before her execution she shall be put to the torture, both ordinary and extraordinary, to make her confess her accomplices.'

The following eye-witness account of Madame de Brinvilliers' ignoble death was contained in a letter between Madame de Sévigné and her daughter:

Paris, Friday July 17th, 1676

. . . It is all over, Brinvilliers is reduced to ashes, her poor little body after her execution was thrown into a very great fire, and her ashes into the air; so that we shall draw them in with our breath, and by the communication of the small particles we shall be seized with an inclination to poisoning, which will do a great deal of mischief.

She was tried yesterday; this morning her sentence was read to her and the torture shown to her, but she said there was no need of it for she would confess everything. And indeed, for four hours together she gave an account of her life which was shocking beyond imagination. Ten times successively did she poison her father, and yet had much ado to kill him. Love and intrigues had always a share in her crimes . . .

At six in the evening she was carried in a cart, without any clothing but her smock, with a halter about her neck, to the church of Nôtre Dame where she made the *Amende honorable*. Then she was put again in the cart, where I saw her lying on some straw that was in it, with the doctor on one side and the executioner on the other. I confess the sight made me tremble . . .

She got upon the scaffold alone and barefooted, and the executioner spent a quarter of an hour shaving and placing her head, which the people complained of as a great cruelty . . .

BRODERICK, Elizabeth   Daniel Broderick III was big in law, in fact he was reckoned to be one of the most powerful lawyers in San Diego. Dan had started in medicine, qualified from Notre Dame in 1969, and decided to continue his studies. In 1975 he graduated from Harvard law school.

Dan Broderick had met seventeen-year-old Betty Biscelgia in 1965; she was a freshman student from New York, who had gone to Notre Dame for the college football match. They married in 1969 and over the subsequent years had four children. Their second son was called Rhett, after Dan's all-time idol from *Gone with the Wind*; which says a lot about Dan. Life was none too easy in those days, money was always short. But by 1979 Dan had his own medical-malpractice law firm bringing in close to $1 million a year. The family home was now a five-bedroomed house in its own grounds in La Jolla. The problem was that Betty's home life was not up to much – if before Dan had spent all his time studying or with his friends, he now spent it working. She was not a woman scorned yet, but Betty Broderick was feeling distinctly ignored, increasingly trapped by what amounted to single-parenthood.

In 1983 Betty took the kids camping. Nothing strange in that, it happens in a lot of busy families when one partner can't get away from work. The trouble was, Dan never seemed to be at home when Betty called him. It was about this time that Dan Broderick took on a new legal assistant, twenty-two-year-old Linda Kolkena. Betty put two and two together and came up with the right answer – though Dan insisted there was nothing going on between them.

Despite persistent rumours of the affair which were reaching her ears, Betty was determined to hang on. The eleventh of November 1983 was Dan Broderick's birthday, his thirty-ninth; and by way of a surprise Betty called unexpectedly at his office bearing a bottle of champagne. It was a surprise all right, but the surprise was on Betty. Dan and Linda had already had their party and were now out at lunch. What they did after lunch is anybody's guess, but they certainly didn't go back to the office. What Betty Broderick did is no secret – she went straight home, took her husband's wardrobe-full of expensive tailor-made suits out into the yard, doused them with petrol and lit a bonfire.

During the latter part of 1984 the Brodericks moved out of the La Jolla house temporarily while the builders were carrying out repairs; the family took a short lease on another house. The acrimony followed them, and by February 1985 Dan had had enough and moved back to the family home. Uninvited and unwanted, Betty followed and indulged in an orgy of destruction, smashing glass and spraying graffiti on the walls.

In September 1985, Dan Broderick filed for divorce. And for the next five years the civil courts became the Brodericks' battleground. When Dan wanted to sell the family home, Betty refused her consent. Dan sold it anyway, by an unusual legal manoeuvre involving getting a judge to authorize the sale. Not, you understand, that Betty Broderick was left entirely destitute. In fact, Dan had voluntarily awarded his wife alimony of $9,000 a month (later increased to $16,000) and bought her a new home with an ocean view at La Jolla for an estimated $650,000.

But it had all become more personal than that. For a start

there was Linda Kolkena; or rather, Linda *Broderick* as she now was. As soon as the divorce papers had come through, Dan Broderick had married his former mistress at a sumptuous front-lawn ceremony at his new luxury home in Marston Hills. Betty's name was notably absent from the guest list, and somebody joshed that perhaps the bride and groom should be married in bullet-proof vests. It wasn't altogether a joke.

On one occasion Betty sped her car across the lawn and rammed it straight into the front door of Dan's Marston Hills home. When he opened the car door to pull his ex-wife out, Dan saw an ugly-looking butcher's knife on the seat beside her, and the incident turned into a public brawl.

Betty was mad all right; maybe not crazy mad, but she sure was angry mad. From her viewpoint she had been deprived of everything she had ever worked for, including her children.

On 5 November 1989 Betty Broderick woke early. At around 5.30, before dawn, she climbed into her car. She later claimed her intention was to drive to the beach for a solitary walk, but that she instead found herself outside Dan and Linda's home. Betty insists that despite the early hour all she wanted was to discuss the custody issue. And the only reason she was carrying a loaded pistol was that if Dan refused to cooperate, 'I wanted to splash my brains all over his goddamned house.' Rather unconventionally for a 'business' visit, Betty Broderick let herself into the dark and silent house with a key borrowed from one of her daughters, and made her way up the stairs to Dan and Linda's second-floor master bedroom. There she took out the .38 Smith and Wesson and opened fire apparently randomly. Linda Broderick was struck by one bullet in the neck and another in the chest and died instantly. Daniel Broderick received a shot which punctured his lung and he fell from the bed to the floor where he lay drowning in his own blood. Then, according to Betty's later statement, she left the house in a daze: 'I didn't have any idea if I even hit them.' It wasn't until 7.30 the same morning that the bodies were found by friends of the Brodericks (one of them was Betty's current boyfriend), who had been unable to raise them on the telephone.

Less than half an hour later the police were at the scene, and shortly after that detectives were on the trail of Betty Broderick. Before long she was in custody in the Las Colinas Women's Detention Facility, and taking every opportunity to give her side of the story to anybody prepared to listen – especially if they were from the media. 'He traded me in for a younger model and stole my kids,' Betty lamented. 'He sued me to death.'

Betty Broderick's first trial opened in June 1990 and occupied the following three months. Her attorney, Jack Earley, presented his client in a sympathetic light as a woman scorned, and dragged down by a spiteful and insensitive husband, which had left Betty in a depressed state: 'The anger was as much at herself as at others; she just couldn't get out from under the avalanche, she couldn't escape.' After a lengthy retirement the jury could not agree on a unanimous verdict.

Mrs Broderick's second trial took place before Superior Court Judge Thomas J. Whelan in October 1991 and lasted until the end of the year. The attorneys were the same as for the previous trial, with Jack Earley retaining Betty's brief and prosecutor Kerry Wells presenting the case against her. By this time Betty had become a media *cause célèbre* – a star almost. Already two major books were awaiting an ending and so was a CBS film on the case. The American women's movement had adopted Betty as an example of the wronged wife fighting for justice.

Judge Whelan felt obliged to present the other side of Betty Broderick; he reminded the jury of the evidence of Deputy Maria McCullough, who said that after the previous year's trial Mrs Broderick had bragged about the impact of her evidence: 'I had such a good day at court; I had the jury eating out of my hand,' she had said, adding: 'I think my crying had a really good impact on the jury – they ate it up.'

The jury once again had a difficult time making up their minds, but did manage to agree unanimously in the end, and presented the judge with a verdict of guilty of second-degree murder. Early the following year, in February 1992, Judge Whelan sentenced Betty Broderick to the maximum penalty of thirty-two years in prison; this means that she will serve at least eighteen years before she can apply for parole.

In the meantime, Betty Broderick still enjoys considerable celebrity status, and in the wake of her sentence made a taped interview for broadcast on the high-rating 'Oprah Winfrey Show'. The CBS film became a TV blockbuster, netting 28.4 million viewers and selling to twenty-eight countries around the world. The feminists still see her as a victim, and the Alliance for Divorce and Marriage Reform group have used Betty's case as an argument in its campaign for divorce laws that are fairer to women.

Not everybody agrees, of course. Prosecutor Kerry Wells, who was responsible for presenting the case which put Betty behind bars, is reported as complaining: 'I've had my fill of Elizabeth Broderick; she was not a battered woman. She was getting $16,000 a month in alimony, she had a million-dollar La Jolla house, a car, a boyfriend. I see abused women every day with broken bones and smashed faces. Give me a break.'

BRUHNE, Vera   It came as a most bitter blow to Vera to be suddenly and quite unexpectedly asked to leave. It was the year 1960, and she had been the pampered mistress of Dr Otto Braun for some time, her every whim indulged and more besides – alternating between the luxury mansion outside Munich and the equally luxurious estate on the Costa Brava which, in a moment of generosity, Braun had given Vera. Braun was at the time an uncannily well-preserved sixty-five, and Vera still trim and attractive at fifty; indeed, many considered her remarkably beautiful, including Dr Braun.

Although he was a distinguished physician, it was through

other, decidedly crooked activities, that Braun acquired the riches which he bestowed on a succession of mistresses – drug smuggling, illegal abortions, and so on. He also had a rather short attention span, particularly when it came to female companions. A number of attractive mistresses had passed through Munich, many of them had been given the villa in Spain, along with furs and jewels; and when Braun had tired of them they had been cast out and the villa repossessed. Most of these women had, with greater or lesser grace, gone quietly, probably counting their blessings as they packed the furs, expensive gowns and jewellery. Vera Bruhne was less sanguine about being deprived of her future luxury; in fact she was absolutely furious, especially when she was asked to remove her toothbrush from the villa. Braun was, so he said, going to sell it. The doctor was almost certainly surprised when Vera offered to find him a buyer; it was not the way dismissed lovers usually behaved, but given Braun's conceit, he probably put it down to his charm and power over women.

Anyway, Vera came up with Herr Johann Ferbach. She and Ferbach had first met in 1944, while he was on the run after deserting from the German Army. She hid him until it was all over, and then kept him on as a sort of all-purpose companion, sometimes lover, more often minder. The lumbering, none-too-bright Johann stuck with her through her many love affairs including the one with Otto Braun, and at least a couple of marriages. Now he was to add a further service, that of hired assassin. It was Johann Ferbach, posing as Herr Doktor Schmitz, a prospective purchaser of the villa, who, with a note of introduction from Vera, got into Braun's Munich house, murdered the housekeeper and lay in wait for the master.

When the police were called to the scene of the crime they found the housekeeper in the basement dead from a bullet wound; Dr Otto Braun, equally dead from gunshot wounds, lay in the master bedroom. For reasons best known to themselves, the police initially concluded that Braun had suffered a brainstorm, killed his housekeeper and then turned the gun on himself. The theory lasted only until Braun's body was exhumed and a post-mortem was carried out. The pathologist discovered that Dr Braun had two bullet wounds in his head – either of which would have been instantly fatal. Besides which, the bungling Ferbach had left behind his letter of introduction, the handwriting of which was later identified as being that of Vera Bruhne. The seal was set on Vera's fate by her own daughter, Sylvia, a degenerate teenager who was more than happy to describe to the police how Vera had planned the whole Braun affair and sent her dogsbody Ferbach to do the dirty work.

Both Vera Bruhne and Johann Ferbach were jointly convicted of murder and sentenced to life imprisonment.

BRYANT, Charlotte   At the age of twenty-five Frederick Bryant had been a corporal in the military police serving in Ireland during 'The Troubles' of 1920–21. Despite the savage guerrilla warfare that had been waged against the British troops, the awful bloodshed that was to result in a divided Ireland, Bryant had come through unscathed. It was to be another fifteen years before one of Erin's children would be the cause of his untimely death.

During his service in Londonderry, Frederick had met Charlotte McHugh, at the time just nineteen, illiterate, and careless both in appearance and morals. Quite why the sober, upright corporal found her attractive is a mystery; but he did, and brought her back home to Somerset where, in March 1922, they married.

But life for Frederick Bryant, a soldier without a battle to fight, was proving a sad disappointment. After the glamour and camaraderie of the Service, to find himself unemployed was more than his dignity could stand. Desperately clutching at the respectability of honest toil, Bryant accepted a job as a labourer on a farm at Over Compton, on the Somerset/Dorset border. In

1925, he and his new wife moved into the tied cottage that had come with the job.

Before long, Charlotte had settled down and resumed some of the old daily routines that she had enjoyed in Ulster – mainly drinking and sex; both in varying degrees of excess. Squalid as she was in both mind and appearance, toothless and verminous, her reputation grew; as did her list of amours and her brood of children. Not that Frederick Bryant was in much of a position to complain – feeding seven mouths on a labourer's wage was not easy; as he once confided to a neighbour: 'Four pound a week is better than thirty bob – I don't care a damn what she does.'

Around Christmas 1933, an eighth mouth was sitting at table in the Bryants' shabby abode; a lodger in the person of Leonard Parsons, itinerant gypsy horse-dealer and peddler. Needless to say, Charlotte's favours were included in the rent.

When even the tolerant people of Compton tired of the 'goings-on' of the Bryant household, and Frederick was thrown out of job and home, he simply removed his rag-bag of family and possessions on to Coombe, to another farm, another cottage. Life here resumed its familiar pattern, though by now Leonard Parsons was spending less time at the Bryants' hovel and more time with his 'wife' Priscilla Loveridge – also a gypsy, and the mother of his four children. Thus did jealousy become an aggravating complication in Charlotte Bryant's life.

It must have been about this time that she made up her mind that Frederick alone was the obstacle in the path of her true happiness with Leonard Parsons. On 14 May 1935 Bryant fell ill with vomiting and acute stomach pains, diagnosed – wrongly as it turned out – as gastro-enteritis. On 6 August of the same year he had a further similar attack. Now whether it was because he suspected foul play and feared for his own safety, or that he simply tired of Charlotte's sluttish ways, Parsons packed his bags and made it clear that he was going for good. Between the eleventh and the twenty-first of December

Frederick Bryant was once again in pain, his suffering becoming so acute that he could barely move or speak. On Sunday the twenty-second he died in the Yeatman Hospital at Sherborne.

Suspicious now, Dr MacCarthy refused to sign the death certificate, and quickly made known his misgivings to the local police. As a result, Frederick's earthly remains were given into the charge of Home Office analyst Dr Roche Lynch, who would have been blind not to have noticed the lethal 4.09 grains of arsenic in the body. Scotland Yard had meanwhile been alerted to this possibility, and were already making an exhaustive search of the Bryants' cottage. Of the 146 samples of dust and dirt collected from various surfaces in the building, an astonishing thirty-two were later to show traces of arsenic. In a pile of rubbish found outside, the police also recovered a battered tin that had once contained 'Eureka', a weed-killer with a high arsenic content.

Charlotte Bryant appeared at the Dorset Assizes in May 1936, charged with the murder of her husband. While she sat in the dock munching caramels, the chief witness for the prosecution, Leonard Parsons, recalled for the benefit of the court an occasion in the previous October when Mrs Bryant had assured him that she was soon to become a widow. Mrs Lucy Ostler, a recent lodger with the Bryants, told how on 21 December Charlotte had almost forced her husband to drink a cup of Oxo meat extract, and subsequently disposed of a tin of weed-killer with the words: 'I must get rid of this.'

On Saturday 30 May 1936 Charlotte Bryant was found guilty and sentenced to death. On 15 July that sentence was carried out at Exeter Prison. The priest who attended Mrs Bryant in her final hours said later: 'Her last moments were truly edifying.'

BYRON, Kitty   Kitty Byron, a twenty-four-year-old milliner, had been living with Arthur Reginald Baker at his lodgings in London's Duke Street for several months before tragedy overtook them. Baker, a stockbroker, could hardly have been described as the perfect partner – for a start he was married; but this fact, he assured Kitty, would prove no obstacle to their future happiness, he would simply divorce Mrs Baker. For another thing Baker was a violent alcoholic, and it was usually Kitty to whom he showed the violence. He was also utterly disloyal, and it was this unfortunate characteristic which led to his untimely death.

It was the year 1902, and a time when morals, on the surface at least, were a little stricter than now. The 'arrangement' upstairs had never pleased Baker's landlady, despite the couple calling themselves Mr and 'Mrs' Baker; add to this the frequent quarrels and fighting, and the good lady decided that she would rather have peace and quiet than the rent. After a particularly bad bout of squabbling on the morning of 7 November, Mr and Mrs Baker were asked to leave. Baker made some mealy-mouthed apology, confessed that Mrs Baker was really Miss Byron, and promised that he would kick Kitty out if only he could keep his room. Unfortunately, through a gossiping house-maid, Kitty got to hear of this arrangement.

That was on the morning of 10 November, shortly after Baker had left for work in the City. Kitty Byron, feeling bitter and betrayed, followed him into town, purchasing on the way a spring-bladed knife. When she reached Lombard Street post office Kitty sent a telegram to Baker insisting on seeing him there and then. And he came. What was said on the steps of the post office we can only guess, but the meeting soon turned into the familiar unseemly quarrel. Kitty became more and more agitated and tearful, more and more angry. Then suddenly she drew the knife from her muff and, in full view of passers-by, stabbed Arthur Baker once in the chest and once in the back. As he fell to the ground, Kitty threw herself down on top of Baker's body, sobbing: 'Reggie, dear Reggie, let me kiss my Reggie.' Later, in a statement to the police, she said: 'I killed him willingly, and he deserved it.'

Well, I am not sure that people deserve to be killed just because they are a thoroughly bad lot, but it was obvious in what odium 'Reggie' Baker was generally held when his fellow-brokers at the Stock Exchange held a collection to pay for Kitty Byron's defence. Her case was handled by 'Harry' Dickens, son of the novelist Charles Dickens.

Kitty was tried before Mr Justice Darling, and despite her attorney's impassioned plea for a manslaughter verdict she was convicted of murder and sentenced to death. However, acknowledging the great strength of public feeling in her favour, proved by a 15,000 signature petition, the Home Secretary first commuted Kitty Byron's sentence to life imprisonment and then to ten years. After serving six years of her sentence, Kitty entered a benevolent institution for women.

C

CAILLAUX, Henriette *Le Figaro* is one of France's most highly regarded daily newspapers, and in those far-off days at the beginning of the last century, before television stripped them of much of their immediacy, such newspapers were capable of exercising considerable power. At that time *Le Figaro's* editor was the august and brilliant Monsieur Gaston Calmette; and Calmette was not hesitant to use the influence which that position bestowed on him. In particular, he developed a barely rational dislike of the country's Minister of Finance, Joseph Caillaux. And via *Le Figaro's* editorials accused him of a range of scurrilous misdemeanours ranging from womanizing to working with enemy agents from Germany, a country against which France would soon be at war. During the early months of 1914, Gaston Calmette published more than a hundred such articles, culminating in March with the reproduction of a number of letters from Caillaux to his former mistress Henriette Rainouard. They were inflammatory not so much for their sexual content, though there was plenty of that, but for their revelation that Caillaux had been less than straightforward in his activities in the Chamber of Deputies. This earned Minister Caillaux the vilification of the French people, and Gaston Calmette the mantle of a fearless defender of the truth. The only person smarting more than Caillaux from this public roasting was the former Henriette Rainouard – she was now the second Madame Caillaux.

On 16 March 1914, Madame Caillaux visited Maître Monier, a family friend and respected high-court judge; despite Henriette's genuine anger and distress, there was nothing Monier could do to help – public figures such as her husband could not issue libel writs against the press. Which is why, on the afternoon of the same day, we find Madame Caillaux in the showroom of the celebrated Parisian gunsmiths Gastinne-Renette; the neat parcel she carried out with her contained a Browning revolver.

That evening, Henriette Caillaux left a hasty note for her husband, telling him that she was going to 'obtain justice', and took a car to rue Druot where *Le Figaro* had its headquarters. Gaston Calmette courteously received Madame Caillaux in his office. And then it happened. By the time the office boy had wrestled the Browning from her hand, Henriette had fired four bullets into Calmette's body. While the editor was being rushed to the hospital at Neuilly for emergency treatment, Madame Caillaux was being rushed to the gendarmerie to be charged with attempted murder. When Calmette succumbed to a wound in his abdomen at midnight on the same day, the charge was changed to murder.

Madame Caillaux faced her accusers on 20 July 1914, and spoke so eloquently in her own defence that the jury believed her every word. No matter that she had calculatedly bought a gun, with only one purpose in mind; no matter that she had written to her husband telling him what she was about to do; no matter that she shot not once but four times into the unfortunate Gaston Calmette – the jury believed that it was the unpre-meditated act of a woman who found herself, as she described it, 'in the presence of the monster who has ruined our lives . . . the gun went off accidentally'. To everybody's surprise, and alarm, Calmette's assassin was found innocent of murder and freed by the court to return home.

Until her death in 1943, Henriette Caillaux never again mentioned the incident. Her husband remained at the top of his political career until, ironically, he was charged with the very crime of which Calmette had accused him – treason.

CALVERT, Louie   Early in 1925, a night-watchman by the name of Arthur ('Arty') Calvert was living at No. 7 Railway Place in Hunslet, now a district of Leeds. In addition to his wages, Calvert was also in receipt of a small pension from the Army in consideration of wounds sustained at Passchendaele during the Great War. He had, at any rate, sufficient funds to engage a housekeeper in the person of 'Louisa Jackson', and sufficient funds for that housekeeper to manipulate Arty into marriage.

After six months housekeeping for Calvert, during which time Louie's duties clearly went beyond the merely domestic, she decided that it was time Arty married her, and to this end she claimed (quite untruthfully) that she was pregnant by him. Just before the August Bank Holiday of 1925 they were standing in front of the registrar at Hunslet Register Office in Glasshouse Street. On her wedding certificate, Louie described herself as 'Louie Gomersal, spinster, aged twenty-nine, a weaver'. Which must have been somewhat bewildering for Arty Calvert, who was under the impression that her name was Jackson, and that she had been widowed as the result of an accident and had a five-year-old son of that marriage named Kenneth. Nor was she, in truth, twenty-nine, but thirty-three years old, though with her wizened, toothless appearance she could have passed for even older.

After the wedding, the Calverts and Kenneth returned to Railway Place to await the birth of the new baby. Month succeeded month and there was still no signal of the happy event; until at length Calvert became rightly suspicious and continued to pester his wife for news until March of the following year. Louie's bizarre way of solving the problem was to procure a child and present it as her own. Heaven knows why she could not simply have said she had been mistaken, or even claim to have had a miscarriage, but on the eighth of the month Louie left Hunslet to go to her 'sister's' – for her 'confinement'.

In fact, her 'sister' was Mrs Lily Waterhouse, a forty-year-old spiritualist living in Amberley Road, Dewsbury, where Louie rented a room. Next she inserted an advertisement in the local paper offering adoption of a new-born baby. The daughter that was subsequently presented to Arty Calvert as his own, was in fact the illegitimate offspring of a seventeen-year-old girl from Wrangbrook, near Pontefract.

The trip to Dewsbury had served a double purpose for Louie, for she took the opportunity to transfer some of her landlady's humble possessions into a suitcase. Realizing what was going on, but reluctant to confront her with it, Mrs Waterhouse went to the police and swore a summons against Mrs Calvert. On the day before the summons was due to be taken up, Louie Calvert, the new baby, and the suitcase containing the ill-gotten gains returned to Railway Place. Later that day – it was April the first – the police called upon Lily Waterhouse to see why she had not appeared at the magistrates court, and discovered her body lying strangled and bludgeoned on her bedroom floor.

When officers arrived to arrest Mrs Calvert they found her wearing her victim's boots – several sizes too large but, Louie claimed, 'serving a turn'. At the Leeds Assizes on May sixth and seventh, Louie Calvert faced the evidence of twenty-five prosecution witnesses; for her defence, Dr E.C. Chappell could find not one.

When she had been duly found guilty and sentenced to death, Mrs Calvert returned to a former ruse; once again she claimed that she was pregnant, a claim which the 'jury of matrons' empanelled to oversee the doctor's examination emphatically pronounced 'not proven'.

Louie Calvert, dressed all in black, attended her process hearing at the Court of Criminal Appeal in London only to hear it dismissed. With her appearance on the gallows a certainty, Mrs Calvert made a startling and unsolicited confession: she had been responsible for the murder of one John William Frobisher who had lived at Mercy Street in Leeds, and had employed 'Louisa Jackson' as housekeeper. Frobisher's bludgeoned body had been found on 12 July 1922, floating in the canal at Water Hall, to where it had no doubt drifted after being cast off the Wellington Bridge upstream.

It is characteristic of the sharp-tongued Louie Calvert that after her conviction she called for a meeting with her husband in the cell below the court, at which she reviled him in the most foul-mouthed manner for being the cause of her present situation, to which the long-suffering, thoroughly confused, Calvert could only reply:

'Well lass, it can't be helped.'

Mrs Calvert was hanged at Strangeways prison on 26 June 1926.

CARSON, Susan and James (aka Suzan and Michael BEAR)   In 1981 James and Susan Carson (for some reason calling themselves Michael and Suzan Bear) were living in San Francisco, and mixing comfortably in the sub-culture of drug dependency and drug dealing. One of their close acquaintances of the time – and a regular customer – was former Hollywood actress Keryn Barnes. When Keryn went missing her landlord let himself into her apartment with his pass key and found her body slumped in the kitchen, her skull smashed and savage knife wounds to her face and neck. There was no evidence of a sexual motive and robbery was ruled out when Keryn Barnes' purse was found near the body with the money intact. It was when police found the name 'Suzan' scrawled around the flat that they put out an alert for the Bears.

By now they were in Humboldt County where Michael

encountered Clark Stephens, a friend of a man who had earlier assaulted him, and shot him dead. The couple tried unsuccessfully to burn Stephens' corpse, and eventually settled for covering it with rocks and chicken manure. By the time he was found in his makeshift grave the Bears were on the move again, resuming a nomadic existence that was to take them into Oregon and then back to California.

In January 1983, the couple were picked up as hitch-hikers by Jon Hillyar who drove them to just outside Santa Rosa. Unluckily for him, Suzan Bear had taken it into her drug-dazed head that Hillyar was a witch, and must be killed. Suzan failed to stab him to death so Michael was obliged to deliver the *coup de grâce* with a bullet. But such activity cannot go unnoticed on a public roadside, and Michael and Suzan Bear were overtaken by the police, arrested and charged with murder.

Following their arrest the Bears insisted on holding a press conference from the California jail where they were being detained, and announced to the world that their instructions to kill had been personally given by Allah. Michael Bear admitted murdering Keryn Barnes, a witch who had just put a spell on Suzan and was too dangerous to live. They both admitted complicity in the Stephens and Hillyar killings, but again as a benevolent gesture to rid the world of evil.

Tried in San Francisco first for the Barnes murder, Michael and Suzan Bear were convicted and sentenced to twenty-five-years-to-life. Further trials for the other murders ended in convictions and similar sentences.

CHANNEL, Mary Mary was the daughter of one Mr Woods, a person of excellent repute, who resided in a little village near Dorchester, in the county of Dorset. He was a person of known wealth and good credit, who, by his industry and diligence, daily increased his riches. Perceiving his daughter to be of a promising disposition, and amiable both in body and in mind, he gave her a liberal education in order to refine by art and study those good qualities with which she was endowed by nature. Mary made such speedy progress in her learning that she soon outshone her school- fellows, and the strong imagination, polite behaviour and majestic grace of her carriage so displayed themselves that she became the mirror and discourse of all who knew her.

Her charms did not consist in adorning and dressing herself in magnificent and gay attire, decked with pearls and diamonds – which gives a false gloss of beauty to persons whose natures are opposite, and only serves to brighten the lustre of their pretended fine qualities. In a word, she was generally esteemed the most celebrated wit and accomplished beauty of her age.

Being now in the flower of her youth and full bloom of her beauty, Mary had several suitors of good repute who all became captives to her beauty – and hardly did they find themselves ensnared but had the boldness to flatter themselves that one day they might possess so charming a prize. Among the rest was Mr Channel, a wealthy grocer of Dorchester, who came to pay his respects to Mary. For the riches he enjoyed Channel was gladly accepted by her parents, but by Mary he was altogether condemned and slighted. He had nothing to recommend him but his wealth, his limbs and body being in some measure ill-proportioned, and his features in no way agreeable; but what rendered him the more detestable and ridiculous in her sight was his splay-foot, which did not in the least appeal to her sublime sense of design.

Mr Woods, clearly perceiving that the addresses made by Mr Channel were accepted by his daughter with scorn and reproof, entreated her to receive him with less disdain. However, being weary of his attentions, Mary determined never again to entertain her unwelcome admirer. Still her father, with increasing impatience endeavoured to seal the match between them, and finally by virtue of invoking her duty to him, Mr Woods secured his unhappy daughter's marriage to Channel by moral blackmail.

Having now gratified her parents' desire, and yielded to their incessant pressure, still Mary continued to slight her husband most contemptuously, and she embarked upon a study of what measures might be employed to get rid of him. Finally it was resolved; nothing short of his death would fully ensure her freedom and happiness; and with this in mind she despatched her maid to the apothecary for white mercury – on the pretence of killing mice.

The vehicle for this vicious poison was an innocent-looking break- fast bowl of rice milk, personally served by Mary to her husband, who, finding the taste to be what he called 'amiss', gave it in turn to his brother-in-law to try, but Mary snatched it away from the youth, and did so with such speed as to cause no little suspicion. So Mr Channel next required the maid to take a draught, and again her mistress flew to snatch the bowl from her hand. But for the unhappy Channel there was no salvation; presently his body began to swell. A doctor was summoned, but so great a hold had the mercury taken of Channel's body that no remedy could expel it, and the master of the house resigned his last breath. Just as there was no doubt that Channel had perished from poison, so was it certain from her own behaviour that his wife had been its source, and she was immediately lodged by the magistrate in Dorchester Jail.

At the ensuing Dorchester Assizes Mary offered a defence (whether real or pretended) of such wit and ingenuity, and spoken with such an extraordinary courage and humility, that it caused admiration in the judges, and pity and compassion in all who heard her trial. But this availed her nothing; for the evidences appearing plain against her, and the friends of her late husband being people of some substance, she received sentence to be burned at the stake till she was dead.

On the day of her execution, Mary Channel was led by soldiers to the fatal place, her face veiled; after some private words, she took off her gown and white silk hood and handed them to her maid, who with great tenderness accompanied her to the stake. There she declared her faith in Christ, and to the last railed against her parents' constraints which had been the cause of her horrid death. And so, at a small distance from the town of Dorchester, in or about the month of April 1703, in the eighteenth year of her age, she perished in the flames.

(The Annals of Newgate, 1776)

CHESHAM, Sarah

SARAH CHESHAM'S LAMENT
For the Murder of Richard Chesham, her Husband, by Poison

Tune: *The Wagon Train*

Behold a wretched married woman,
    The mother of a family,
For the murder of her husband,
    Doomed to die upon a tree;
Oh! Whatever could possess you,
    On that sad and fatal day,
For to prepare the fatal poison,
    And take your husband's life away.

Chorus
See a wretched wife and mother,
    Borne down by grief and misery,
Because she did her husband murder,
    Doomed to die upon a tree.

Sarah Chesham is the wretched culprit,
    At Clavering, near Newport, she did dwell,
Her husband was an honest labourer,
    Respected and esteemed full well.

A husband kind – a tender father,
    He was unto his family,
Besides he was an upright member
Of a Burial Society.

On the twenty-eighth of May,
    The wretched woman she did go,
To a shop to buy the fatal poison,
    Which has proved her overthrow;
The dreadful dose she gave her husband,
    Soon after which Richard Chesham died,
And she when taxed with the foul murder,
    Strongly the deed denied.

At length suspicion fell upon her,
    And to justice she was brought,
That no one would the crime discover,
    The sad and wretched murdress thought;
She slew the partner of her bosom,
    It was, we read, for cruel gain,
And made her darling children suffer,
    Distressed and overcome with pain.

For a paltry sum of money,
    She did her lawful husband slay,
And for no other cause but lucre,
    Did she take his life away;
The judge on her pronounced her sentence,
    Sarah Chesham you must hanged be,
At the front of Chelmsford gaol,
    On the dismal fatal tree.

When she was at the holy altar,
    She did a solemn vow then give,
Her husband dear, to love and cherish,
    Whilst God permitted her to live;

But she the solemn vow has broken,
　　Wicked, base, deceitful wife,
Barbarous and cruel mother,
　　Doomed to die in prime of life.

The solemn knell for her is tolling,
　　Numbers flock her end to see,
A cruel wife, a wretched mother,
　　To approach the fatal tree;
From whence her frame when life is ended,
　　Will in disgrace be borne away,
And placed within Chelmsford gaol,
　　To lie unto the judgement day.

Males and females take a warning,
　　By Sarah Chesham's dreadful fate,
Ponder well, night, noon and morning,
　　Before, alas! it is too late;
Let not even Satan tempt you,
　　To desert from virtue's way,
And think upon that wretched woman,
　　Who did for gain her husband slay.

CHEVALLIER, Yvonne   Yvonne Chevallier was the wife of Dr Pierre Chevallier, member of the French Cabinet and former mayor of the town of Orléans, where the couple lived with their four-year-old son Matthieu. In 1951 Madame Chevallier fired five bullets into her husband's body in what she claimed was a fit of jealous rage against his affair with Madame Jeanette Perreau.

Although public disapprobation had been so strong as to have necessitated the removal of the trial from Orléans to Rheims in the hope of finding an impartial jury, no sooner did the court find out that it had a mistress to hiss at, than Madame Chevallier was restored to popularity and, amid tumultuous cheers in court, she was acquitted.

CHRISTIE, Susan On the afternoon she died, 27 March 1991, Penny McAllister had left her job in the shop at Drumadd Barracks, where her husband Duncan was a captain in the Royal Corps of Signals, for a lunchtime stroll in the woods with her two dogs. She had arranged to meet up with a friend, Susan Christie.

At about one-thirty, two boys saw Susan Christie in a state of great distress come stumbling from the edge of the trees, her clothing stained with blood. One of the lads stayed with the distraught woman while his companion ran for help. When the police arrived, Susan claimed that she and Penny had been attacked and Penny had been killed. She gave a detailed description of their attacker which was circulated as a Photofit. Meanwhile, a massive hunt was launched for the killer using a helicopter to search the woodland from the air. It was not until four days after the murder, when Captain Duncan McAllister admitted having an affair with Susan Christie, that the police began to suspect her story. At first Christie had denied a sexual relationship with McAllister, but eventually she made a statement in which she claimed she could remember nothing of the circumstances surrounding the murder, concluding: 'I must have done it; I don't remember. There was no one else there. Oh God, I could not kill Penny.' Susan Christie was charged with murder.

The couple had met when Susan Christie, then a twenty-one-year-old private in the Ulster Defence Regiment, joined the sub-aqua club run by Duncan McAllister. A friendship developed between the captain and Private Christie which was at first purely platonic, with Susan taking the role of admiring pupil and McAllister that of the flattered instructor. But in Susan Christie an unhealthy obsession was growing. Over the summer months of 1990, as Christie's obsession strengthened her resolve to have Duncan all to herself, so McAllister began to get cold feet.

In October Susan dropped the bombshell; she announced she

was pregnant. McAllister, no doubt mindful of his obligations as an officer and a gentleman, responded with support and understanding; which Susan interpreted as love and affection.

In the spring of 1991, after a convenient 'miscarriage', Susan Christie was accepted for officer training, necessitating her spending some time in England at Sandhurst. It was the opportunity Duncan McAllister had been waiting for. A few days before Susan was due to go he told her he was never going to leave his wife, and that their affair was over. Surprisingly, Susan seemed to take it well, almost resignedly. No tears, no hysterics, no threats of exposure, no more pregnancies; in fact, she and Penny McAllister became closer than they had been. On 27 March, Susan suggested they should meet up in the afternoon and take their dogs for a walk in Drumkeeragh Forest Park . . .

Susan Christie's trial opened in the Downpatrick Crown Court on 1 June 1992; she denied murder, entering a plea of not guilty.

Mr John Creaney QC, for the Crown, described the obsessive jealousy which overcame Susan Christie: 'She had reached a stage where she regarded the captain's wife as an obstacle, and she was determined to remove that obstacle'; and on 3 June, a tearful Susan Christie sat in the dock while her lover, Duncan McAllister, gave evidence of their short, stormy affair.

The moment the crowded court had been waiting for arrived on 8 June, when Susan Christie gave evidence in her own defence. Here at last was an opportunity to present her side of the affair with Duncan McAllister. It started when she joined the sub-aqua club at Armagh. She and McAllister always got on well and often flirted with each other. Then, while they were on a diving trip: 'He told me it was obvious that I fancied him and said that he felt the same way about me. I said that I needed to think about it. I was very attracted to him, but he was married and I wasn't sure what I wanted. As the months went by,' she continued, 'he was all I ever thought about. I had never felt this way about anyone in my life.'

Susan Christie claimed that she had become pregnant late in 1990, but when she told her lover he gave her an ultimatum – either she had an abortion, in which case he would support her all the way, or, if she insisted on having the child, he would deny being the father and leave her. In December 1990 she suffered a miscarriage.

Cross-examined by prosecutor Creaney about Penny's death, Susan was asked: 'Do you now accept that you killed her?' She replied: 'I would say I killed her for Duncan. I meant to get Duncan for myself. I was that in love with him that I would have done anything.' She later admitted that 'it took me over a year to accept it. I have never felt able to say "Yes I did kill her." I really believed that at the time I never killed her; that it was somebody else . . . When I was talking to the police I really believed that I was innocent and that there was a man out there to look for.'

And so this trial of what had become popularly known as the Fatal Attraction Killing drew to a close. The judge, Lord Justice Kelly, summed-up favourably to the defendant, posing this question to the jury: 'Can you conceive of a girl of her background going to a shop and sharpening a knife and carrying out this vicious act of killing if she had not taken leave of her senses?' The Crown prosecutors had refused to accept a plea of diminished responsibility, but the judge clearly hadn't. And neither, for that matter, had the jury. After a retirement of three and a half hours, they found Susan Christie guilty of manslaughter with diminished responsibility.

In what was to be a most controversial sentencing, Lord Justice Kelly gave Susan Christie a five-year prison sentence – which meant that, allowing for the fifteen months she had already spent on remand plus full remission, she could have been free within a year. He told the prisoner: 'You will still be a young woman when you are released from prison. I hope you will find some degree of the happiness which has eluded you so far.'

If it was meant to be provocative, then it succeeded. A spokesperson for Susan Christie was reported as saying: 'She is an extremely relieved young woman indeed, because even up until the moment before she was sentenced she was expecting far worse.' And well she might have been. Few people with any concern for justice could have taken comfort from the fact that Susan Christie had, in effect, been sentenced to two and a half years for a murderous attack on a person who had offered her no provocation. What was more puzzling, perhaps, was that Lord Justice Kelly, while invoking Susan Christie's unstable mental state as a mitigation of sentence, failed to make an order requiring her to undergo psychiatric treatment.

One person who was not entirely happy with the outcome of the trial was Duncan McAllister. According to one report he felt 'she should have been put away for ever'.

Although the Crown could not appeal against a verdict, it could ask the Northern Ireland Court of Appeal to review the sentence. Which it did. In October 1992 Mr Brian Kerr QC presented the case for the Attorney-General, emphasizing the aggravating features of the killing such as the degree of responsibility, the violence used, and the innocence of the victim. It was his view that the sentence should be doubled. One month later a decision was announced by the Northern Ireland Court of Appeal; it held few surprises. Susan Christie sat impassively in the dock while Sir Brian Hutton, Northern Ireland's Lord Chief Justice told her that, by a majority decision, he and his colleagues intended to increase the length of her sentence from five to nine years.

Lord Justice Murray stated his opinion that: 'The killing of young Mrs McAllister by Susan Christie was an indescribably wicked and evil deed, prompted not by any grievance, real or imaginary, which she felt against her victim, nor by any hatred towards or even dislike of her victim, but by the jealousy which she allowed to find entrance to her heart and mind.'

CHRISTOFI, Styllou Pantopiou   Jealousy is an emotion of limitless strength – as overwhelming as love; as all-consuming as hatred; and more destructive than both. This is the story of a woman whose intense and unreasoning jealousy caused her to kill not once, but twice; caused her to kill with unimaginable brutality; caused her to kill two members of her immediate family.

The tyrant is Styllou Pantopiou Christofi, and at the time that this episode of her life opens, she is living in a small village in Cyprus. She already looks old beyond her fifty-three years, wrinkled and dried out by the heat of the sun and overwork. With little help from her reluctant husband, she spends most of her waking life squeezing a small and indifferent existence from a small and indifferent olive grove. She had suffered enough of that relentless, debilitating poverty to have become a sour, envious old woman. And beyond this, Mrs Christofi carries in her heart a terrible guilt. She has already committed one horrible crime – in 1925, when two fellow-villagers had held open the mouth of the victim while Styllou Christofi rammed a blazing torch down her throat. The victim died; she was Styllou's mother-in-law. Incredibly, Styllou Christofi was acquitted at her trial.

Styllou Christofi's only son Stavros, has already left the claustrophobic, bitter atmosphere of the village; left the unproductive olive grove, and walked all the way to Nicosia where he worked as a waiter while he saved the money for his boat fare to England. By 1953, he has been in England for twelve years. During this time he has made a happy match with a thirty-six-year-old German girl named Hella, a daughter of the Ruhr. The couple have three healthy children, and live in South Hill Park, a stone's throw from Florence Nightingale's former home. The street, the house, the family, all fit easily into the civilized, very English life that is lived here on the edge of Hampstead Heath. To complete their contentment, Stavros holds a respected post as wine waiter at the internationally renowned Café de Paris in London's West End. That life of contentment is about to end abruptly and explosively. The peace is about to be shattered by the arrival of Stavros's mother.

Were it not for the mean, intractable nastiness that characterized Styllou Christofi's personality, one could go some way to sympathizing with her position. An ignorant peasant woman set down in the sophistication of London, unable to speak a word of English – illiterate even in her native Greek – confronting a daughter-in-law and three young grandchildren for the first time, without the means to communicate with them directly. It would overwhelm anyone. And Stavros understood this; Hella understood it too; the whole family spared no effort to make the recently arrived member as welcome as they were able.

But the old woman had been wrapped up in her own resentment for too long; the bitterness allowed to take too firm a grip. The mother began to cling to her son like an emotional limpet; began to develop a fanatical and jealous hatred of her daughter-in-law. She developed a hatred for the house; for Hella's stylish way of dressing, and her 'extravagance' in buying make-up; for the way Hella brought up her children. All this and more Styllou Christofi hated, and was not slow to say so – to shout it, in Greek, often. So oppressive did life become at South Hill Park, that Stavros twice arranged for his mother to live elsewhere; where Styllou rendered herself so objectionable that she was asked to leave on both occasions.

By now, by the July of 1954, even the good-natured Hella felt that she had endured enough. 'Next week,' she told her husband, 'I am going home to Wuppertal for a holiday. I am taking the children, and when we get back your mother must be gone.' 'But where can she go?' 'Back to Cyprus!'

It cannot have been easy for Stavros to break the news to his mother; harder still for her to accept it. To her it must have sounded like the announcement of the end of her world. She must surely have thought, this is all the fault of that girl; without her, I could be living here happily with my son.

When Stavros kissed his wife good-bye as he left for work on the evening of 29 July, he had no idea of the horror that was to greet his return.

The children were in bed. Alone at last with the woman who was destroying her family, Styllou Christofi struck. Struck from behind, smashing the cast-iron ash-plate from the kitchen stove down on to Hella's skull. Struck again, winding a scarf around the unconscious girl's throat, twisting, pulling. Dragging Hella's now lifeless corpse into the area behind the house, Styllou Christofi, insane in her revenge, made mad with jealousy, soaked the body and a pile of newspapers in paraffin and lit a match. It is possible that she remembered another fire, twenty-nine years before.

At the time, John Young, a neighbour, happened to be looking in the direction of No. 11, and saw the sudden blaze followed by the red glow of the fire. Thinking that the house might have caught light, he went to investigate. What he saw when he looked over the garden fence must have seemed so incredible that Young's mind refused to register the obvious truth. Instead it looked to him as though someone was trying to burn a 'wax dummy'. 'All I could see was from the thighs down, and the arms were raised and bent back at the elbow like some of the models you see in shop windows. There was a strong smell of wax.' At that point it was about 11.45 p.m.; Mrs Christofi reappeared to stoke up the fire, which seemed to reassure Mr Young, and he returned home.

Shortly before 1.00 a.m. a local restaurateur named Burstoff and his wife were returning home when they were forced to halt by a gesticulating figure in the road, shouting incoherently: 'Please come, fire burning, children sleeping.' By the time they had got Mrs Christofi back to the house the fire was out, but the body was still there, like a charred shop-window dummy on the paving slabs of the area. Wisely, Mr Burstoff decided to telephone for the police.

Three months later, Styllou Christofi stood in the dock at the Old Bailey listening, through a court interpreter, to the catalogue of evidence painstakingly collated by the police in support of their prosecution. The blood-stained kitchen, the petrol-soaked rags and papers, the fractured skull, the marks of strangulation around the neck. Most damning of all, the discovery of Hella's wedding ring, wrapped in paper and hidden in the old woman's bedroom.

Styllou's defence was as pathetic as had been the rest of her life. As desperate an attempt to survive as had been her cultivation of the obstinate olive grove. She had gone to bed before Hella, she claimed, leaving the girl to 'do some washing' (it had been a never-ending source of puzzlement to Styllou that her daughter-in-law washed her body every day – clearly not a feature of her previous experience in the village). The next thing she was aware of was waking to the smell of smoke; she recollected going to the bedroom door, looking out and noticing that the street door was open; remembered going to Hella's room and not finding her there; rushing downstairs where the kitchen door was open revealing the body of her daughter-in-law lying on the ground in the yard, flames licking around her and blood staining her face. She had splashed water on the girl in an attempt to revive her, and when this failed to get a reaction had run in search of help – which was when she met the Burstoffs.

The trial did not last long. Had Styllou Christofi pleaded insane – as she almost certainly was – it might have been even shorter. In the event, in a final defiant gesture of dignity, she had claimed, 'I am a poor woman, of no education, but I am not mad woman. Never. Never. Never.'

And so Styllou Christofi, on 13 December 1954, gave herself

up to be the first woman to be executed in England since Edith Thompson (see p. 263), thirty years before. And she was nearly the last woman to hang; but Ruth Ellis (see page 121), who also committed murder in South Hill Park a few months later, was to earn that distinction.

CHUBB, Edith Daisy It is a curious fact that the great majority of murders are committed within the close confines of the family; and frequently in the communal home. But a closer examination is rewarded by at least one useful observation – that members of a family, unlike friends, can rarely choose each other, and a family created cannot, like a failed friendship, be easily undone. Which may help us understand why, though blood may be thicker than water, quite a lot of it seems to get spilled.

Edith Daisy Chubb was a drudge. She had not been born so, but at the age of forty-six she found herself with sole responsibility for a thoughtless, ill-tempered husband, an elderly mother, five children and a domineering sister-in-law. In addition to her seemingly endless domestic commitments, Edith Chubb kept the family just this side of poverty by working a gruelling twelve-hour three-day-a-week shift as a cleaner in the Haine Hospital near her home in Broadstairs; ironically she was a trained nurse. Edith was constantly tired, constantly in debt and, like too many women forced into this position, an eternal silent martyr. That was probably the cause of the trouble that was building up for the Chubbs; had she allowed herself now and again to express her rightful indignation at her lot, the pressure might have eased. As it was, something obviously had to break under the strain. It happened to be Edith Chubb's reason, and the violent outrush of all her frustrations, all her disappointments, had to go somewhere; it happened to be in the direction of Miss Lilian Chubb.

Sister-in-law Lily was a maiden lady of a type popularly characterised on the English comedy stage – that is to say, she was middle-aged, prim, opinionated and overbearing. Miss Chubb was employed as a sales assistant in the ladieswear department of a big store in Cliftonville, and in perfect keeping with the rest of her character, she left home on the dot of 8.40 every morning, and left work on the dot of six every evening.

The morning of 6 February 1958 was the one time she varied the routine – and then it could hardly be said to be the result of a temporarily wayward spirit. Because this was the day that Edith's mind chose to seize up. Her husband had left for work, the children for school; the two women were alone in the house. 'I felt irritated by the way she put her tea-cup down,' recalled Mrs Chubb; 'I followed her down the stairs, and pulled hard on her scarf . . . I didn't mean to hurt her . . . just to shake her up. She fell backwards on to the floor, striking her head on the banister.' Outside the front door, the milkman could be heard making his daily delivery; inside, Lilian made a low, groaning sound, and Edith put her hand over her mouth to stop it.

That evening there was great surprise in the Chubb household – Lilian was late home! Consternation when she did not come home at all; and it was Edith Chubb who next morning went to Broadstairs Police Station to report her missing. That was at around 10 a.m. One hour later the police returned her visit; Lilian Chubb had been found, in a hedge in Reading Street Road. She was dead; the doctor said it was strangulation. Edith could hardly believe her ears: 'I just can't imagine anything like this happening; we are a very happy, united family.'

It was only after Miss Lily had been given the questionable privilege of a post-mortem by one of the country's leading forensic pathologists, that Edith Chubb's story was seriously doubted. Professor Francis Camps confirmed that Lily Chubb had died from strangulation, and he also identified the probable cause of the strangely situated patches of lividity on the body. The state of lividity, or hypostasis, is simply the result of the blood in the body – no longer circulating after death – finding its own level and coagulating in the vessels; thus, those parts of the corpse that are in contact with a hard surface, such as the floor, or constricting pressure, such as collars and waistbands, will not show the characteristic livid patches where the blood lies. Based on this principle, it was Camps's contention that the body of Lilian Chubb had been sat upon a chair shortly after death and left on it for some time before disposal. Incidentally, Camps suggested, the pressure on the throat could easily have been exerted by a woman.

The victim's movements on the day of the crime were the next to come under police scrutiny; or rather, it was the lack of movements that started Chief Inspector Everitt and his team looking for a killer literally closer to home. It had already been established that Lilian Chubb had not reported for work on the morning of the sixth; what is more, none of the neighbours, who were familiar with her punctual nature, had seen Miss Chubb leave at her customary time that morning. So, reasoned the officers, she must have died in the house.

Edith Chubb made her confession to Chief Inspector Everitt without too much prompting: 'I knew,' she said, 'that I should have to tell you before long.'

At the trial, the forlorn, long-suffering Mrs Chubb stepped into the witness box and with the help of her defence counsel began the long recitation of depressing events in a deeply depressing life: 'Lily was so smug; nobody knows what she was like. . .' Poor Lilian, she became the focus, rightly or wrongly, for all Edith's discontent. Then finally: 'Something came over me. I pulled the scarf tightly round Lily's neck. She didn't struggle . . . When I realized she was dead I was horror-struck.' Edith Chubb put her victim in the old invalid chair that was in the garden shed, and pushed it back into the shed. Next morning early she covered the corpse with a rug and wheeled it down to Reading Street Road where she dumped it: 'It didn't take me long.'

And it didn't take the jury long either, to reach their verdict.

They had heard medical evidence from Edith's doctor, Gordon Marshall, who testified that she was a woman close to breaking-point. Mrs Evelyn Cook, the matron of Haine Hospital, where the prisoner had worked, agreed that Mrs Chubb was a sick woman. Mr Justice Jones, however, was careful to redress this balance of sympathy when he spoke about the incident of the milkman on the doorstep: 'This woman is a trained nurse, and you may think that the simplest thing in the world would have been for her to deal with the situation and the deceased would have recovered quite quickly . . . You must ask yourselves whether the most natural behaviour on the part of a nurse would have been to render some first-aid.' He added that, at the very least, the jury must return a verdict of manslaughter. And that is what they did.

The next four years, during which Edith Chubb was a guest of Her Majesty, were probably the most relaxed of her life.

CLARK, Lorraine   A crime more sad than bad, the shooting of Melvin Clark was the almost predictable consequence of a disintegrating marriage and sexual infidelity. Lorraine and Melvin Clark didn't do much of anything together any more; he had his pursuits which kept him away from home a lot, and she had hers which kept her at home a lot. Lorraine Clark was a member of the local wife-swapping group. The gang would all get together, put their front-door keys in a bowl and then pick a key; whoever owned the key you got to go home with. Tacky? Maybe, perhaps more the last resort of the bored. And besides, this is middle-class suburban Massachusetts in the 1950s. They did that sort of thing then.

On 10 April 1954 Melvin Clark came home unexpectedly and found Lorraine in bed with the man who picked her key. Having dispatched the bewildered bed-partner out of the front door, Melvin and Lorraine got on with what they did best – quarrelling. Lorraine got very angry indeed and stabbed her husband with a knitting needle. It didn't do much harm but the shock value gave Lorraine Clark the valuable seconds she needed to grab the gun they kept in the house and put two bullets in Melvin's body.

Mrs Clark made a very good job of disposing of the corpse. She trussed it up all neat and tidy with chicken-wire, securely attached some weights, and threw it off a bridge over the Merrimack river. It was her hope and expectation that the bundle would be washed down to the sea. But it wasn't, it was washed instead to some marshland where it was found seven weeks later by a birdwatcher.

Meanwhile, Lorraine had told anyone who asked that her husband had left her after one too many rows. So how come he ended up in the river with two bullets in him?

In the end Lorraine Clark confessed, and the jury took a lenient view, convicting her only of second-degree murder; she was sentenced to life imprisonment.

CONROY, Teresa Miriam On Monday 19 October 1953, a coroner's jury at Twickenham sat in silence as Detective Superintendent Leslie Watts described finding the body of thirteen-year-old John Michael Conroy – the subject of the current inquest – in what had become popularly known as The Ritual Burial Murder.

On 26 September, Watts had gone to the house in Denton Road where he saw the body 'buried' in the base of a divan; the bed had been ripped open along the centre, forming two flaps. The boy had been wrapped in a dark brown blanket, placed in among the upholstery of the bed and the flaps closed over it, but folded back in the area of the head rather like the lapels of a jacket. Two mattresses, four blankets, an eiderdown and sheets were piled in a heap on the floor.

Subsequent to the examination by pathologist Dr Donald Teare, the boy's mother, forty-four-year-old Teresa Miriam Conroy, had been accused of his murder. In mitigation, it was later observed that Mrs Conroy was not very sound in her mind at the best of times, and in all probability the police were dealing with a case of diminished responsibility; the principal Medical Officer of Holloway Prison, Dr Thomas Christie, stated: 'She is of low intelligence, only slightly above the level at which certification as a mental defective would be considered.'

The circumstances that emerged from the evidence of the father, Michael Oliver Conroy, were that on Friday 25 September his wife announced that she intended to visit a cousin of hers in Muswell Hill, and that she was taking their son with her. When he asked to see the boy that evening she told her husband not to worry him as he was sleeping, and that he would see the child in the morning. The following morning, however, there was no sign of Mrs Conroy or of John, and Michael Conroy assumed that they had left early for Muswell Hill. The family's unusual sleeping arrangements makes this a reasonable explanation – Teresa Conroy and her son occupied beds in one room, and Mr Conroy slept in another.

'When I did my shopping,' continued Conroy, 'and returned on Saturday afternoon, I thought the boy was enjoying himself on Muswell Hill, but I found him dead in his own bedroom.' He immediately called a doctor to the house, and the physician pronounced that the boy had been dead for about forty-eight hours. It was at this point that police and pathologist took over the responsibility for making some sense of the bizarre discovery in the bed.

Dr Teare was provisionally of the opinion that the symptoms of death were consistent with asphyxia during an epileptic fit, from which John Conroy was known to suffer; the subsequent post-mortem, however, had a more sinister tale to tell. Asphyxia it certainly was, but an examination of blood samples revealed from fifty-five to sixty per cent carbon monoxide saturation – a fatal concentration. John Michael Conroy had been gassed to death. Furthermore, a quantity of a barbiturate drug used to treat epilepsy was found in the body in far too great a concentration for normal use; this almost certainly resulted in unconsciousness before death.

On 27 September Teresa Conroy made a statement in which she claimed: 'Last Tuesday he had a fit. About midnight he had a bad turn for about an hour. Then he went off to sleep. I was awake practically all night looking after him. The next day he had another bad turn while he was still in bed. He just choked, and his hands and legs shook. This lasted five minutes, and then he appeared to go to sleep. I know I should have gone for a doctor, but I was so tired and worn out I did not know what I was doing. I did nothing to him or about him until Thursday morning, by which time I realized he was dead. I stripped my bed [the divan] and ripped the covering with a pair of scissors. I don't know why I did this. I lifted him from his bed and wrapped him up in the blanket, and put him on the divan. I put the divan mattress on top of him, and made the bed in the usual way.'

On 15 October Leslie Watts arrived at Denton Road to arrest Mrs Conroy on a charge of murder. She replied simply: 'Shall I have to stay at the police station long?'

Teresa Conroy appeared before the bench at the Old Bailey on 8 December 1953. In its essentials, the prosecution case was outlined by Mr Christmas Humphries as follows:

It may be that in her mind was a mixture of three reasons as a motive for killing her son. The boy, who was epileptic, was getting worse. She was bound to him as a person whom she had nursed night and day. It would be a relief to her to be rid of the burden of the boy. There may have been some element of mercy killing, and that would seem to be true of some of the phrases in her statement to the police. There is a less kind allegation, but it is a fact that the boy had in a Post Office savings bank account more than £600 which had come to him in a will. Only he could touch that money. On his dying without making a will his next of kin would get it. If the police did not discover he had been murdered, the mother would be rid of a burden and she and her husband would be £600 better off. Possibly she gave the boy a dose of the drug, which was used for treating epilepsy, in a drink. Finding that he did not die, she carried him into the kitchen and put his head into the gas oven. When she turned on the gas he would die in three to four minutes. Then she probably took him back to the bedroom and ritually buried him in the divan by cutting open the top cover, pressing the body between the springs, and putting the mattress back on top of the divan.'

In her defence, Mr Elliott Gorst QC said of Mrs Conroy: 'She was a loving mother who cared for her child by day and by night. She must have got to breaking point. There was never a tear to the very end . . . this woman had no apprehension of what she was doing.' Mr Gorst said that the defence could not contest the facts of the murder, but asked for a verdict of 'Guilty but Insane'.

And it was an insanity verdict that the jury returned, after a twelve-minute retirement. The prisoner was ordered to be detained during Her Majesty's pleasure, and it is unlikely that we will get any more help in making our selection from Christmas Humphries' three options; or of ever understanding the significance, if there was any, of the ceremonial 'burial'.

COTTON, Mary Ann

> Mary Ann Cotton
> She's dead and she's rotten
> She lies in her bed
> With her eyes wide oppen.
> Sing, sing, oh, what can I sing?
> Mary Ann Cotton is tied up wi' string.
> Where, where? Up in the air
> Sellin' black puddens a penny a pair.

She wasn't always Mary Ann Cotton; the notoriety of that name came later. Mary Ann Robson was born in 1832, in the pit village of East Rainton, near Durham. At the age of twenty, she became Mrs William Mowbray, and while Mowbray followed his occupation as a navvy, Mary Ann devoted herself to producing five children. All these, the four sons and one daughter, died in infancy, victims, so it was said, of 'gastric fever'. Then William Mowbray died unexpectedly of diarrhoea, not long after taking out sizeable insurance.

Mary Ann made a fresh start with George Ward, who died fourteen months later of 'gastric fever'. Within weeks, the widow Ward had taken up new responsibilities as housekeeper to John Robinson and his five children. The scope of Mary's duties was obviously very broad, for she quickly became pregnant and then even more quickly became Mrs Mary Ann Robinson.

Already one of the Robinson children had contracted a fatal dose of 'gastric fever' when, in 1867, three more children died. John Robinson, it must be recorded, was lucky. On previous experience he, too, might have lost his life; as it was, Mary Ann simply helped herself to his savings and fled.

Mary next met Mr Frederick Cotton and his sister Margaret. Some months later when Mary was expecting his child, she married Cotton. She now bore the name which was to become notorious – Mary Ann Cotton. Margaret Cotton, the sister, went down with 'gastric fever' and died shortly before her brother's wedding.

Now a significant number of pigs belonging to Mary Ann's neighbours mysteriously began to die, and those uncharitable farmers started to point an accusing finger in Mary's direction; indeed, such was the acrimony over the deceased pigs that the Cottons – Frederick, Mary Ann, two offspring of Cotton's earlier marriage and Mary's baby – found it wise to remove to West Auckland.

Once settled, the family rapidly decreased in number;

Frederick went first, on 19 September 1871. He was followed into the grave by Mary's ten-year-old stepson Frederick and baby Robert. Joseph Nattrass, a lodger who had been imprudent enough to become Mrs Cotton's lover, and unwise enough to make a will in her favour, became the fourth victim of 'gastric fever'. This left only little Charles Edward, a stepson, who had managed to survive the 'illnesses' to attain his seventh birthday. He would never see his eighth; on 12 July 1872 he died.

Mary Ann was arrested when a post-mortem on the boy's body revealed abnormal traces of arsenic. Exhumation was ordered for the four previous victims, and the autopsies proved that they too had met their end through arsenical poisoning.

Mary Ann Cotton was finally tried only for Charles Edward's murder, at the Durham Assizes in March 1873. Her defence was that her stepson had been accidentally poisoned by some wallpaper in his bedroom, the green pigment of which was derived from arsenic. And it was a defence that stood at least a chance of succeeding had the judge not allowed evidence of the four previous poisonings in order to refute the proposition of accidental death.

The jury were in retirement for barely an hour before returning a verdict of guilty. Mary Ann Cotton died on the scaffold at Durham County Gaol at 8 a.m. on Monday 24 March 1873.

COWE, Mary   In a sleazy back-street hotel in London on 29 September 1913, a desperate woman was sinking into the welcome oblivion of death. Beside her on the grey sheets lay the body of her eleven-year-old son Alexander, whom she had killed in a moment of hopeless and insane compassion. A pocket handkerchief was stuffed into the boy's mouth – tablets of morphine, a hypodermic syringe and an empty chloroform bottle littered the floor.

Suddenly the door was forced open and a babble of harsh

voices penetrated the deathly silence of the room. Then the police were called, and the dying woman was rushed to the Royal Free Hospital. She had failed even in this, her last desperate bid for peace; and while she recovered, the inquest on her son reached its verdict of 'wilful murder by morphine accelerated by suffocation'.

Mrs Cowe was brought to trial before Mr Justice Ridley at the Old Bailey charged with the murder of her son, and the drama that unfolded during the proceedings was that of a woman broken by human tragedy. The whole of her married life had been a battle against misfortune and crippling poverty; eleven years earlier her husband's ailing drapery business had finally failed and he had drowned himself in the bath, leaving his penniless widow with two young sons to rear. She managed to scratch the barest of livings as a midwife and general nurse, sending the two boys to a Blue Coat charity school. Then the elder lad, a sensitive and intelligent seventeen-year-old, fell victim to overwork and the strain of his scientific studies; he too committed suicide, by coal gas inhalation.

His mother sank into an understandable depression, continuing the fight now only for the preservation of her remaining child. They struggled along together somehow, until, just before the tragic action for which she was now on trial, Mrs Cowe had managed to scrape together the sum of twelve pounds to pay their overdue hotel bill and keep them going for a few more weeks. With the money in her pocket, she made her way home through the crowded streets; pausing to window-shop, no doubt to dream about how it must feel to be blessed with some of life's luxuries. It was while she was in this reverie that a passing pickpocket relieved her of all she had in the world.

That had been at the end of September. Already the nights were drawing in, and with no hope of replacing the stolen money, she and her son were faced with a hungry and homeless winter. A blackness of despair clawed its way into her head; she could think of nothing save escape from a life which promised only endless struggle, endless misery. It was in this state that she had committed that awful deed for which the jury must now try her.

The verdict, when it came, was as bleak and unpromising as she might have expected – 'Guilty, but insane and not responsible for her actions'. But for the first time in years Mrs Cowe would have a permanent roof over her head, and food which she had not had to scrimp and save for – all this 'at His Majesty's pleasure'.

CRANE, Cheryl   At the age of nineteen, screen actress Lana Turner entered into the first of what would be a long succession of less than ideal marriages. Within two months of the ceremony she had parted from band-leader Artie Shaw and later they divorced. Lana's second husband was businessman Stephen Crane; they met at a night-club, danced together, and were married the following week. Unfortunately, Crane was not yet divorced from his previous wife and the marriage to Lana was temporarily anulled; by this time she was pregnant. Lana and Crane finally married and baby Cheryl was born five months later. When this marriage also collapsed Lana Turner became Mrs Henry 'Bob' Topping, and millionaire Topping was succeeded by one of the screen's most famous Tarzans – Lex Barker. The relationship with Barker came to an acrimonious end provoked, it is said, by Cheryl's jealousy, and Lana married in fairly quick succession Fred May, Robert Eaton and Ronald Danse. Cheryl was now a confused and insecure ten-year-old with no very high opinion of her mother or her mother's morals. Just how seriously their relationship had deteriorated was illustrated by an incident at one of Cheryl's many expensive boarding schools. Told by a teacher that if she did not write a letter to her mother she would go to bed without supper, Cheryl wrote: 'Dear Mother, this is not a letter, it is a meal ticket . . .

Lana, meanwhile, had fallen for the smooth patter of part-time gigolo, part-time crook Johnny Stompanato. Lana, more impulsive than discriminating, became obsessively infatuated with her new lover and, it has to be said, he with her. Indeed, Johnny became violently and irrationally jealous, and when Lana was obliged to travel to England to film *Another Time*, *Another Place*, he followed her out of jealousy of her co-star Sean Connery. The quarrels between Lana and Johnny became so aggressive that the English police were finally forced to deport Stompanato after he had tried to strangle Lana. Still they clung desperately to each other, and surprisingly the relationship actually brought young Cheryl closer to her mother than she had been for a long time; and of all her mother's husbands and lovers Johnny was the one Cheryl seemed to take to.

On the evening of Good Friday, 4 April 1958, Cheryl, Lana and Johnny were at home in North Bedford Drive when one of the frequent quarrels erupted, during which Stompanato became his usual threatening, bullying self. Cheryl slipped into the kitchen and picked up a carving knife; she said later that she was afraid Johnny would hurt her mother.

Events were beginning to take on a menacing physical threat, with Stompanato flailing his fists around . . . but before he or Lana realized what was happening, Cheryl rushed up to Johnny and drove the nine-inch blade of the carving knife into his stomach. Although he was still alive when the doctor arrived, by the time the police got to the scene Johnny Stompanato was dead.

The coroner's inquest opened on 11 April and was broadcast live on national television. Lana Turner gave the performance of her life as the abused and terrified mother fearful for her own and her child's safety from a man insane with violent jealousy. There was scarcely a dry eye in the court, and after a token retirement the jury returned a verdict of justifiable homicide; Cheryl Crane was released to the apparent joy of all.

Unlike many stars whose careers were shattered by personal

scandals, Lana Turner survived the Stompanato affair, and many have observed that the sensation had actually revived a flagging career. Cheryl Crane became a successful business-woman in the field of real estate, and later published her autobiography.

CRIMMINS, Alice At first it looked like the nightmare scenario that runs through most parents' minds at some time or another – that their children have been abducted, or worse. On 14 May 1965 Edmund Crimmins received a telephone call from his estranged wife asking if he had taken the children. She had gone into their bedroom as usual that morning and they were missing. Crimmins had not taken the children.

When detectives arrived at twenty-six-year-old Alice Crimmins' ground-floor apartment in the Queen's district of New York they found the children's beds apparently slept in, and the bedroom window wide open. Mrs Crimmins said she had last seen five-year-old Eddie and his four-year-old sister Alice Marie (called 'Missi') at around four the previous evening, 13 May, when they went to bed. On the afternoon of 14 May Missi's strangled body was found on a waste lot. Two things puzzled the police. First, Alice Crimmins' seeming indifference to the discovery; second, the medical examiner's report that undigested food in the child's stomach indicated that she was already dead seven hours before Alice claimed to have seen her last. A week later young Eddie's decomposed body was also found dumped.

Routine house-to-house inquiries had turned up a sighting of Mrs Crimmins in company with a man in the early morning of 14 May. She had been carrying a bundle under one arm and leading a small boy. However, it was not until two years later that Alice Crimmins was charged with the murder of her daughter. She stood trial first in May 1968 when she was convicted and sentenced to five-to-twenty years for first-degree murder. A subsequent appeal saw this conviction quashed. In

1971 Alice Crimmins appeared before a jury again. This time she was charged with the murder of her son and the manslaughter of little Alice Marie. One of the most damaging witnesses against her was one of Alice's former lovers, who claimed that she had confessed to him that she had murdered her children; it was a particularly powerful piece of evidence because it got close to providing a motive for an otherwise inexplicable crime. As part of this bedroom confession Alice was supposed to have said that she 'preferred to see the children dead than allow her husband to get custody of them'.

It convinced the jury, and Alice Crimmins was found guilty on both counts against her. Eventually another appeal overturned the murder conviction, and Alice's life sentence was shortened. In early 1976 she was released into a residential work programme where she studied to be a secretary.

D

DADDOW, Jean Jean Blackman met financial adviser Terry Daddow in 1985 when she walked into the Tenterden branch of Lloyd's Bank to report the theft of her credit cards; within a short while the couple were involved in an affair, and Daddow left his wife and children and moved in with Jean. On 6 June 1989 they married at Gretna Green.

It was never a particularly happy union – Daddow was inclined to violence, and had a history of depression which eventually necessitated his early retirement in June 1991, nudging him further into his already destructive drink problem. If Daddow had been difficult to live with before his marriage, now he became intolerable, with his increasingly frequent anxiety attacks and alcoholic depressions spilling over into violence that on more than one occasion resulted in Jean Daddow calling out the police. As for Jean, she tended towards waywardness, and during her previous marriage had entertained a succession of lovers. It is not certain that Jean Blackman had her eyes on Daddow's money from the start, but it seems to have provided a pretty strong inducement to marriage, and it was not long before the new Mrs Daddow was scheming to transfer 'their' assets to her control. During the time between the wedding and Daddow's untimely death, Jean had opened a network of thirty bank and building society accounts.

Quite when she hatched the plot to have her husband murdered we do not know, but she was enthusiastically abetted by twenty-three-year-old Roger Blackman, a son by her previous marriage and said to be a small-time drug dealer. The man chosen for the job was Robert Bell, a thirty-three-year-old ex-Legionnaire and former soldier in the British Army. He did the job because he owed Roger Blackman money for drugs and Blackman was putting on the pressure – including, it was alleged, making threats against Bell's family.

The first attempt had taken place in the early hours of 11 October 1991, when Blackman and Bell arrived at the Daddows' home. Disguised in his full-face crash helmet and armed with a metal bar, Bell crept across the blackness of the front lawn and up to the front door. As he stood just across the threshold Bell froze. He had heard a noise from the bedroom upstairs; and like a startled rabbit he turned on his heel and fled.

There followed a series of burlesque attempts to persuade Bell to shoot Terry Daddow – while he was driving his car, as he took a stroll at Dungeness . . . all of which he failed to do. Towards the end of November, the reluctant hit-man was told to wait in his car out of sight in a side road when Jean Daddow drove her husband to visit her parents. The plan was for Jean to stop the car in a quiet spot and persuade her husband to get out; Bell was supposed to drive round the corner at speed and knock him down. Once again Bell's courage deserted him.

On 11 November 1991, Robert Bell arrived at Daddow's door and announced that he was, of all things, a conservation officer specializing in the welfare of badgers. While he engaged Daddow in a discussion on the creatures, Bell slipped Jean a packet containing drugs sent by Roger Blackman – though why Blackman could not have given them to his mother in person is anybody's guess. The packet contained a mixture of LSD and amphetamines. The drugs were duly introduced into the unfortunate Daddow's food which, quite oblivious of the desperate plans to end his life prematurely, he ate with apparent enjoyment. The drugs did not kill him, but they did make him very ill, and the hallucinations could have done nothing for his already frail mental health.

On the morning of 26 November 1991, the following inexplicable advertisement appeared in *The Wealden Advertiser*;

> DADDOW, Terry and Jean. Because of malicious gossip would like it known that they are happily married and together. All have been proved by solicitors, etc. NOT guilty of fraud, theft or senility. Thanks to the few true friends who believed in us; perhaps the rest could find themselves to criticize or work for their sick minds.

Time ran out for Daddow and Robert Bell that night. Bell arrived at the door of Chapelfield Cottage this time armed with a 12-bore shotgun which had been pressed on him by Roger Blackman. When the sleeping Daddows heard the ringing of the doorbell, it was Terry who got up to answer it. It is unlikely he even got a good look at his visitor as a mass of molten shot blasted its way through his chest at point-blank range, killing him instantly. Hearing the explosion of the gun from the bedroom, Jean Daddow came slowly down to the hall where the bleeding body of her husband lay, just inside the doorway. She waited; five minutes, ten, fifteen . . . Bell should be well away by now. Time to call the police.

When the police arrived they found Jean Daddow apparently beside herself with grief. They learned that the Daddows' neighbours nicknamed them 'Terry and June' after the affectionate middle-class couple in the television sit-com of the same name; and until the peculiar advertisement appeared in the local paper on the morning of Terry Daddow's death they had attracted very little attention in the small East Sussex village of Northiam.

But detectives had begun to probe behind the 'Terry and June' image which had been created for the rest of the world; they had found rumours of malpractice aimed at Terry Daddow, and accusations that his wealth had been secured by coercing his clients into giving him 'presents' of money. At the trial it would be said that Daddow had concocted a scheme for getting elderly ladies drunk and then taking compromising sexual photographs to use as blackmail.

Meanwhile, Terry Daddow's mortal remains had been buried beneath a polished black marble headstone; the inscription read:

'Treasured Memories of Terence John Daddow.
Taken suddenly on 26 November 1991, Aged 52 years.
In God's house but in my heart, Your wife, Jean.'

In early March 1992, the police caught up with Robert Bell, who had recently fled to the United States. An arrogant man who clearly believed in the power of his own silver tongue, he volunteered to return to Britain and explain his innocence. Instead, he was arrested and charged with murder. So was Roger Blackman. Mrs Daddow would have been taken into custody as well – but in a final desperate gesture to 'prove' her innocence she took an overdose and almost killed herself.

From the dock at Hove Crown Court fifty-three-year-old Jean Daddow, her son Roger Blackman, and Robert Bell pleaded not guilty to conspiracy to murder; Bell also pleaded not guilty to a charge of murder. The trial opened on 24 February 1993 before Mr Justice Hidden. In his opening speech to the jury, prosecuting counsel said that Mrs Daddow had milked £7,000 from the bank account she held jointly with her husband and kept the cash in a shoe box in order to pay a contract killer to murder Terry Daddow. That killer was Robert

Bell, Mr Pratt continued, though Bell still protested his innocence and blamed Mrs Daddow's son Roger for the murder. He listed the incredible bungled attempts to dispose of Daddow before his life was eventually taken with a single blast from a shotgun.

On 8 April the jury returned a unanimous verdict of guilty on all charges. Neither Jean Daddow nor her son showed the slightest emotion. Freed now from the legal requirement not to make prejudicial comments during the trial, Detective Superintendent Brian Foster, who had so successfully led the inquiry, was reported as saying of Mrs Daddow: 'It is difficult to believe someone would be so cold and calculating for so long a period . . . Throughout the case we thought we were getting close to the truth; then Jean Daddow threw out another piece of information.' Mr Foster added: 'The motive was a mixture of greed and dislike of Terry Daddow. She stood to inherit a fortune of around £300,000 if he died, and she and her son had grown to hate him throughout their marriage.'

DARTSCH, Sylvia, and SABEIKOV, Heidemarie   Otto Moerre was sixty-eight when he encountered the Grim Reaper; not an age when one contemplates too distant a future, but even in the atmosphere of austerity of pre-unification East Berlin Herr Moerre was counting on a few more years. There was nothing very special about him, except perhaps that he had only one leg – the other had been lost in an accident longer ago than he cared to remember – and had it not been for this infirmity it is quite possible that Otto Moerre's corpse would have remained undiscovered for longer than three days. It happened like this.

Old-age and handicap had deprived Herr Moerre of any inclination to hop down several flights of stairs from his apartment in the city's Floriengasse and get his own shopping. As convenience would have it, this duty was undertaken by fourteen-year-old Willi Kastner, an enterprising youth who lived with his parents in the same building and who, for a few pfennigs, fetched and carried from the shops on behalf of a number of elderly residents.

It was on 6 August 1971 when, for the third day in a row, Willi was unable to attract Herr Moerre's attention by knocking on his door, that he mentioned it to his mother. Frau Kastner in her turn tried to summon the old gentleman, also without success. Knowing that it was by no means rare for elderly people living alone to pass away unnoticed and unmourned, Frau Kastner called the police; after all, decomposing bodies do not make the best of neighbours. And that, in fact, was exactly what the police found when they broke down Herr Moerre's front door. At first sight it looked as though he had died of a heart attack. The truth of the matter is that he was sprawled across the sofa with his trousers open and his genitals exposed, and it seemed likely that he had been indulging in a spot of auto-eroticism when the excitement had become too much for his heart. Certainly, the police agreed among themselves, there were worse ways to go. That was before they examined the dead man's head. The way he had been lying, with his head thrown back, almost obscured the bloody wound which identified this as a job for the murder squad.

Which is how Herr Otto Moerre found his exit from this life interrupted by an ignominious appointment with a mortuary slab and a pathologist's scalpel. The post-mortem examination revealed a number of potentially important pieces of information. Herr Moerre had indeed experienced a sexual orgasm just minutes before he died, and it was very probable that somebody else had been helping him. Also, an attempt had been made to strangle Herr Moerre manually before the attacker had given up and battered him to death first with a bottle and then with his own crutch. There was every likelihood that, given the sexual element and the failed attempt at strangulation, the killer was a woman. What's more, Otto Moerre was known to be fond of young girls, and there were reports from fellow residents in the apartment block that adolescent females had occasionally been seen visiting the old man. Motive was proving difficult to establish, because although no cash had been found on the body or in the flat, a number of valuables such as a coin and stamp collection and a bank-book had been left behind after the place was ransacked. If robbery was the motive, what was the thief after, and did she (or he, or they) find it? Or perhaps it was just inexperience or ignorance that made the killer leave behind the valuable collections.

To the hard-bitten members of Berlin's murder squad there was one likely type of suspect that might fit all the criteria. As in the broken-down slum areas of all major cities there existed an underground population of young, homeless, rootless drug addicts, many barely in their teens; you could find them haunting the main railway stations like frail ghosts, offering sex for the price of their next fix of heroin, interested only in relieving the pain and misery of reality. So, apart from a few fingerprints which were not on record, that was as far as the investigation had got when Otto Moerre's assassin made a fatal mistake. It is common for amateur crooks to boast about their 'achievements', and that is exactly what she did – or, rather, what they did. Quite why anybody would want to brag about beating to death a sixty-eight-year-old cripple is difficult to fathom, but word began to reach the police that two young women described as being aged about twenty and calling themselves Sylvia and Heidemarie were doing just that. Although this information did not prove immediately useful, Germany being well stocked both with Sylvias and with Heidemaries, detectives were to hear one of the names again very soon, and from a completely different direction.

It transpired that police on the other side of the city had received an anonymous report from a man who had picked up a young woman in his car and taken her to a secluded spot where she exchanged her sexual favours for his financial ones. When they had finished their *al fresco* romp, the woman had jumped into the car and attempted to drive off leaving its startled owner behind. Unfortunately for her enterprise, a tree was in the way and the woman was obliged to get out of the car and run before her client caught up. It was a salutary experience for the victim, though he seemed to bear no special grudge; indeed, his only reason for contacting the police was to return the girl's handbag which she had abandoned in the car in her hurry to escape. The anonymous nature of the information, the man said, was on account of his being married. Inside the handbag there was an identity card in the name of Sylvia Dartsch. The address was not a current one, but the landlady was able to tell detectives that Fräulein Dartsch had a close friend named Heidemarie Sabeikov. Sylvia and Heidemarie.

It was only a matter of time before the huge search turned up the two suspects, plus a third, Dieter Jagdmann. Sylvia proved very talkative, particularly on the subject of her companions' guilt. Apparently she and Heidemarie would go knocking on doors seeking elderly men who were interested in young women. The sex rarely developed much further than masturbation, but pickings were satisfactory, supplemented by occasional thefts from the client's apartment, Sylvia keeping him 'occupied' while Heidemarie looked around for goodies. Jagdmann's job was to act as look-out. However, infirm and old as he was, and grateful of the sexual relief, Otto Moerre was not willing to part with his possessions; and for that he died. The reason why the coin and stamp collections had been left behind was simple – none of the villainous trio had the slightest idea that they were valuable.

Sylvia, Heidemarie and Dieter Jagdmann faced an assortment of murder and conspiracy charges, were found guilty and sentenced to terms of life imprisonment.

DE LA MARE, Gertrude Gertrude de la Mare, accompanied by her three-year-old daughter, had been in service on the Channel Island of Guernsey since the break-up of her marriage some year or so before. It was now 1935, and although she was a rather clumsy, dull-witted woman her housekeeping services seemed to satisfy the elderly farmer for whom she kept house, and on the face of it both Gertrude and Alfred Brouard appeared to fulfil each other's expectations.

Then on the morning of 6 February 1935 Mrs de la Mare rushed to her neighbour in a state of agitation, shouting: 'The old man's dead. He's cut his throat.' When the police arrived shortly afterwards they found Alfred Brouard lying on the bed, a savage slash across his throat. What at first appeared to be a suicide note gratuitously offered the information that 'no blame attaches to Mrs de la Mare', and left all funeral arrangements in her capable hands. Another document, penned in the same semi-literate hand, purported to be Mr Brouard's last will and testament leaving all his worldly goods – valued at about £60 – to that same housekeeper. It was later said that the handwriting and style of these documents most closely resembled those of Mrs de la Mare.

Further suspicion was aroused when police interviewed Mrs de la Mare who told them that Brouard had been sharpening the bread knife and had said to her daughter: 'We will be able to butcher ourselves with it.' Then, three days before the event, Mrs de la Mare had told her own mother that Alfred Brouard had already committed suicide.

At the opening of Gertrude de la Mare's trial the prosecution, led by Attorney-General Ambrose Sherwill, transferred proceedings to the farmhouse where Alfred Brouard died. There the judge and jury were treated to a re-enactment of the incident in which a police officer playing the part of Brouard demonstrated the impossibility of the victim being able to cut his own throat in the way it had been done.

Back in court the jury were told how scientists had found bloodstains on the dress worn by Mrs de la Mare's daughter, and it was suggested that these marks had been transferred from the mother's hands after the murder.

Although there was some attempt at an insanity defence, the jury clearly knew the difference between a dullard and a lunatic. Even so, it was a close decision dividing the jury six to five. But that was enough to earn Gertrude de la Mare the mandatory death sentence. In the event, King George VI exercised the royal prerogative of mercy, and Mrs de la Mare's sentence was commuted to life imprisonment.

DE MELKER, Daisy Louisa   The obituary which attracted Alfred Sproat's attention was published in the *Rand Daily Mail* in March 1932; it commemorated the death of Rhodes Cecil Cowle, only surviving child of Mrs Daisy De Melker, Sproat's former sister-in-law. Because he was puzzled, Alfred wrote a letter addressed to the police authorities at Germiston, in the Transvaal. The letter drew attention to the suspiciously bad luck suffered by Mrs De Melker in losing yet another close member of her family. Alfred's own brother Robert had been Daisy's second husband and had died five years previously on 6 November 1927. Her first husband, William Alfred Cowle (Rhodes' father), had also died suddenly in January 1923. In addition, counting Rhodes, all five of their children had also died long before their time.

After some investigation, the Johannesburg police discovered that Rhodes Cowle and his mother had regularly quarrelled over the question of his father's estate, which Rhodes thought he should inherit on attaining the age of twenty-one. He was a surly and deeply unpleasant youth, fond of threatening suicide to get his own way, and not above dealing his mother a few hefty blows during their increasingly frequent disagreements.

In April 1932 a decision was made to exhume the bodies of Rhodes and William Cowle and Robert Sproat; arsenic was found in Rhodes Cowle's body and minute traces of strychnine in his father's and that of Robert Sproat. A warrant was immediately issued for the arrest of Daisy De Melker, and she was charged with murder, though at this time there was no evidence linking her with the purchase or possession of poisons. However, following extensive newspaper publicity a chemist named Spilkin came forward and identified Daisy as having bought arsenic from him six days before the death of Rhodes Cowle.

Mrs De Melker was tried before Mr Justice Greenberg and two assessors (in this instance Mr J.M. Graham and Mr A.A. Stanford, both experienced senior magistrates). The trial lasted thirty days (then the longest trial of a European in the legal history of the Union of South Africa), and Daisy spent a total of more than eighteen hours in the witness box. One man closely involved with her defence, Henry Harris Morris KC, has described Mrs De Melker under cross-examination: 'She spoke rapidly and with animation; when in difficulties or on the defensive, her voice was raised in a whining pitch which gave the impression that she was not telling the truth . . . Her most striking feature was her mouth, which was strongly suggestive of a cruel disposition. She seemed almost incapable of emotion.'

Although the charges of poisoning her husbands remained unproven, Daisy was convicted of poisoning her son. In sentencing her, Mr Justice Greenberg said: 'Daisy Louisa Melker, this court has come to the decision that you are guilty of the crime of having administered poison to your son and murdering him. There is only one sentence I can pass. Whether that sentence will be carried into execution or not is a matter with which I have nothing to do; that rests with the Governor-General in Council, who will decide whether the sentence is to be carried out or not after having considered all the records in the case together with a report from the prosecutor and myself. But in the meantime the only sentence I can pass on you is that you be taken back to custody and that you be hanged by the neck until you are dead.'

It was a sentence which, in the case of a poisoner, was never commuted in South Africa. Daisy De Melker was hanged in Pretoria Central Prison on 30 December 1932.

DEAN, Minnie   Minnie was born Williamina in Edinburgh in 1847, and in 1865, when she was only eighteen years old, arrived at East Winton, near Invercargill, New Zealand. Later, but not much later, Minnie married Charles Dean, and settled down to rural domesticity in a modest shack that the Deans had cobbled together themselves; their, or rather Minnie's, flower garden became the envy of her neighbours.

To supplement Dean's by no means reliable income, Minnie decided to take up the profitable side-line of baby farming – not always the sinister occupation that it became at the hands of such practitioners as Mrs Dyer (see page 115). Whether through bad luck or inadequate care, one of her charges, young May Irene, died in her care; and so did six-week-old Bertha in 1891. Although the deaths were certified as due to 'natural causes', the medical authorities were far from happy about the squalid conditions in which the children had been kept.

In April 1895, a Mrs Hornsby replied to one of Minnie's advertisements in the New Zealand *Timaru Herald,* the result of which was that Minnie was given charge of a one-month-old baby. When the child disappeared after having been seen in Minnie Dean's arms in a railway carriage, awkward questions began to be asked, and Minnie denied ever having set eyes on the child – a lie quickly exposed by the discovery of the mite's clothing at her home.

Both Minnie and her husband were placed under arrest, giving detectives greater freedom to undertake a more thorough search of the Dean household and 'estate' – in particular the newly turned patches of earth among Minnie's prize chrysan-themums into which cut flowers had been inexplicably pushed in imitation of their growing neighbours. Beneath the scented blooms, in a shallow grave, were two small bodies – one was the recently missing baby. From under the dahlia patch the almost skeletal remains of a third child were unearthed. Autopsy confirmed that one of the children had died from morphia poisoning, and quantities of the drug were also found about the house.

It had been established early on that Charles Dean was quite unaware of what had been going on, and so on 18 June 1895, Minnie Dean stood alone in the dock at Invercargill Supreme Court. She was found guilty of murder, and on 12 August Minnie Dean became the first and the last woman to be hanged in New Zealand. A reporter for *The Times* described how Mrs Dean went to the scaffold: 'without flinch or falter; she died a brave, a wonderful woman'.

DICK, Evelyn   Evelyn Dick was not so much evil as totally without morals. She had been spoiled and pampered as a girl, her expensive education in Toronto being sponsored – unwittingly – by the Hamilton Transit system. Her father, Donald Maclean, was a tram conductor who stole unused tickets from the street cars, passing them on to Evelyn who sold them to immigrant workers. She got used to a certain style of life, and by the time she left school was an attractive, wilful and thoroughly promiscuous young woman. She claimed to have had sexual relations with more than two hundred men – obviously a woman who knew what she wanted. And what, on the other hand, she could do without.

She had a go at marriage in 1945, not a very committed or solemn undertaking it would seem, for the couple parted within a few months. His name was John Dick, a tram conductor by occupation, and on 16 March 1946 his headless torso was discovered near Albion Falls, south-east of Hamilton, Ontario. He had been missing for ten days – since the evening when he had an appointment with his estranged wife.

The tram conductor's equipment found in Evelyn Dick's house was positively identified as belonging to John. The fragments of bone in the furnace were not so easy to identify, were indeed never proven to belong to John Dick, although certainly they were human. And other tell-tale clues were not hard to find: the nauseous smells from the chimney which the neighbours complained about; bloodstains in the shed, and on the gear lever of Evelyn Dick's car; not least, John Dick's sweater in the boot of the car, with a bullet hole blown through it.

But that was not all. In the lumber room, in among all the bags and cases, was a small but weighty suitcase. It contained the body of a baby boy, strangled with a length of hemp, and encased in concrete. When this unspeakably horrific discovery was relayed to Evelyn Dick by Inspector Charles Wood, she is reported to have leaned forward, quite deadpan, pulled at the lapel of his jacket and demanded: 'Would you please get me a sandwich? I'm starving.'

Evelyn Dick, her father, her mother and her current lover, one William Bohozuk, whom she named as the father of the baby, were all arrested. No evidence was offered against the mother, who was dismissed from the trial, as was Bohozuk when Evelyn refused to give evidence against him. Donald Maclean pleaded guilty to being an accessory after the fact in the murder of John Dick, for which he was sent down for five years. But it was Evelyn who was the principal figure in the case, and justice seemed to have been done when she was sentenced to be hanged.

This, however, was to reckon without Mr John Robinette. The young defence lawyer took up the case and steered it through the appeal court with such vigour and passion that a second trial was ordered, where he was able to dent the prosecution's case sufficiently for his client to be acquitted. Acquitted, but not freed: Evelyn Dick was found guilty on a charge of the manslaughter of her son, and received a well-deserved sentence of life imprisonment.

DONALD, Jeannie Jeannie Donald was the thirty-eight-year-old wife of an Aberdeen hairdresser. Her victim, eight-year-old Helen Priestly, lived with her parents in a flat on the first floor of a tenement at 61 Urquart Road, Aberdeen. Below them on the ground floor lived the Donalds, although they were neighbours only in a strict locational sense, Mrs Donald and Mrs Priestly having not spoken to each other for five years, the result of some long-forgotten grievance.

Just after midday on 20 April 1934, young Helen arrived home from school for the lunchtime meal; she finished her food and rushed round to visit a friend, and returned home at about ten minutes past one, when she was immediately sent out again to the local Co-op store to buy her mother a loaf of bread. Helen was seen by several people walking back from the shop with her purchase – it was around one-thirty. Helen Priestly was never seen alive again.

When her daughter failed to return home, Mrs Priestly alerted the neighbours, and the well-oiled machinery of working-class community spirit burst into action. During the whole of the rest of that day and through the night, the police searchers were assisted by parties of local people anxious to offer their support in the Priestlys' hour of crisis. At five in the morning, one volunteer who had been home for a few hours' sleep, entered 61 Urquart Road to tell Mr Priestly he was ready to resume the hunt for missing Helen. Here, in the half-light of the communal lobby, his search ended; in a recess under the stairs was a brown sack, and as his eyes became accustomed to the gloom, he saw the hand and foot of a child protruding from it. Within minutes people had collected, it seemed, from far and wide in the neighbourhood. Helen Priestly had been found – dead.

At first sight it appeared to police officers that little Helen had been strangled and sexually assaulted; only when a thorough post-mortem had been conducted was it established that, despite some instrument having been intruded into her body, there were no signs consistent with rape or attempted rape; the most logical conclusion being that Helen had been slain by a woman who faked the abuse in order to deflect suspicion. The post-mortem revealed that the victim's death had taken place around two o'clock on the afternoon of her disappearance, and the cause of death was asphyxia, possibly from manual strangulation, although vomited particles were found in the wind-pipe and smaller air tubes.

By the middle of the week following Helen Priestly's death, gossip had reached the ears of the police about the long-standing feud between Mrs Donald and the Priestlys (Helen had often taunted Mrs Donald with the nickname 'Coconut'). After lengthy questioning Jeannie Donald was taken into custody at midnight on 25 April and later committed for trial.

The evidence against Jeannie Donald proved to be a damaging jigsaw of interlocking facts collated from the reports of pathologists, chemists and bacteriologists. Bloodstains and bacteria found on the child's garments matched those on articles in the Donald home, as did various hairs and fibres.

In her own defence, Mrs Donald said only that she had nothing to do with Helen Priestly's death, and saw no reason to go into the witness box and repeat the fact. The trial occupied six days, but at the end of it the jury required no more than eighteen minutes to return a majority verdict of thirteen 'guilty' and two 'not proven'. Jeannie Donald was sentenced to death, although that grim sentence was subsequently commuted to life imprisonment – which for Mrs Donald was ten years. She was released on special licence on 26 June 1944.

DOSS, Nannie   A prolific familicide, Nannie Doss of Tulsa, Oklahoma, notched up at least eleven murders including several husbands, her mother, two sisters and two of her children.

She married for the first time to George Frazer, in 1920, though Nannie's numerous affairs, conducted in the pursuit of 'Mr Right', did little to cement the union. The final straw for George was when he came home from work to find his two children lying dead on the floor – 'accidentally' poisoned. Not waiting around to see who might be next, Frazer wisely took a speedy leave of his wife. Husband number two, Frank Harrelson, died of 'stomach trouble' later the same year. Arlie Lanning lasted a bit longer – from 1947 until his death from 'stomach trouble' in 1952. A comfortable insurance of $1,500 ensured that marriage to Richard Morton lasted no longer than necessary, and finally Nannie's fifth husband, Samuel Doss, contracted his 'stomach trouble' after eating a bowl of his wife's stewed prunes. In this last case, Nannie came up against a more painstaking doctor, who not only refused to sign a death certificate but insisted on an autopsy and called in the police. When post-mortem examination proved without the least doubt that Sam Doss had died of a massive dose of arsenic, Nannie confessed all.

Nevertheless, the defiant Mrs Doss who had freely admitted her misdeeds, indignantly denied the prosecution attorney's suggestion at her trial that she had murdered solely out of greed. It had been, she insisted, a search for true love: 'I was looking for the perfect mate, the real romance of life.' Nannie Doss was convicted and sentenced to life imprisonment in 1964. She died in prison of leukaemia the following year.

DOWNS, Elizabeth Diane   It is not exactly a rare motive, but it is always slightly shocking to read of people, particularly women, killing their own children because they have become a nuisance. In 1983, twenty-seven-year-old Diane Downs was divorced with three children; and she had a new boyfriend who made it quite clear what he thought about kids – he didn't like them. One evening towards the end of the year, Mrs Downs put eight-year-old Christie, seven-year-old Cheryl and three-year-old Danny into the car and drove to the outskirts of her hometown of Springfield, Oregon. There she took a gun out of her purse, shot each of the children and then put a bullet through the fleshy part of her own arm. (Although she killed

Cheryl, Mrs Downs had only wounded her two other children, albeit critically.) According to her statement to the police, the car had been flagged down by a man she described as 'shaggy haired', who started shooting at them.

At her trial, Elizabeth Diane Downs was convicted on one count of murder, two of attempted murder and two of first-degree assault. The sheer cynicism of the crime earned Downs maximum penalties on each count, clocking up terms of life plus five years (murder with a *firearm*), two of thirty years (attempted murder) and two of twenty years (assault). Following sentence Judge Foote told Downs: 'The court hopes the defendant will never again be free. I've come as close to that as possible.'

In fact Diane Downs was free for a brief period of ten days when she escaped from Salem prison in July 1987. Since her recapture she seems to have come to terms with her fate and in 1989 her autobiography *Diane Downs: Best Kept Secrets* became a bestseller.

DRYLAND, Christine The Drylands were to all appearances made for each other, at least in the rather artificial, close-knit world of the professional Army. Tony Dryland had joined the Royal Electrical and Mechanical Engineers (REME) at the age of sixteen, determined to make the service his career. He had served almost five years when he met seventeen-year-old Christine Caine, the only daughter of Warrant Officer 2nd Class Michael Caine who had coached Tony Dryland in boxing. They were married on 4 February 1967. The couple were moved from posting to posting more than a dozen times over the years of their marriage, but coming as they did from service families accustomed to such a nomadic lifestyle, both coped, and as their wedding anniversaries came and passed there were no obvious signs of discontent. However, things were not quite what they seemed.

The Drylands had not long arrived in Soltau, near Hanover,

Germany, from their previous posting at Paderborn when, in August 1990, the major met thirty-four-year-old Marika Sparfeldt. Tony Dryland was an enthusiastic and expert horseman and the proud owner of two magnificent black Hanoverian horses; two horses that required stabling. Marika Sparfeldt was a riding instructor at the stable he chose, and an equestrian journalist; before long their mutual love of riding had developed into a strong personal attachment, only a short step from becoming lovers. Their affair had been interrupted by the advent of the Gulf War, when Dryland served with the REME corps attached to the Seventh Armoured Brigade in Saudi Arabia and Iraq. During his service in the Middle East Major Dryland sent no fewer than forty-seven passionate letters to Marika; it was at this time that he made a fatal decision. Less than a week after his return from the Gulf, Tony Dryland announced his intention, after twenty-four years of marriage, to divorce his wife and marry Marika Sparfeldt. With that curious mixture of stoicism and resignation common to so many service wives, Christine Dryland seemed to take the news in her stride; in fact, she offered to clear her husband's path by taking their sons Robert, aged sixteen, and three-year-old James to stay with her parents in Australia. For her part, Marika Sparfeldt moved out of the apartment she had shared for five years with her partner Joachim Oetjens.

And so it might have ended. Two relationships torn apart, a new one joined. It was hardly unusual, not exactly newsworthy; just rather sad.

But if she had shown an unnerving calmness at the time, Christine Dryland gradually came to resent her self-sacrifice; perhaps she thought being an Army wife wasn't so bad after all – even the wife of an unfaithful major.

Exactly what was in her mind at that time we may never know; but it is certain that she had no fond feelings for Marika Sparfeldt, and over the following weeks there are reports of bitter exchanges between the two women. The acrimony culminated in tragedy on 27 July 1991. It was Tony Dryland's forty-sixth birthday, and he had decided to spend it with Marika at the riding club. For Christine Dryland it was the final indignity. At some point in the late afternoon she climbed into her green Saab 9000 and drove the short distance to the stables, where she proceeded to ram the car into her husband's Mercedes. When Dryland and Marika ran out of the clubhouse to see what was happening, Christine aimed the Saab at her rival and put her foot down hard on the accelerator. The car hit Marika's legs, throwing her over the bonnet, and she struck her head on the windscreen before falling to the ground. When he tried to help his lover to the safety of two horseboxes, Major Dryland was also struck by the car and thrown up on to the bonnet. According to witnesses Mrs Dryland then ran once over the injured woman's body. Marika Sparfeldt was alive when she reached hospital but died later from massive internal injuries.

After her arrest on 27 July, Christine Dryland was taken into the custody of the military police at Falling Bostel Barracks, where she would remain for six months awaiting trial.

The court-martial opened on 25 February 1992 at the First Armoured Division's headquarters at Verden near Bremen, North Germany. If an unusual tension was felt in the courtroom it may be because it was witnessing a 'first' – the first time a soldier's wife had been tried for murder in a military court. In keeping with services policy, because the defendant was a woman there was a female majority on the seven-strong panel of officers and civilians.

To the charge of murdering Fräulein Sparfeldt, Mrs Dryland, close to tears, pleaded not guilty, adding 'guilty of manslaughter by reason of diminished responsibility'. The plea was accepted by the court after Mrs Dryland was reminded that by entering such a plea she was accepting that she either intended to kill her victim or cause serious bodily harm.

When the hearing was reconvened on 27 February the judge advocate reminded the panel that, consistent with Mrs

Dryland's plea, the only evidence they would be hearing was medical testimony in mitigation of sentence. Dr Paul Bowden, a psychiatrist attached to the Maudsley Hospital in London, described the fragile state of Christine Dryland's mental health and listed three serious attacks of depression. The first had been the result of a physical problem associated with a surgical operation back in 1970; in 1974 she became suicidal over her husband's affair with another woman and tried to end her life with an overdose, and then she became depressed again in 1990, and rumours of her husband's liaison with Marika Sparfeldt had worsened her mental state: 'By 27 July 1991 she felt she was going mad; that she could not believe what she saw with her own eyes. She felt she could not turn to anyone because of the effect it would have on her husband's career. She was confused and uncertain.'

The professional opinion of both Dr Bowden and Lt-Col Coogan, a psychiatrist with the Royal Army Medical Corps, was that Mrs Dryland should 'receive psychiatric treatment in a hospital for a substantial period of time'. They emphasized that she was not in any way a danger to society.

Summing up for Mrs Dryland, Ann Curnow QC described the case as 'a tragic one in which everyone concerned has already suffered enough'. The court could hardly deny the truth of that, and their compassion was reflected in the sentence. Christine Dryland could have faced a maximum of life imprisonment, but instead was ordered to undergo up to twelve months' psychiatric treatment in a London hospital, concurrent with a one-year Rhine Army probation order.

DUBUISSON, Pauline   It is well known that in France, and certain other countries for that matter, a special leniency is exercised by the law courts in the face of a *crime passionnel*, or 'crime of passion'. It is not quite so loose a term as is popularly believed, and is enshrined in British law as the defence of 'temporary insanity' – that is, the accused person must prove that he or she acted in a moment of passionate jealousy, or anger; a betrayal between lovers is a common scenario. But what if that 'passionate jealousy' ferments over a period of time? Does it then become premeditated murder, and not a *crime passionnel*? The case of Pauline Dubuisson put this distinction to the test.

Pauline was born in Dunkirk in 1926, which made her sixteen when the Nazis occupied France during the Second World War. Her father was an unashamed collaborator and openly worked for the Germans, while for her own part, Pauline 'entertained' the German troops and was for a period the mistress of a fifty-five-year-old colonel named von Domnick. After the liberation of France Pauline Dubuisson, in common with other women who had fraternized with the enemy, was dragged into the town square, had her head shaved and was paraded through the streets to the scorn and abuse of the crowds gathered with the sole purpose of humiliating her.

Whether this had any lasting effect on Mademoiselle Dubuisson we will never know. One thing is certain, Pauline left the town of her birth in 1946 and enrolled in the department of medicine at the University of Lille. Whereas before she was promiscuous with soldiers, she was now promiscuous with students, recording their varied sexual prowess and preferences in a secret diary. At the same time, Pauline was conducting what she seemed to regard as a 'serious' affair with fellow medical student Felix Bailly. The relationship continued for two years until Felix transferred his studies to Paris.

Pauline did not bother to keep in touch and neither, as far as we know, did Felix. But eighteen months later, in March 1951, a mutual friend brought the news back to Lille that Felix was engaged to be married to an attractive young woman named Monique Lombard. Quite suddenly, Pauline Dubuisson decided she wanted Felix back. Of course it may have been that she realized what she had lost and how much she really cared for him; but with the benefit of hindsight it is more likely that

Pauline was simply peeved, and still saw Felix as a possession. Anyway, she journeyed to Paris and made some histrionic attempt to force her way back into his life. As for Felix Bailly, he was not interested; he was in love with Monique Lombard and was determined to marry her.

Pauline, however, was a very bad loser. On 10 March 1951 she purchased a .25 calibre pistol. Four days later she put the gun in her handbag and wrote a letter which could be interpreted as a suicide note; in it she made clear her intention to kill Felix Bailly and herself. Then Pauline headed for Paris. Now, concierges being what they are, Pauline Dubuisson's gun and letter had already been scrutinized, and the inquisitive landlady had immediately telegraphed Felix that his life was in danger. Felix knew Pauline well enough to take the warning seriously.

On the night of 15 March, Felix stayed over with his friend Georges, and the following day Georges acted the role of bodyguard. Later, to accommodate his friend's previous appointment, Felix telephoned fellow student Bernard Mougeot to take over as his temporary 'minder'. Sadly, Bernard was late; which gave Pauline Dubuisson, who had been waiting for just such a chance, the opportunity to pounce. When her knock came at Felix Bailly's apartment door he quite naturally thought it was the arrival of M. Mougeot. It was not; it was the pistol-waving Mademoiselle Dubuisson, and she shot him three times, any one of which would have been instantly fatal. Pauline later claimed that she then turned the gun on herself, but the mechanism jammed. Certainly the murder weapon found by the police was stuck after the third bullet. Pauline instead tried to gas herself in the kitchen, but the eventual arrival of Bernard Mougeot deprived her of that exit.

Pauline Dubuisson recovered in hospital, but was not due to stand trial until more than eighteen months later. On 28 October 1952 she once again delayed due process by hacking at her wrists with a small piece of glass. Finally, at the end of November, Pauline Dubuisson found herself in the dock of the

Seine Assizes trying to support a defence of *crime passionnel*. But how, the prosecutor wanted to know, was this a crime of passion when the prisoner had calculatedly planned the assassination, stalked her prey and then chosen a moment when he was alone and vulnerable? Besides, would a woman with her record for promiscuity – and with Nazi soldiers at that – ever know what real love felt like? Surely, the prosecutor continued, her love for Felix Bailly could not have been very strong if, for eighteen months after their separation, she had not once tried to contact him; no, this was a case of simple malice.

There was really little that could be said in Pauline's defence. Any suggestion of previous good character would have been quite fatuous in the face of her wartime record and the much publicised sexual diaries. Nor did her own obviously unrepentant attitude throughout the trial help; she had sat so indifferent to the evidence brought against her that the press had nicknamed her 'The Mask of Pride'. But juries can be unpredictable even in the face of the clearest evidence. In this case they returned a verdict of guilty of killing Felix Bailly, but *without premeditation*. Perhaps it was just a squeamish jury; perhaps they feared that Pauline Dubuisson was so publicly reviled that France would relax its tradition of sixty years and send a woman to the guillotine. As it was, she received the maximum penalty of life imprisonment.

DUFFY, Renee Because it has, quite rightly, been subjected to considerable legal and media attention over the past decade, the plight of the battered woman who resorts to killing her partner in order to escape the torment, has been seen as a modern phenomenon. This is not so; for just as 'wife-beating' is as old as humankind, so there have always been instances of women who fight back. One of those who turned on her abuser was nineteen-year-old Renee Duffy.

In 1948 Renee had been married to twenty-three-year-old George Duffy for just a year, and they had one son. Despite the fact that they lived under the same roof as Renee's mother, Duffy saw no reason to let that restrain him from beating her daughter regularly and viciously. Although with misplaced loyalty Renee explained away her black eyes and bruises as 'accidents', her mother threw George out of the house on more than one occasion. Always he pleaded to come back, always Renee took him back, and always she was rewarded with another beating.

Eventually even the long-suffering Renee had taken enough. On 7 December 1948, after receiving a particularly savage assault, she packed her bags and prepared to leave. But George had other ideas – after all, what would he use as a punchbag if Renee walked out? As she got to the front door, Duffy began to attack his wife again, grabbing their bewildered, screaming child and refusing to let her take him. Blind rage now compounding her panic, Renee pushed her way back into the kitchen and grabbed a hammer. She remembered hitting him only twice, but it was probably more. Duffy was still alive when he reached hospital, but he died the following day. Renee Duffy was picked up by the police at her sister's house, and charged with his murder.

The trial took place in March of the following year, 1949, at the Manchester Assizes. In a summing-up reminiscent of recent similar trials, Mr Justice Devlin warned the jury against taking into consideration George Duffy's past history of violence towards his wife, and instructed them to consider only those elements which contributed to his murder: 'What matters is whether this girl had time to say "Whatever I have suffered, whatever I have endured, I know that Thou Shalt Not Kill".'

After an hour-and-a-half's deliberation, the ten men and two women that made up the jury rejected Renee Duffy's plea of self-defence and found her guilty of murder as charged, adding a strong recommendation to mercy. It was not for judges to act upon these recommendations, their duty was laid down in law, and the only sentence that could be passed on a convicted murderer was death. It was in the judge's report to the Home Secretary that he passed on the jury's recommendation, along with any observations of his own, and it was up to the minister to exercise the power to reprieve. In the case of Renee Duffy, she was shown the mercy asked by the jury and her sentence was commuted to one of life imprisonment.

DURKIN, Diana Jade   That a killing can be, and sometimes is, excused, can be seen as a requisite of any compassionate legal system. For it is often only when a person's life reaches the open forum of a public court that the full background, perhaps of unendurable provocation, can be fully appreciated, and the clemency of the law mobilized in the protection of the 'innocent'.

On 28 November 1984, Police Constable Pat Durkin of the South Yorkshire force was shot dead by his wife Diana Jade just a week after their wedding. Neighbours had been startled awake at dawn by the sound of a shot, followed by what one witness described as 'a cry, a death cry'. Then all was silent.

On the face of it, the couple's relationship was stable enough. They had met in rather romantic circumstances when Diana accidentally locked herself out of her flat, and Pat Durkin answered her SOS call in his panda car. Twenty-five-year-old Diana, a clerk with the DHSS, had moved into Durkin's house in Kilnhurst six months before their wedding at Rotherham register office – a ceremony which was interrupted so that the bride and groom could go out into the street to find two people to act as witnesses.

Eight days later, Mrs Durkin was in another of Rotherham's official buildings – the magistrates court, where she was remanded in custody charged with the murder of her husband.

When Diana Durkin appeared before Mr Justice Hodgson at the Crown Court in Sheffield in July 1985, a quite different kind of relationship was exposed to public scrutiny; a relationship dominated by Pat Durkin's extreme sexual demands, overstepping the border into perversion. Mr George Tierney, speaking in Mrs Durkin's defence, told the court that her husband exercised a 'Svengali-like' hold over her, which was amplified by her deep love for him. Mr Tierney went on to say: 'There is reference in her statement to the police of porno-graphic films, allegations of bestiality and sickening perversions.' Many of the allegations were translated into such innocuous language – 'perverse', 'pornographic', 'kinky' – that it is difficult to know the true extent of Diana's Durkin's 'night-mare'. Mr Justice Hodgson actually refused to read out in court statements relating to the case, defending his action with the words: 'I could hardly accept it until I saw things found in their house' (presumably a coy reference to the paraphernalia of sexual sado-masochism), and in deciding not to jail Mrs Durkin he said: 'There seems no reason to blacken anyone's name by going into details of their marriage. One doesn't want to be seen covering up, but it is encapsulated in the phrase that she was subjected to sadistic behaviour over a lengthy period of time which she accepted because she was in love with him.'

Mrs Durkin was put on probation for three years on condition that she remained an in-patient at a psychiatric hospital.

DYER, Amelia Elizabeth   It was in the early spring in 1896 – to be precise, Monday 30 March – and a barge was making its languorous way up the Thames between Kennet's Mouth and the Caversham Lock. With little else to look at, the bargeman's eye was attracted by a brown-paper parcel lying on waste ground between the towpath and the water. Stretching out his punt-hook to catch up the bundle, and in the process tearing the wet paper, the unfortunate man was treated to the unwelcome sight of a baby's leg protruding from the soggy wrapping.

With the speed that such a discovery demands it was not long before Police Constable Bennett, the local bobby, arrived on the scene to add authority to the proceedings. Bennett took the parcel, discreetly tied up in a sack, back to the station, and in company with Inspector J.B. Anderson removed it to the more appropriate surroundings of the mortuary. There the sad little bundle was carefully unwrapped, layer upon layer of anonymous scraps of paper until, immediately covering its pathetic contents, was a sheet of paper bearing a name and address: Mrs Harding, 20 Wigotts Road, Caversham. There was also a Midland Railways label with the address 'Temple Mead Station, Bristol'. When this vital clue had been removed the body of a baby girl was revealed, a piece of tape knotted tightly around her tiny neck.

Taking immediate action, Inspector Anderson checked the Caversham address only to find that there was no Wigotts Road; however, there had been a Mrs Harding living at Pigott's Road and she had moved to 45 Kensington Road, Reading, to take up residence with her daughter Mary Ann (called Polly) and son-in-law Arthur Palmer. The Palmers had apparently departed for London, though neighbours remembered seeing Mrs Harding leaving No. 45 carrying a carpet bag on the morning following the discovery of the little corpse; and neighbours being what neighbours are, that is not all the detective learned – it transpired that Mrs Harding had been in the habit of adopting children.

Inspector Anderson now used a ploy that indicated his already deep suspicion of the woman calling herself Mrs Harding. The detective arranged for a trustworthy young woman of his acquaintance to visit the Harding home with the story that she was looking to have a baby adopted. When she arrived on the doorstep, the young woman was greeted by a crone of very advanced years announcing herself as 'Granny Smith'. The old woman made it clear that, though she was not presently at home, Mrs Harding would be most interested in the proposition, and an appointment to discuss the delicate matter was made for two days later.

Accordingly, Mrs Harding met the spy, and after the customary bargaining consented to take the child for a reward of £10, no questions asked. The transaction was to take place under cover of darkness on the following evening.

The appointed hour arrived; but it was not a young woman and infant child that knocked at the door in Kensington Road – it was Inspector Anderson and Sergeant James. Furthermore, they sufficiently intimidated Mrs Harding that she confided her real name: Dyer; Mrs Amelia Elizabeth Dyer. The story is enlarged by Mr Anderson in his own account of the Reading case*:

> We began to make a close examination of the place, and in a cupboard under the stairs we found a very important clue – a quantity of baby clothing, and we noticed a most unpleasant odour, as if some decomposing substance had been kept there. Doubtless, as subsequent events showed, the body of a little child had been concealed in this cupboard for some days before being taken out and disposed of.

On 2 April Mrs Dyer was taken to Reading police station where she was charged. Despite two attempts to end her own life – once with a pair of scissors and once with her own bootlace – she was quickly remanded by the magistrates to take her trial.

While this had been going on, Mrs Dyer's daughter and son-in-law had been traced to 76 Mayo Road, Willesden, where they were subsequently arrested. Sergeant James had been back to Kensington Road to have words with Granny Smith, and had the opportunity not only to meet some of Mrs Dyer's 'adoptees', but to examine certain of the official documentation of a girl-child apparently born in Hammersmith, but whose vaccination papers had not been returned for registration. The child was nowhere in the house and Granny Smith could give

*Survivors' Tales of Famous Crimes, ed. Walter Wood, Cassell, London, 1916.

no adequate account of her whereabouts; however, via the Hammersmith district registrar, James was able to trace Elizabeth Goulding, an unmarried barmaid, and discover that she had responded to a newspaper advertisement announcing Mrs Harding's adoption service. She had later handed over her baby and £10 to Harding and a young man answering the description of Arthur Ernest Palmer. Thus did Polly and Arthur find themselves in the same official company as their parent.

The river was being dragged for other bodies by now, and on 8 April the decomposing body of a male baby was pulled out; two days later a carpet bag was dragged up containing two bodies later identified as Doris Marmon and Harry Simmons. The ten-month-old baby of Elizabeth Goulding was next to be brought up from the river bed, and a week later, at the end of April, another unidentified infant boy was recovered.

While she was in Reading Gaol, Mrs Dyer made her single charitable gesture; she wrote a letter to the Superintendent of Police confessing her guilt and clearing her daughter and son-in-law:

> I feel my days are numbered . . . But I do feel it is an awful thing, drawing innocent people into trouble. I do know I shall have to answer before my Maker in Heaven for the awful crimes I have committed, but as God Almighty is my Judge in Heaven as on Earth, neither my daughter, Mary Ann Palmer, nor her husband, Arthur Ernest Palmer, I do most solemnly swear that neither of them had anything at all to do with it. They never knew I contemplated doing such a wicked thing until too late.

Mrs Amelia Dyer, then fifty-seven years old, appeared at the Old Bailey on 21 and 22 March 1896 charged with the murder of little Doris Marmon. The presiding judge was Mr Justice

Hawkins, and the prosecution and defence were led by Mr A.T. Lawrence and Mr Kapadia respectively.

Mr Kapadia acknowledged that his client was guilty on her own admission of the crimes, but attempted to set up a defence of insanity. Dr Logan of the Gloucester Asylum testified that in 1894 he considered Mrs Dyer to have been suffering from delusions (one of which was that birds spoke to her), and Dr Forbes Winslow agreed that she suffered from delusional insanity complicated by depression and melancholia.

For the prosecution, Dr Scott said that as medical officer of Holloway Prison, where Mrs Dyer had been recently confined, he had had the opportunity of observing the prisoner daily, that he could find no evidence of clinical insanity, and that it was his belief that any delusions were feigned. With which conclusion the jury obviously agreed, for it took them a bare five minutes to find Amelia Dyer both guilty and sane; she last saw the light of day on 10 June on the scaffold of Newgate Gaol.

Mrs Dyer never revealed how many children she had murdered – if indeed she even remembered – but she did confide with some pleasure: 'You'll know mine by the tape round their necks.'

It is said that from the condemned cell Mrs Dyer wrote this poem:

> By nature, Lord, I know with grief
> I am a poor fallen leaf
> Shrivelled and dry, near unto death.
> Driven by sin, as with a breath.
> But if by Grace I am made new,
> Washed in the blood of Jesus, too,
> Like to a lily I shall stand
> Spotless and pure at His right hand.

It was signed: 'Mother'!

E

EDMUNDS, Christiana Jealousy can be a most terrible thing, and combined with an aggressive nature is sure to end in destruction. Christiana Edmunds had an aggressive nature; she has been described variously as an 'ill-tempered', 'waspish', 'spiteful' spinster of forty-odd years. It is difficult to be precise about her age on account of her tendency to prune the years as they advanced. This was in 1871, and Christiana was just about to add jealousy to her other unlikeable characteristics.

Miss Edmunds lived in the Kemp Town district of the elegant Regency town of Brighton, on England's south coast. It was, in those days, a place much favoured by the middle classes, who sought its quiet respectability for their retirement. Christiana lived with her elderly mother, and while Mrs Edmunds suffered from nothing so much as advancing years, her daughter had become a martyr to sick headaches. And this is how she first met Dr Charles Beard, a general practitioner in the town. It was, for Christiana, love at first sight, and, she told herself confidently, there was more warmth in his manner than is usual between a doctor and his patient – he must, she was convinced, entertain feelings much like her own. In fact, Christiana couldn't have been more wrong; if if there was anything more than commonly solicitous in Dr Beard's treatment of her, then it arose from a sense of kind-hearted pity. It was obvious to the doctor that most of Miss Edmunds' ailments were in her mind, the product of lonely frustration broken only by her walks on the prom with her mother, and that good lady's infrequent supper parties. Truth to tell, Christiana Edmunds desperately needed a bit of romance in her life; unfortunately for Dr Beard he was to become the focus of that desperation.

Following that first visit to the Edmunds house, Charles Beard was the unwilling recipient of a barrage of passionate letters. Too much a gentleman to reject his admirer, a bewildered Dr Beard did nothing but observe the courtesy of a polite, if very brief, reply. Christiana took this as a sure sign of his deep love for her. Time passed, and all Christiana's days were now filled with the thought of how desperate dear Charles must be to escape from his unworthy wife, and how cruel fate was that it could not be Christiana who filled that role. She decided to help him out.

It was in March 1871 that Christiana Edmunds paid a teatime visit to Mrs Emily Beard. As well as a thin veil of bonhomie, Christiana had also brought a box of chocolates with her, and insisted that Mrs Beard eat one there and then; which the unlucky woman did. No sooner had she bitten into the confection than Emily Beard unceremoniously spat it out; the chocolate, she declared, was so bitter as to be inedible. Dear, dear, Christiana clucked, she really must reprimand that shopkeeper. But Mrs Beard was not fooled for a minute, and as soon as her husband had finished surgery, complained that what had until then just been a nuisance was now becoming dangerous – Charles would have to do something about it. And he did. He went straight round to Christiana's home and accused her of trying to poison his wife; what was more, he insisted that she pester him no more, and that she find herself another physician.

It should have occurred to Christiana Edmunds that she was very lucky not to have received a visit from the police, but it didn't. In fact, it was not long before she had developed a new paranoia – what if Mrs Beard should spread the news around that she was a potential poisoner; the gossip might get back to her mother. So Christiana hit upon another wicked plan. She would arrange for somebody quite unconnected with her to die after eating a chocolate from the same shop. Here was the ruse: Christiana bribed a young lad in the street to buy half a pound of chocolates for her at Maynard's; then she carefully injected them with strychnine before getting another small boy to take the chocolates back and say they were the wrong kind. Mr Maynard cheerfully exchanged the goods and put the poisoned candies back on sale. This routine was repeated several more times – it could only be a matter of days before they found their way into somebody's mouth.

It happened that the somebody was a four-year-old child, and on 12 June 1871 he died. The confectioner's stock was checked and other chocolates were found to contain strychnine. Luckily for him, nobody suspected Mr Maynard of trying to kill off his customers; it was, everyone agreed, a tragic and inexplicable accident. For Christiana Edmunds, things couldn't have turned out more successfully; all she had to do now was sit back and wait for Dr Beard to pay a visit and humbly beg her forgiveness. Dr Beard did not call. But some weeks later the police did.

It was inevitable after the death of young Sidney Baker that an attempt would be made to try to locate recent purchasers of strychnine in the town, and Christiana began to panic. She had bought strychnine several times from Mr Garrett, the pharmacist on North Street. True she had used the name 'Wood', but better safe than sorry. Christiana once again employed a young lad to carry a message to Garrett; the note was supposedly signed by the coroner and asked the druggist to send over his poisons register for official inspection. Garrett obliged, and the book found its way back to Christiana Edmunds. When the same youth returned the register to the pharmacy one of its pages had been torn out. But Christiana had made her one fatal error – she had torn the wrong page out. When police compared the 'Mrs Wood' signature and address, it matched Miss Edmunds' handwriting exactly.

At her trial at the Old Bailey in January 1872 Christiana Edmunds was confronted by the string of young boys who had carried out her deadly errands, by the pharmacist, by the confectioner and by Dr Charles Beard. Worse still, she was confronted by her own family history. In an attempt to have Christiana certified insane, her mother stood in the witness box and recounted the long catalogue of madness in the immediate family – her husband, Christiana's father, had died in a lunatic asylum, another child, Arthur, was confined to Earlswood Asylum, and Christiana's sister had been suicidally insane and died at an early age. As for Christiana herself, she too had undergone treatment. In short, it would have been surprising if Christiana had not been a little mad.

In the end the trial judge, Mr Baron Martin, made it clear that he would have no truck with namby-pamby excuses like insanity, and promptly sentenced Christiana Edmunds to hang. However, the intervention of the Home Secretary secured the wretched woman a reprieve, and she was committed to Broadmoor Asylum for the Criminally Insane, which had been opened just a decade earlier. Christiana died in Broadmoor in 1907, at an advanced age.

ELLIS, Ruth Ruth was the unremarkable, rather brassy nightclub hostess-turned-manageress of The Little Club, a tawdry late-night drinking establishment in London's West End. Her life had not been entirely a bed of roses, having been born in 1926 into a large impoverished family and become pregnant at the age of sixteen by a married French-Canadian soldier, who had left her to bring up her son alone. To pay the bills, Ruth took up modelling for a camera club until, at nineteen, she was taken on as a Mayfair club hostess by one Morris Conley, a man much involved in the leisure industries of drinking, gambling and prostitution. Then Ruth married a violent alcoholic named George Ellis, a Southampton dentist. She gave birth to his daughter, Georgina, just before Ellis filed for divorce – it was almost a year to the day after their wedding. Ruth returned to London and willingly into the clutches of Morris Conley again. She briefly hopped back upon her bar stool at Conley's Carroll's club, before being offered the job as his manageress at The Little Club in 1953. Not a bed of roses by any means – so if Ruth drank just a bit too much and enjoyed the loud company that gravitated to the club, who could deny her these modest pleasures?

David Blakely was a member of The Little Club, and Ruth was later to claim that he was the first customer she served there. However that may be, there was instant sexual attraction; a good-looking, if somewhat degenerate youth, with a generous manner, a romantic occupation – he was a racing driver – and an above average appetite for drink, Blakely was probably just what Ruth needed at the time.

The romance lasted for about a year, during which time Ruth became pregnant and had an abortion, and seemed to be going about as well as such a match might reasonably be expected to go. And then things began, some said inevitably, to sour. Blakely had started seeing other women, Ruth had started to object; Blakely began to plan his escape.

Nevertheless, he and Ruth still saw each other, and despite the fact that she was by then living with a man named Desmond Cussen, they seemed to be getting on. They arranged to meet on Good Friday 8 April 1955, when David was to pick Ruth up and take her back for drinks at Tanza Road, Hampstead, where his friends Anthony and Carole Findlater lived. In the end, Blakely decided not to collect Ruth, and went back to Tanza Road with Linklater alone. At about 9.30 p.m. Ruth telephoned and was told by Anthony Findlater that David wasn't there. At midnight she presented herself on the doorstep, ringing furiously on the bell; nobody answered. So Ruth attacked

Blakely's van parked outside. It wasn't long before the police were advising Mrs Ellis to go home and stop making a nuisance of herself.

Early the following morning, 9 April, Ruth telephoned the Tanza Road number and whoever answered just hung up. On Easter Sunday she made an early-morning telephone call which was answered by 'Ant' Findlater. Ruth just had enough time to blurt out: 'I hope you're having an enjoyable holiday . . .' before he put the receiver down. She was going to add 'because you've ruined mine'. That evening, after a day spent with the Findlaters, they ran out of beer, and David and a friend named Clive Gunnell obligingly drove down to the local, a pub called the Magdala, to stock up. When they came out of the pub at around 9.20 p.m., they saw Ruth standing there. Ignoring her, Blakely walked to the driver's door of his car. As Ruth followed him, she pulled a revolver from her handbag and shot at him. Blakely ran, then fell, and Ruth stood over him and emptied the chamber into his back.

Ruth was escorted to the Hampstead police station in 'S' division, where she gave her initial statement – in prosecution terms the most co-operative confession imaginable. The interview room played host to Detective Superintendent Leonard Crawford, Detective Chief Inspector Leonard Davies and Detective Inspector Peter Gill; and Ruth Ellis. Ruth, after being told for the third time that day that she 'did not have to say anything, but if she did . . .', made this statement:

About two years ago I met David Blakely when I was manageress of The Little Club, Knightsbridge. My flat was above that. I had known him for about a fortnight when he started to live with me and has done so continuously until last year, when he went away to Le Mans for about three weeks motor racing. He came back to me and remained living with me until Good Friday morning.

He left me about ten o'clock a.m. and promised to be

back by eight p.m. to take me out. I waited until half past nine and he had not phoned, although he always had done in the past. I was rather worried at that stage that he had had trouble with his racing car and had been drinking.

I rang some friends of his named Findlater at Hampstead, but they told me he was not there. I was speaking to Findlater, and I asked if David was all right. He laughed and said 'Oh yes, he's all right.' I did not believe he was not there, and I took a taxi to Hampstead, where I saw David's car outside Findlater's flat at 28 [sic; it was actually No. 29] Tanza Road. I then telephoned from nearby, and when my voice was recognized they hung up on me.

I went to the flat and continually rang the door bell, but they would not answer. I became very furious and went to David's car, which was still standing there, and pushed in three of the side windows. The noise I made must have aroused the Findlaters, as the police came along and spoke to me. Mr Findlater came out of his flat, and the police also spoke to him.

David did not come home on Saturday, and at nine o'clock this morning (Sunday) I phoned the Findlaters again, and Mr Findlater answered. I said to him: 'I hope you are having an enjoyable holiday' and was about to say: 'because you have ruined mine', and he banged the receiver down.

I waited all day today (Sunday) for David to phone, but he did not do so. About eight o'clock this evening (Sunday) I put my son Andrea to bed. I then took the gun which was given to me about three years ago in the club by a man whose name I do not remember. It was security for money, but I accepted it as a curiosity. I did not know it was loaded when it was given to me, but I knew next morning when I looked at it. When I put the gun in my bag I intended to find David and shoot him.

I took a taxi to Tanza Road, and as I arrived David's car drove away from the Findlaters' address. I dismissed the taxi and walked back down the road to the nearest pub where I saw David's car outside. I waited outside until he came out with a friend I know as Clive. David went to his door to open it. I was a little way away from him. He turned and saw me and then turned away from me, and I took the gun from my bag and shot him. He turned around and ran a few steps around the car; I thought I had missed him so I fired again. He was still running and I fired the third shot. I don't remember firing any more, but I must have done. I remember he was lying on the footway and I was standing beside him. He was bleeding badly and it seemed ages before an ambulance came.

I remember a man came up and I said: 'Will you call the police and an ambulance?' He said: 'I am a policeman.' I said: 'Please take this gun and arrest me.'

This statement has been read over to me and it is true.

(Signed) Ruth Ellis

It is almost certain that if Ruth Ellis were to be put on trial today, charged with the same offence, she would advance a plea of 'diminished responsibility'. This defence was made possible by the Homicide Act of 1957, which states that: 'Where a person kills or is a party to the killing of another, he shall not be convicted of murder if he was suffering from such abnormality of mind (whether arising from a condition of arrested or retarded development of mind or any inherent causes or induced by disease or injury) as substantially impaired his mental responsibility for his acts or omissions in doing or being party to the killing.'

In practical terms this converts the murder charge into one of manslaughter, a considerable advantage in the barbarous days when a capital sentence was mandatory for murder. The plea of diminished responsibility puts the burden of proof on the defence and, as in the case of Insanity pleas, the proof need not be 'beyond reasonable doubt' but 'on a balance of probabilities'. Medical evidence must obviously be presented on the defendant's behalf as to their state of mind, but it is for the *jury* and not expert witnesses to decide, on the basis of the evidence offered, whether the 'abnormality' amounts to diminished responsibility.

As it was, Ruth Ellis was predictably found guilty of murder and, according to the law of the time, sentenced to death. Ruth rejected all attempts to persuade her to appeal, and despite petitions galore calling for commutation of the sentence she was hanged at Holloway Prison in London at nine o'clock in the morning of Wednesday 13 July 1955. Among her last words, on being told of the people petitioning on her behalf, were: 'I am very grateful to them. But I am quite happy to die.'

Of course it can have been of no consolation whatsoever to her, but Ruth's execution had finally sickened politicians and public alike of the capital sentence. Ruth Ellis was the last woman to be hanged in Britain, and a decade later, with the double execution of Peter Allen and Gwynne Evans in 1965, hanging effectively ceased.

F

FAHMY, Marie-Marguerite Within the personalities and the lifestyles of its two leading characters lay all the ingredients that together make either a great Romance, or a great Crime of Passion. It was to be the meeting of two quite alien cultures that set this runaway train of emotions hurtling towards the latter course.

He was Prince Ali Kamel Fahmy Bey, a volatile young Egyptian playboy, holding a nominal diplomatic post with his Government's embassy in Paris, and heir to his father's immense fortune. She was a beautiful, sophisticated Parisienne ten years his senior.

When they met in Paris in 1922 Fahmy instantly fell in love with the beautiful Marie-Marguerite Laurent, a recent divorcée, and pursued her relentlessly and passionately. He followed her to Deauville, where they became lovers, and in December Marguerite was converted to the Muslim faith and the couple married, embarking on a life that revolved around the fashionable high-spots of Egypt and Paris. Subsequent events were to illuminate the dark recesses that lay behind this outwardly bright and carefree extravagance.

The beginning of July 1923 found the Fahmys ensconced in a luxury suite at London's famous Savoy Hotel. On the evening of the ninth the couple fell into bitter disagreement over an operation that Marguerite wished to have performed in Paris, but her husband insisted be carried out in London – or he would not provide the money to pay for it. The quarrel accompanied them to supper in the hotel restaurant, where Madame Fahmy was overheard threatening to crack a bottle over Prince Ali's head.

Later on, as part of his customary courtesy, the leader of the restaurant's small orchestra approached the Fahmys' table to ask Madame if there was any particular tune that she would like them to play. 'I don't want any music,' she replied. 'My husband has threatened to kill me tonight.' With a polite bow the conductor made a tactical withdrawal with the words 'I hope you will still be here tomorrow, Madame.'

Twice during that tense evening Fahmy asked his wife to dance with him; twice she refused; twice she accepted the same invitation from his personal secretary, Said Ernani. They returned to their fourth-floor suite at about 1.30 a.m., the squabbling clearly continuing to escalate. John Beattie, a luggage porter, walking past the Fahmy rooms was startled to see the door fly open, and the Prince launch himself into the corridor complaining, 'Look at my face; look what she has done.' The porter recollected seeeing nothing more alarming than a small red blemish on the Egyptian's face, but before he could gather himself for a response Madame Fahmy came out of the room talking loudly, excitedly and in French. With what must be considered great tact, Beattie persuaded the warring couple to return to their room and stop making a public nuisance of themselves. Turning his head as he resumed his way along the corridor, the porter caught a glimpse of Fahmy, still outside his room, crouched down whistling and snapping his fingers at a small dog. Before he had reached the end of the passage, three sharp, loud noises obliged him hastily to retrace his steps. The sound was from a gun; Madame Fahmy's gun; and when he arrived back at the entrance to the Fahmys' suite it was Marguerite Fahmy herself holding it. Her husband lay on the floor, bleeding from the head.

Ali Fahmy was to die shortly after admission to hospital; at about the same time Madame Fahmy was being charged with his murder.

By the opening of the trial at the Central Criminal Court on 10 September 1923, sufficient information was already publicly available to ensure that the case was a sensation even before the first witness took the stand.

That first witness (for the prosecution), under the expert cross- examination of popular defender Sir Edward Marshall Hall, began to reveal the grim story of repression, mental cruelty and physical abuse which had led poor Marguerite to her most desperate method of escape. The witness was Fahmy's secretary, Said Ernani, and he agreed that the couple were always in dispute because of his master's strong views on the position of women; that having wooed her with sugar-coated promises and elegant flattery, Fahmy forced her to become a Muslim before their wedding as it was a condition on which a large legacy from his mother depended. Despite Fahmy's promise that a clause would be entered into the marriage contract allowing Marguerite the right to initiate a divorce if things became intolerable, he had this agreement struck out of the document, so that only he could annul the marriage. As to the physical side of things, Said Ernani denied that Fahmy had sworn on the Koran to kill his wife, but reluctantly admitted there had been a series of incidents of physical assault – once occasioning Marguerite a dislocated jaw.

Warming to his defence, Marshall Hall read out to the court a letter written by Fahmy to Marguerite's younger sister: 'Just now I am engaged in training her. Yesterday, to begin with I did not come in to lunch nor to dinner and also I left her at the theatre. This will teach her, I hope, to respect my wishes. With women one must act with energy and be severe – no bad habits.

We still lead the same life of which you are aware – the opera, theatre, disputes, high words, perverseness.'

Sir Edward then touched on the bizarre (certainly in the eyes of 1923) sexual appetites of the Prince, and in particular the homosexual relationships which he enjoyed with (among others) the witness himself – a liaison which had become popular gossip in Egypt. Referring to Fahmy's sexual use of his wife, the defender elicited such information as to suggest that the very complaint for which she wished to attend a Paris clinic, and which had initiated the quarrel on the night of the murder, almost certainly arose from complications associated with persistent anal intercourse.

Marshall Hall's closing speech – as indeed his whole handling of the defence – has gone down as one of his most outstanding, relying as it did on emphasizing the fatal consequences of intermarriage between the sons and daughters of East and West. He told the jury:

> She made one great mistake, possibly the greatest mistake a woman of the West can make. She married an Oriental. I dare say the Egyptian civilization is, and may be, one of the oldest and most wonderful civilizations in the world. But if you strip off the external civilization of the Oriental, you get the real Oriental underneath. It is common knowledge that the Oriental's treatment of women does not fit in with the way the Western woman considers she should be treated by her husband . . . The curse of this case is the atmosphere which we cannot understand – the Eastern feeling of possession of the woman, the Turk in his harem, this man who was entitled to have four wives if he liked for chattels, which to us Western people with our ideas of women is almost unintelligible, something we cannot deal with.

He then came to the night of the murder, and in one of those moments of dramatic brilliance which illuminated his career, Marshall Hall took up the pistol which had shot Fahmy dead. He crouched in imitation of Ali Fahmy, stealthily advancing towards his wife, about to spring like a wild animal upon her; 'She turned the pistol and put it to his face, and to her horror the thing went off'; the jury found themselves momentarily looking down the barrel of that same gun. Then, as his words died in the silence, he dropped the weapon with a deafening clatter on to the courtroom floor.

'I do not ask you for a verdict,' he told the jury, 'I demand a verdict at your hands.'

Mr Justice Swift, at the time the youngest judge sitting on a High Court Bench, followed with his summing-up. It concluded: 'A person who honestly believes that his life is in danger is entitled to kill his assailant if that is the only way he honestly and reasonably believes he can protect himself. But he must be in real danger, and it must be the only way out of it.'

Quite clearly the jury found this the perfect description of Madame Fahmy's predicament; at any rate it took them a little over an hour to return a verdict of 'Not guilty'. Those two words were all but drowned by the outburst of cheers from the court, and taken up by the huge crowd outside, all awaiting just such a result.

For Marshall Hall, the undying gratitude of a beautiful woman, and the unstinting respect of his peers. Only the Egyptian Government was less than impressed, and cabled the Attorney-General, complaining bitterly about the derogatory remarks made about Orientals. For Marie-Marguerite Fahmy, the love and admiration of a nation; and now, the freedom to 'be forgotten by everybody except my own friends'.

FALLING, Christine   It is a strange fact that some people take up baby-sitting because they are fond of children, others because they want to kill them; in the files on serial murder, Christine Falling is not alone in this second category. In all, five infants died in her care, and three others nearly died. Then, for variety, there was the old gentleman who passed away the day after Christine entered his home as housekeeper.

The killings – 'smotheration' she later called it – started with two-year-old Cassidy Johnson in February 1980. Cassidy became unconscious while in Christine Falling's care and died three days later in Tallahassee Hospital, Florida. A year later, Christine was baby-sitting little Jeffrey Davis when he too died; the autopsy indicated death by myocarditis. Three days later Jeffrey's cousin Joseph Spring was left in Christine Falling's care while his parents attended Jeffrey's funeral. They soon had a funeral of their own to attend. Again death was attributed to myocarditis complicated by a virus infection. Far from suspicion being cast in Christine's direction, she enjoyed a great deal of sympathy – how absolutely dreadful to have all those babies dying in your care! Perhaps not wishing to seem ungrateful for this show of confidence, Christine suspended her baby-sitting operation and took up housekeeping. The death of her first employer so soon after she took up residence seems to have convinced Christine that she might as well go back to baby-care.

And the 'bad luck' returned with her. First the eight-month-old daughter of Christine's stepsister died in June 1981. Travis Coleman, ten weeks old, died in July 1982. Conveniently both these inexplicable deaths were at first attributed to 'infant death syndrome'. The Coleman autopsy, however, had a different tale to tell – the severe internal ruptures along with other indicators proved that Travis Coleman had been the victim of 'smotheration'.

Christine Falling entered a psychiatric hospital where she eventually confessed to the killing of Cassidy Johnson, her stepsister's baby and Travis Coleman; for reasons known only to herself, she denied responsibility for the other deaths. And who knows, perhaps they were, after all, innocent if tragic deaths from natural causes. At any rate, the three murders were quite enough to earn Christine Falling life imprisonment, with no prospect of parole for twenty-five years.

FAVRE-BULLE, Jeanne It was the kind of *crime passionnel* for which the French, with some justification, have become famous. In 1924 Madame Jeanne Favre-Bulle was forty-two years old, though wealth and careful handling had preserved much of the radiant beauty she enjoyed in youth. Cultured, and thoroughly spoiled, Madame was looking for something else – excitement. And excitement arrived in the person of Monsieur Léon Merle, a pleasant enough man ten years Jeanne's junior.

The couple had met on the Paris Metro, and after more than a year during which they coyly smiled at each other across the carriage, they began talking and meeting for coffee. In 1927 they became lovers. To complicate matters, Merle was at the time living conjugally with a cousin named Juillard. As their mutual passion deepened, Madame Favre-Bulle and Monsieur Merle vowed to leave their respective partners and live together.

Jeanne announced her intention to desert her husband in September 1929 and left her luxury Paris apartment, staying temporarily with her parents. Despite her husband's pleas for her to return, Jeanne turned up at Merle's house in Boulogne-sur-Seine on 15 October, where she found him still ensconced with 'Madame Merle'. It need hardly be said that Jeanne Favre-Bulle was not pleased. Having sacrificed a loyal and loving husband, not to mention wealth and luxury, she was now told by Merle that she must join in a ménage à trois – Jeanne, Merle and Madame Juillard. For a girl brought up in a convent, this new level of 'excitement' was more than Jeanne had bargained for, and after a couple of weeks during which the rather bohemian sleeping arrangements became more and more distasteful to her, Jeanne returned to Paris and bought a gun. Two days later she was back with Merle, and in an exchange of angry words, Léon explained his need for two mistresses. If she disagreed, Jeanne didn't show it. Not until they were in bed that night.

For hours Jeanne Favre-Bulle lay awake, turning matters over and over in her head. Then, quietly, she got up, crossed the room and took the pistol out of her bag; she aimed it towards the sleeping figure lying there in the dark, and pressed the trigger twice. As the bullets hit him, Léon Merle lurched and screamed . . . and that woke Madame Juillard, who was also startled out of her bed. She didn't have time to scream though, before a third bullet from Jeanne's gun cut her down. Jeanne Favre-Bulle then tried to shoot herself, but the mechanism of the gun failed and she simply fled from the house. Hours later, Jeanne was found huddled in a doorway, the gun still in her hand; ironically it was the doorway of a police station.

On 25 November 1930, the President and jury of the Seine Assize Court heard more or less the same narrative. There was little to deny as far as the basic facts of the story went; what the court had to decide was whether or not the killings had been premeditated murder or whether it was, as Jeanne's defence attorney claimed, a true crime of passion – the result of a temporary loss of sanity. In the end the jury chose a compassionate middle path – they found Madame Favre-Bulle guilty of murder, but with 'extenuating circumstances'. She was sentenced to twenty years' hard labour.

FERRARA, Florence   Dr Marion Klinefelter was one of the best known and most highly respected bone surgeons of his generation; he was also one of the kindest and most generous, earning his nickname 'the poor man's doctor' due to the charitable work he did and his 'forgetfulness' about sending bills to his less well-off patients. Everybody liked Dr Klinefelter. Except Florence Ferrara. But there, Florence knew something nobody else did. Didn't she?

On 28 November 1942 Florence Ferrara walked determinedly

into Dr Klinefelter's office at the Missouri Baptist Hospital in St Louis. As she approached his desk, Ferrara sneered: 'Well, Mr Mad Man, how are you?' Then she shot him through the head. As she left, the assassin called back over her shoulder: 'Now you're exposed, Mr Wilder.'

Florence Ferrara was picked up by the police where she had been since the shooting, sitting in her car in the hospital car park. The story she had to tell was this:

Dr Klinefelter is not the man I shot. The man I shot is named Meldrum Wilder and he is the one who killed Dr Klinefelter in 1904. He has been posing as Dr Klinefelter ever since and has been chloroforming and crippling people for years. In 1936 I had an infected finger and he treated me for that, but he didn't get me, and he's been trying to get me ever since. So last summer I went over to East St Louis and bought a pistol for my own protection, and this morning I decided to go and see him face to face. I said: 'Mr Wilder, here I am', and he grabbed the telephone. He wanted to get someone to use ether on me, so I shot him in self-defence. He had been having me followed, watched, and the men who were following me were trying to place a cloth filled with chloroform on my face so they could take me to the doctor and he could break my bones.

Of course it was all a delusion, and twenty-nine-year-old Florence Ferrara was never put on trial; she spent the rest of her days in a mental institution.

FULLAM, Augusta Fairfield   At the turn of the last century, when the continent of India was ruled by A.O. Hume's National Congress, and law and order was maintained by the British Army, Lieutenant Edward Fullam, a military accounts examiner, was posted to Agra, in the north of the country;

accompanying Fullam was his thirty-five-year-old wife Augusta. In the early part of 1911 Mrs Fullam met Dr Henry Lovell William Clark at a military ball. Clark was a forty-two-year-old Eurasian physician with the Indian Subordinate Medical Service, and was beginning to find his own marriage as tiresome as Augusta found hers. The pair were soon embarked upon an illicit love affair conducted mainly by correspondence; Dr Clark wrote letters by the dozen, letters which, in less than two years, would hang him. Matters were not helped in the Clark household when Henry, seconded temporarily to another district, began to write strange and sinister letters to his wife; one ended: 'I am fed up with your low, disgusting ways; I am sure you don't care a damn about what becomes of me. With fond love and kisses to self and the rest at home, I remain your affectionate husband, H.L. Clark.' Mixed sentiments indeed.

In the autumn of 1911 Mrs Fullam resolved to dispose of her husband permanently, and consulted Dr Clark on the most efficient poison for the job. Clark suggested that arsenic poisoning would be most appropriate, because its symptoms closely resemble those of heatstroke, a common complaint among Europeans exposed to the Indian climate. Lieutenant Fullam, though, was obviously made of sturdy stuff, and stubbornly refused to succumb to the heavily poisoned soup. And so, on 19 October 1911, Clark was obliged to inject him with gelsemine, an alkaloid poison which induces muscular weakness, general fatigue, slow pulse and eventual death by respiratory failure. Its effect, too, shares many outward similarities with death by heatstroke; and that is exactly what Dr Clark wrote on Fullam's death certificate.

There remained one obstacle to the future happiness of Dr Clark and Mrs Fullam – Mrs Clark. On the night of 17 November 1912, four Indians crept into her bedroom and hacked her to death with swords; for this service Clark is believed to have paid them a miserly 100 rupees. When he was questioned about his movements on the night of his wife's murder, Dr Clark made a very big mistake: he said he was dining with Mrs Fullam. Quite naturally officers were dispatched to confirm the story, and it was during this interview that Mrs Fullam seemed so anxious as to arouse the detectives' suspicions. Which in turn resulted in the police taking a closer look at the Fullam residence and finding the small tin trunk in which Augusta had faithfully preserved the almost four hundred letters between herself and Dr Clark. The correspondence alone would have been enough to convict the pair, so meticulously did it document the murder plans; but lest there were any room for doubt the body of Lieutenant Fullam was exhumed and subjected to autopsy; the analyst's report quantified abnormally high traces of both gelsemine and arsenic.

Dr Henry Clark was tried at Allahabad in March 1913; he was found guilty and, after making a full confession, was hanged on the twenty-sixth of the month. Mrs Augusta Fullam turned King's evidence and testified against her lover, thus earning herself a reprieve from the death sentence. She was sentenced to life imprisonment and shortly afterwards gave birth to Clark's child. On 29 May 1914 Mrs Fullam died in prison – ironically the cause of death was heatstroke.

G

GARVIE, Sheila   In many respects Maxwell Robert Garvie was a quite extraordinary man. In the 1960s he became interested in flying and quickly established a club near his home in Aberdeen, flying the light aircraft on regular trips around the cities of Europe. He also founded a local naturist club, and the area branch of the Scottish National Party. By occupation Garvie was a farmer, and since his marriage to Sheila Watson in 1955 they had worked the farm at Carnbeg, Kincardineshire. At the time of the dangerous liaison which would cost Max Garvie his life, the couple had three children and the marriage was beginning to falter.

Brian Tevendale was twenty-two years old, and an enthusiastic Scottish Nationalist; which is how he met the Garvies. Soon both Tevendale and his sister Trudy Birse were regular weekend guests at the farm. For good measure, Trudy was married to a policeman serving with the Aberdeen force. What actually went on during those days at the farm is anybody's guess, but one of the results was that Sheila Garvie and Brian Tevendale ran away together. Mrs Garvie later returned to her husband, but clearly the rot had set in and it was only a matter of time before the final showdown was reached. On 14 May 1968 Max Garvie attended a meeting of the SNP, left around ten o'clock, and disappeared. It was not until a week later that Garvie's sister reported him missing. Mrs Garvie was apparently quite unconcerned and assured the police that he would 'turn up'. He did not, and after Garvie's car was found abandoned at the flying club a full-scale search was mounted for the missing man.

For reasons not immediately clear, though it may have had something to do with a guilty conscience, Sheila Garvie confided to her mother a belief that Max was dead, and that somehow his death had been engineered by Brian Tevendale. After some soul-searching, Mrs Watson took her story to the police. As a result both Sheila and Brian Tevendale were arrested; they were later joined by Alan Peters, a close friend of Tevendale's. In August, the body of Maxwell Garvie was found in a tunnel at Lauriston Castle; he had been bludgeoned and shot through the head.

In November, Sheila Garvie, Brian Tevendale and Alan Peters stood their trial in Aberdeen, and the revelations disclosed by the evidence turned the case into an overnight sensation. It was alleged that during their weekends at the farm Tevendale, his sister and the two Garvies engaged in more than milking and mucking-out. Tevendale was to claim that he felt Max was more interested in him than in his wife, and Mrs Garvie accused her husband of making a nuisance of himself by demanding that she indulge him in 'unnatural' sexual acts (a coy reference to anal intercourse); however, it appears that Trudy was more than willing to comply. By their own account there were no permutations that the quartet had not experienced, and when that became passé, Trudy's policeman husband, Alfred, was invited along, provided with a woman, and all half-dozen of them enjoyed the romp. But there is a vast difference between group sex, however bizarre, and murder; and that, after all, was what the court wanted to hear about even if the press was happy to hear more tales of sexual indiscretion.

It was Brian Tevendale's claim that Sheila had called him to the farm after another row with Max over his 'unnatural' demands, and he had threatened to kill her if he couldn't have his way. As they struggled for the gun, Garvie was accidentally shot dead. According to Tevendale, Garvie was lying dead when he arrived at the farm, and he had simply helped hide the body.

However, Alan Peters and Sheila Garvie had a different account of the events of 14 May. According to their version, Peters and Tevendale had gone to the farm together, and when Mrs Garvie had gone to bed, Brian Tevendale murdered her husband. It was difficult to know what to believe; none of the defendants made a particularly good impression in the witness box, and the tangled web of sexual intrigue had served only to alienate those members of the jury who, like many of their countrymen, still held dear the puritanical beliefs of John Knox. In the end, and without much surprise, Sheila Garvie and Brian Tevendale were convicted of Max Garvie's murder. But to everyone's disbelief, the case against Alan Peters was found 'Not Proven', that unique Scottish verdict – which spoke volumes for the jury's bewilderment at the evidence they had heard.

GBUREK, Tillie *see* **KLIMEK, Tillie**

GIBBS, Janie Lou   Everybody liked Janie Gibbs. She ran the day-care centre for children of working mothers in the small Georgia community of Cordele, and was well known for her patience with children. Whenever a member of her family died, Mrs Gibbs received nothing but kindness and sympathy. Oh, and insurance money; a portion of which she assiduously donated to the local church. What nobody seemed to notice was that in Mrs Gibbs' family deaths seemed to occur rather more frequently than in other families.

The first death had been that of thirteen-year-old Marvin, Janie's son; he died on 29 August 1966 from what was diagnosed as 'kidney disease'. Melvin, the sixteen-year-old, took seriously ill in January 1967, and died of 'hepatitis'.

The Gibbses' eldest son, Roger, was already married, though he and his wife still lived in his family's home. In August 1967, Janie became a grandmother. Baby Ronnie Edward fell sick shortly after birth, and despite the best of care did not live beyond six weeks. Then, two weeks after the infant's death, his father was taken ill with stomach cramps and nausea; two days later he too died. The death was inexplicable enough to warrant a post-mortem examination, and the doctor was so unhappy with the results, displaying as they did severe damage of the liver and kidneys, that he ordered tissue samples to be dispatched to the Georgia State Crime Laboratory for analysis.

After two months of exhaustive tests, the lab reported evidence of unusually high quantities of arsenic. With the indication of foul-play in Roger Gibbs' death, an exhumation order was obtained to subject the other deceased members of the Gibbs family to autopsy.

Janie Lou Gibbs was taken into custody and put under the care of a psychiatrist to whom she confessed the poisonings. All the evidence indicated that Mrs Gibbs was suffering from schizophrenia, and although she was capable of distinguishing right from wrong, believed the world to be a very bad place in which her loved ones should not be forced to live. Declared unfit to plead, Janie Gibbs avoided the immediate ordeal of trial and was instead committed to the state mental institution. However, in 1976, Janie was re-assessed and considered sane enough to stand trial; after conviction she was sentenced to five consecutive life terms.

GODFRIDA, Sister Wetteren is a small Belgian town not a dozen miles from the old city of Ghent, in East Flanders. It is unremarkable, save perhaps for its show of piety, for Wetteren can boast no fewer than seven Roman Catholic churches and the Convent of the Apostolic Order of Holy Joseph, called the

Josephites. Attached to the convent is an old people's home administered by the nursing nuns. At the time events around Wetteren are of interest to us – the early part of 1977 – the Mother Superior of the convent was a rather severe woman in her mid-forties named Sister Godfrida. This was her adopted religious name of course; Godfrida, born into a fiercely Catholic family from Overmere, had been christened Cecile Blombeck, and packed off to join the Josephites at the age of fifteen.

Cecile, at first a reluctant penitent, soon took to life around the cloisters and found herself, in no time at all it seemed, in the exalted position of Mother Superior. And she may well have continued to exert her benign, if strict, influence over her sisters and the elderly in her care, had it not been for a brain tumour. Sister Godfrida was taken into hospital, where she lost the tumour but acquired an addiction to morphine. To say that the good sister underwent a change of personality as the result of her drug dependence would be to understate matters. She became a veritable monster – a demon in nun's habit. For a start, Godfrida began to display a prodigious sexual appetite, with partners of both genders. To their credit, most of the convent sisters strenuously resisted Godfrida's demands to fondle and kiss her body, and in turn be fondled and kissed. A few succumbed reluctantly, and one at least responded enthusiastically and passionately. Sisters Godfrida and Mathieu became quite an item around the cloisters of the Holy Joseph, with their open displays of lust; and they were a well known couple in the bars, clubs and restaurants of Ghent and Brussels. But such little luxuries have to be paid for, not least Sister Godfrida's escalating dependence on drugs. One simple source of funds, and one that Godfrida found pleasurable, was selling her sexual favours to such of her elderly male charges as were still interested in such things. Later there would be revelations of worse activities than this; much worse.

One might have thought that a convent was the last place to

get away with such overt behaviour – the company of nuns does not encourage carnal desires and heroin abuse. In fact, the reverse proved true here. When one or two of the more courageous sisters mentioned Godfrida's activities to the priest responsible for hearing their confessions he immediately ordered the sisters to undertake a vow of silence on the matter. They said nothing; to have done so would be a sin. But the exposure of Sister Godfrida's less spiritual activities did have one benefit – the Mother Superior was removed from the convent to a place where, it was hoped, she would be cured of her addiction. And so life settled down once more around the cloisters, and the little sisters of Holy Joseph got back to their humdrum routine. That was until they received a postcard at Christmas 1977. It read: 'I shall be with you soon.' It was from Sister Godfrida. Still, they thought, after her rehabilitation Godfrida was probably back to normal, back to her old self, before the operation. But she was not; she was back to her old self *after* the operation. Back to . . . The prospect was too awful to contemplate, even by nuns under a strict vow of silence.

And that is why, on the grey Monday morning of 16 January 1978, Sister Godlive, Sister Franziska and Sister Pieta sat in an office at the police station talking to a dumb-struck Inspector Dyke van Horn. You see, it wasn't only the drugs, not just the sex and the lavish excursions to Ghent; there were other offences, not only against God's law, but against those of man. In short, Sister Godfrida had been killing elderly patients in order to get her hands on their savings and possessions.

The Inspector realized that he faced a difficult job, one that would require not only all his tact, but all the luck he could lay his hands on. He could hardly treat this accusation in the same way he would cover a routine case of murder – to begin with, the accusations were being made against one of the senior officers of the local Roman Catholic Church; secondly, the Church had already effectively put a blanket of silence over Sister Godfrida's misdemeanours – there was no reason why it should not do so again. In the end it was sheer good luck that carried Inspector van Horn through to a solution. It just happened that Sister Godfrida was either mad enough or proud enough to take full credit for her murders. She recalled, in particular, the death of Maria van der Gunst: 'I sent her to Heaven because she was too noisy; she disturbed my sleep.' Maria also had some jewellery which Godfrida had her eyes on. There were two other cases which she remembered with clarity – eighty-two-year-old Pieter Diggmann, and seventy-eight-year-old Leonie Maihofer. All three victims had been dispatched to Paradise with an overdose of insulin. Then there were the cases which Sister Godfrida couldn't remember at all well, though research in the medical records of patients who had died since Godfrida's reign of terror began indicated that she could have been responsible for as many as thirty murders.

The Mother Superior of Wetteren's Order of Holy Joseph was considered too mad to stand trial, and was instead confined indefinitely to a mental institution, where she remains to this day.

GONZALES, Delfina and Maria de Jesus   By the time the two Mexican sisters were brought to justice in 1964 they had been responsible for the deaths of a staggering eighty-plus young girls in ten years. The Gonzales sisters ran a brothel at their Rancho El Angel, to which the girls, many of them in early teenage, were abducted, forced into drug dependency and made to endure unspeakable humiliation and deprivation. Those who became ill, lost their looks, or became troublesome were killed.

It had been going on for heaven knows how long; it would have gone on for heaven knows how much longer if police had not finally caught up with the woman with a mole on her cheek. A familiar figure in the twilight world of prostitution, drugs and much else that is evil, Josefina Guttierez had been suspected for years of being behind the disappearance of very many young women from around Mexico's west-coast city of Guadalajara. In custody, Josefina proved willing enough to talk, though what persuaded her we can only guess – perhaps it was simply an uneasy conscience. The girls, it transpired – dozens of them – were destined for the Rancho El Angel, somewhere near the town of San Francisco del Rincón.

When police officers arrived at the ranch they found the Gonzales sisters had fled, leaving the pathetic dormitory of young girls, broken down by ill-use and narcotics, in the care of a handful of thugs. When investigators put a team in to dig over the ground around the ranch, they found the remains of more than eighty young women, plus the foetuses that had been forcibly aborted from those unlucky enough to fall pregnant.

But it was not only the enslaved and unwilling prostitutes who met a grim end; migratory workers returning from America with fat wage packets also fell victim to the insatiable greed of Delfina and Maria Gonzales when they stopped off at the ranch for a little 'recreation'.

The Gonzales sisters were tried and sentenced to forty years' imprisonment; some might say it was rather lenient – a few months each for all those miserable lives and horrible deaths.

GONZALES, Maria de Jesus *see* **GONZALES, Delfina and Maria de Jesus**

GOOLD, Maria Vere   The two passengers arrived with their luggage at Marseilles off the Monte Carlo Express on the morning of 5 August 1907. Their first stop, having secured the services of a porter, was the baggage office where they deposited their large trunk in the care of a clerk named Pons. It had been labelled for dispatch to London's Charing Cross station, and Pons was left to complete the paperwork while the trunk's owners took up their reservations at the Hotel du Louvre de Paix, carrying with them a heavy bag which had not left the woman's maternal grasp since they disembarked from the train.

As young Monsieur Pons attended to his duties he became uncomfortably aware of a strange, not entirely pleasant odour circulating about the office, the origin of which turned out to be the London-bound cabin trunk. As he attempted to move it, the clerk's hand met a sticky patch of reddish-brown liquid which appeared to have seeped from the luggage. Perhaps he was just being efficient, or perhaps he was simply inquisitive, but the youth made straight for the Hotel du Louvre to confront his customers with the twin problems of the smell and what looked like blood emanating from their property. 'It must be the poultry,' the woman snorted. 'They might bleed a little.' If she were him, the lady went on, she would get the trunk off to London as quickly as possible.

Instead, Pons went to the railway police where an inspector listened to his story and decided that on no account should the owners of the trunk leave Marseilles until it had been opened and checked. For some extraordinary reason known only to himself, the inspector sent the youth Pons back to the hotel to persuade the mysterious couple to return to the railway station. It may seem a funny way to go about things but it worked! And so the unlikely trio took a cab back to the baggage office. En route the woman tried to buy the clerk off with several thousand francs, but Pons was too deeply involved now, even if he felt tempted.

Before long the cause of the smell coming from the cabin trunk was explained; it arose from the dismembered human torso and arms which were putrefying inside it. As for the kit-bag which had seemed so precious to its owners, that contained the legs and head belonging to the same body. It was later identified as that of a lady named Emma Erika Levin.

More important, who exactly were the apparently aristocratic couple who were trying to send one half of a corpse across the channel to England, and carried the other half around with them? The woman introduced herself to the police as Lady Vere Goold, and her companion as Sir Vere Goold – in reality neither of them had any right whatever to such titles. Maria Girodin had been born in Switzerland in 1877, and had already been widowed twice in suspicious circumstances when she met an Irishman named Vere Goold in London. For a year or so after their marriage the Goolds sponged off relatives, and when they had worn out their welcome, transferred their activities to Monte Carlo where they drank and gambled away such funds as remained. Things were beginning to look decidedly bleak on the financial front, when 'Lady' Vere Goold cultivated the acquaintance of Madame Levin, a wealthy Swedish widow. How was Maria to know it would be so difficult to prise Madame's money from her? How was she to know that even when she did manage to scrounge fifty pounds the wretched woman would want it back?

On 4 August 1907, a Sunday, her Ladyship invited Emma Levin out to the Villa Menesimy where she and 'Sir' Vere Goold rented rooms. Lured on the pretext of having her loan repaid Madame Levin was attempting to engage in conversation with an as usual inebriated host, when her hostess snuck up behind and stunned the poor woman with a blow from a fire-poker, finishing the bloody deed with a knife. After helping themselves to Madame's jewellery, the couple dismembered her body in the bath, packed the parts into the trunk and the hold-all, and fled to Marseilles . . . which is where they had the misfortune to encounter baggage clerk Pons.

'Sir' and 'Lady' Vere Goold were put on trial in Marseilles, and after scenes of histrionics that earned her the popular soubriquet *La Grande Comédienne,* Maria was sentenced to death for being the dominant force in the killing. The sentence was later commuted, and both she and her husband were condemned to life imprisonment on the French penal colony of Cayenne in French Guyana. In July 1908 Maria contracted typhoid fever and died; Goold committed suicide the following year.

GOTTFRIED, Gesina Margaretha As a young woman Gesina was an attractive blue-eyed blonde, with no shortage of eligible suitors; from among them she happened to choose a man named Mittenberg, good looking enough but inclined to be prodigal. Despite warnings that the man was a drunkard, Gesina was determined to marry him, and in 1815 she did. From the beginning the marriage was a disaster. Mittenberg drank increasingly large volumes of alcohol, and almost certainly as a result of this, was unable to perform his marital functions. At first Gesina simply took a lover, in the person of a young man named Gottfried, but finally she entertained a notion to dispose of her unwanted spouse permanently. Within the week the arsenic was in Mittenberg's beer, and Mittenberg was in his grave. His death was assumed to be the result of drinking – which in a way it was!

Although Gesina was now free to marry Gottfried, he declined to take on the responsibility of the two children fathered by Mittenberg. The solution was simple, and before long the mites were lying alongside their father. When Gesina's parents got to hear of the impending marriage they – with good reason or not – took against Gottfried and tried all they could to sabotage their daughter's plan. But by now Gesina had a ready answer to such minor irritations as these; she simply invited her parents to lunch at her home to discuss the matter, and poisoned them. Their deaths were certified as 'inflammation of the bowels'.

Still Gottfried would not say 'I do', and in a fit of pique Gesina decided that he should not ouly be her husband but also her next victim. Day by day she spiked Gottfried's food until he was confined to bed with only Gesina to nurse him. Feeling the chilly hand of death on his shoulder, Gottfried summoned a priest and a solicitor – the cleric to perform a sick-bed wedding, the lawyer to draw up the will that would transfer his every possession to Gesina. Within hours, Gottfried was dead and Gesina was rich.

The widow Gottfried's soldier brother was her next victim, for no other reason than that his habits 'disgusted' her. A doctor attributed his death to venereal disease. A love-lorn suitor followed him into the grave as soon as he had settled his worldly goods on Gesina. Then she travelled to Hamburg to visit one of her creditors – and settled her debt with arsenic.

In 1825 Gesina Gottfried took a large house in the Pelzerstrasse in Bremen, and when she could no longer afford to keep up the payments, the bank foreclosed on her, and Gesina was obliged to sell the property to a wheelwright named Rumf. A generous man by nature, Rumf could not see Frau Gottfried on the streets, and asked her to stay on as his house-keeper. During the early months of this arrangement Mrs Rumf gave birth to a son, and only days later died; it was certified as 'complications of childbirth'. Then the Rumf children began to die one by one of mysterious illnesses, and by early 1828 nobody was left in the house except Gesina, a few servants and Rumf. But although Rumf was himself chronically sick, he had not lost his powers of observation, was not entirely blind to the strange white powder that seemed to coat every meal his house-keeper prepared. In March 1828, he took a sample of meat to the police, tests were made, and the powder quickly found to be white arsenic. A magistrate arrested Gesina Gottfried and charged her with the murder of Frau Rumf.

Gesina offered no defence at her trial, during the course of which she proudly admitted to killing the Rumfs and *at least* thirty other people. The murders, she said, had given her great satisfaction, an ecstasy not unlike a sexual orgasm. Found guilty and condemned, Gesina was led up the steps to the scaffold where the executioner waited, masked and leaning on his heavy axe . . .

GRAHAM, Barbara   Barbara Elaine Wood was born in Oakland, California, in 1923. When she was just two years old, her teenage mother was confined in a reformatory, leaving neighbours to bring Barbara up as best they could. Whether Barbara might have enjoyed a brighter future if she had stayed with the neighbours is debatable; we will never know because after a few years her mother was released and took the child back into the squalid and unstable home life into which she had been born. One thing is certain, Barbara couldn't have had a much worse life, as she suffered constant beatings at her mother's hands, eventually becoming so brutalized that she was confined to the self-same reformatory.

When she was released in 1939, Barbara made a half-hearted attempt to embark on some sort of normal life. In fact, to be fair, she made quite a good start, enrolling at secretarial college, marrying and giving birth to a son. The problem was that Barbara wasn't a sticker, and by 1941 she was divorced and had exchanged college for prostitution. In 1945 she married again and almost as quickly divorced. But if her domestic life was in tatters, then Barbara's professional life was taking off. She began work as a call-girl for San Francisco's most notorious madam, Sally Stanford. As a result Barbara met, and in 1952 married, Henry Graham. Henry was a crook in a small way of business, and soon Barbara was not only hooked on the drugs he peddled, but becoming actively involved in robbery. Barbara Graham was about to get into a higher league altogether.

On 9 March 1953 Barbara and three other petty crooks broke into the house of Mrs Monohan, an elderly and reputedly wealthy widow of Burbank, California. If they thought they were going to get rich quick, our hapless hoodlums were mistaken; in fact, there was nothing much of value at all, which made Barbara so cross she battered Mrs Monohan to death with the butt of a pistol.

There is little honour among thieves, especially petty crooks who find themselves involved in murder. Within days John L. True was in police custody and singing like a canary. Barbara was taken in for questioning, and after pleading her innocence was put in a police cell. Here she was approached by a 'gangster' who offered her an alibi for the sum of $25,000. Barbara jumped at the offer of course; how was she to know her benefactor was an undercover police officer?

When Barbara Graham appeared in court, this damaging evidence plus the eye-witness testimony of John L. True, who had turned state's evidence, was too much for a jury to ignore. On 3 June 1955, Barbara Graham was introduced to San Quentin's gas chamber.

GRAHAM, Gwendolyn Gail, and **WOOD, Catherine** It was one of the most extraordinary motives ever revealed by a serial killer, or in this case killers; so they said, it had all been part of an elaborate game by which the first letter of succeeding victims' names would spell the word MURDER. What was worse, Gwendolyn Graham and her lesbian lover Catherine Wood had the raw material of this crazy scheme at their disposal; they were both on the care staff of the Alpine Manor Nursing Home in Walker, Michigan. It happened that the spelling game proved too complicated, so Wood and Graham settled for just killing the old ladies, and stealing some trinket or other as a souvenir. The *modus operandi* had been for Wood to act as look-out, while Gwendolyn Graham suffocated the victims by pressing cloths over their nose and mouth. How long the killings would have continued, no one could tell; but they ended when Gwendolyn Graham found herself a new lover and Catherine Wood became passionately vindictive. She simply confided everything to her ex-husband, who wasted no time getting the story to the ears of the police.

By the time the investigators caught up with her, Catherine Wood had fled to her native Texas, whence she was extradited after agreeing to testify against her former partner in exchange for a reduced charge of second-degree murder for herself. For her own part, Wood confessed her involvement in six murders, the victims' ages ranging from sixty to ninety-eight; she claimed she was relieved to have everything out in the open because she feared Graham was about to start murdering babies in the hospital which now employed her; whether this was true or not, the revelation certainly impressed the court. According to Wood's evidence, her former lover had expressed a feeling of 'emotional release' when they killed, and afterwards when they washed the bodies down. Even talking about killing was sufficient to fill both of them with an uncontrollable desire for sex.

Gwendolyn Graham and Catherine Wood were jointly charged with the murders, though because she turned state's evidence Wood got away with the comparatively light sentence of twenty-to-forty years. Gwendolyn Graham, charged in December 1988, denied the killings, but was nevertheless convicted on six counts of first-degree murder and sentenced to six life sentences without possibility of parole.

GRILLS, Caroline   In 1947, Caroline Grills' mother-in-law, Christina Mickelson, died suddenly at the advanced age of eighty-seven; it was probably a relief to Caroline because she had never really seen eye to eye with Mrs Mickelson since she married her son in 1908, and besides, she got possession of the old lady's cottage.

Shortly afterwards a family friend died, Mrs Angeline Thomas – another venerable octogenarian. Sixty-year-old sailor John Lundberg, Caroline's brother-in-law, was the next in her circle of family and friends to fall ill; first his hair fell out, and in October 1948 he died. In early 1953 Mary Ann Mickelson, a sister-in-law, was taken ill with similar symptoms, and became the next to die. The late John Lundberg's widow, Eveline, son-in-law John Downey and daughter Chrissie Downey, began to lose their hair and feel a heavy deadness in their limbs.

They were nursed in their sickness by Caroline Grills, who seemed never happier than when soothing her patients with cups of tea. As the two women slowly weakened, John Downey began to put two and two together and arrived at the answer 'poison'. And when one of the cups of tea was analysed in the police laboratory it was found to contain the metallic poison thallium – just in time to save the Downeys' lives.

Following a short investigation, Mrs Grills was arrested and charged with murder, though in advance of her trial, the prosecutor elected to proceed only on the charge of the *attempted murder* of Mrs Eveline Lundberg – who had now gone blind as the result of her experience with thallium. Although from an observer's point of view there was little in the way of motive for the murders, the prosecution contended that the pivotal reason for murder could have been gain, but was more likely Caroline Grills' clear desire to exercise the power of life and death over her victims; in other words, she enjoyed killing people. She was found guilty of the charge against her and sentenced to life imprisonment.

In jail, Mrs Grills became affectionately known as 'Aunt Thally' by her fellow inmates.

GROESBEEK, Maria   It is said that Friday the thirteenth is a most unlucky day; for Maria Groesbeek it was the unluckiest day of her life. On Friday 13 November 1970, she was hanged.

Marginally less unlucky, but bad enough, was 28 March1969, also a Friday; that was the day Christiaan Buys died; and at the time Maria was Mrs Buys. The couple had married in 1953 and the subsequent decade had been sheer hell, for Maria at least; according to her account of things she was subjected to continual deprivation and assault. Then, in 1969, she became attached to twenty-year-old Gerhard Groesbeek, a dozen years her junior and at the time the Buys' lodger. About a month afterwards Christiaan Buys, a railway worker from Harrismith in the Orange Free State, died at the Voortrekker Hospital after several weeks' illness. Although Buys had been treated for pneumonia, a subsequent autopsy revealed a high deposit of arsenic in his organs. The unseemly haste with which

Maria married Gerhard Groesbeek was bound to spark off rumour, and shortly after the wedding the Groesbeeks were taken into custody and questioned by the police. Maria confessed that she had fed her late husband arsenic-based ant poison, but only after he had adamantly refused to divorce her: 'I just wanted to avenge myself on Chris,' she told detectives. 'I wanted to make him thoroughly sick, so he would give me permission to divorce him.'

Maria went on to tell the sorry story of a broken marriage and a cruel husband. The fact was, as any number of witnesses would testily, Christiaan Buys had been a singularly mild and sensitive man, generous to a fault, and kindness itself to his wife and children. Besides, more than one person had heard Maria grumbling that she was bored with her husband and that if he would not divorce her then she would poison him. All this came out at Maria Groesbeek's trial at the Bloemfontein Criminal Sessions, and the judge and two assessors who heard her case found Maria guilty of premeditated murder. As for young Gerhard Groesbeek, he was tried separately, and although there was some evidence that he was aware of Maria's murderous intentions it was not conclusive enough to convict him beyond reasonable doubt, and he was acquitted. Meanwhile, Maria Groesbeek, sustained by prayer and self-pity, languished in Pretoria jail awaiting her appointment with the hangman.

GUNNESS, Belle   Bella Poulsdatter was born in Norway, in 1859, showing no early signs that she would become one of America's busiest murderers. She arrived in the New World in 1883, married Max Sorensen, and took occupation of a homestead in Austin, Illinois. In 1900 Max Sorensen died.

Helped by the $100 she realized selling up the ranch, Belle moved to Chicago to invest in a lodging-house. Within weeks a fire had destroyed her prospects as a hotelier, leaving Belle with no more than a huge insurance claim for comfort. This capital was put into a bakery business, and it too fell victim to the mysterious fire-bug; which was one blaze too many for the suspicious minds of the insurance investigators, and Belle was obliged to seek some less risky means of turning a dishonest dollar.

Marriage proved a satisfactory, if temporary, tactic, and Belle took herself to Laporte, Indiana, where she became Mrs Belle Gunness. Tragically, Peter Gunness did not long survive his wedding, a hatchet slipping from a high shelf and dealing him a mortal blow on the head. Fortunately, he had taken out a large enough insurance to allow his widow few regrets.

Belle now realized that her future relied upon having a man about the house – or rather his money:

Rich, good-looking widow, young, owner of a large farm, wishes to get in touch with a gentleman of wealth with cultured tastes. Object, matrimony.

A specification not entrusted to print was that prospective husbands be without kith or kin. Surprisingly, there seemed no shortage of suitably unattached individuals, and Belle turned a tidy profit over the succeeding years. Of the many that arrived bearing money, none ever left, none was ever asked after. It was bad luck then, when Belle chose a suitor named Andrew Holdgren, who not only had an undisclosed brother, but one to whom he had confided his marital aspirations. After several months, Holdgren's brother was unimpressed to learn that Andrew had disappeared from Mrs Gunness's life, and announced his imminent arrival.

Mr Holdgren was too late. On 28 April 1908, Belle's old adversary struck again. Police arriving at the conflagration found four charred corpses – one without a head was later identified as Mrs Gunness, the others as those of her children.

On 23 May Roy Lamphere, employed by Belle to help out on the farm as well as to perform other more 'personal' duties, was indicted on four counts of murder and one of arson. He was convicted only of arson.

Meanwhile, the authorities were investigating the farm with picks and shovels. They solved the enigma of Andrew Holdgren – his dismembered body, wrapped in oil-cloth, was one of the first to be dug up. There were thirteen others, maybe more if they had looked.

Years later, Roy Lamphere talked about that fatal night in 1908. He confided that he not only knew about the murders at Laporte, but had helped dispose of the victims. A more startling revelation was that the corpse identified as Belle Gunness was not his former employer and lover, but a female vagrant who had been lured to the farm.

If this were true, where was Belle?

H

HAHN, Anna Marie   Anna Marie Hahn emigrated from her native Germany along with husband Philip and young son Oscar in 1929. They arrived in Cincinnati and settled into the city's well established German quarter. Anna was a pleasant and obliging young woman, and soon earned the trust and affection of the area's elderly gentlemen, acting as a sort of unofficial (and unqualified) 'nurse'. Anna was later to describe herself as an 'angel of mercy'.

The wealthier these old gentlemen were, the more accommodating Anna was. And if their attentions sometimes passed beyond the merely paternal, then who was Anna to deny these harmless grandfathers their last fling? 'Last' being the crucial word. And if they felt that the best way to reward these 'services' was by a small gift or bequest, then who was Anna to deny them the pleasures of giving? In 1933, for example, Ernst Kohler left Anna his large house.

On 1 June 1937, Jacob Wagner was taken on as a patient only to pass away on the following day; later that same week another patient, seventy-year-old Georg Opendorffer also died suddenly.

However, there were those uncharitable souls among Anna Hahn's neighbours who thoroughly resented her ostentatious lifestyle, and were only too ready to back-bite and gossip; some went as far as to gossip to the police – about how the previously robust Herr Wagner and Herr Opendorfer died after suffering acute stomach pains and vomiting. Eventually exhumation orders on a number of 'nurse' Hahn's deceased patients were requested, and in each instance the autopsy revealed that death had been accelerated by various poisons, most often a mixture of croton oil (a strong purgative) and arsenic. Anna's home was found to be equally well stocked with poisons, which is how the 'angel of mercy' found herself in custody.

Anna Hahn's defence, which was that she was merely embezzling the old gentlemen, suffered a severe set-back when Philip Hahn testified that his wife had on several occasions tried to persuade him to insure his own life for large sums. When he refused, he unaccountably began to suffer stomach cramps and vomiting. Anna's future was looking bleak indeed.

She was finally convicted of murder and sentenced to death. She perished in the electric chair on 7 December 1938. For all it might have cheered her last hours, Anna Hahn had the doubtful privilege of being the first woman in the state of Ohio to be judicially electrocuted.

HARPER, Katie   It was a balmy night in June 1959, in the Winnipeg suburb of Old St James, when Leading Aircraftsman John Down, aged twenty-four, fell from a dormer window to his death on the concrete path below. Unlucky, his widow Katie remarked, that he should have stepped out for a cigarette. Either that or he was sleepwalking. And he had taken quite a large dose of sodium amytal, a sleeping pill. At the funeral in Newfoundland Katie, a nurse, handed out some capsules to calm grieving relations. Capsules of sodium amytal.

Katie got married again in 1960, to a hospital orderly called Sandy Harper. The couple had two children, to add to the two from Katie's first marriage, before separating in 1976. It was not long after this that the police received a tip-off that John Down had been murdered by Sandy Harper.

Katie's story was that on the fatal evening Harper had come
to the house and made sexual advances. When she protested
that her husband was asleep upstairs, Harper had gone up to the
bedroom and suffocated John Down with a pillow. The two of
them had gone downstairs, finished what Harper had come to
do, and only then launched Down's body out of the window.
And what did Harper have to say? Nothing. He refused to talk,
to co-operate in any way, and with nothing to pin on him the
police were obliged to put Katie Harper in the dock alone.

Inexplicably, no witnesses were called for the defence. In the
absence of any alternative, the jury swallowed the prosecution's theory that Katie Harper, unaided, had drugged her
husband, smothered him, and shoved him headlong out of the
window. At the age of forty-four she was sentenced to life
imprisonment, with no parole for a minimum of twenty-five
years.

A reporter who had covered the trial, Peter Carlyle-Gordge,
began his own investigation, which told a rather different story.
Sandy Harper was cruel and abusive, an alcoholic with a police
record for violence. He'd married Katie to keep her quiet, had
been heard threatening her if she said anything about Down's
death, had subjected her and her children to sixteen years of
hell, sexually molesting daughter Kathy over a period of years.
Eventually, in 1981, Carlyle-Gordge and his wife Cathy had
enough evidence to file an affidavit in the Manitoba Court of
Appeal. More than that, they put up their home as surety so that
Katie could be released on bail.

In early 1982 Katie and Sandy Harper appeared in the dock
together, both charged with murder. It seemed to be going well
for Katie until the prosecution called, out of thin air it seemed,
a witness by the name of Sister Norma Johnson, who 'had the
impression' while visiting Katie in prison that she had
confessed to the murder and said she would do it again.

Katie was found guilty of first-degree murder and Sandy of
second-degree murder. At appeal both convictions were

reduced to manslaughter. A sentence of two years? Three, at the most? The sentences were returned: twenty years each. Peter Carlyle-Gordge shredded the book he was compiling about the Harper case, whose happy ending would never be written now; while Katie Harper was returned to Portage-la-Prairie correctional centre.

HARTSON, Dorothy Dorothy Hartson appeared to be a mere bit-part player in this drama of jealousy and betrayal and it was only her own uneasy conscience that finally identified her as a passionate killer.

On 13 August 1978, thirty-six-year-old farmer Wilford Cahill was found dead in bed by his wife Laura. Sudden, unexplained deaths in South Africa, as elsewhere, have to be notified to the coroner and it is customary to perform a post-mortem examination to determine the cause of death. In Cahill's case it was a massive dose of strychnine. When police began the investigation triggered by the farmer's murder, Cape Town detectives unearthed a complex tangle of relationships which were a certain recipe for disaster; indeed, it would have been surprising if the situation had not erupted in violence. In their search of Laura Cahill's bedroom, police discovered a bundle of passionate letters that left no doubt that Mrs Cahill had been engaged in an affair with the farm's manager, Denis Hartson. Hartson had been taken on at the farm in 1974 and shortly afterwards had married Dorothy Ekquist; the affair with Laura Cahill began a year before the murder. Also resident at the farm were two servants, Buster Diggens, a mechanic, and Melanie N'Gomo, the maid.

On the face of it, the most likely suspects were Laura Cahill and Denis Hartson, partly because of their love affair and partly because Laura stood to inherit the whole of the Cahill estate. A minor red herring was cast into the pool of iniquity when Melanie the maid accused Buster Diggens of the murder, but once his alibi had been established, Mrs Cahill and Mr Hartson were taken into custody and questioned at length. They strenuously denied any part in Wilford Cahill's death.

However, the police were confident enough of their case to proceed with charges of murder and conspiracy, and who knows but that two perfectly innocent people might have been tried and convicted. But on 1 September 1978, just as the prosecutor's office was drawing up the committal papers, the police had a strange visit from Hartson's wife Dorothy. She explained to detectives that she was well aware of the affair between her husband and his employer's wife, and not surprisingly she resented it very deeply. By way of revenge, and in an attempt to remove temptation from Denis's way, Dorothy had poisoned Cahill in the anticipation that Laura would be executed for his murder. It did not seem to have occurred to her either that she was condemning an entirely innocent man to an agonizing death, or that her beloved Denis would be at the top of the suspect list.

Early the following year it was Dorothy Hartson who stood trial at the Cape Province assize. She was found guilty on her own confession, but the spirit of compassion was clearly still alive to the woman wrong'd, and Dorothy was sentenced to a reasonably lenient twenty years.

HAYES, Catherine   When Catherine Hall left Birmingham and entered the employ of Farmer Hayes in Worcestershire there was hope that she had left her shady and dissolute past behind her. So agreeable and charming did she present herself that young John Hayes, the son of the house, lost no time in leading her to the altar – much to his father's consternation and, had he only known it then, to his own greatest detriment.

For six years until 1726 Catherine managed to maintain the appearance of domestic diligence, though what wild urgings smouldered inside her we can only now guess; her growing restlessness was only assuaged when she and Hayes migrated to the excitement of the country's teeming capital. There they took up residence in Tyburn Street (now Oxford Street), where Catherine started up a boarding house, among whose inhabitants were Thomas Billings and Thomas Wood. Billingsist was who satisfied Mrs Hayes' carnal needs in her husband's absences from town on business. Soon Wood's gratitude to John Hayes – whose kindness had rescued him from destitution – was subordinated to Catherine's greed and debauchery, and he was enlisted in a terrible and treacherous plot by the illicit lovers to assassinate the unfortunate Hayes.

The following contemporary texts take up this story in which four lives are sacrificed to one woman's lust:

When Hayes was asleep, his wife apprised her associates that this was the opportune time to strike, and accordingly Billings entered the bed-chamber with a hatchet, with which he struck Hayes so violently that he fractured his skull. At the time, the unfortunate Hayes' legs were hanging over the edge of the bed, and so great was his anguish that his feet repeatedly stamped on the floor, which aroused Wood from his drunken reverie and he too joined in bludgeoning Hayes. The murderers now consulted on the best manner of disposing of the body so as most effectively to prevent discovery. Mrs Hayes proposed cutting off the head, because if the body were found intact it would likely be identified. This plan agreed to, the assassins returned to the room with a candle and a pail. Sliding the body partly off the bed, Billings supported the head while Wood cut it off with his pocket knife; Catherine held the pail underneath to catch the head and to prevent the blood marking the floor. The deed being done, they emptied the blood out of the pail into a sink by the window. The woman now suggested boiling the head until the flesh should part from the bones, but it was thought that this would consume too much time, and it was decided to cast the grisly relic into the Thames where the tide would hopefully carry it off; the head was thus put into the pail, and Billings took it under his greatcoat, accompanied by Wood, to the river.

The head being thus disposed of, the murderers returned home. The next object of their endeavour was the disposal of the body, and Mrs Hayes proposed that it should be packed in a box and buried. The plan was decided upon, and a box purchased, but being found too small, the corpse had to be dismembered in order to admit of being enclosed within it. However, the inconvenience of manhandling the heavy box soon became apparent, and the bits of mangled body were unpacked and wrapped in a blanket, this collection being deposited in a pond in the middle of a field in Marylebone.

In the meantime the head had been discovered, and the circumstances of a murder having been committed being obvious, every measure was taken to secure the discovery of its perpetrators. The magistrates, with this view, directed that the head should be washed clean, and the hair combed, and that it should be displayed on a pole in the churchyard of St Margaret's, Westminster, that an opportunity might be afforded to the public to identify it.

Thousands witnessed this extraordinary spectacle; and there were no few among that crowd that expressed the belief that the head belonged to John Hayes. When the head had been exhibited for four days, it was thought expedient to preserve it, and Mr Westbrook, a chemist, consequently undertook to bottle it in spirits.

On the day of her death, Catherine Hayes received the Sacrament, and was dragged on a sledge to the place appointed for execution. When the wretched woman had finished her devotions, in pursuance of her sentence an iron chain was put around her waist, with which she was attached to the stake near the gallows. When women were burned for petty treason, as now, it was usual to strangle them by means of a rope passed around the neck and pulled by the executioner, so that they were mercifully insensible to the heat of the flames. But this woman was literally burned alive, for the executioner let go of the rope too soon, in consequence of having his hand burnt by the flames. The flames burned fiercely around her, and the spectators beheld Catherine Hayes pushing away the faggots, while she rent the air with her cries and lamentations. Other faggots were instantly piled on her, but she survived amidst the flames for a considerable time, and her body was not perfectly reduced to ashes until three hours later.

(The Annals of Newgate, 1776)

HENDLEY, Noeleen   Noeleen Hendley met widower Terry McIntosh when their children became engaged to be married; after the wedding they became lovers – in fact, much of their time together is alleged to have been spent in bed. For reasons best known to herself, though almost certainly as much to do with the business of inheritance as because of her religion, Noeleen refused to divorce her husband. However, she was apparently quite happy to go along with the alternative – killing him; or rather, paying somebody else to kill him. They certainly could have found a more committed, more competent hit-man than Paul Buxton, however. There were to be six murderous plots in all, and even then the victim's death was bungled.

The initial plan was set to be carried out on 7 October 1991, when Noeleen was to take her husband to a cinema where Buxton and an accomplice would lie in wait until the Hendleys left, then pounce out of the darkness and beat Tony Hendley to death. Unfortunately, the accomplice proved less courageous as the time approached, and the 'mugging' was abandoned. The following week Noeleen and Tony Hendley paid another visit to the cinema, but just as Buxton was about to strike the fatal blow a stranger walked by and the assassin took to his heels.

The third script concocted by Hendley and her lover was for Buxton to hide in the Hendleys' house while they were out, having first removed all the light fuses. When the couple returned, Tony Hendley would find the power off and go to check the fuses – at which point Buxton would creep up behind him and do the deed. But Buxton failed to turn up. Still blissfully unaware of the sexual intrigue and the increasingly farcical death plots that were going on around him, Tony Hendley agreed to take his wife for a drink at a local pub; here Paul Buxton was supposed to ambush them, kill Tony, who would be slightly the worse for drink, and rob Noeleen of some inexpensive items of jewellery. This plan fell apart when the Hendleys couldn't even get into the crowded pub.

As all their *al fresco* plots seemed doomed to failure, Noeleen, McIntosh and Buxton settled on another variation of the fuse-box scenario. This time Buxton was to creep into the house after Tony Hendley returned from a works outing; he would remove the fuses, plunging the house into darkness, Hendley would come to investigate, and be bludgeoned to death with an iron bar. And had Buxton's nerve not failed him at the last minute it might have worked.

On the night of 30 November 1991, Noeleen Hendley was entrusted to remove the bulb on the upper landing so that when he arrived home, Tony Hendley would have to walk upstairs in the dark. Waiting for him in the shadows would be Paul Buxton. Meanwhile, Terry McIntosh had lured the unsuspecting Hendley down to the pub for a few drinks, the intention being to render the strongly built Hendley less capable of resisting a murderous attack. As he stumbled up the stairs in the gloom, Tony Hendley had no premonition of what was to come; that is until the first blow smashed down on his head. Then another, and another . . . in total Paul Buxton bludgeoned his victim twenty-nine times, and still Hendley was not dead, but staggering around clutching wildly at his attacker, blood pouring from a smashed skull – it was a sight that would haunt Paul Buxton for ever after. Before he fled in panic, Buxton punched Noeleen Hendley in the face to reinforce the story that a burglar had attacked the couple and then run off. When Noeleen summoned up the courage to walk upstairs, across the landing carpet soaked with her husband's blood, she found him lying there, his head and face she later described as 'just a blob; like a sponge'. Even more awful, he was still alive. There was no turning back now; the plan had to be carried through.

When one of the Hendleys' neighbours was woken from his sleep by Noeleen's dreadful screams, he rushed down to find that 'she was shrieking hysterically and claiming someone had stabbed her husband'.

Tony Hendley was rushed to hospital for emergency treatment and immediately put on a life-support machine. By the following morning it was clear that the terrible battering had destroyed Hendley's brain beyond any hope of recovery, and the life-support was turned off.

There are few things more difficult to hide than illicit love affairs. As Mr Brian Escott-Cox was to observe later at Noeleen Hendley's trial: 'One of the things about having an affair is that you can't help talking to someone.' In Noeleen's case it was at the slimming club she ran that word of the extra-marital fling got out.

Then there was the business of the photograph. When the Hendleys' son Shane married Kay McIntosh they went to live in her father's house at Little Eaton. It was here that Shane quite innocently came across a photograph of his mother; not, one might add, the usual sort of family snapshot, but something almost risqué in a middle-aged kind of way. There stood Noeleen, her trousers around her ankles, proudly and provocatively displaying the tattoo of a butterfly and rose at the top of her left thigh; she was apparently a fan of the rock band Guns 'n' Roses. It was shock enough to find the photograph – but in Terry McIntosh's home!

It did not take the police long to pick up on these revelations, nor the brain of an Einstein to link the affair with the brutal killing of Tony Hendley.

Police now checked the telephone records and discovered a call to Paul Buxton. Under questioning Buxton admitted to the police that Hendley and McIntosh had hired him to dispose of Tony Hendley.

Meanwhile, Noeleen had banked the £70,000 life insurance payout due on her husband's death, and had also been keeping up an impeccable performance as the grieving widow, shedding copious tears at Tony Hendley's funeral, and keeping the sob in her voice while, dressed all in black, she begged the public for information on her husband's killer during a television appeal.

On 17 November 1992, forty-six-year-old Noeleen Hendley stood in the dock at Nottingham Crown Court jointly charged with Terry McIntosh and amateur hit-man Paul Buxton with the murder of her forty-six-year-old husband Tony. Both Mrs Hendley and Buxton denied any part in the killing, but McIntosh had already made a full confession and because of his guilty plea was not tried with them. When Noeleen Hendley gave evidence on her own behalf at the trial, she admitted that she became obsessed with Terry McIntosh:

'He was like a sex drug. We made love as often as possible. I couldn't get enough of him.' And according to Noeleen, there was quality as well as quantity: 'Terry just took me over completely. I had never experienced such sexual practices before.' Mrs Hendley also blamed McIntosh for the plot to kill her husband: 'He suggested hundreds of schemes . . . I thought it was a joke – he was always playing jokes. It was just like the films. Things didn't happen like this in real life.' Asked why she had appeared on television pleading for help to find her husband's killer, Noeleen replied, somewhat lamely: 'I forgot it was Paul Buxton.'

As for Buxton himself, the prosecution claimed that in a statement he had insisted that all he had done was hit Tony

Hendley a couple of times before running off in panic – if you asked *him*, it was Mrs Hendley who had finished the job off.

Following a twelve-day hearing, the jury of seven men and five women needed a retirement of less than three hours to return guilty verdicts against all three defendants.

Sentencing the prisoners to life, Mr Justice Holland told them: 'This case has been distinguished by a wickedness which will long be in my memory, and all others who have listened to it. It was not just the fundamental wickedness of plotting to murder a man, but the fact that it was persevered with over the period of a month. It culminated in a murderous attack, the brutality of which I suspect surprised even you.' As the judge pronounced his sentence, Noeleen Hendley collapsed in the dock and was helped from the court by two prison officers.

HILLEY, Audrey Marie   Audrey Marie Frazier was born in Anniston, Alabama, in 1933, the only daughter of a mill worker. She married at the age of eighteen, and over the following decade produced two daughters. In 1975 Marie's husband, Frank Hilley, died at the young age of forty-five. He had suffered extraordinary agonies during the illness leading to his death, though medical tests could find no cause. The autopsy report suggested that Frank had succumbed to infectious hepatitis. Marie was left with a pile of debts and the sum of $31,140 on the life insurance.

Over the following two years the local police were pestered almost daily by reports from Marie that her home had been burgled or that threatening letters had been left in her house. In January 1977, Marie's mother, Lucille Frazier, who had been living with Marie since contracting cancer, died; she left Marie $600. In July 1978 Marie Hilley took out a policy on the life of her eighteen-year-old daughter Carol. The following year Carol fell sick with a mysterious illness which the hospital were unable to diagnose, and which more than once brought her close to death. And Carol might well have died, had she not mentioned to a friend that her mother had been giving her injections; just as she had given injections to her father and grandmother. This immediately aroused the suspicion of poisoning, and urine and hair tests did indeed prove that Carol Hilley's body contained an unusually high concentration of arsenic. The bodies of Frank Hilley and Lucille Frazier were exhumed and they too revealed abnormal levels of arsenic. Marie was arrested, and a search of her house turned up a bottle of arsenic hidden in her jewellery case.

Although Marie was charged only with the attempted murder of Carol Hilley, the circumstances surrounding the other deaths in the family might be thought suspicious enough to have warranted keeping Mrs Hilley in custody. Apparently not; Marie was released on bail and promptly disappeared from sight, first to Florida where, in 1980, she married, and thence to New Hampshire, where she took a position as a secretary. The nationwide hue and cry was still on, of course, and to save possible embarrassment Marie decided she had better 'die'. She contrived to have her death announced in the newspaper obituary columns, and to discourage potential mourners let it be known that Marie had left her mortal remains to medical science. Then Marie reappeared as her twin sister Teri Martin. It was in this masquerade that she was arrested in 1983.

Marie Hilley was now facing two charges, the murder of her husband and the attempted murder of her daughter. The whole trial was riddled with incompetence. Considering the ingenuity of Marie's deceits she deserved a less bungling defence than she got, but she was convicted on both counts and sentenced to life and twenty years respectively. As if they had not learned their lesson, the authorities released Marie Hilley for a weekend's leave in February 1987; of course she disappeared. Marie was found on open ground four days later suffering from exposure. She died in hospital.

HINDLEY, Myra, and BRADY, Ian   Born in Manchester in 1942, Myra Hindley met Ian Brady in January 1961, when she went to work as a typist at Millwards Merchandising, where Brady was a stock clerk. The mousy nineteen-year-old became heavily infatuated with the black shirt wearing, Marlon-Brando-esque young man. They started to date and Brady quickly seduced her (on her grandmother's sofa). A manipulative admirer of Hitler and the Marquis de Sade, Ian Brady was soon moulding Myra's mind like wax.

Brady was born in Glasgow in 1938, and became a burglar as a child. Sent to Manchester to join his mother as a teenager, he was soon sentenced to two years in borstal for helping a friend load some stolen lead onto a lorry. A perhaps understandable sense of injustice filled him at this harsh sentence, and Brady became obsessed with a desire to take revenge on what he saw as a stupid and unjust society.

Just as in the Leopold and Loeb case, 21 years before, Brady believed his (self-defined) intellectual superiority to his fellow citizens put him morally above their petty laws. But where Leopold and Loeb had murdered to prove their own superiority to the common herd, Brady murdered as an act of self-gratifying revenge. The world had made him suffer, he believed, so the world was going to pay.

Brady and Myra Hindley's chosen 'pound of flesh' payment was to be taken from the children of Manchester. The sadistic pair kidnapped, sexually assaulted and murdered Pauline Reade, aged sixteen, on July 12, 1963. A similar fate befell John Kilbride, aged twelve, on November 23, and Keith Bennett, also twelve, on 16 June, 1964.

On December 26, 1964, ten-year-old Lesley Anne Downey was picked up – like the earlier victims – by the harmless looking Myra Hindley. She was taken back to the house in Wardle Brook Avenue, that Hindley and Brady shared with Myra's grandmother, and made to undress, after which Brady took pictures of her. Her pleas to be allowed to return home were tape-recorded. Then she was raped by Brady, and strangled – Brady claims – by Hindley.

The fifth and final known victim, Edward Evans, was a seventeen-year-old homosexual who was picked up by Brady on October 6, 1964, and was taken back to Wardle Brook Avenue.

Towards midnight, Hindley called at the home of her sister Maureen, and asked Maureen's husband, David Smith, to walk her home. Smith, aged seventeen, was another admirer and disciple of the charismatic Brady.

A few minutes after he had arrived at the house on Wardle Brook Avenue, Smith heard Hindley shout 'Dave, help him!' and ran into the sitting room to find Brady hacking at Evans' head with an axe. When this failed to kill him, Brady strangled Evans to death with an electric light flex, commenting casually: 'This one's taking a time to go.' After the murder, Smith was asked to help carry the corpse upstairs.

The whole scene was doubtless concocted, at least partially, with an aim to make Smith a member, willing-or-no, of Brady's killing club. But later, when Smith arrived home, he vomited and told his wife what had happened; she told him to go to the police. Evans' corpse was discovered and Brady was arrested the next day, Hindley a week later.

Brady told the investigators that the murder of Edward Evans had been in self-defence, and that Lesley Ann Downey had been brought to the house in Wardle Brook Avenue by 'two men', who had taken her away after taking the paedophilic photographs (which had already been found).

On April 19, 1966, Brady and Hindley appeared at the Chester Assizes. The tape, made by Brady, of Lesley Ann Downey's pathetic pleas for mercy was played in court and shocked the nation. On May 6, 1966, both Brady and Hindley were sentenced to life imprisonment (the death penalty had been abolished the previous year.)

The actual number of victims may never be known. All but

Evans were buried on Saddleworth Moor, but Brady and Hindley claimed to have forgotten where Keith Bennett's grave was and refused to admit involvement with the disappearance of three other children who went missing in Manchester during the period of their killing spree. It is probable now that we may never know.

Myra Hindley died of a combination of bronchial pneumonia and heart disease on 15 November 2002, aged sixty. Ian Brady to date remains in a maximum-security mental hospital and has sued for the right to starve himself to death, free of protective intervention by the authorities.

HOUSDEN, Nina   Jealousy has been the powerful motive behind some of history's most terrible crimes, and it was the same passion which motivated Nina Housden to murder and dismember her husband. In 1947 Nina and Charles Housden were living in Detroit where he drove one of the city's buses. Despite his obvious loyalty and fidelity, poor Charlie Housden had suffered his wife's irrational jealousy for years. She spied on him, she pestered him at work, and always there were the constant violent accusations. Finally Housden could take no more and sensibly filed for divorce and moved out. On 18 December, just days before the divorce was due to be granted, Nina called her husband on the telephone and invited him over to the former matrimonial home at Highland Park – just for old times' sake. Having got Housden incapably drunk – indeed unconscious – Nina strangled him with a length of washing-line. Then, being careful to roll back the carpet and put a layer of newspaper on the floor, Nina hacked his body into manageable portions with a meat cleaver. Next she wrapped the pieces up carefully in bright Christmas paper, loaded the packages on to the back seat of the car and drove off to dispose of them.

'The best laid schemes . . .' as Robert Burns reminds us. It was Nina Housden's bad luck that her previously reliable car chose to break down in Toledo, Ohio. The garageman reckoned it would take a couple of days to fix, and Nina insisted on camping on the front seat until the job was done. If he thought it was peculiar the repairman said nothing and got on with his work. What he did mind was the awful smell that was coming from inside the car; in fact, he complained about it stinking his garage up. Nina's story about taking parcels of venison as Christmas presents to her family didn't sound entirely convincing, and her suggestion that the meat was going off because he was taking his time over his work hurt the mechanic's professional pride. Late that night, while Nina was grunting and snoring across the front seats, the man took a peek into one of the gaily wrapped packages; and immediately wished he hadn't. The dismembered human leg was decomposing rapidly.

Having been tried, convicted and sentenced to life imprisonment, Nina Housden is supposed to have told newsmen: 'Charlie wasn't a bad egg. He just made the mistake of running around with other women.'

HULME, Juliet *see* **PARKER, Pauline Yvonne**

J

JEFFS, Doreen In November 1960, at the English south-coast resort of Eastbourne, Mrs Doreen Jeffs killed her baby daughter Linda, and then fabricated a kidnapping story. When the child's body was found later, Mrs Jeffs was subjected to further police questioning, during which she broke into tears and admitted killing Linda in a fit of depression. When Doreen Jeffs' case came before a court, this explanation had been expertly moulded into a defence by her attorney. Mrs Jeffs was, he told the jury, 'a woman who committed an offence under the stress of childbirth'. It was certainly an unusual plea, but it was clear that the jury agreed – Mrs Jeffs had been unbalanced as the result of the premature birth of her child.

For a while Doreen Jeffs received treatment in a psychiatric hospital, but shortly afterwards, when she was released on probation, she tried unsuccessfully to commit suicide by gassing herself. In January 1965, Mrs Jeffs took a short trip along the sea-front from the town of Eastbourne to the coastal beauty spot known as Beachy Head, a majestic, sheer chalk cliff dropping down to the sea 590 feet below. Here Doreen Jeffs removed her outer clothing, folded it neatly on the grass, and then hurled herself over the edge.

JEGADO, Hélène   Following a most unpromising start in life
as an orphan – and a particularly unattractive specimen at that
– Hélène was, as were so many similar unfortunates, taken into
domestic service to endure a future of endless drudgery
followed by bleak old age. Revenge for the cruel lot cast for her
passed through Hélène Jegado's mind when she was thirty
years old. Within a period of three months, she had disposed of
seven members of the household, including her own sister,
through the simple expedient of poison. But such a pretence of
devoted care had this cunning maid shown that even the long-
headed local authorities could not bring themselves to think her
capable of such infernal wickedness as murder.

It is clear that Hélène derived considerable pleasure from
killing people, for no sooner had she found a new position, than
the family 'upstairs' and her fellow servants began to drop like
flies. Hélène Jegado was a committed and, one might almost
say, 'professional' poisoner, for no matter how long her list of
victims grew, by a judicious combination of hurt innocence
('Wherever I go, people die,' she would moan), and keeping on
the move, she was never once suspected. When she tired of the
rigours of the world, Hélène entered a convent and became
Sister Hélène. It was a brush with the godly that did not last
long, and she was thrown out for breaking that commandment
which cautioned against stealing.

She was asked to leave her next convent for breaking that
other commandment that forbids poisoning one's fellow nuns,
and though in the interests of preserving the Order's good name
no official inquiry was ever held, Hélène was once again
looking for employment. It was 1833, and during her wander-
ings here and there over the next ten years, there can be traced
a trail of corpses that number at least twenty-four, but almost
certainly more – a fitting testimony to Hélène Jegado's grudge
against the world.

Then in 1849 things started to go awry, and the world began
to get its own back. Hélène was in service with a Monsieur

Rabot at Rennes, and when the gentleman of the house found
Hélène helping herself to a few trinkets he did not hesitate to
give her notice. On the following day the entire family was
stricken with nausea, vomiting and excruciating stomach pains
– mercifully, none of them died.

Hélène seemed to be losing her touch, and it was at the home
of Professor Theodore Bidard, also at Rennes, that she gave her
farewell performance. Here, on 1 July 1851, Hélène Jegado
poisoned fellow servant Rosalie Sarrazin; the doctor, far from
issuing a death certificate without question as she had become
accustomed to, made the result of his very thorough examination known to the police – Mademoiselle Sarrazin had been
poisoned with arsenic. Murdered.

Still Hélène *might* have got away with it had she not made
her first words to the visiting magistrate: 'I am innocent!' 'Of
what?' questioned the magistrate. 'Nobody has accused you.'
But they soon did; soon Hélène Jegado was on trial for her life.
Despite the surprisingly scant amount of direct evidence that
could be proved against her on most of the seventeen charges,
in December 1851 the world had the last laugh when Hélène
Jegado laid her neck upon the guillotine's lunette and heard the
blade rushing down to meet it.

JONES, Elizabeth Marina, and HULTEN, Karl Gustav It
was a late afternoon in the October of 1944, towards the end of
the Second World War, when the man who liked to call himself
Second Lieutenant Richard Allen, of the 501 Parachute
Infantry Regiment, US Army, walked into a small cafe in
Queen Caroline Street on London's Hammersmith Broadway.
Coincidence was about to cross his path with that of a young
woman; between them they would commit one of the most
cold-blooded, senseless killings of the twentieth century.

Karl Gustav Hulten, who for no honest reason was
masquerading under the sobriquet 'Ricky Allen', recalled at his
subsequent trial, 'I saw Len Bexley [an acquaintance] sitting there

with a young lady. I took another seat, but he asked me to come over and join them, which I did.' Bexley introduced 'Ricky' to Elizabeth ('Betty') Jones, an eighteen-year-old stripper who worked under the name Georgina Grayson; in this latter name she rented a room at 311 King Street, not far from where she now sat. Born and brought up in South Wales, Betty was married when she was only sixteen to a soldier, a man ten years her senior with a quick temper and a brutish manner. When he punched her on their wedding-day it was for the last time; she walked out on him then and there, making her way up to London and a succession of seedy, unfulfilling jobs – waitress, barmaid, cinema usherette and striptease dancer at the Blue Lagoon Club, an occupation from which she had recently emerged unemployed.

Hulten further remembered, 'We were there a while in the cafeteria, and afterwards we all got up and left together. Mrs Jones and I walked towards the Broadway. I asked her if she would care to come out later on.'

At 11.30 that same evening – Friday 13 October 1944 – Betty Jones was just about to give up her wait outside the Broadway Cinema, when a two-and-a-half-ton ten-wheeled US Army truck pulled up in front of her; Hulten was in the driver's seat. Betty was soon sitting up beside him in an appropriately bizarre start to an affair which was to destroy them both.

In a sense they were still children; still locked in the world of celluloid fantasy that comprised wartime entertainment. We know from subsequent statements that the conversation on that first date was not the normal run of boy-girl talk. 'Ricky' opened by telling his new friend that the truck was stolen, and that he was a lieutenant in the US paratroops (in fact Private Hulten was a deserter). This obviously appealed to Betty's sense of the romantic, and she responded that she had always wanted to do something exciting 'like becoming a gun moll like they do in the States'. Hulten then boasted, quite untruthfully, that he had 'carried a gun for the Mob' in Chicago, and started to brandish a stolen pistol.

Perhaps the point of no return had already been reached, with both now committed to act out the roles they had chosen for themselves, and admired in each other. At any rate, a sequence of events had been put into motion that would not stop short of murder.

Past midnight on the road outside Reading, Berkshire; the truck overtakes a lone girl on a bicycle. Stopping the vehicle, Hulten steps down and waits for the girl to pass and as she does, pushes her off her machine and grabs the handbag which had been slung over the handle-bars. Before their startled victim could regain her feet, these modern highway robbers were speeding back to London; the proceeds of their crime – a couple of shillings and some clothing coupons. At 5 a.m. Betty Jones was tucked up in bed at King Street; Hulten in a near-by car-park in the truck.

On Thursday the fifth the wartime Bonnie and Clyde again climbed into the cab of the ten-wheeler. Robbery was once more on their minds. First, a decision to 'do' a pub; mission abandoned. Betty suggests robbing a taxi-cab; Ricky forces one to stop, and with a gun at the driver's head, 'Let me have all your money.' Luckily – as future events would show – the cabbie had a passenger, whose evident alarm panicked Hulten and this robbery too is abandoned in an undignified scramble to escape. We next find the Hammersmith outlaws driving back into London's blackout along the Edgware Road. At Jones' suggestion they picked up a young woman who was making her way to Bristol via Paddington station; Hulten offered to drive her out as far as Reading (which seemed to have some magnetic attraction for him), and the girl climbed gratefully into the truck between them. Hulten later recollected, 'When we were almost through Runnymede Park going towards Windsor I stopped the truck off the road. I told the girl we had a flat tyre. We all got out . . . I hit the girl over the head with an iron bar.' While Hulten held her face-down on the ground, Jones rifled the girl's pockets. 'By this time the girl had ceased struggling. I picked up her shoulders and Georgina [Jones] picked up her feet. We carried her over and dumped her about three feet from the edge of a stream.' Proceeds of this crirne? Less than five shillings. The victim, thankfully, survived.

The next day, Friday, Hulten once again called for Jones at King Street, and in the early hours of the following morning they decided to try another taxi robbery. By 2 a.m. they were approaching the Chiswick roundabout in the back of George Heath's hire car, a grey Ford V8 saloon, registration number RD 8955.

'We'll get out here.'

Heath pulled into the kerb. According to Elizabeth Jones' later statement: 'As Heath was leaning over [to open the door for Jones] I saw a flash and heard a bang . . . Heath moaned slightly and turned a little towards the front. Ricky said, "Move over or I'll give you another dose of the same." I heard [Heath] breathing very heavily and his head slumped on his chest.'

Hulten now replaced Heath behind the wheel of the saloon, and while he drove off towards Staines his companion systematically emptied the dying man's pockets. Heath struggled to keep hold of his life for just fifteen more minutes before succumbing to a massive internal haemorrhage. His corpse was unceremoniously cast into a ditch by Knowle Green, just outside Staines. The couple arrived back in home territory at 4 a.m., and after wiping the car of fingerprints, dumped it in the cinema car-park behind Hammersmith Broadway. After a quick snack in the Black and White cafe, they went back to Jones' room to look over the loot.

Six hours after it had been discarded, George Heath's body was discovered in its resting place by auxiliary fireman Robert Balding. Heath's less immediately useful possessions, such as his cheque book and driver's licence, lay where they had been thrown out on to the Great West Road by Betty Jones the night before; they were found by John Jones, an apprentice electrician. This gave a possible identity to the recently found corpse, and a description of George Heath and his car were circulated to all police units.

In the meantime, the gunman and his moll had been disposing of their victim's marketable possessions: his fountain pen and propelling pencil were snapped up by Len Bexley; a wristwatch to Hulten's hairdresser, Morris Levene. They passed the afternoon spending the proceeds at the White City greyhound track, and in the evening they watched Deanna Durbin in the film *Christmas Holiday*. But bravado had become the new name of their dangerous game, and on the night of Sunday 8 October, the couple were openly driving around in George Heath's V8. After spending the next morning in bed at King Street, Hulten again climbed behind the wheel, and took a trip to Newbury, to his old army camp; in the evening he returned to London and the arms of another girlfriend, Joyce Cook.

Patrolling his customary beat on this Monday night, PC William Walters spotted a Ford saloon parked in Lurgan Avenue, off the Fulham Road. The car's number was RD 8955.

In response to his call, Walters was soon joined by Inspector Read and a sergeant, who kept watch on the car. At about 9 p.m. Hulten left Joyce's house and got into the stolen V8.

'Is this your car, sir?' inquired PC Walters.

At Hammersmith police station, Hulten introduced himself as Second Lieutenant Richard Allen, 501 Parachute Regiment. In his hip pocket had been found a Remington automatic and a handful of ammunition. 'Allen' claimed that he had found the car abandoned out at Newbury. In the early hours of Tuesday morning Lt Robert Earl de Mott of the American CID took Hulten to their headquarters in Piccadilly. This was in perfect accord with wartime protocol, which recognized the 'sovereignty' of American servicemen while stationed in Britain, and did not permit them to be tried in a British court. The Americans, however, in an almost unprecedented act of disdain for Hulten, waived this right and returned him to the ministrations of British law and justice.

Meanwhile, Hulten had given police Jones' address at King Street, and she had been interviewed at Hammersmith police station, where she made a statement and was released. Clearly haunted by her part in what had become known as 'The Cleft-Chin Murder' (descriptive of George Heath), and prompted by a chance meeting with an old friend, Henry Kimbelly (who coincidentally was a War Reserve police constable), Elizabeth Jones made a full confession of her part in the crime, albeit laying much emphasis on Hulten's dominant role. She later enlarged the point by claiming that she was afraid of Hulten – terrified by his threats of violence. Karl Hulten gave as good as he got, and blamed Betty for egging him on to the final deed: 'If it hadn't been for her, I would never had shot Heath.'

Six months before VE Day, Hulten and Jones appeared at the Old Bailey before Mr Justice Charles. Six days later, on 21 January 1945, sentence of death was pronounced on them both. Appeals were dismissed in February.

For Karl Hulten, the last reel of the third-rate gangster movie he had made of his life came to an end on 8 March 1945. At the end of a rope; a week after his twenty-third birthday.

His co-star, too, had made her last appearance. Reprieved just two days before her execution date, Betty Jones spent the next decade in gaol, and was released on licence in 1954.

JONES, Genene Babies admitted to the intensive care unit of San Antonio's Bexar County Hospital had begun dying at an alarming rate. Between May and December 1981, they had lost as many as twenty infants, apparently through cardiac arrest or runaway bleeding. Suspiciously, the majority of fatalities had occurred while the babies were in the care of nurse Genene Jones; Miss Jones, however, was widely regarded as the very paragon of her caring profession.

Internal inquiries were held without reaching any positive conclusion, and finally a panel of experts was appointed to look further into the deaths. Members of the Bexar's staff were routinely interviewed, and the team were surprised when one of the nurses bluntly accused Genene Jones of murder. The panel failed to reach any firm conclusion but did suggest that the hospital dispense with the services of both Jones and the nurse who had accused her of killing babies. As a result, Genene Jones resigned from the hospital. She obtained her next appointment at the Kerrville Hospital, where within months of her starting work a number of children began to experience breathing problems; however, they all recovered. When fourteen-month-old Chelsea McClellan was admitted to the hospital for regular immunization against mumps and measles, it was Jones who administered her first injection, and it resulted in an immediate seizure.

On her way to San Antonio for emergency treatment, the McClellan baby went into cardiac arrest and died. By now the health authorities had become troubled by the deaths at both hospitals and Jones was dismissed pending a grand jury investigation. News reports had begun to talk of as many as forty-two baby deaths under investigation. Finally Genene Jones was charged with murder following the discovery of succinyl-choline, a derivative of the drug curare, in Chelsea McClellan's body.

In February 1984 Genene Jones was found guilty and sentenced to ninety-nine years. She was subsequently tried for administering an overdose of the blood-thinning drug heparin to another child, and this time she was handed down a concurrent term of sixty years. Although we are unlikely ever to know what really motivated Genene Jones to kill the babies entrusted to her care, there is general agreement that she took pleasure in creating life and death dramas in which she could play an influential role, so indicating a power motive.

JUDD, Winnie Ruth   The 'Phoenix Trunk Murders', as they have become known, took place in an apartment in the Arizona capital on the night of 16 October 1931. The flat had been occupied by Hedwig Samuelson and twenty-seven-year-old Agnes LeRoi; on the night in question a former flat-mate and colleague at the local clinic, Winnie Judd, had been with them. A quarrel seems to have arisen over men-friends which erupted into physical violence, and Hedwig, in true bar-room style, had pulled out a gun and shot Winnie in the hand. Winnie grabbed the gun and – in self-defence she later claimed – shot both girls dead.

Agnes LeRoi fitted comfortably into one large trunk, but Miss Samuelson needed to be reduced to her constituent parts before being packed into a smaller piece of luggage. On 18 October Winnie Judd, together with the two trunks, embarked on a west-bound train for the Southern Pacific station of Los Angeles. By the time Mrs Judd, accompanied now by a young man she identified as businessman Carl Harris, was ready to claim her baggage, one of the trunks had begun to leak a sticky, foul-smelling liquid. Asked to open the trunks, Winnie and Carl left the office on pretence of getting the keys and never returned. It was the baggage man who prised open the luggage, launching a nationwide hunt for double-killer Winnie Ruth Judd (by now nicknamed the 'Tiger Woman').

Following a plea from her doctor husband, Winnie turned herself in, and at her trial was found guilty of murder and sentenced to death. At a retrial just ten days before the execution date, Mrs Judd was judged insane and committed to the Arizona State Hospital, from which she was paroled in 1971.

K

KENT, Constance Constance was born in 1844, ninth of ten children, to Samuel Savile Kent, a factories inspector, and Maryanne, his wife. Of the previous eight children, three had survived – two daughters and a son named Edward. In the following year a further son arrived, though Maryanne finally succumbed to a steadily worsening mental complaint for which her husband, to avoid the stigma of 'insanity in the family', had not wished to have her certified. She died in 1852.

During Mrs Kent's 'illness', the family governess, a Miss Mary Pratt, had taken every opportunity to inveigle herself into the family, and into Samuel Kent's affections in particular; so successful was she that in 1853 she was fully prepared to become the second Mrs Kent. Between them, Samuel and Mary produced a second set of offspring – two girls and a boy, Francis Savile. Of her stepchildren Mary had never been fond, and when not engaging in active abuse, she ignored and neglected them; a characteristic seemingly acquired from their father.

On the night of 29 June 1860, in the family home at Road Hill House, near Trowbridge in Wiltshire, Mary Kent's four-year-old son Francis was taken from his cot, probably asphyxiated, and then had his throat savagely cut through to the vertebrae. His body was found the following morning where it had been crudely hidden in an unused outside privy.

The killing seemed as inexplicable as it had been brutal. There had been no other observable disturbance to the house, and nothing had been stolen; and for these reasons the finger of suspicion pointed inevitably at a member of the Kent household. Most notably, it was at the nursemaid Elizabeth Gough and the sixteen-year-old Constance that that finger was directed. There seemed little tangible evidence to support a case in either instance; indeed, the only tangible evidence – a bloodstained nightdress recovered from the boiler flue by another servant – had already been carelessly lost by the police. The coroner's jury returned an open verdict.

The unfortunate Constance was hastily packed off to France, where she was cloistered in a convent at Dunat. Two months later Elizabeth Gough was re-arrested, and then, once again, released.

By the time Constance returned to England, to enter St Mary's, a convent in Brighton, the tragic fate of Francis Savile Kent had been all but forgotten. And might have continued so had it not been for the strength of Constance's religious faith, and the zeal of her Mother Superior and the founder of the 'retreat', the Rev. Arthur Wagner. By a process of persuasion (with the promise of her confirmation as spiritual 'bait') Wagner extorted out of Constance a confession to the murder of her little stepbrother which he promptly communicated to *The Times* newspaper of 30 August 1865 in the form of a letter:

A few days before the crime she obtained possession of a razor from a green case in her father's wardrobe and secreted it. This was the sole instrument she used . . . Soon after midnight she went downstairs and opened the drawing-room door and shutters . . . She took the child from his bed and carried him downstairs through the drawing room . . . Having the child on one arm, she raised the drawing-room

sash with the other hand, went round the house and into the
closet, lighted the candle and placed it on the seat of the
closet, the child being wrapped in the blanket and still
sleeping. While the child was in this position, she inflicted
the wound in the throat. She said she thought the blood
would never come . . so she thrust the razor into the left side
and put the body with the blanket round it into the vault . . .
She went back to her room, examined her dress and found
only two spots of blood on it . . . She thought the bloodstains
had been effectively washed out . . . but afterwards she found
the stains were still visible . . . She eventually burned it [the
dress] in her bedroom . . . As regards the motive for her
crime, it seems that although she entertained at one time a
great regard for the present Mrs Kent, yet if any remark was
at any time made which in her opinion was disparaging to
any member of the first family, she treasured it up and determined to revenge it. She had no ill will against the little boy
except as one of the children of her stepmother. She declared
that her father and her stepmother had always been kind to
her personally.

Subsequent upon her additional confession to the police (again
prompted by the Rev. Mr Wagner), and her brief trial at
Salisbury Assizes on 21 July, sentence of death was passed on
Constance; a sentence later commuted to life imprisonment.
For Constance, the sentence ended twenty years later. It is said
that she changed her name and emigrated to Canada to become
a nurse, where she died. But for this fact, as with so much else
in the case, it is not possible to find any evidence. As in many
of the classic murder mysteries, there will always remain a
question mark over the identity of the murderer.

What is certain is that for the whole of her life, Constance
Kent was a sad victim of the times in which she was unfortunate enough to grow to womanhood.

KLIMEK, Tillic (aka Tillie GBUREK)   Tillie Klimek's two outstanding qualities were that she was a superb cook, and that she possessed an uncanny accuracy in predicting the deaths of neighbourhood dogs; a strange distinction it is true, but one which led to her being considered something of a 'wise woman' among the more superstitious residents of Chicago's Polish district.

Tillie had been married for almost twenty-eight years when, in 1914, she told a neighbour that her powers of prediction bore sad tidings – her husband, John Mitkiewitz, would soon be passing into the next world. Inside three weeks, according to the voices, she would be a widow. Almost three weeks to the day later, she was; comforted only by the one thousand dollars insurance money.

Six weeks later, she was Mrs John Ruskowski. After three months, Tillie had another premonition, and two weeks after that she became, quite suddenly, the widow Ruskowski.

Next she took up with Joseph Guszowski, though they never married. Actually there wasn't all that much time for matrimonial plans, because after all too brief a spell of being treated to Tillie's culinary expertise he suddenly died. Displaying infinite good taste, Tillie nevertheless had him buried next to her late husbands in the cemetery.

It was thirteen months after the death of John Mitkiewitz, about eight since Ruskowski's decease, and almost no time at all since Joseph Guszowski had handed in his dinner pail, but Tillie was set to marry again. The unfortunate groom this time around was one Frank Kupczyk. At the wedding reception a distant relative of Tillie's, Rose Chudzinski, asked her how long she thought Frank would live, which given her previous record was not an entirely inappropriate question. The bride replied that the spirits hadn't told her about that yet, but for what it was worth Rose herself would be giving up the ghost in about six weeks. In six weeks she did.

It was not until 1920 that Tillie was privy again to the Grim

Reaper's personal plans, and then it spelled sorrow for a couple with whom she had been quarrelling. Their three children died one by one. Tillie had told them they would. Then Frank Kupczyk began to get on her nerves, and shortly he died – fortunately the spirits had given Tillie plenty of warning and she was able to order his coffin well in advance. On the day of Kupczyk's death she confided in a friend that she hoped she would have better luck with her next husband, Anton Klimek.

In fact, he brought her considerable ill-luck, because when Anton took sick a few months after the wedding, Klimek's brother went to the police. An analysis of one of Tillie's celebrated stews revealed her secret ingredient – arsenic.

At her trial for Frank Kupczyk's murder, Tillie Klimek declared that her spirit guides would not allow her to be executed. And they were right, she was instead sentenced to a lifetime's imprisonment. Her suggestion that she might be allowed to work in the kitchens was politely declined . . .

L

LABBE, Denise   When Denise Labbe's two-and-a-half-year-old bastard child drowned in a wash-basin at Blois in November 1954, people couldn't help recalling the two previous occasions on which the unfortunate infant had almost met a similarly watery end while in its mother's care. The result of the combined wagging of tongues was that twenty-eight-year-old Denise was taken in for questioning at the gendarmerie and thence before the examining magistrate; here she confessed to what she enigmatically described as 'a ritual murder' of her daughter. Denise had, it transpired, fallen under the spell of Second Lieutenant Jacques Algarron of the St Cyr military school; he in turn had fallen under the spell of Friedrich Nietzsche and arrogantly supposed himself to be a representative of that philosopher's breed of 'Supermen'. At any rate, he exerted an unhealthy and total control over Denise Labbe, who was informed on 1 May 1954: 'The price of our love must be the death of your daughter . . . an innocent victim must be sacrificed.' The idea seemed to be that only through suffering could their union become strong.

Exactly one year after the 'monstrous act', Labbe and Algarron stood their trial, she receiving a lifetime of penal servitude, he collecting twenty years' hard labour.

LEE, Jean Like many of her Antipodean countrymen, Jean Lee made her own modest contribution to the smooth running of allied operations during the Second World War. At a time when Australia was playing host to friendly troops from around the globe, Jean set herself up in the 'entertainment' business. A naturally companionable redhead, Jean left her child to be cared for by relatives, bade farewell to her soldier husband, and departed Sydney for Brisbane where she worked in the canteens of a number of army camps. In her time off she drank and . . . 'entertained'.

When military hostilities were over, and Jean's source of fun dried up, she returned to Sydney where she threw her lot in with one Bobby Clayton, a little, weasely man with a record of petty crime. First Jean became Clayton's mistress, then she went on the game for him, returning from her nocturnal endeavours to pour the proceeds into his bottomless pocket. And when that proved inadequate for their needs, the couple took a second bite at the same cherry through blackmail. Having first secured the fee for her 'services', Jean would entice her client into a compromising position. At this stage Clayton, playing the enraged husband, would burst into the room and threaten to call the authorities unless the bewildered man handed over more of his money. Sometimes Clayton would beat the clients up a bit – just for the hell of it really – he was that kind of man. So was Norman Andrews, and when he joined the couple in their business venture in 1949 he fitted in just perfectly.

It was in November of that year that we find the unlovely trio up to their tricks in the Melbourne industrial suburb of Calton. Jean had been routinely scouting for clients in the lounge of the University Hotel where they were staying, and had settled on a seventy-three-year-old bookmaker named William Kent. Kent, despite his age, had retained a healthy appetite for wine and women and, a little woozy from the evening's drinking, he took Jean and a bottle back to his lodgings. Once there, Jean proceeded to try to relieve William Kent of his money. The problem was, the drunker he got the tighter he hung on to his wallet, until in the end Jean was obliged to crack him over the head with the now empty wine bottle. Then she let Clayton and Andrews into the room to join the party. The two thugs immobilized Mr Kent by binding his legs and tying his thumbs tightly together; then they tortured him to death, kicking the helpless man senseless and slashing at his face and body with shards of the broken bottle. When lodgers and staff found the victim later, the room had been ransacked and the bound and bloody corpse of William Kent had been unceremoniously cast on to the bed.

When they arrived on the scene, fingerprint experts set about dusting the room for latent prints, while detectives questioned the other residents and put together a vague description of the redhead Kent had brought home with him that night. This was confirmed by bar staff at the University Hotel, and the hotel detective gave officers the name of Norman Andrews, who was a crook well known to him.

Meanwhile, after a quick celebratory drink, Jean Lee, Bobby Clayton and Norman Andrews had left the hotel (without paying, of course), and returned to Sydney. Which, once the police had sorted out names, descriptions and fingerprints, is where they were arrested.

At first the killers denied ever having met William Kent; when it became clear that there was strong evidence that they had, Clayton accused Jean and Andrews of the murder. Surprisingly, Jean Lee made a confession; not surprisingly, Norman Andrews did not.

Still, all three were arraigned on charges of murder and robbery at Melbourne Criminal Court in March 1950. By this time Clayton had felt pangs of conscience over letting Jean take all the blame, and made a confession of his own exonerating her from any part in the killing; Jean was happy to go along with that, and retracted her confession. Norman Andrews said nothing. On 26 March the jury found all three defendants guilty, and they were sentenced to death. Over the following eleven months, various legal procedures resulted in a successful appeal, followed by a retrial, another conviction, an unsuccessful appeal, and finally an execution. On the morning of 19 February 1951, Jean Lee, Bobby Clayton and Norman Andrews followed each other on to the gallows at Pentridge Jail.

LEHMANN, Christa   Christa Lehmann was born in Worms, Germany, in 1922, and from her teenage years (when Christa's mother was confmed to an asylum and her father lost interest in everything but drink) embarked upon the petty criminality that was to lead to murder and her own life imprisonment.

In 1944, at the age of twenty-one, Christa married Karl Franz Lehmann, a man it turned out with as few redeeming features as the alcoholic father she had escaped from, and who drank even more. Lehmann died in September 1952, and not surprisingly responsibility for his early demise was laid at the door of the demon drink. The following January Christa's mother-in-law Kathe Lehmann died, and not long afterwards her father-in-law Valentin Lehmann simply fell off his bicycle in the street and after several agonized twitches, also perished. Neither drank particularly heavily, but still the decimation of the Lehmann family aroused no suspicion.

In February 1954, Christa visited a neighbour, seventy-five-year- old Eva Ruh, bearing a gift of chocolate truffles. Frau Ruh took one, and put it in the fridge for later. So much the worse for Anni Hamann, Christa's best friend and Eva Ruh's daughter. When Anni returned home from work she found the truffle, took a bite, and immediately spat the bitter chocolate out of her mouth. Minutes later she died. The family dog, which lapped up the scraps was also found with its legs in the air. Of course, both Anni and the luckless canine had been poisoned, but with what nobody could tell. It was only after all the tests for all the known poisons had proved negative that analyst Kurt

Wagner recalled that there was a new phosphorus compound known as E605 which had been developed as a chemical insecticide. It was also the deadly poison that had robbed Anni Hamann of her life.

Christa Lehmann was the obvious suspect, though nobody could think of any reason why she should kill her best friend. That was until a bright detective remembered the unexpected and remarkably similar death of Valentin Lehmann. Following exhumations and post-mortem examinations of all three Lehmanns, E605 was identified as their killer; or rather, E605 helped by Christa Lehmann.

On 23 February 1954, she confessed to all four murders. The poisoned truffle was, of course, meant for Eva Ruh and not Anni. At her trial in September 1954, Christa stubbornly refused to retract her confession, leaving her counsel to flounder along as best he could with a none too convincing defence that while Christa Lehmann was not insane in the legal sense she was, in the opinion of a psychiatrist, a 'moral primitive'. The jury just thought she was guilty. Frau Lehmann was sentenced to life imprisonment.

Before Christa was taken to prison, she had these words for the waiting reporters: 'I don't suppose I should have done it. But with the exception of Anni, they were all nasty people. Besides,' she added, 'I love to go to funerals.'

Following the publicity that the case generated, more than twenty murders and seventy-seven suicides were reported in West Germany, all using the fashionable new poison E605.

LINE, Elizabeth   'She would wait for him to come to bed at three or four in the morning to be assaulted, to be buggered, to be raped. She endured having her kitten killed. She was pushed over the limit by a man who no doubt when sober was a loving and caring husband, but when drunk was rather like Dr Jekyll and Mr Hyde.'

That was Mr Stephen Leslie speaking in the defence of Mrs

Elizabeth Line at Southwark Crown Court in 1992. But it is a description which has become all too familiar in Britain's courts as one defendant after another seeks to defend herself against a charge of murder. The ingredients rarely vary – drunkenness, violence, sexual degradation, often over a period of many years. What does seem to vary, in a qulte alarming way, is the manner in which these desperate women are sentenced. Despite the prevalence of the syndrome, there is still no official recognition under British law of a 'battered woman' defence, and the attempts to apply existing laws such as those of self-defence and provocation have proved inconsistent and unreliable, resulting in defendants who killed in similar circumstances being given sentences as widely different as a couple of years' probation and life imprisonment. Elizabeth Line was one of the fortunate ones.

Elizabeth had been born in Poland in 1963 to a strict Roman Catholic family. At the age of seventeen she entered a convent where she stayed for three years before becoming a nurse. She arrived in Britain in 1986, and four years later married forty-nine-year-old Ronald Line. Although their relationship began happily enough, Line's increasing dependence on alcohol resulted in an escalating spiral of violent abuse, not only against his wife but anything else which got in his way; the court heard how on one occasion Line had hurled the family cat from the balcony of their tower block flat in west London.

In June 1991, after a particularly heavy encounter with the bottle, Ronald Line pinned his wife against the kitchen wall, yelling: 'I'll show you, you bitch. Which knife shall I use to cut your throat so you will shut your gob for ever?' Instead, it was Mrs Line who grabbed a knife and plunged it several times into her husband's body. As he lay dying on the floor she rushed in to a neighbour, crying: 'Call the police, I have just stabbed my husband.' In court, Elizabeth Line explained: 'I was so terrified. I was one hundred per cent sure he had a knife. I'm sorry, but the knife went in. I probably pushed it. I was just so scared. I did not think that he had died.'

But what is the court to do faced with evidence like this? How can it acknowledge the plight of the abused spouse – male or female – without sanctioning homicide as a solution to marital strife? In the case of Elizabeth Line the judge, Mr Justice Butler, ruled: 'Any unlawful killing is always a matter of the utmost gravity. Only in the most exceptional circumstances can it be dealt with by other than an immediate sentence of custody. These exceptional circumstances exist here. The final act of provocation was itself sufficient to reduce the charge to manslaughter. You had been subjected to months of violence and sexual abuse of the worst kind. You have been in prison for several months awaiting trial; you have suffered enough.'

After being sentenced to eighteen months' imprisonment suspended for two years, Mrs Line replied: 'Thank you very much. I hope this country will not be disappointed with me again.'

LYLES, Anjette When Anjette's husband Ben died suddenly in January 1952, she suffered a great shock. Not because she was particularly fond of him, nor because she would miss him, but because Mrs Lyles had felt sure he was insured for more than the $3,000 she eventually received. Still, it was better than nothing, and at least it would supplement the uncertain income she got from the practice of voodoo. In fact, it was just enough to open a modest restaurant in her hometown of Macon, Georgia. She called it, not without a certain black humour, the Gay Widow.

One of the restaurant's regulars was an airline pilot named Joe Neal Gabbert who became as fond of Anjette as he was of her cooking, and after a whirlwind romance they married in June 1955. Three months later, Gabbert fell seriously ill, was rushed to hospital and died soon afterwards. This time Anjette was happier with the insurance settlement; after all, she had seen to the policy herself. Anjette's former mother-in-law, Julia Young Lyles, died on 29 September 1957, and she too was suitably well covered.

Eight months after Julia Lyles' untimely loss of life, Anjette's nine-year-old daughter Marcia suffered an agonizing death in hospital. It is not certain exactly how much the poor child's life was worth, but her death had been so worrying that the hospital authorities ordered an autopsy; cause of death was attributed to arsenical poisoning. A police search of Anjette Lyles' home revealed no fewer than six bottles of arsenic-based rat poison together with several empty poison bottles.

In the evidence against her at the Gay Widow's trial it was said that all told she had netted some $47,750 from the four deaths she had engineered, including the estate of her mother-in-law which had been secured with a forged will. The money was said to have been spent mainly on men and supplies and equipment for her black-magic practices.

Although she was sentenced to die in the electric chair, Mrs Lyles was eventually declared insane and committed to a secure mental hospital.

M

McCULLOUGH, Muriel, COLLINGWOOD, James, and
KAY, Alan   Bill McCullough was Muriel's second husband,
and she brought with her two children from her first. What she
did not realize in December 1980, when she accepted him for
better or worse, was that Bill's worse was very bad indeed; the
forty-eight-year-old insurance executive turned out to be a
drunk, a squanderer, and to top it all, a wife-beater.

Had it not been for the £110,000 life insurance policy, it
might have been possible to believe Muriel McCullough's story
that she just hired a couple of heavies to beat Bill up – 'I wanted
him to have a taste of his own medicine, and I thought they
would give him a good bashing. I wanted him to know what it
was like to be on the receiving end.' But then, you might think
that a bullet through the head was a bit severe for a 'bashing'.

The call came through to the police station at Ailsworth,
Cambridgeshire, on the morning of 18 November 1981. Fifty-
two- year-old business-woman Muriel McCullough claimed
that she had been staying overnight with a friend in Hale,
Cheshire, and when she returned she 'felt' the house had been
burgled. When a police constable made his routine investigation he found a distressed Mrs McCullough sitting in the
lounge; she had not, and would not, go upstairs. Which is not

entirely surprising, because there in the bedroom lay Bill McCullough, a bullet through his skull. The officer decided to play a hunch of his own. It seemed surprising to him that a woman who was convinced her jewellery had been stolen would not want to check whether it was missing; so he told Mrs McCullough that her husband was upstairs in bed feeling poorly. Still she made no move to go up and see him. When the constable told her the truth – that he was dead – Mrs McCullough made a histrionic show of grief that would have fooled nobody.

The result of a surveillance on Mrs McCullough was the introduction to the picture of two bully-boys named James Collingwood and Alan Kay, petty crooks operating out of Liverpool; under questioning, Collingwood obligingly told detectives that Muriel McCullough had offered him £8000 to kill her husband. Who was he to refuse? Business, after all, is business. On the night of 18 November Alan Kay had driven Collingwood to the McCullough house where he entered through the door left open for him, and using a plan of the house made for him by Muriel, made his way up to the master bedroom where he shot Bill McCullough as he slept.

All three conspirators stood trial at Birmingham Crown Court in November 1982, all three were found guilty as charged, and all three were handed down life sentences.

MAJOR, Ethel Lillie   It is a fact of every police officer's life that he receives his share of letters, telephone calls and visits from cranks and attention-seekers. It is very rarely that the officer will ignore such seeming red herrings, for though many police hours may be lost chasing wild geese, at least a small percentage of such tips prove, on previous experience, to be vital clues.

In the case of the death of Arthur Major the police would have been unaware that there had even been a crime to solve had it not been for an anonymous letter – the writer of which remains unknown to this day.

On 26 May 1934 Inspector Dodson of the Horncastle force received the following letter:

> Sir, have you ever heard of a wife poisoning her husband? Look further into the death (by heart failure) of Mr Major, of Kirkby-on-Bain. Why did he complain of his food tasting nasty and throw it to a neighbour's dog, which has since died? Ask the undertaker if he looked natural after death? Why did he stiffen so quickly? Why was he so jerky when dying? I myself have heard her threaten to poison him years ago. In the name of the law, I beg you to analyse the contents of his stomach.
>
> 'Fairplay'

A quick check revealed that forty-four-year-old lorry driver Arthur Major had indeed died – on 24 May – of what had been diagnosed as an epileptic fit. The symptoms – violent spasms and muscular contortions – had begun two days before. Dodson acted swiftly in getting a coroner's order to prevent the funeral taking place at its appointed time on 27 May, and it must have been a uniquely disturbing experience for mourners to look on as the police removed the coffin from before their very eyes.

Meanwhile, Dodson's officers had confirmed that a wire-haired terrier belonging to the Majors' next-door neighbour had died during the night of 23 May after suffering muscular spasms. The direct cause of the unfortunate beast's untimely death could not elude the redoubtable Dr Roche Lynch, distinguished analyst to the Home Office. Nor could the reason for Arthur Major's recent demise; both had succumbed to a fatal dose of strychnine – in Major's case, probably two doses.

So what of the wife who had been anonymously accused of the terrible crime? What of Ethel Major? An account is appropriately supplied by the Scotland Yard officer who was placed in overall charge of the case, Chief-Inspector (later Commander) Hugh Young:

> She impressed me as a cool and resourceful woman suffering no pangs of sorrow at the loss of her husband. In fact, she seemed quite callous about the whole affair, and even informed me that she felt 'much better in health since he was gone'. She began, however, by telling me that she was sure her husband had died through eating corned beef. She appeared over-eager to impress me with the fact that she had nothing to do with providing his meals, explaining that for a fortnight before her husband's death she and her young son had not slept at home, but had stayed with her father . . . 'My husband bought his tinned beef himself,' she went on, adding with great insistence: 'I know that I never bought any. I hate corned beef and think it is a waste of money to buy such rubbish.' This obvious desire to dissociate herself from any provision or purchase of corned beef seemed to me rather important, because corned beef was the last meal eaten by Arthur Major before he was seized with his fatal illness on the night of 22 May.

> (Commander Hugh Young,
> *My Forty Years at the Yard*, 1955)

Further investigation began to colour in many of the details of the Majors' unsettled married life; for a start, they couldn't stand the sight of each other – in fact Ethel, a cantankerous, arrogant woman, was pretty much disliked throughout the neighbourhood. Arthur was also sinking financially as a result of what he saw as his wife's extravagance. It was a development worthy of note in the circumstances that Major had, the very week he died, arranged to have a notice published in the *Horncastle News* dissociating himself from all the debts accumulated by his wife – an arrangement countermanded by Mrs Major immediately her husband died. Jealousy also emerged as a potential motive. Ethel claimed to have found two letters written by Mrs Kettleborough (a neighbour) to her husband; to her detriment she showed these letters to her doctor with the accompanying comment: 'A man like him is not fit to live, and I will do him in.'

When Chief-Inspector Young next interviewed Mrs Major she claimed: 'I did not know my husband died from strychnine poisoning.'

'I never mentioned strychnine,' the detective replied. 'How did you know that?' 'Oh, I'm sorry. I must have made a mistake.'

When she came up for trial at Lincoln Assizes, Ethel Lillie Major was defended by Mr Norman (later Lord) Birkett. He could not have faced a more daunting task in the whole of his long career. The evidence against his client was overwhelming. The police had proved access to the poison when they found a key in Ethel Major's purse that opened a box containing strychnine belonging to her ex-gamekeeper father. He had used the poison to exterminate vermin, and vaguely remembered having mislaid his spare key some years before. The corned beef from which Mrs Major had been at such pains to distance herself was proved to have been bought by the couple's fifteen-year-old son – on his mother's instruction.

Norman Birkett would surely have been one of the first to concur with the claim made by his learned colleague for the Crown, Mr Edward O'Sullivan KC: 'The case is really on the evidence unanswerable.' The defence called no witnesses, and Ethel Major did not take the witness stand. When the jury filed back into court with their verdict after one hour, Birkett already knew that he had lost.

Mr Justice Charles passed sentence of death on the prisoner, and relayed the jury's inexplicable recommendation to mercy. This latter was not acted upon by the Home Secretary and Ethel Lillie Major was executed at Hull Prison on 19 December 1934.

MANNING, Maria and Frederick   Maria de Roux was born in Switzerland in 1819. Her early means of livelihood was as a lady's maid, and in 1846, while travelling from England to the continent to join her mistress, Lady Blantyre, she first met Patrick O'Connor. O'Connor was a forty-nine-year-old Irishman, a customs officer in the London docks, but earning a considerable second income from money-lending. Shortly afterwards, Maria met Frederick George Manning, a railway guard on the Great Western Railway and a man of somewhat dubious reputation.

In the following year, 1847, Maria married Manning and the couple moved to Taunton, in Somerset, to run the White Hart Inn; Maria, though, persisted in her previous close friendship with O'Connor. Manning himself was still working on the railway, but after being implicated first in a £4,000 bullion theft, then arrested and released following a mail robbery, he and Maria decided that a move to London might be advisable, and they opened a beer shop in Hackney Road. Shortly afterwards Maria took it into her head to abscond with O'Connor, Manning in hot pursuit. He was clearly able to effect some kind of reconciliation, because we next encounter the Mannings living in Minver Place, Bermondsey, where to make ends meet, it was necessary to take in a lodger, in the person of a medical student called Massey. Manning suddenly developed a previously undeclared interest in medicine, and seemed anxious to question Massey about various matters related with that youth's intended profession. The effects of chloroform for example, and whether a person could sign cheques under the influence of narcotics; the effects of shooting somebody with an airgun, and where the weakest point of the skull is. These were prominent among the queries which began to arouse Massey's suspicion; Massey's suspicion in its turn resulted in the unfortunate man being thrown out of the house. It was about this time that Manning took delivery of a crowbar and a quantity of quicklime.

O'Connor had throughout continued to be on terms of some intimacy with Mrs Manning, and on 8 August 1849, he was invited to tea; it was on the same day that Manning bought a shovel.

O'Connor was never seen alive again.

Mrs Manning had shot him through the head, and according to Manning's final confession, 'I found O'Connor moaning in the kitchen. I never liked him very much, and battered in his head with a ripping chisel.' He was then buried under the flagstones in the kitchen, well covered with the quicklime.

On the following day Maria Manning visited O'Connor's lodgings and removed a quantity of money and shares, and two gold watches. Frederick was sent out to sell the shares, on which he raised £110. At this point Mrs Manning decided to ditch her husband and, after putting her belongings in the left-luggage at London Bridge station, she fled to Edinburgh. Manning sat it out at Minver Place a couple more days and then he also fled; to the Channel Islands.

O'Connor's acquaintances were quick to notice his disappearance and contacted the police, and an official search of the house at Minver Place revealed two newly cemented slabs in the kitchen floor; Patrick O'Connor's remains beneath them. Mrs Manning was speedily arrested in Edinburgh, but Manning was able to lie low until 21 August, when he was recognized and taken near St Helier, in Jersey.

The trial of Frederick and Maria Manning opened on 25 October 1849, before Mr Justice Cresswell, with the Attorney-General prosecuting. The case aroused huge public interest, with Frederick and Maria each trying to put the blame for the murder on the other. It was all to no avail, and both were duly sentenced to death. At the end, just before the day of execution, Manning confessed; but Maria still maintained her innocence, claiming, 'There is no justice and no right for a foreign subject in this country.'

At the appointed hour Frederick Manning was led out, head

bowed and unsteady on his feet, accompanied by William Calcraft, the executioner. The white hood was put over Manning's head and the rope positioned around his neck. Then it was Maria's turn to appear, dressed in respectable black satin with a black silk veil; she was blindfolded at her own request. Her demeanour was proud and steady as she was led to the scaffold and the preparations were made. A warder brought the couple's hands together as they stood over the trapdoor. The chaplain asked the unrepentant Maria one more time if she had anything to say regarding her guilt. 'Nothing, but thank you for your kindness,' she replied. Thus two callous and calculating killers were launched into eternity.

Maria and Frederick Manning were executed on 13 November 1849 in front of Horsemonger Lane Gaol. A crowd of fifty thousand spectators witnessed the hanging, including Charles Dickens, who complained to *The Times* about the levity of the crowd and the barbarity of the scene.

Maria's wearing of a black satin dress on the scaffold is said to have put the material out of fashion for ladies' dresses for a period of at least twenty years.

MAREK, Martha   Martha's start in life was not auspicious. We do not know when she was born, nor do we know who her parents were; and nor did Martha. Around 1904 she was adopted by a poor but industrious couple named Lowenstein and raised in Vienna. We next encounter Martha Lowenstein at the age of sixteen working in a dress shop, where she caught the eye of a wealthy businessman named Moritz Fritsch. Fritsch became her guardian, lavished love and presents on her and, when he died, left her his not inconsiderable fortune; which she squandered.

So much for Martha's early life. In 1924 she married Emil Marek, who was as penniless as herself; which is why between them they plotted a most grotesque insurance fraud. Martha first took out an accident policy on her husband; then she chopped away at one of his legs with an axe (with his agreement). Although Martha put in her insurance claim, the surgeon treating Emil Marek's leg injuries was suspicious that the angle of the cuts was not entirely consistent with his account of injuring himself while felling a tree. The couple were arrested and charged with fraud; to make matters more grimly ironic, infection set into Emil's leg and it had to be amputated. Martha later tried to bribe the hospital staff but succeeded in doing no more than lengthening her prison sentence.

On their release from jail, the Mareks flirted unsuccessfully with a business venture in Algiers, and ended up destitute in Vienna once again, with two children to feed and Martha selling vegetables from a barrow in the street market. In July 1932 Emil Marek died, apparently of tuberculosis; in August baby Ingeborg also died.

Less encumbered, Martha next became a nurse-companion to one of her adoptive parents' relatives, Suzanne Lowenstein; and so pleased was Frau Lowenstein with her services that when she died she left Martha her small estate. Unfortunately it was too small, and having frittered away the lot, widow Marek was obliged to take in lodgers. One of these paying guests, a Frau Kittenberger, died not long after moving in; and while this was not in itself suspicious, gossip started to spread when it was learned that she passed on within days of Martha insuring her life. A post-mortem examination carried out at the insistence of Frau Kittenberger's son revealed that the cause of her death had been thallium poisoning – which put something of a question mark over other deaths that had taken place around Martha Marek. When the bodies of Emil and Ingeborg Marek and Frau Lowenstein were dug up and autopsied it was found that they too had suffered death as a result of the metallic poison thallium.

For her misdeeds Martha Marek died no less surely than her victims, but rather more quickly. On 6 December 1938 her head was judicially struck off with an axe.

MASSET, Louise   In October 1899, Louise Masset had been living at a married sister's house in Stoke Newington for eighteen months, and was earning her living as a private tutor in music and French. Louise was half French herself, and while living in that country had conceived a child by a young Frenchman out of wedlock. When she came to England Louise had put little Manfred into the care of a foster mother with the comforting name of Helen Gentle, who lived in the Tottenham district of north London. Miss Gentle's fees were paid by Manfred's father, and everything had about it an air of gentility and respectability.

At least it did on the surface; look a little closer and a deeper, more darkly passionate picture is revealed. The fact was, Louise had fallen desperately in love, the object of her desires being a nineteen-year-old medical student named Eudore Lucas who lived next door. Partly because of the difference in their ages – Louise was thirty-six – and partly because she had already committed one indiscretion, Louise and her beau conducted this affair with as much secrecy as possible – snatched moments together, stolen kisses behind the garden wall. But this could never be enough for a woman like Louise, who lived for the grand romantic gesture. They must get away for a weekend, she decided, and chose the seaside town of Brighton as the place to get away to. The plan was this: first Louise would tell her sister she was taking Manfred to France for a few days to see his father and would pick the boy up from Miss Gentle. According to what she told Lucas, Louise was making 'other arrangements' for her son.

On 16 October 1899, Louise wrote to Helen Gentle advising her that Manfred's father wanted him to be brought up by a cousin, and that she would collect the child and take him to London Bridge railway station and thence to France. On 24 October Louise bought a black shawl and instructed Eudore Lucas to meet her at Brighton on the twenty-eighth. The boy Manfred was duly collected amid some tears from the kindly

Miss Gentle, and both mother and son were later seen sitting in the waiting room at London Bridge; one witness later described the child as being 'fretful'.

Three hours later, at around 6.30 p.m., the naked body of a young boy was found, wrapped in a black shawl, in another railway waiting room at Dalston Junction, over in north London and the nearest station to where Louise was living. The child had been battered over the head and then strangled. Beside the body lay the brick used to bludgeon him; it was similar to others found in the garden rockery at the Masset home in Stoke Newington.

Louise Masset arrived at Brighton, so she later claimed, off the 4.00 p.m. train from London, but did not book into her hotel until around 9.45. In the meantime, she said, she had strolled along the sea-front and then taken a light supper in a restaurant. On the following afternoon, Saturday 28 October, Louise was at Brighton station again, this time to meet Lucas off the 3.30 train. They embraced, and then sped back to Louise's hotel room. What they did there was entirely their own business. Back at the station something of far more importance was going on. In the waiting room – the one in which Louise had been waiting for her lover – a bundle of children's clothing was found wrapped up in a brown parcel; the clothing had belonged to little Manfred Masset.

Louise and Lucas had their weekend of passion and returned to London on Sunday evening; Louise did not go back to Stoke Newington, but went instead to stay with another sister in Croydon.

Meanwhile, the publicity surrounding the child found dead at Dalston had aroused Miss Gentle's worst fears, and she had gone to the police and identified Manfred's body. Two days later, on the Monday, Louise Masset was arrested in Croydon and charged with her son's murder.

On the face of it, the case against Louise was a strong one. For a start she had told everybody that she was taking Manfred to France, and she was doing no such thing. It was then claimed that instead of taking the four o'clock Brighton train she had returned to Dalston Junction from London Bridge, there killed Manfred and wrapped his body in the shawl bought just days previously, tying his clothes in a bundle which she took with her first to London Bridge and thence to Brighton. There was even a sighting of Loulse by the waiting-room attendant, who claimed she saw the same woman that had been sitting with the fretting child earlier in the afternoon, but this time she was alone. Louise, the prosecution said at her trial, took a later train to Brighton, which is why she only checked into the hotel at 9.45. After her weekend with Eudore Lucas, during the course of which she had carelessly left the bundle of Manfred's clothes in the waiting room, Louise Masset returned to London, not to her home in Stoke Newington but to another address.

But why, Louise Masset's attorney asked? Why *should* she go through this elaborate and unconvincing charade in order to dispose of a child for whom she had never shown anything but the greatest affection? Why expose herself to scorn and ridicule by making public her affair with a boy almost young enough to be her son?

Here is what Louise Masset had to say about the events leading up to that Saturday. It had all begun, she told the court, the previous month, in September 1899, when she had taken Manfred to the park. There she met two women named Browning; one of them was accompanied by her young daughter, and the other was her sister-in-law. During the conversation, Louise confided that she was not entirely happy with the way in which Miss Gentle was handling Manfred's education. The women replied that, by a great coincidence, they were at that very time setting up a small private school in King's Road, Chelsea. At a second, apparently unplanned meeting, Louise decided to remove her son from the care of Miss Gentle and place him with the Brownings. It was arranged that they should meet 'half-way', at London Bridge station. It was unfortunate, Louise said, that she was late meeting the Browning women, because it meant that she did not have time to accompany them and settle little Manfred in before catching the four o'clock to Brighton. She just had enough time to hand over the £12 deposit on the boy's board and education before her son was hurried off between the two women.

Needless to say, there was no private school in King's Road, and Mrs Browning and her sister-in-law were never traced, nor, if they existed, did they come forward to speak in Louise's defence. Could the jury really believe that the Brownings would carry out the sequence of actions surrounding little Manfred's tragic death just in order to frame Louise; did they really follow her down to Brighton and leave the child's clothing in the waiting room? Had they gone secretly to the house in Stoke Newington in order to collect a murder weapon from the rockery? The jury thought not, and it required a retirement of less than fifteen minutes before they returned a verdict of guilty. Louise Masset was hanged at Newgate on 9 January 1900. The jury was vindicated in their decision when, just before she went to the gallows, Louise is supposed to have told Ellen Hayes, an Inspector of Prisons, that she had killed Manfred to preserve him from the shame illegitimacy would bring him in later life.

I am sure, given the facts, that Louise *did* murder her son; but for a far more cynical reason than to shield him from ridicule. Louise was in love, and no matter the difference in their ages, it is not impossible that she saw a very real prospect of marriage to Eudore Lucas; the last thing she needed was to be burdened with another man's child.

MERRIFIELD, Louisa   By the time she knocked on Sarah Ricketts' front door applying for a job, Loulsa Merrifield already had quite a colourful history. She had been born Louisa Highway, one of five daughters, to a miner from Wigan. Although the family were brought up in the Methodist tradition, Loulsa showed early signs of rebellion by joining the Salvation Army. At the age of twenty-five, Louisa became Mrs Joseph Ellison and between them they had four children. Sadly for everybody, Louisa preferred the gin bottle to the baby bottle, and very soon Mrs Ellison was a permanent fixture in the Wigan pubs and her children were permanent guests of the local council children's home.

In 1949 Joseph Ellison passed away, leaving Louisa free to marry their lodger, seventy-eight-year-old Richard Weston. The difference in their ages – Louisa was then forty-two – made financial speculation at least a possible motive for wedlock. Especially as the old man died less than three months later. In 1950, the widow Weston remarried; this time to Alfred Merrifield, twenty-four years her senior. It is obvious that Alfred did not provide the hoped for financial rewards, because we next find the Merrifields taking up a succession of domestic posts, Louisa as housekeeper, Alfred, as far as he was able, as handyman. Their lack of success in these roles is attested by the fact that the Merrifields were obliged to move on no fewer than twenty times in three years. During this period Louisa also managed to acquire a modest prison record for ration-book fraud.

This, then, was the couple that presented themselves at the door of a three-roomed bungalow in Devonshire Road, Blackpool, in the early part of 1953. They were answering an advertisement placed in the local newspaper by Mrs Sarah Ricketts. Mrs Ricketts, at the age of seventy-nine, felt the need for a housekeeper-companion. She was clearly no judge of character, because out of more than fifty hopeful applicants she chose Louisa Merrifield. Alfred, now seventy-one and showing distinct signs of slowing down, was a bit superfluous, but loyally Louisa insisted that he was part of the package.

It was an uneasy relationship from the start. Mrs Ricketts was a difficult woman and had already lost two husbands to suicide. Mrs Merrifield was a truculent dullard with a taste for drink.

Before long Mrs Ricketts was complaining to anybody who cared to listen about how badly she was being treated, how she was kept short of food: 'I don't know what they are doing with all my money,' she told the milkman. Well part of it at least was disappearing down Louisa's throat on regular excursions to the local ale-houses. And with her tongue loosened, Mrs Merrifield began to say some very strange things – about an elderly lady who had just died and left her a bungalow worth £4,000. Sometimes she made the same claims when sober: 'I've just had a bit of luck,' she told one acquaintance, 'where I've been living the old lady has died and left me the bungalow.' That was on 25 March.

The fact is, much of this was true. For some inexplicable reason Mrs Ricketts *had* made Louisa and Alfred beneficiaries of her will. They *had* been left the house. But Mrs Ricketts was certainly not dead. Not then anyway.

When Sarah Ricketts did die, on the night of 13 April, it might well have passed without fuss – but for Mrs Merrifield's odd predictions. One woman, a Mrs Brewer, read about Sarah Ricketts' death in the local paper, and it caused her to remember a conversation with Mrs Merrifield: 'We're landed,' Louisa told her friend. 'I went to live with an old lady and she died and left me the bungalow worth £4,000.' The conversation had taken place three days *before* Mrs Ricketts died. Which is why Mrs Brewer paid a visit to the police station.

A post-mortem examination of Mrs Ricketts' body was carried out by Dr G.B. Manning, and it was his opinion that she had died as the result of phosphorus poisoning. Meanwhile, the police were searching the bungalow and digging up every inch of the garden in their hunt for the phosphorus-based rat poison, Rodine, known to have been purchased by Alfred Merrifield. For Mrs Merrifield's part, she decided to add a touch of eccentric solemnity to the proceedings by arranging for the Salvation Army band to play *Abide with Me* outside the bungalow while the digging was going on. In fact, not a trace of poison was ever found in the house or the garden which might account for Mrs Ricketts' death. Not so Louisa Merrifield's handbag, for in here police found a sticky teaspoon, coated, the analyst said, with a mixture of rum and phosphorus.

Mr and Mrs Merrifield stood trial jointly charged with murder at the Manchester Assizes on 20 July 1953. The trial lasted eleven days, during which the jury heard about the last hours of Sarah Ricketts' life. She had actually been examined by a doctor on 13 April, the day before she died, and was found to be as healthy as a person of her age might expect. That night, however, Mrs Ricketts fell sick: 'I was up and down with her five or six times that night,' Mrs Merrifield told the court. 'I heard her go to the bathroom again, she was under the tap. I asked her if she was sick and she said "No". I got her into bed again. She went to the toilet and cried bitterly and said "You don't know how ill I am." I got her to bed, and she seemed to go quieter. She said she thanked both my husband and me for what we had done. Those were her last words; she had lost her speech by that time.' A most touching account by a devoted housekeeper you might have thought. That is until it was revealed in cross-examination that despite the obvious serious-ness of Mrs Ricketts' condition, Louisa Merrifield did not summon medical help until nearly eleven hours later. Asked why, Mrs Merrifield replied: 'Well it was not such a nice time in the morning to go out on the streets and call a doctor.'

The Merrifields' defence was that Sarah Ricketts died of natural causes – of cirrhosis of the liver – though even Professor Webster, the defence medical expert, had to agree that phosphorus was present in her body.

The jury found Louisa Merrifield guilty of Mrs Ricketts' murder, but could not agree about Alfred. In the end, the Crown decided not to pursue a retrial and Merrifield was discharged. After having her appeal dismissed, Mrs Merrifield was hanged at Strangeways Prison, Manchester, on 18 September 1953.

Alfred went back to live in his rightfully inherited bungalow in Devonshire Road, and earned a little extra money appearing in Blackpool side-shows; he died in 1962, aged eighty.

METYARD, Sarah, and her daughter, Sarah Sarah Metyard was a milliner, and her daughter her assistant, in Hanover Square, west London. In the year 1758 the mother had five apprentice girls bound to her from different parish workhouses, among whom were Anne Naylor and her sister.

Anne Naylor, being of a sickly constitution, was not able to do as much work as the other apprentices of about the same age, and therefore she became the more immediate object of the fury of the barbarous Metyards, whose repeated acts of cruelty at length occasioned the unhappy girl to abscond. She was dragged back, and confined in an upper apartment, where she was allowed each day no other sustenance than a small piece of bread and a little water.

Seizing an opportunity of escaping from her confinement, unperceived she got into the street, and ran to a milk carrier, whom she begged to protect her, saying that if she returned she must certainly perish through the want of food and severe treatment she daily received. Being soon missed, she was followed by the younger Metyard, who seized her by the neck, forced her into the house, and threw her again upon the bed in the room where she had been confined. She was then seized by the old woman, who held her down while the daughter beat her in a most cruel manner with the handle of a broom.

They afterwards put her into a back room on the second storey, tied a cord round her waist, and her hands behind her, and fastened her to the door in such a manner that it was impossible for her to either sit or lie down. She was compelled to remain in this situation for three successive days; but they permitted her to go to bed at the usual hours at night. Having received no kind of nutriment for three days and two nights, her strength was so exhausted that, being unable to walk upstairs, she crawled to the safety of the garret on her hands and knees.

While she remained tied up on the second floor the other apprentices were ordered to work in an adjoining apartment, that they might be deterred from disobedience by being witnesses to the unhappy girl's sufferings; but they were enjoined, on the penalty of being subjected to equal severity, against according her any kind of relief.

On the fourth day she faltered in speech, and presently afterwards expired. The other girls, seeing the whole weight of her body supported on the strings which confined her to the door, were greatly alarmed and called out: 'Miss Sally! Miss Sally! Nan does not move.' Then the daughter came upstairs, saying: 'If she does not move, I will make her move!'; and then beat the deceased on the head with the heel of a shoe.

Perceiving no signs of life, she called to her mother, who came upstairs and ordered the strings that confined the deceased to be cut; she then laid the body across her lap and directed one of the apprentices where to find a bottle with some hartshorn drops. When the child had brought the drops, she and the other girls were ordered to go downstairs. The mother and daughter, being convinced that the object of their barbarity was dead, conveyed the body to the garret. They related to the other apprentices that Nanny had been in a fit, but was perfectly recovered, adding that she was locked in the garret lest she should again run away; and in order to give an air of plausibility to their tale, at noon the daughter carried a plate of meat upstairs, saying it was for Nanny's dinner.

They locked the body of the deceased in a box on the fourth day after the murder, and, having left the garret door open and the street door on the jar, one of the apprentices was told to call Nanny down to dinner, and to tell her that, if she promised to behave well in the future, she would be no longer confined. Upon the return of the child, she said Nanny was not above-stairs; and after a great parade of searching every part of the house they reflected upon her as being of an intractable disposition and pretended she had run away.

The sister of the deceased, who was apprenticed to the same inhuman mistress, mentioned to a lodger in the house that she was persuaded her sister was dead; observing that it was not probable she had gone away, since parts of her apparel still remained in the garret. The suspicions of this girl coming to the knowledge of the inhuman wretches, they, with a view of preventing a discovery, cruelly murdered her and secreted the body.

The body of Anne remained in the box two months, during which time the garret door was kept locked, lest the offensive smell should lead to a discovery. The stench became so powerful that the Metyards judged it prudent to remove the remains of the unhappy victim of their barbarity; and therefore, on the evening of 25 December, they cut the body in pieces, and tied the head and trunk up in one cloth and the limbs in another, excepting one hand, a finger belonging to which had been amputated before death*, and that they resolved to burn.

When the apprentices had gone to bed, the old woman put the hand in the fire, saying: 'The fire tells no tales.' She intended to consume the entire remains of the unfortunate girl by fire but, afraid that the smell would give rise to suspicion, changed that design, and took the bundles to the gully-hole in Chick Lane and endeavoured to throw the parts of the mangled corpse over the wall into the common sewer; but being unable to effect that, she left them among the mud and water that was collected before the grate of the sewer.

Some pieces of the body were discovered about twelve o'clock by the watchman, and he mentioned the circumstance to the constable of the night. The constable applied to one of the overseers of the parish, by whose direction the parts of the body were collected and taken to the watch-house. On the following day the matter was communicated to Mr Umfreville, the

*And so would serve as a means of identification.

coroner, who examined the pieces found by the watchman; but he supposed them to be parts of a corpse taken from a churchyard for the use of some surgeon, and declined to summon a jury.

Four years elapsed before the discovery of this awful murder, which at length happened in the following manner. Continual disagreements prevailed between mother and daughter; and, though the latter had now arrived at the age of maturity, she was often beaten, and otherwise treated severely. Thus provoked, she sometimes threatened to kill herself, and at others give information against her mother as a murderer.

At last information concerning the affair was given to the overseers of Tottenham parish, and the mother and daughter were committed to the Gatehouse. At the ensuing Old Bailey sessions they were both sentenced to be executed on the following Monday, and then to be conveyed to Surgeons' Hall for dissection.

The mother, being in a fit when she was put into the cart, lay at her length till she came to the place of execution, when she was raised up, and means were used for her recovery, but without effect, so that she departed this life in a state of insensibility. From the time of leaving Newgate to the moment of her death the daughter wept incessantly. After hanging the usual time [one hour] the bodies were conveyed in a hearse to Surgeons' Hall, where they were exposed to the curiosity of the public, and then dissected.

MILLER, Charlotte   Charlotte Miller was born in 1962 in Melbourne, Australia, to Hilda Miller and her husband. The marriage had not lasted, and Charlotte was brought up by Hilda and her new partner Arthur Housdon. On 10 January 1980, when Charlotte was eighteen, her mother was discovered dead, apparently from a self-administered overdose of barbiturates; it was known that Mrs Miller believed, quite wrongly, that she was dying of cancer.

At least that was the theory until Thomas Hunt, a sharp-witted detective with the Melbourne Police, found there were no fingerprints on the pill bottle; it was a rare suicide indeed who wiped the evidence clean before dying! Inspector Hunt was also suspicious of the relationship between Housdon and Charlotte; and he was later proved to have good reason. Under questioning, Arthur Housdon's already loose grip on his self-control broke, and he confessed that while Hilda was in hospital undergoing one of her tests, Charlotte had seduced him. He also told detectives that, out of jealousy, the girl had killed her own mother. Confronted with her stepfather's statement, Charlotte Miller fully admitted – without the least show of remorse – to murdering the woman she believed stood in the way of her future happiness with Arthur Housdon. Charlotte was a juvenile according to Australian law, and was thus committed to the care of the juvenile authorities.

MITCHELL, Pauline, and **HEADLEY, Peter** The discovery of a motive is vital to the speedy solution of a homicide case. Any detective will tell you that if you can find the motive, a suspect won't be far behind. And by and large this is true. But so is the reverse – a wrong interpretation of motive will lead to entirely the wrong suspect.

The first the Sydney police department knew of James Mitchell's death was a telephone call received at their communications centre from an ambulanceman's radio-telephone. It was around 6.40 on the morning of 27 May 1981. Fifteen minutes earlier, Mrs Christine Lane was woken from her sleep by an insistent, almost insane, hammering at her front door. Having first checked through a window that she was not the focus of a homicidal maniac, Mrs Lane put on a wrap and hurried down to let in her frantic neighbour Pauline Mitchell. Mrs Mitchell, barely able to speak for sobbing, said that she had woken up to find her husband slumped on the floor beside the bed, blood trickling from his mouth. Mrs Lane telephoned the ambulance service who discovered on their arrival that James Mitchell was bleeding not only from his mouth, but also from what looked like a stab wound in his side; he was dead.

When he arrived at the scene, the assistant coroner confirmed the paramedic team's assessment, stating in a subsequent report that Mitchell had been lying on his back in bed asleep when the unknown assassin stabbed him just once, penetrating the heart. Body spasm would have caused the victim to fall off the bed.

Undoubtedly murder. So what about motive? The motive would appear, on the face of the evidence, to have been robbery – at least that was Pauline Mitchell's best guess; a burglar interrupted in the execution of his crime. Jim Mitchell had, by the age of fifty-one, amassed the just rewards of building up a successful chain of garages, and his expensive lifestyle might well attract the criminous. But satisfying as this simple explanation was, it did not explain why nothing was missing from the house – despite the fact that a quantity of cash and Mrs Mitchell's jewellery were there for the taking. Besides, why would any burglar want to stab a sleeping man, and expose himself to the risk of a struggle and of waking the sleeping wife next to him and having to kill her as well – and then flee empty-handed? It did seem a bit far-fetched when looked at like that.

Given the high percentage of domestic killings, the police were quite justified in next taking a serious look at Mrs Mitchell as a suspect. Perhaps elimination was the motive; perhaps Pauline had a lover and wanted to cancel out the opposition. It was certainly an attractive theory – it would explain why nothing was stolen, why Mrs Mitchell was unharmed, and why there was no evidence of a forced entry. But as a motive it also had serious flaws. The most scrupulous investigation of her past and present revealed Pauline Mitchell as decidedly not the type to have lovers. Despite the difference in their ages – Mrs Mitchell was thirty-one – the couple had seemed genuinely devoted to each other, and Pauline wanted for nothing, she had total access to the family funds.

The next motive detectives tried out was revenge. Nobody – not even a warm-hearted, generous, Mr Nice Guy like Jim Mitchell – could build such a prosperous business empire without upsetting a few people. It was a long, tedious job for the officers of the Sydney force, but in a matter of days they had assembled profiles of all Mitchell's business contacts, his employees and his ex-employees. It was in this last category that detectives found what they were looking for: The Suspect. He was a twenty-two-year-old motor-car mechanic named James Cox; Cox had at one time been employed in the Mitchell workshops, but had been fired recently for joy-riding in a customer's car. He hadn't taken the sacking too well, and threatened all manner of violence. The fact that James Cox already possessed an impressive police record for offences involving violence sealed his fate. So there it was. Find the motive and you will find the suspect.

It was while the police effort was being diverted into the search for a fugitive James Cox, that Sydney detectives received an extraordinary letter. In it, the woman said that her husband was having an affair with Pauline Mitchell. More intriguing still was the claim that the affair had started fifteen years ago, and that in those early days an illegitimate child had been born to the couple. Now, most murder cases attract their share of eccentrics and timewasters, seeking the spotlight, making false confessions, making telephone calls with bogus information, sending anonymous letters . . . The difference about this letter was that it wasn't anonymous, it had been signed by Mrs Joan Headley, the wife of the allegedly errant Peter Headley, and it gave the Headleys' address. The senior officer who visited Mrs Headley reported back that it was her theory that Pauline Mitchell and Peter had planned and carried out the murder in order for Pauline to inherit the business; Headley would then divorce Joan and marry Pauline. They had to admit, it made sense. Motive, you see, the motive was there. Or it was if what Joan Handley told them was true.

Pauline Mitchell and Peter Headley were invited to make separate statements about their alleged affair. At first Pauline denied ever having set eyes on Headley, and he in his turn claimed he only knew her as the boss's wife – apparently he had worked for Mitchell for a while. But the police had been putting in overtime on the history of the Mitchell-Headley saga, and had traced their child. The girl had been brought up by Pauline's mother, as Pauline's sister – not even the child knew who her real mother was. Suddenly Pauline Mitchell remembered; yes, she did know Peter Headley, yes, they had produced a daughter from their relationship fifteen years ago, but *no*, she had emphatically not seen Headley since. As for Peter Headley, his memory was improving too; it had improved so much that he was able to remember *still* being involved in an affair with Pauline, after a chance meeting in 1980.

In the end, both Pauline and Peter were accusing each other of planning the murder of James Mitchell. They convinced the police, they convinced the jury; and on 27 July 1981 they were both sentenced to life imprisonment for that murder.

MOORE, Helen Patricia   In December 1980 at the Supreme Court in Parramatta, Sydney, Australia, eighteen-year-old Helen Moore stood trial accused of the murder of three children and the attempted murder of two others.

Moore, who was living with her mother and stepfather, had been trusted to mind her seven-year-old stepbrother while the adults went out for the day. This was not an unusual family pattern, but today, while the boy was innocently watching television, Helen inexplicably put her hands over his mouth and attempted to suffocate him. The terrified child struggled fiercely and almost broke free, but in the end his physical strength was no match for his spiteful teenaged attacker, and he was soon made captive; Helen then pressed her hands over his nose and mouth until her small victim breathed no more. After this uncommonly strenuous and exhausting exercise, Miss Moore calmly went upstairs for a shower.

Questioned by the police, Helen admitted that she had also, three months previously, suffocated a two-year-old girl asleep in her cot and, a few months prior to that, had suffocated a baby girl of sixteen months. Back in the previous year, Helen confided, she had tried to kill two other youngsters, the baby boy being left totally blind and without the use of his legs as a result. Helen Moore had been baby-minding!

By way of explanation for this extraordinary wickedness, Helen insisted that she had attacked the children out of anguish over the death of her own baby brother; the difference was that he had died of natural causes. Helen also maintained, truthfully or not, that she had been having sex since she was eight years old with an 'uncle' (in fact, he was the father of one of the children she killed). The uncle, hardly surprisingly, vehemently denied the allegation.

In spite of a convincing submission by her defence counsel that Helen should be found not guilty by reason of insanity, the jury nevertheless convicted her on all charges. Helen Moore was sentenced to life imprisonment for the three murders, with concurrent terms of ten years each on the indictments for attempted murder.

MOORS MURDERS *see* **HINDLEY, Myra**

MYRTEL, Hera (aka Hera BESSARABO) Mexico at the turn of the last century; a mysterious country soaked in the exotic glamour of its Aztec history; a land of opportunity for those with the courage and determination to carve themselves a place beneath the sun. It was here that Madame Bessarabo spent the first years of her married life. She was Madame Jacques then.

She had been born Hera Myrtel in Lyon, France, on 25 October 1868. A sensitive, creative girl, she both read and wrote poetry eagerly, and until the bankruptcy of the family business, Hera had worked as an assistant to her father. It was in her twenty-sixth year that Mlle Myrtel had voyaged to South America and there met Paul Jacques, a traveller in silk who was twenty years her senior. It was shortly after their return to Paris in 1904 that, as Madame Jacques, she became mother to baby daughter Paule, and as Hera Myrtel became mother to a series of literary works of dubious quality which she had printed at her own expense. She clearly felt that this entitled her to collect a 'salon' – mostly of young men, most of whom became her lovers.

The Jacques marriage, to give it credit, had lasted for almost twenty years before succumbing dramatically on 8 March 1914. Despite a previous attempt by his wife to poison his soup with corrosive sublimate, Monsieur Jacques had stayed put at 107 rue des Sèvres. On the eve of his leaving for a business trip to Mexico, he became the victim of a fatal shot, fired, so the coroner's court ruled, by his own hand. The following year Hera Jacques returned to Mexico.

One day, the police in Mexico City were confronted by an apparently distraught Madame Jacques sobbing out a somewhat preposterous story of four hooded horsemen who had ridden up to the ranch, dragged her head ranch hand from the house, and with the verbal receipt: 'This settles the account,' shot him dead and rode off.

It was undeniable that Mexico was – and is – a violent place; and ranchers and travellers were troubled with more than their share of 'bandidos'. Despite strenuous police efforts, the four killers were never traced.

However, sympathetic as the authorities had been, local gossip was far less charitable.

As time went lazily by, Madame made the acquaintance of a Romanian wood merchant named Bessarabo. Actually, Bessarabo was not his real name, but to him at least, it seemed preferable to the less romantic Charles Weissman with which he had been christened.

With almost indecent haste, Madame sold the Jacques hacienda and moved into Mexico City, where her beauty and Bessarabo's wealth made her the toast of the French colonists.

After their marriage, the Bessarabos and young Paule returned to France and a life of civilized gaiety mingling in Parisian society. But the good times were not to last, and by the time the rumbling thunder of 'the war to end wars' rolled over Paris, Madame was preoccupied with a young French soldier, while Monsieur sought refuge in the comforts of a young typist whom he had installed in a discreet country retreat.

Despite the end of the war, there was no ceasefire for the battling Bessarabos, and when the couple were obliged to be in each other's company there were spiteful quarrels. On one occasion – it was the evening of 8 July 1920 – Madame Bessarabo in a particularly violent fit of pique, pulled a gun on her husband and with words roughly translating as: 'Get out or I'll lay you out', fired at him – a shot which would surely have found its mark if the quick-thinking Charles had not thrown himself to the floor.

By now it must have seemed to observers that the late World War had transferred to the Bessarabo household. And then, out of the blue, a letter bearing a South American postmark created further upheaval, throwing the family into panic. Extra security locks were put on doors and windows which were kept shut at all times. To those few confidants who spoke to Bessarabo during the following weeks, all he would say was: 'a man from the past is seeking my life'.

On 30 July, a second letter threw the unfortunate businessman into a further panic. A couple of days after that, Charles Bessarabo disappeared.

A man like Bessarabo cannot be missing for long before people begin to ask uncomfortable questions – like 'Where is he?' And it seemed appropriate, in the first instance at least, to ask the person most likely to know his whereabouts – his wife. Charles Bessarabo's mistress asked her; his chauffeur asked her. And when the chauffeur reported his master missing, the police asked her. To all, she answered that he had gone to Mexico.

Less than satisfied, the police began to make discreet inquiries, during the course of which they interviewed a boatman with a strange story to tell, of two women who had hired a craft late at night and rowed it to the centre of the dark lake to throw a heavy bundle overboard.

In the heat of the late summer of 1920, the contents of a trunk held for collection at Nancy railway station had begun to make their presence known over a large area of the left-luggage office. So offensive did the smell become that the local gendarmerie were called in to remove the luggage before anyone actually passed out.

The contents of the trunk, trussed up with rope and wrapped in a waterproof sheet, proved to be a man's body, naked save for a red flannel waistcoat, a bullet hole in the head through which his brains were seeping. The remains were deposited in the mortuary to await identification.

Unlike what happened in many of the celebrated trunk murders, in this case the police had no trouble at all identifying the contents of the Nancy baggage. The trunk had been dispatched by train from Paris by a woman giving her name as Bessarabo, whose handwriting was Paule's. That her stepfather was missing was a coincidence that the police could not ignore.

When Madame Bessarabo was invited to the morgue to view the Nancy remains she was emphatic: 'That,' she declared, 'is not my husband. He was a young man, and a handsome one. This is old and ugly.' Even so, it did beg the question why her daughter should have sent a corpse – *any* corpse – to Nancy packed in a trunk.

Now that was something Madame *could* explain, though it sounded as fanciful as the apocalyptic riders who had put an end to her rancher in Mexico. It involved a secret agent by the name of Becker, and a Mexican secret society who had sent the letters threatening her husband's life.

But what about the body in the trunk?

Madame told the police that Bessarabo had contacted her some weeks after his disappearance and asked her to meet him at Paris's Gare du Nord at eleven in the morning, whence they would journey to Montmorency where the Bessarabos had their summer house. After loading two trunks into a taxi – one containing papers which her husband wished to go through – Madame arrived at the station. Charles Bessarabo kept the appointment, arriving by taxi with a trunk. He stopped only long enough to greet his wife and promise to return shortly. The taxi did come back, with the trunk but without Bessarabo; only his letter directing her to send the trunk by train to Nancy, which instruction Paule later carried out. For all Madame knew of it, the body was that of the elusive enemy agent Becker who had been tracking her husband. Bessarabo, she insisted, was alive and well in South America, though unable to declare himself for fear of the secret society!

It wasn't really much of a defence to present to the jury, especially as Paule had already been proved to have purchased the waterproof sheet and cord used to pack the body. It was the prosecution's contention that Madame Bessarabo, in a fit of jealousy over her husband's infidelity, and probably aggravated by drink and drugs, had shot her husband, and with the help of her daughter had disposed of the body.

In fact, it was not that far from the truth. We know, because on the last day of the trial, a previously silent Paule Jacques suddenly burst out: 'The truth, the truth. I must speak the truth.' Her version of the truth, which is about as close as we are likely to get, was that her stepfather had been making her mother's life a misery for years, and that one night she had awakened to the sound of a shot. Rushing to her mother's room, she had cried out: 'What have you done?'

'It was his life or mine. I cannot reveal the terrible secret of what has passed here tonight, but believe me, I did not kill him,' her mother had told her.

Paule, who had clearly inherited many of the histrionic genes from her mother then recalled that in the period of drowsiness just before the shot was fired, she heard two male voices, one of which was a familiar voice from long ago – it was her father, the once-deceased but now returned Monsieur Jacques! After an impassioned plea on her mother's behalf, Paule concluded: 'Although I can tell you all I heard and saw that night, I cannot tell you all I suspect – nay, what I know, for it is my secret. I understand that my father was still alive, and imagine him to be the cause of the crime.'

So what *was* the truth of the matter? Whose *was* the body in the trunk? Who killed him? And why? And what of the secret society?

The French jury decided that it was really far simpler than that; in fact, it was as the prosecution had contended, and they returned a verdict of guilty under extenuating circumstances. Madame Bessarabo was sentenced to twenty years' imprisonment. Her daughter, unaccountably, was acquitted. But Justice is a hard mistress, and it was recounted by one senior police officer involved in the case that Paule Jacques, 'An unhappy waif, lost in Paris, lives in misery.'

NEWELL, Susan   The sight was not an unusual one, not on the streets of this soot-grimed suburb of Scotland's second city, with its skyline of foundries and tube works. Not the sort of thing to remark on – a thin, shabby woman of indeterminable age pushing a rickety perambulator full of clothing with one hand and steering an eight-year-old child with the other. Susan Newell, her daughter Janet and the pram had emerged from the single room they occupied with her husband at 2 Newlands Street, Glasgow, in the early light of a June morning in 1923. Their route took them along Dundyvan Road, through Whifflet Street, and on to the North Road in the direction of the city's centre. Here a lorry driver, seeing her struggling with the load (which now included young Janet atop the clothing) stopped and gave Susan and her belongings a lift. Between them, they lifted the pram into the back of the vehicle, and Susan and Janet climbed into the driver's cab with their good samaritan. When they reached the Parkhead Cross and turned into Duke Street, Mrs Newell, daughter and pram parted company with the lorry, and in the same shambling fashion as before resumed their journey.

Mrs Newell had now reached a part of Glasgow where such behaviour does attract attention. It had certainly attracted the attention of one woman who, looking through her kitchen window, had watched with horrified fascination while Susan Newell had off-loaded her pram from the truck. It was not the strange-looking woman herself, or even her ragamuffin child that held her gaze. It was the bundle; or, rather, the small human foot which protruded from one corner. The poor woman was just telling herself that she must be mistaken when a head popped out of another part of the package. It was all over in seconds; the bundle was retied, and the odd party set off once again up Duke Street as though nothing untoward had happened. Enlisting the support of her sister, the horrified housewife followed the Newells at a distance, on the way picking up reinforcements in the persons of a passing man and a police constable.

Susan Newell and her bizarre cargo had by now entered one of the small courtyards off Duke Street. Susan set down her bundle and was preparing to depart without it when she came face to face with the law. After a brief chase round the yard, during which she attempted to scale a six-foot wall, Mrs Newell was taken firmly into custody. It remained the unpleasant duty of the constable to tackle the bundle. Untying the knots at the corners, and removing an assortment of rags and clothing, the shocked officer revealed the body of a small boy trussed up like a chicken.

At the police station, an indignant Susan Newell explained that it had been her husband who killed young John Johnstone, despite all her best efforts to prevent it. Although she clearly considered him a thoroughly worthless bully of a man, Mrs Newell had, for her husband's peace of mind, sought to remove the ghastly evidence of his impetuous crime.

The story seemed about as plausible as anything else in this most implausible scenario, so John Newell became a wanted man. As it was, the police did not need to look for him; Newell, reading of the murder in the following morning's newspaper, went straight to the nearest police station and told them that he knew nothing of the killing, and indeed had been nowhere near Coatbridge when it was supposed to have occurred.

Nevertheless, John Newell stood beside his thirty-year-old wife in the dock of Glasgow's Justiciary Building when her trial began. Slowly, through a procession of more than three score witnesses, the prosecution pieced together the appalling crime committed on the person of thirteen-year-old John Johnstone. John had come home from school in Coatbridge at four o'clock on the day in question, and after tea went out saying he was going to the cinema. On the way he met a friend who gave him some newspapers which John went off to sell. He never returned home, and on the following day Robert Johnstone went to the mortuary to identify his son's body. Death had resulted from manual strangulation, and his spine had been dislocated. In addition, there were burns on the side of John's head consistent with his coming into contact with fire while he was still alive.

Mrs Young, the Newells' landlady, told the jury that on that Wednesday evening she gave notice to Susan Newell to vacate her room; there had been many disagreements during the short three weeks of her tenancy, and the noise of the Newells' fighting and arguing had become intolerable. Between 6.30 and 7.00 p.m., John Johnstone had come to the house selling his newspapers, knocked on Susan Newell's door and was invited in.

Mrs Young had gone about her business, and for all she knew the boy left. She heard some banging about upstairs, but assumed that it was Mrs Newell packing to leave. During the early hours of the following morning, Susan Newell was heard to go out of the house twice, once just after midnight and again at about 1.45 a.m., returning at 2.30. After this all was quiet until about 7.30 a.m., when Mrs Young heard Newell and her daughter go out of the front door. The sequence of events which followed have already been detailed.

So much for Mrs Newell's movements. But what of the man

who stood beside her? John Newell was a slightly built man of thirty-three, a worker at the local tube factory; in his evidence to the court, Newell gave the following account of his whereabouts during the days preceding the murder.

For a start, on the Monday he had quarrelled violently with his wife and she, in characteristic form, had dealt him a couple of severe blows to the head. On the following day he attended his brother's funeral, and afterwards had another row with his wife; that night he spent at his father's house. On Wednesday, the day John Johnstone was murdered, Newell was in Glasgow from noon until 9.00 p.m., and a number of people had testified to speaking with him. Between 9.00 and 10.30 he was travelling between Glasgow and Coatbridge to visit a sister, where he sat chatting for about an hour. After this, John Newell could not have had a better alibi – he was at Coatbridge police station discussing what could be done about his wife assaulting him.

This timetable had already been thoroughly checked by the police, and witnesses had been interviewed who confirmed Newell's statement. In that light, it is extraordinary that he should ever have been charged alongside his wife with a murder which he could not possibly have had any part in. The error was soon rectified when the trial judge, Lord Justice-Clerk Alness, ordered John Newell to be formally acquitted.

There followed a further, even less excusable feature of this trial which can, with hindsight, only be seen as a gross error of good taste. Eight-year-old Janet Newell was put in the witness box to testify against her mother. It would not happen now, small children are not subjected to such potentially traumatic ordeals; besides, there was already ample evidence of Susan Newell's guilt.

Janet had previously – on the wicked instructions of her mother – told police officers that John Newell had killed the boy. Now she told the truth; about the way her mother had killed John Johnstone, and after failing to hide the body under the floorboards, wrapped it up in a 'bag' and put it into the pram for subsequent disposal.

Susan Newell's defence of insanity was successfully disposed of by John Glaister, at the time Regius Professor of Forensic Medicine at Glasgow University. Glaister testified that, in his opinion, the prisoner had not exhibited the slightest sign of insanity – only markedly low intelligence. The fact that she had committed an unspeakably cruel and callous killing did not of itself prove madness in the sense required by law to uphold a defence of insanity. After a retirement of thirty-seven minutes, the all-male jury returned a verdict of guilty – though only by a majority, and with a strong recommendation to mercy.

Susan Newell received no more mercy than she had shown to young John Johnstone. On 10 October 1923 she became the first woman to be hanged in Scotland for fifty years (and in Glasgow for seventy).

NOZIÈRE, Violette   Poor Violette Nozière was one of those all too common products of an over-indulged childhood. In the eyes of Monsieur Nozière and his wife, little Violette could do no wrong, no matter how beastly her behaviour. So it was not surprising that little Violette grew up into a young woman who *believed* she could do no wrong. And that is very dangerous indeed.

Another result of her unfortunate upbringing was that nothing was ever good enough for Violette, and not content with an honest hard-working railway engineer for a father, she reinvented him as the railway's director. Unhappy with her own modest place in the scheme of things, Violette laid claim to being an heiress. Harmless really, rather sad; but Violette Nozière became so attached to her fantasies that she had to act them out. And of course, heiresses have lots of money, whereas Violette had very little. In order to keep up her pretence among her student peers, Violette took to prostitution by night and dishing out largesse during the day. Matters became complicated when Violette met a young man named Jean Dabin, eighteen years old, and a student like herself. To Dabin she made the most extravagant claims of all; soon, she promised, she would be taking him on a luxury holiday, soon she would inherit 200,000 francs. What she failed to mention, even had it seemed important to her, was that in order to inherit she would have to murder her parents.

Early in 1934 Violette had a run-through of her plan. First she powdered up a handful of Veronal tablets and spiked the elder Nozieres' coffee. They didn't die, but it made them very drowsy; so drowsy that they didn't notice Violette setting fire to the living room; so drowsy they didn't hear her run into the street shouting 'Fire! Fire!' Neighbours helped the dazed couple out into the fresh air and the blaze was soon under control. It was later put down to an electrical fault.

Monsieur and Madame Nozière were not so lucky the next time. For a start, Violette upped the dose of Veronal quite considerably. Having doctored their coffee, Violette sat and waited for them to die. In the early hours of the morning Violette was again out in the street yelling for help – 'Gas!' she was shouting. 'The gas pipe has burst.' When neighbours responded they turned off the gas tap which Violette had earlier turned on, and once more carried the Nozières to safety. By the time they reached hospital Monsieur Nozière was dead; Madame unexpectedly survived.

Violette, meanwhile, was out on the town squandering what ready cash she had managed to plunder from home. But Nemesis was never far behind, and when one of Violette's consorts recognized her photograph in the newspaper he turned her over to the gendarmerie.

The trial was brief – after all, there was not much to be said in Violette Nozière's favour, and anyway she really couldn't see a lot wrong with murdering her father. It was no doubt with this shocking truth in mind that the judge passed on Violette the ancient sentence of decapitation: 'That you will have your head cut off upon a public place in Paris. That you be taken there barefoot and wearing only a chemise, your head hidden beneath a veil. Before the execution is done, let this Judgement be publicly read.'

In fact, when emotions had settled, the awful Mademoiselle Nozière received the mercy she had no right to expect, and her sentence was commuted to life imprisonment.

P

PAPIN, Christine and Lea They called them 'Les Diaboliques', The Devils of Le Mans, though they could hardly have looked less diabolical. As they sat there in the small Palais de Justice at Le Mans, the sisters Christine and Lea Papin looked more like bewildered convent girls, their faces clouded, their eyes fixed to the floor. It was the morning of 20 September 1933, and after six months of escalating press hysteria the trial of the decade was about to begin. But that is to jump ahead.

Twenty-eight-year-old Christine Papin and her twenty-one-year-old sister were live-in servants in the employ of the Lancelin family. They were rather dull young ladies really, or perhaps 'unworldly' would be a more generous description. They seldom went out and had no real friends besides each other. If they were unexceptional as domestics then at least they were hard-working, honest and dutiful.

On the evening of 2 February 1933, Monsieur René Lancelin, a lawyer, returned home from his office expecting to collect his wife and his daughter Geneviève and go on to dinner with an old family friend. When he received no response to knocking on the door, René Lancelin walked round the corner to a public telephone and tried to get through to his wife; there was no reply. Lancelin went back to the house and tried knocking again. It was at this point that he became aware of something else not quite normal; all the lights in the house were out save for a small glimmer coming from the attic room occupied by the maids. Without wasting any more time Lancelin called the police.

Assisted by an inspector from the local force, Maître Lancelin broke into the house, switched on some lights, and began to search for some clue as to where his wife and daughter had gone. The ground floor of the house was deserted. It was on the first-floor landing that René Lancelin found them. Lying next to each other were the grotesquely mutilated bodies of Madame and Mademoiselle Lancelin. The carpet and stairs were soaked with their blood, and heavy bloodstaining stretched to the tops of the doors and walls. So badly had the two victims been slashed, stabbed and bludgeoned that they were virtually unrecognizable; Madame Lancelin's face had been completely crushed, and one of her eyes and several of her teeth were found some distance from her body.

Behind the locked door of their attic room, cowering naked in a single bed were Christine and Lea Papin. When the police inspector broke down the door and questioned them, Christine confessed to the killings without hesitation, making a long statement which would ultimately form the basis for the prosecution case when the sisters came to trial later in the year:

When Madame Lancelin came home to the house I told her the electric iron had broken again [there was, apparently, a longstanding problem with the fuses] and I had not been able to do the ironing. I saw Madame Lancelin was going to jump on me, so I leapt at her face and scratched her eyes with my fingers . . . No, that is not right, it was Mademoiselle Lancelin that I leapt on and her eyes I scratched out. My sister was jumping on Madame Lancelin and scratching her eyes out in the same way. As they lay cowering on the floor I went to the kitchen and fetched a hammer and a knife, and with these we attacked our mistresses. We exchanged weapons several times, striking at the head with the knife, hacking the body and legs, then hitting them with the hammer . . . They cried out, but I can't remember what they said. After that I bolted the entrance doors, I wanted the police to find the bodies before our master. Then we went to our room, took off our bloodstained clothes, locked the room door and lay down together on the bed. I have no regrets – or, rather, I can't tell you whether I have any regrets or not . . . I did not plan my crime, or feel any hatred towards them.

Lea Papin confirmed her sister's account of the savage attack, adding: 'The idea came suddenly when we heard Madame Lancelin scolding us . . . I would rather have had my mistresses' skins than they had ours.'

The trial of the 'Lambs who become Wolves' failed to get any closer to a motive for the dreadful killings. It was explained to the court how very well the maids were treated by the Lancelins – a state of affairs by no means common in other households at the time. They were paid well, ate the same food as the family and were not overworked; in fact, the Papin sisters freely admitted they were happy in their work. One has to wonder, though, whether there were not at least occasional confrontations between the two servants and the women of the house. Christine had already said that the fatal incident had been provoked by a problem with the electric iron. It had been a month earlier, in January 1933, that Lea had clumsily damaged it. On 1 February, the day before the killings, Madame Lancelin had deducted five francs from the girl's wages to pay for it, which seems a singularly petty act from a mistress who was supposed to have been so generous and considerate. On the following day, the second, the faulty iron had fused the lights in the house; this no doubt caused Madame no end of irritation, and it is at least possible that a mistress who would make a servant pay for a damaged iron would strike out at her in a moment of anger. Christine claimed that she simply 'jumped on' Madame Lancelin to prevent Madame jumping on her. Which seems to indicate that 'jumping on' was a not infrequent consequence of misdemeanours in the Lancelin ménage. Even so, such a savage response was hardly appropriate.

In the Papins' defence, Dr Logre, a celebrated psychiatrist of the time, gave his opinion that both Christine and Lea were insane. However, overwhelming counter-testimony that they were perfectly sane and indeed rational, persuaded the jury to return a guilty verdict on both sisters. Christine, thought to be the dominant partner in the crime, was sentenced to death; Lea was imprisoned for ten years. In accordance with French custom, Christine Papin was reprieved and her sentence commuted to life imprisonment. Ironically, after a few years reason began to desert her, and Christine Papin died in a mental hospital in 1937.

PAPIN, Lea *see* **PAPIN, Christine and Lea**

PARKER, Pauline Yvonne, and HULME, Juliet It was Tuesday afternoon, 22 June 1954, when two hysterical teenage girls rushed into a tea-shop in Canterbury, New Zealand, claiming that the mother of one of them had accidentally slipped, fallen and struck her head fatally on the pavement. When the police arrived to investigate they found Mrs Honora Parker lying dead on a pathway in the local park. And if she *had* tripped and banged her head, then how come there were more than forty separate wounds on her head and assorted abrasions on other parts of the body? The two girls had a bit of explaining to do; and explain they did, if not terribly convincingly. It was like this, sixteen-year-old Pauline Parker said, her mother had fallen just as they described it, and cracked her head on the ground. They decided the best thing to do would be to drag the unfortunate woman to help – Pauline took one leg and her fifteen-year-old friend Juliet Hulme took the other, and they pulled. As they made their laborious way along the path poor Mrs Parker's head kept 'bumping and banging'. So they left her and ran for help.

Not entirely surprisingly, the police found the story hard to believe, and even Pauline Parker must have seen the futility of pursuing it. After a bit of gentle persuasion, Pauline admitted to killing her own mother. She and Juliet had lured Mrs Parker to the secluded spot and bludgeoned her to death with a brick wrapped in a ladies' stocking; they had even left the weapon behind in the park. Everything fitted with the pathologist's report, and now the police knew who and they knew how. What they didn't know was why.

A partial lead to the motive was found when Pauline Parker's diary was discovered in a search of her bedroom. In the entry for 13 February 1954 she had written: 'Why could not mother die? Dozens of people, thousands of people, are dying every day. So why not mother and father too?' A later entry read: 'We discussed our plans for murdering mother and made them a little clearer. I want it to appear either a natural or an accidental death.' But it still didn't explain *why?*

To do that the background of these strange young women had to be pieced together. They were, it transpired, very close. Close may not even be the best word to describe it – they bathed together, they slept in the same bed whenever possible, and they discussed sex endlessly. Whether they had yet embarked on a serious lesbian relationship has always been in doubt, though they may have begun to experiment with their sexuality. But understandably the girls' parents would have been concerned, and Mrs Parker and Mrs Hulme resolved to separate them. To this end, Mr and Mrs Hulme were planning to emigrate to South Africa taking Juliet with them. When Pauline heard the news, she announced that she intended to go to South Africa as well; and Mrs Parker announced that she most certainly would not be going to South Africa. So Pauline and Juliet killed her.

And now they were facing a joint murder charge before a jury at the Christchurch High Court. The court was treated to the intimate details of Pauline and Juliet's relationship, and the defence claimed that they were insane. However, it was almost certainly the arrogant and unrepentant attitude displayed by the girls in the dock that persuaded the jury to incline towards the prosecution contention that they were 'highly intelligent and perfectly sane, but precocious and dirty-minded girls, who callously planned and premeditated murder'. As juveniles, Pauline Parker and Juliet Hulme were sentenced to be detained during Her Majesty's pleasure; in 1958 they were released.

PEARCEY, Mary Eleanor Jealousy can be a powerful emotion and the murder of Mrs Phoebe Hogg and her eighteen-month-old daughter by Mrs Pearcey stands as a classic instance of that passion transformed into consuming fury.

Mary Eleanor Wheeler was not, in fact, married, but took the name Pearcey from a carpenter with whom she had lived for a period of time. In the two years before 1890 she resided at 2 Priory Street, in London's Kentish Town district, in a ground-floor flat which was paid for by a gentleman admirer. At the same time, she had developed a further intrigue with a local furniture remover named Frank Hogg. Hogg seems to have had an equally relaxed attitude to relationships, and contrived to get another girl, Phoebe Styles, pregnant and, constrained by family pressure, married her and set up house at 141 Prince of Wales Road, Kentish Town. This, though, did not bring the affair with Mrs Pearcey to an end. Indeed, when Mrs Hogg was poorly after the birth of her daughter Phoebe, Mrs Pearcey was introduced into the household to nurse Mrs Hogg and look after the baby. At the same time, Hogg was still visiting Mary Pearcey regularly at Priory Street.

On Friday 24 October 1890, Mrs Pearcey sent a message to Mrs Hogg, inviting her and her baby daughter to tea. Mrs Hogg arrived at Priory Street, wheeling her child in a perambulator, at a quarter past four.

At seven o'clock of the same evening the body of a woman was discovered a mile away on a building site in Crossfield Street. Her throat had been cut, nearly severing the head from the body, her skull had been fractured and there was considerable bruising around the face. At first rumours circulated that Jack the Ripper was at work again.

At 8 p.m., a further mile away, in Hamilton Terrace, St John's Wood, an empty perambulator was found covered with blood; it was clear that the pram had been used to transport the body. On the following Sunday morning the corpse of a small child was discovered on waste ground in the Finchley Road. She had been suffocated.

Frank Hogg was not immediately concerned about the disappearance of his wife, thinking that she had gone to visit her sick father. On the Saturday, however, he became considerably worried by a description in the newspaper of the body found in Crossfield Road and sent his sister, Clara, round to see if his friend, Mrs Pearcey, had any idea where his wife might be. The two women then visited the mortuary to view the corpse. Clara immediately recognized the clothing but Mrs Pearcey tried to pull her away, saying 'It's not her – it's not her, let's go! Let's get out of this.' The police, most suspicious at this behaviour, took the women to Hampstead police station, picking up Frank Hogg on the way. When Hogg was searched and a latch key to Mrs Pearcey's lodgings was found in his pocket, he broke down and admitted his affair with the lady, prompting the police to search the houses at Priory Street and at Prince of Wales Road.

While Mrs Pearcey sat in her parlour playing the piano and humming to herself, the officers discovered in the kitchen all the evidence that they needed. Blood spattered the walls and ceiling, two window panes had been broken, two carving knives were found to have blood on their handles, and a very ineffectual attempt had been made to clean blood from the rug with paraffin. Asked to explain the blood, Mrs Pearcey muttered 'Killing mice, killing mice, killing mice.' She was taken into custody and formally charged with the murder of Phoebe Hogg and her infant daughter.

Further police inquiries began to piece together the gruesome events of that tragic afternoon and evening. Neighbours had noticed that Mary Pearcey's curtains were drawn for most of the day, and they confirmed the presence of a perambulator in the hallway. Mrs Pearcey had 'talked very funny and looked boozed'. Later she was seen wheeling the pram, heavily laden, under the railway arch at the end of Priory Street. Passers-by had witnessed her progress along the busy streets of North London on her diabolical errand. It seems likely that she made a separate journey to dispose of the child; an extraordinary round trip of six miles!

The funeral of the two victims attracted large crowds, who hissed and cursed the hapless Frank Hogg. He attracted similar treatment at the coroner's inquest and the magistrate's hearing. The trial began on 1 December 1890 at the Old Bailey, with Mr Justice Denman presiding, Mr Forrest Fulton for the prosecution and Mr Arthur Hutton representing Mrs Pearcey. It lasted for three days, and the result was never in doubt, the jury taking just fifty-two minutes to reach a verdict of guilty. A petition was submitted suggesting that Mrs Pearcey had been of unsound mind when the crime was committed, and there was evidence that she had suffered from epilepsy and had twice in the past tried to commit suicide; but such psychological subtleties were briskly rejected.

To the end, Mrs Pearcey sent impassioned but fruitless appeals to Frank Hogg to comfort her last hours in the death cell. His only positive action was to sell off the contents of her kitchen and the infamous perambulator to Madame Tussaud's

Waxworks Museum for £200. Thirty-thousand people attended the grand opening of the tableau in the Chamber of Horrors on the day of her execution.

Mary Pearcey was executed by the hangman, James Berry, in Newgate Prison on 23 December 1890. On the same day, by arrangement with her solicitor, Mr Freke Palmer, an enigmatic message was placed in the Madrid newspapers, 'M.E.C.P. Last wish of M.E.P. Have not betrayed.'

There is one final twist to this bloody tale. Almost a decade earlier, on 30 November 1880, Mary Pearcey's father, Thomas Wheeler, had hung from a noose at St Albans, convicted of the murder of a farm labourer.

PEARSON, Elizabeth Murder by poison, in the popular imagination at any rate, is seen as being a peculiarly female enterprise – a fiction much encouraged by such notorious Victorian 'lady-killers' as Adelaide Bartlett (see page 32) and Madeleine Smith (see page 247). And it is due, no doubt, to these representatives of the genre, that a certain romance has grown up around the 'lady in black' and her *crime passionnel*.

Elizabeth Pearson was female – if not obviously feminine – and she was a Victorian, in that she took her first and last breath during that indomitable monarch's reign. But that is where any correspondence to romantic fiction ends. Elizabeth Pearson represents the real face of that most ugly of crimes; a crime considered so vile that its perpetrators were by tradition prosecuted by one of the law officers of the Crown, either the Attorney-General or his deputy, the Solicitor-General, the two most powerful advocates in the kingdom.

The case of Elizabeth Pearson, brief and sordid as it is, is typical of the majority of murders – a narrative of greed, incompetence and treachery.

It was in the year of 1875, the thirty-eighth of Victoria's reign, that Elizabeth Pearson, her husband and child came to the small village of Gainford, half-way between Darlington to the east and Barnard Castle to the west. Some time in March, the family arrived to 'care' for Pearson's uncle, a seventy-five-year-old widower afflicted with severe lung disease. There was never any altruism in this seemingly charitable gesture – certainly not on the part of Elizabeth, who saw the proximity of the old man's demise as proximity to a much craved inheritance.

Deprived of even the most rudimentary nursing, it was not long before old Pearson made plans to transfer himself and all his worldly goods to the home of his son in Barnard Castle. When the parent failed to arrive, the son dutifully visited the cottage at Gainford to investigate. There he found the place had been stripped of every movable object save the bed, on which lay the old man's body, twisted in the final grotesque contortions of strychnine poisoning. Elizabeth Pearson – like old Pearson's possessions – had disappeared.

Retribution, however, was swift. The carefree manner in which Mrs Pearson had bought quantities of 'Battle's Vermin Killer' (a mixture of flour, prussian blue and strychnine) put her culpability beyond reasonable doubt. But as if that were not sufficient, her mother-in-law – who had colluded in the old gentleman's murder – turned Queen's evidence and appeared at Elizabeth's trial as a witness for the prosecution.

Unlamented, Elizabeth Pearson lost her miserable life to the hangman at Durham Gaol in August 1875.

PIVAIN, Hugette, and **MONTIGNY, Emile** 'Opposites attract', according to the laws of magnetism, and rarely can more opposed characters have been attracted than those of François Jeanne and Hugette Pivain. He was a gentle giant of a man, six foot four and two hundred and fifty pounds, enormously strong, well-liked, affectionate, never in trouble, responsible and dutiful. She, a vicious little slut of a woman, reached barely to his waist, was dirty in her habits, dishonest, promiscuous, savage and malicious. Yet in 1973 the couple set up home together in Cherbourg where he worked as a shipyard carpenter and she as a waitress, and in 1976 Hugette gave birth to a daughter, Katia.

Not long after this happy event Hugette took to hanging around the bars in town, picking up men for sex. One of those men, a former workmate of François, was Emile Montigny, a feeble, idle, scruffy layabout. A relationship developed, and in May 1980 Hugette moved into Montigny's apartment at Avenue de Paris, taking Katia with her. She continued to receive the contents of Jeanne's wage packet, and would return to his apartment at Cité Fougère to use the washing machine and raid the fridge.

This beneficial arrangement came to an abrupt end on Monday 23 June 1980. At about ten-thirty that evening the body of François Jeanne was discovered in the entrance hall of his apartment block, lying in a massive pool of blood which drenched the entire floor, and which flowed from a head wound caused by the screwdriver which had been hammered into his skull. Other wounds had been caused by a heavy, smooth object which had split the scalp and caused further profuse bleeding. Amazingly, Jeanne was still alive when the ambulance arrived, but he was pronounced dead on arrival at Caen hospital.

The murder weapon was from François Jeanne's toolbox, which he kept in a kitchen cupboard. As was the 'heavy, smooth object', a twenty-four-inch crescent wrench which was found in the hall. It looked as though the murderer was somebody with access to Jeanne's apartment, somebody with a grudge, and with a vicious disposition. So reasoned Inspector Jules Maréchal of the Department of Criminal Investigations. But why would Hugette Pivain slay her big benefactor? And, to be practical, how?

During interrogation the facts emerged. Hugette had waited behind the door, jumping as high as she could when Jeanne came in and landing him a double-handed blow. He fell, she and Montigny took turns to pound him with the wrench, and then she hammered in the six-inch shaft of the screwdriver. Afterwards they went home and had sex. The motive for the attack? None, that she could think of.

On 5 June 1981 Hugette Pivain and Emile Montigny were sentenced to life imprisonment.

It emerged that over the previous three years François Jeanne had suffered hundreds of cuts, bruises and broken bones at Hugette's hands. Always he claimed the wounds were self-inflicted. Perhaps that was why he was felled so easily: he was used to her perpetual punishment. And perhaps the secret of the strange attraction between these two unlikely specimens lay in their implicit conspiracy of spite.

PLEDGE, Sarah, and WHALE, Ann   Ann Whale was born of respectable parents, at Horsham, in Sussex; but her father died in her infancy, and she was left to the care of her mother. Early in life she showed signs of an uncontrollable disposition and, after a dispute with her mother, she wandered into the country and associated with people of bad character. Her mother, in order to save her from ruin, at length prevailed on her to return home.

Soon after this she was addressed by a sober young man, named James Whale; and as a relation had left her a legacy of eighty pounds, payable when she was of age, and the mother readily consenting to their alliance, the marriage took place. They had not been long wedded when they went to live at a place called Steepwood; but soon returning to Horsham they took up their residence in the house of Sarah Pledge, who was distantly related to Mrs Whale.

In 1752, a misunderstanding happening between the women, Mr Whale forbade Mrs Pledge to come into his apartment – a circumstance that only tended to fuel the quarrel. Soon afterwards, however, the women were privately reconciled; and as the man was remarkably sober, and they were of the opposite character, it is the less to be wondered at that they sought the means of his destruction.

Mrs Whale having lain in, and being tolerably recovered, Mrs Pledge by now deserted by her husband came into her room, saying: 'Nan, let us get rid of this devil!' (meaning Mr Whale). The wife said: 'How can we do it?' To which the other replied: 'Let us give him a dose of poison.' The abandoned woman too readily consented to this horrid proposal; and the only difficulty which appeared to arise was, how the poison should be procured.

They first attempted their purpose by roasting spiders and putting them into his beer, but finding this did not produce the effect desired, Mrs Pledge undertook to purchase something more efficacious, and for that purpose travelled to several market-towns; but as she went into each apothecary's shop she saw, or fancied she saw, some person who knew her, or her conscience interposed. At length she went to an apothecary at Horsham to whom she was a stranger and, though still afraid, she made the purchase.

Hastening back she gave the bane to her more wicked friend, who with equal dispatch administered it; for at the moment her husband was fondling their child, on whom he doted, she mixed it in some hasty pudding prepared for his supper. Unsuspicious, the affectionate but unfortunate man ate, was soon seized with the racking torments occasioned by the deadly poison, and the next day expired; but, the neighbours suspecting that his death was occasioned by some sinister arts, a surgeon examined the body, and the coroner's jury being summoned brought in a verdict of 'Wilful Murder'.

Thereupon Mrs Whale and Mrs Pledge were taken into custody, and carried before a magistrate. The latter wished to turn King's evidence; but being separately examined, and both confessing the fact, they were committed to Horsham Jail.

At their trials the confessions which they had signed were

read and, some corroborative evidence arising, they were convicted, and received sentence of death.

For some time after conviction Mrs Pledge behaved in the most hardened manner, making use of profane expressions, and declaring that she would fight with the hangman at the place of execution. On the contrary, Mrs Whale acknowledged the justice of the sentence which had condemned her, and gave evident signs of being a real penitent.

On the evening preceding the execution the clergyman who attended them brought Mrs Pledge into a better state of mind, and then administered the sacrament to both the convicts.

An immense crowd attended at the place of execution where Pledge was hanged; and Whale, being tied to a stake, was first strangled and then burned to ashes, in the twenty-first year of her age.

POPOVA, Madame One of the world's most remarkable and prolific female poisoners, Madame Popova was a native of Samara, Russia, and was active for about thirty years as a professional killer before her arrest in 1909. Of course, Madame would have hotly denied the implication of the words 'professional killer'. It is true that she killed, and it is also true that she frequently received some trifling reward for her services; but Madame Popova would almost certainly have preferred the term 'liberator', for it was her life's work to unshackle the downtrodden peasant women of her region from the excesses of brutish and violent husbands. This she achieved by poisoning the 'tyrants' – about three hundred of them over her long career. There would no doubt have been more had not one of her overly sentimental clients come to the conclusion that even a pig of a husband was better than no husband at all, and in her remorse gone to the authorities.

There was a rudimentary trial, but so delighted was Madame with her record of success that it was really only necessary to sentence her to death. It is recorded that the military escort taking her to the place of execution had the devil's own job to prevent the mob that lined the route from seizing the prisoner and burning her at the stake. Finally law and order prevailed, and Madame Popova, still protesting that she had been an instrument of salvation for womankind, met her death in front of a firing squad.

PUENTE, Dorothea Kindly, grey-haired Mrs Puente seemed to have just two preoccupations in life. First was the care of those less fortunate than herself, second her immaculately tended garden. Both Dorothea and the garden were sources of inspiration to her Sacramento neighbours, and to the local welfare department which boarded elderly and alcoholic mental patients with her in the sure confidence that they would enjoy the very best of care. And take care of them she certainly did! For though many passed through the doors of Granny Puente's boarding house, few were allowed to overstay their welcome – only their pension cheques remained to keep the old lady company.

For two years, until November 1988, the sixty-one-year-old widow opened her comfortable Victorian house to the homeless and the friendless at the irresistibly low rent of $350 a month, meals included. Surprising then that there should be such a rapid turnover of 'guests', so many deciding, as Mrs Puente phrased it, to 'move on'.

Then a persistent social worker arrived in search of a missing client named Alvaro Montoya. Mrs Puente insisted that he had gone to visit friends in Mexico; which puzzled the social worker, because her client came from Costa Rica, and his only relatives lived in New Orleans. Now the rumours of disappearing boarders began to circulate, and tales of bad smells in the house. John Sharp recalled the night Granny Puente had taken 'Drunken Ben' upstairs to sober up, and how Ben had never been seen again, only that same putrid smell hanging on the air. The smell was particularly strong in the garden; 'dead rats', the landlady declared, and got to work with deodorant sprays.

Now the police took occupation of widow Puente's manicured lawn, and by the time they left little remained of the colourful flower beds, the newly paved driveway and the statuette of St Francis surrounded by luxurious rose bushes. What there was instead were the decomposing remains of seven bodies each lying beside its shallow grave. The headless corpses had been covered with lime, presumably to hasten putrefaction. In the event, like so many amateurs whose knowledge of such matters derives from television gangsters and pulp fiction, Mrs Puente had not realized that in order to burn through flesh and bone, quicklime must be slaked with water. The effect here had been to *retard* putrefaction to an extent that autopsies were able to reveal the cause of death as huge overdoses of the drug Benzodiazepine.

Meanwhile, sweet old Granny Puente had persuaded police officers to book her into a motel so that she need not suffer the heartbreak of seeing the precious garden wrecked. As soon as their backs were turned, the merry widow was on the first bus out of town. It took a seven-day nationwide hunt to track Dorothea Puente to Los Angeles, where she had been recognized by the elderly gentleman she was trying to pick up in a bar!

What became known as the 'Arsenic and Old Lace' trial opened in February 1993. By now the number of murders with which Mrs Puente was charged had risen to nine; the bodies recovered from under the grounds of her Sacramento home were supplemented with the alleged murder of a woman previously thought to have died of an accidental drug overdose in 1982, and another tenant whose body was found in a box in the Sacramento river in 1986. The victims were aged between fifty-one and eighty, and had allegedly been poisoned, though their pensions and social security cheques continued to be cashed.

Already the trial of Dorothea Montalvo Puente had been moved to Monterey because she was unlikely to receive a fair hearing in her home town, feelings against her running as high as they were. Even so, Mrs Puente was reported by her attorney, Peter Vlautin, to be 'looking forward to her day in court'. His client, he said, would plead not guilty, and argue that the deaths of her residents were the result of natural causes or suicide. Hundreds of prospective jurors were interviewed, and due to the complexities of the American jury selection system the process was so lengthy that by the time twelve jurors and substitutes had been found, some of the original members had moved home or otherwise disqualified themselves.

When the trial finally got under way in 1993, prosecutor John O'Mara described the victims – people taken as lodgers by Mrs Puente, after referral by social workers – as 'shadow people', homeless, friendless, jobless, mentally and emotionally disturbed individuals who would not be missed. As jurors watched with horror the police videotape of decomposed and mutilated corpses being dug out of Mrs Puente's rose beds, the lady herself sat quiet and impassive in her neat black cardigan and floral dress. Mr O'Mara explained to the court that in all the bodies recovered, traces of the drug Dalmane were found; that over the years more than $5,000 a month had been fraudulently claimed from the social services. More than two hundred witnesses were expected to be called in what experts have described as America's worst case of female serial murder for decades. The trial lasted a little over six months, at the end of which, quite predictably, Dorothea Puente was found guilty as charged. The problem arose in sentencing; in the United States it is a jury that decides on the matter of the death sentence, and in this case, they were deadlocked at 7–5 against. In October 1993 the judge sentenced Mrs Puente in the only way open to him – to life imprisonment.

R

RABLEN, Eva Described variously as 'a gin-guzzling flapper' or 'a fun-loving wife', the real Eva Rablen probably fell between the two; the one thing you *could* say about Eva was that she liked to enjoy herself. Which made her choice of Carroll Rablen for a husband most puzzling. Older than his wife, Rablen was also profoundly deaf as a result of injuries suffered during the First World War; furthermore, a retiring nature excluded him from most of his wife's activities. And Eva was certainly the very epitome of the 'bright young thing' of the Jazz Age – never happier than when she was dancing and drinking. In the end the Rablens developed the rather eccentric solution of Carroll driving Eva to the dance-hall or speakeasy (remember this is the Prohibition era) and then sitting patiently in the car outside until she had finished enjoying herself, and driving her home to sleep off the booze.

Presumably this docile, dutiful man would have continued to minister to his wife's Bacchanalian needs until he (or probably she) dropped. But Eva was getting restless – and greedy. On the evening of 26 April 1929, it was a Friday, Carroll Rablen had chauffeured his wife to the weekly dance held at the Tuttleton school-house in Tuolumne County, California. As usual he waited outside while Eva stretched her legs doing the latest dance craze, the Charleston. At midnight Mrs Rablen took her husband a cup of coffee which he drank grateftllly. He was less thankful when the first convulsion shot like lightning through his body, and as he screamed in agony the disturbance brought Rablen's father and uncle out of the dance and to Carroll's side. They were just in time to hear him complain about 'bitter coffee' before death released him from further suffering.

Ironically, the investigation which followed such a sudden and inexplicable death revealed no evidence of foul play. An autopsy did not find any trace of poison in Rablen's stomach, and a search of the school-house and surrounding area failed to turn up anything like a poison bottle. Fortunately for the principles of Justice, Carroll Rablen's father, who had never been keen on his son's choice of wife, insisted that Eva had killed him to get her hands on the $3,000 insurance. A new search was made at the school, and this time a small empty bottle which had contained strychnine was discovered hidden under a staircase. The bottle was traced to the Bigelow drugstore in nearby Tuolumne, where the pharmacist identified Eva Rablen as the 'Mrs Williams' who had purchased strychnine in the form of rat killer. The shopkeeper's evidence was later corroborated by a comparison between Eva's handwriting and the signature in the pharmacist's poisons register. District Attorney Grayson now had sufficient reason for suspecting Mrs Rablen to call on the expertise of the forensic chemist Dr Edward Heinrich. A second post-mortem performed by Heinrich found traces of strychnine in Carroll Rablen's stomach, and in the cup from which he drank the 'bitter' coffee. Traces were also found in coffee stains on the upholstery of Rablen's car seat.

Eva Rablen, through her attorney C.H. Vance, strongly denied killing her husband, and by the time of the preliminary hearing the case had become a local sensation. Indeed, so great was the interest that Judge Pitts transferred the preliminaries from his courtroom to an open-air dance pavilion in the middle of town, where the proceedings were watched by hundreds of thrill seekers from miles around.

When the case came to the superior court the process was altogether more sombre, entirely in keeping with the dignity of the law. On 17 May 1929 Eva Rablen stood before Judge Warne in Sonora, California and pleaded not guilty to murder. She was given a trial date of 10 June, but in the meantime Eva's attorney had become so alarmed on reading Dr Heinrich's damning report that he persuaded his client to change her plea to one of guilty. Eva Rablen was committed to life imprisonment to be served at San Quentin Prison.

RANSOM, Florence   In November 1940, at the height of the Second World War, another, smaller, battle was being fought in the austere chambers of London's Old Bailey. It, too, was a battle for life or death. Florence Ransom stood defending herself against the capital charge of murder.

It had all begun on the afternoon of the previous 9 July; for those with an interest in pursuing the military connection, it was the day before the start of the Battle of Britain. The location was the village of Matfield, seven miles or so from Tonbridge in the county of Kent – the county over which much of the Battle of Britain would be fought. But the shots on this day were fired in a different sort of anger. The victims were Mrs Dorothy Fisher and her nineteen-year-old daughter, both of whom had been shot dead in the orchard adjoining their cottage, and Charlotte Saunders, their maid, who lay dead where she had been shot running from the cottage.

When the police arrived at the scene they were faced with a couple of puzzles. Although the cottage seemed to have been ransacked, the killer had made no attempt to steal the jewellery or cash which had been strewn about with other possessions. In her panic to get away from the murderer, the maid had dropped and smashed a tray of crockery; when it had been pieced together there were four cups, four saucers and four plates. This meant that either Mrs Fisher and her daughter were entertaining two guests or, more likely, the Fishers and Miss Saunders, who was as much a friend as a servant, were entertaining one guest. Between the two bodies in the orchard, police searchers found a single, white leather woman's glove; of its companion there was no trace – indicating that the assassin had been a woman and that she had dropped a glove. This theory was supported by sightings of a woman said to have been hanging around outside the cottage on the afternoon of the murder. Witnesses reported seeing her later on the road between Matfield and Tonbridge, where it was ascertained she took the 4.25 p.m. train to London. The woman was described as an attractive redhead, who had been carrying a long, narrow object wrapped in paper – quite probably the shotgun with which the victims had been killed.

It was while they were tracing Mrs Fisher's family that the police came face to face with the mysterious redhead. She was at the time calling herself 'Mrs Julia Fisher', and was living as the wife of Lawrence Fisher, estranged husband of the late Dorothy Fisher. The woman's real name was Florence Ransom, and she and Fisher were working a farm at Piddington, in Oxfordshire. Further investigation revealed an even more tangled set of relationships; Mr Fisher was, it seems, still on excellent terms with his wife and was a frequent visitor to the conage at Matfield; Dorothy Fisher had a new lover in her life and he was known to Lawrence. However, what Lawrence Fisher was in the dark about was the fact that the man whom he had taken on as cowman at the farm was in reality Florence Ransom's brother; and their live-in housekeeper was her mother. And it did not go unheeded by detectives that the cowman had been teaching Florence how to use a shotgun.

Several witnesses from Matfield identified Florence as the woman who had been hanging about the Fisher couage, and the glove that was found at the scene fitted her hand – though it must be added that the other one of the pair was never found. Still, there was enough evidence to support a charge of murder, and Mrs Ransom was remanded for trial at the Old Bailey.

The hearing was brief, and notable for the appearance in the witness box of the elderly housekeeper and the cowman; both testified that Florence had been absent from the farm on the day of the murders, and the cowman told the court that Florence had borrowed his shotgun that same day. Florence denied everything, including the fact that the cowman and the housekeeper were her relatives.

Although Florence Ransom was convicted and sentenced to death, she was later certified insane and committed to Broadmoor.

RATTENBURY, Alma, and **STONER, George Percy** The facts were these. In 1935, sixty-eight-year-old retired architect Francis Mawson Rattenbury was living with his already twice-divorced wife Alma at the Villa Madeira in the refined English south-coast resort of Bournemouth. The ménage was completed by an eighteen-year-old handyman/chauffeur named George Stoner, whom Alma had first seduced at an Oxford hotel and subsequently taken as a permanent lover. If Rattenbury knew of the affair (and he could hardly have avoided it), it seems not to have bothered him as long as he had his hand firmly on the real love in his life – the whisky decanter.

In the small hours of 25 March Alma, so she claimed, found her husband lying on the drawing-room carpet, his head beaten in, but still breathing. When the doctor and the police arrived, summoned by a startled maid, they found Alma Rattenbury apparently much the worse for drink, gibbering hysterically and making what appeared to be a confession: 'I did it with a mallet . . . He's lived too long . . .' and so on. It was just the first of several admissions of guilt, most of which were aimed at protecting her beloved Percy.

Percy himself had begun to make statements, too, the

essence of which were that *he* was the guilty party and Mrs Rattenbury had nothing to do with the dreadful incident. By this time Francis Rattenbury had succumbed to his injuries, breathing his last at the Strathallen Nursing Home, and Alma and Percy – still confessing like mad – were facing a murder charge.

The trial opened on 27 May 1935 at the Old Bailey before Mr Justice Humphreys. By now, Alma Rattenbury had been persuaded by her counsel to stop protecting Percy Stoner, and reluctantly she did so. Percy, with a show of dignity beyond his years, stood by his confession (though he uttered not one single word throughout the trial). Despite attempts by the prosecuting counsel and the judge himself to implicate Mrs Rattenbury in 'leading Stoner astray', she was acquitted. On 31 May, Percy Stoner was convicted of murder and sentenced to death. Heartbroken, Alma Rattenbury committed suicide three days later. Then Percy began to talk; giving notice of appeal he claimed that he had been innocent all along, that it had been Mrs Rattenbury who killed her husband. Stoner was reprieved and served just seven years of a life sentence before being released in 1942 to join the armed forces fighting in the Second World War.

Percy survived the war, married, and settled down to a quiet life in the town one might have thought he would have wanted to forget – Bournemouth. This quintessentially English *crime passionel* has received periodic attention over the succeeding forty-five years, with the debate continuing over who *really* killed Francis Rattenbury. Though still in robust health despite advancing years, Percy Stoner has remained stubbornly silent on the matter.

On 28 September 1990, newspapers reported that Percy Stoner, now seventy-three years old, had appeared before the Bournemouth magistrates. He pleaded guilty to a sexual attack on a twelve-year-old boy in public lavatories near his home. Stoner had been arrested after police found him in the conveniences wearing only a hat, shoes and socks; he was put on probation for two years.

RENCZI, Vera   In the early days of the last century Vera Renczi was born into considerable luxury in the Romanian capital of Bucharest. Before she had reached teenage, Vera was already displaying a prodigious and not entirely wholesome fascination with sex; by fifteen she had embarked on the first of a long succession of lovers. With a thirst for security so frequently exhibited by the sexually promiscuous, Vera married young to a businessman much her senior, and very wealthy. Then one day he simply disappeared. According to Vera he had walked out on her without a word of explanation. Some time later she announced that her errant husband was now her late errant husband; she had received news of his untimely decease in an accident.

This left the merry, and affluent, widow Renczi free to marry again, this time to a younger man. But poor Vera, she did seem to be having a run of bad luck. Hardly had they settled down after the wedding than this spouse also went AWOL – a 'long trip' was the way Vera described it, and later she 'received' a letter signed by her husband and announcing his intention of deserting her for ever. Perhaps to comfort herself for this loss, Vera began to take a series of lovers – there were more than thirty of them over the next few years – and all of them disappeared without trace.

She would probably have gone on to enjoy thirty more had the abandoned wife of one man not reported him missing to the police. When officers visited the Renczi residence, they were able to solve the riddle of the lost lovers. In Vera's cellar, lined up in neat rows, were thirty-five zinc coffins containing thirty-two lovers, two husbands, and the son born of her first marriage who had been silly enough to try to blackmail Vera.

Vera Renczi readily admitted having poisoned each of her victims as soon as she tired of them, or when she felt they might tire of her. Convicted by her own confession, Vera was sentenced to life in jail where eventually she died.

RENDALL, Martha   By 1906, Thomas Morris, a carpenter living in Western Australia, had got a bit fed up with his wife and replaced her with a housekeeper named Martha Rendall. Martha, unlike Mrs Morris, proved to be a strict disciplinarian. She insisted the children call her 'Mother', and frequently thrashed them unmercifully with little provocation. Neighbours had begun to notice that the formerly robust and well-nourished children were mere shadows of their former selves.

The following year two of Morris's children, Anne and Olive, who had been suffering from colds and sore throats, were prescribed throat swabs. Martha, of course, administered the swabs, a treatment which, if the screaming and crying of the children was anything to go by, was extremely painful. Anne Morris died on 28 July and the cause was certified as diphtheria. Three months later Olive died, also from 'diphtheria'. Twelve months after his sisters' untimely deaths, fourteen-year-old Arthur Morris complained of a sore throat, and then complained even louder about the swabbing treatment meted out so unstintingly and with such obvious relish. On 6 October he joined his sisters. Although an autopsy was performed there were no signs of foul play, and 'diphtheria' was once again certified as the cause of death.

In April 1909 George Morris made the mistake of drinking a cup of tea made by 'Mother', which seemed to scald his throat so badly that Martha was obliged to suggest a throat swab. Having already seen the consequences of Martha's swabs, George elected instead to run away from home. It happened that in trying to locate the fugitive boy the police began to question the neighbours, who had a lot to tell and a great willingness to tell it.

An exhumation order was made on the three Morris children, and re-examination established that their throats had been liberally washed with hydrochloric acid – little wonder they screamed; little wonder George took to his heels.

Rendall and Thomas Morris were jointly charged on three counts of murder, though the totally blameless Morris was soon acquitted. At Martha's trial the jury heard how she first laced the children's drinks with acid, and when they complained of a sore throat she swabbed their throats with more of the same. The 'treatment' naturally inflamed the mucous membrane of the throat – a symptom identical to that of diphtheria.

Martha Rendall was convicted of murder and hanged in Freemantle Jail on 6 October 1909, the first and last woman to suffer capital punishment in Western Australia.

RICHTER, Ursula   When Ursula became pregnant by Georg Richter in 1965 she was only thirteen years of age; though to give him credit, Georg married her, and they settled at his home in the town of Meppen, in Germany but close to the border with the Netherlands. The house was shared with a lodger, Kurt Adomeit.

In 1972 Ursula, deprived by motherhood of her adolescent years, was getting bored; she was twenty and had never known any other life than domesticity with Georg. Then, on 30 May 1972, he went missing. Ursula dutifully reported her husband's disappearance to the local police. It so happened that they had already been keeping a casual eye on Herr Richter; he was awaiting trial for some petty crimes, and it was not beyond the bounds of possibility that he had skipped across the Dutch border. When Georg's car was found abandoned by the border it simply confirmed their worst suspicions. Although the police would dearly have loved to catch up with him in the interests of justice, Georg Richter's case was filed away. After twelve months Ursula initiated divorce proceedings on grounds of desertion, although she had already openly taken up with lodger Adomeit who, at the age of twenty, was rather closer to Ursula's own age.

In June 1975 Kurt Adomeit became involved in peddling fake drugs, and was taken into police custody. It was just a hunch, really, but detectives were still not entirely satisfied that Georg Richter would have left home and family for more than three years just to escape the minor consequences his misdemeanours would have incurred. So Adomeit was joined in his cell by a 'drunk and disorderly' case, in reality a police informer planted to get what information he could. The 'drunk' spun Adomeit a story about an attractive girl in the nearby town of Meppen who was being very liberal with her sexual favours while her lover was in prison. The girl's description, of course, fitted Ursula exactly. The ruse couldn't have worked better. An angry and jealous Kurt Adomeit summoned the inspector and confessed that with Ursula's encouragement and help, he had murdered Georg Richter and buried his body. When they searched the spot, police diggers unearthed Georg's skeleton. According to Adomeit's statement, Ursula had first tried to dispose of her husband with rat poison, but he survived; Adomeit had then killed him by the more certain means of a sharp hatchet.

According to German law both Adomeit, at nineteen, and Ursula, at twenty, were considered to be juveniles at the time of the murder. They were therefore tried under the juvenile code and sentenced to a maximum ten years' imprisonment.

ROUSSEAU, Rosella City dwellers on the mainland of Europe understandably have different attitudes from those insular nations such as the English. This is never more apparent than in their approach to 'vertical' living – living in apartment buildings. There are few areas of continental cities where row upon row of small residential houses can be found, as distinct, say, from London. There is a tendency to use some of these apartments for business purposes – as offices, sometimes as combined offices and domestic premises. It is necessary to explain this in order to appreciate the logistics of the Rousseau case.

Albert Oursel was a Parisian employment agent, unmarried, but living with a teenaged girl from Brittany named Germaine Bichon. Attached to the agency offices on the first floor of the apartment block, Oursel had his living accommodation. Below the flat, at ground level, was a restaurant. The obligatory hawk-eyed concierge had her apartment off the building's main entrance hall.

A short distance from the Oursel enterprise lived Rosella Rousseau, who had once been employed as Albert Oursel's housekeeper, but now lived with a man named Martin and his daughter. When they hit financial difficulties in July 1909, Rousseau decided to rob her former employer. She remembered that Oursel left Paris for the country at weekends, and one Saturday Rosella Rousseau managed (heaven knows how) to slip past the concierge and up the stairs to Oursel's office. Avoiding the receptionist she let herself in to the adjoining apartment and was about to look around for money and valuables when she was obliged to take cover; Mademoiselle Bichon had returned home. Following brief visits to the kitchen and the bathroom, Germaine went to the bedroom and locked and bolted the door behind her; that, thought Rosella Rousseau, must be where the valuables are kept. After an uncomfortable night half-sleeping, half-alert with one eye on the bedroom door, Rousseau was waiting to pounce as soon as Germaine Bichon opened the door. Seeing her looming there, the girl screamed and ran into the kitchen closely pursued by the intruder. Germaine picked up a small hatchet used for chopping wood, and the two women wrestled fiercely for possession of it. Not surprisingly the older, heavier Rousseau finally overcame the spirited fifteen-year-old, and began to bludgeon the poor child about the head with determination. Before long she was dead. It seemed a lot of effort for a small gold coin and a watch chain, but against all expectations, that is all Rosella Rousseau could find. On the way out her luck deteriorated, for she walked straight into the concierge. 'My name is Angèle,'

Rousseau claimed. 'I am looking for my friend Arlette; she is not home.'

Imagine the concierge's horror when the proprietor of the restaurant called her in to look at the steady drips of what looked suspiciously like blood falling from the ceiling on to the aluminium top of his bar. It is moments like this that concierges all over Paris live for. In no time at all, her parlour was busy with attentive policemen listening to the life-story of Albert Oursel. Which is how they came to learn of a former house-keeper named Rousseau and a stranger who called herself 'Angèle'. The boys from the lab had been working in the Oursel apartment and had come across a clue which they thought might or might not be of some importance. During the struggle with her attacker, Germaine Bichon had obviously pulled at her hair and wrenched a handful out; it was still clenched tightly in her dead fist.

When detectives from the Sûreté tracked down Madame Rousseau she matched the description given by the concierge of 'Angèle', and that redoubtable lady was later also able to identify the clothing belonging to Rousseau as that worn by the mysterious stranger. Better was to come. The suspect had long light-brown hair, like the strands held in the dead girl's hand;. and the laboratory proved that, under a powerful microscope, they matched exactly. This was the first time the forensic analysis of hair was used in a court of law.

The result of Rosella Rousseau's trial, predictably enough, was a verdict of guilty. She was sentenced to death but later reprieved and spent much of the rest of her life in prison.

RUMBOLD, Freda   Timber merchant Albert Rumbold was, even by his own mother's estimate 'a peculiar person'; and he was never more eccentric than at the time of the full moon. His wife Freda was even worse off – she had to endure Albert's demands for what she described as 'abnormal' sexual habits – which on more than one occasion had forced her to sleep in their fourteen-year-old daughter's room; or out on the landing. But if Albert was eccentric, then Freda was devious; and for some time she had been forging Bert's cheques and taking out loans in his name in order to put by a small nest-egg to finance her escape. Indeed, it is thought that the tragedy that befell Albert was brought about mainly by Freda's belief that he was on the verge of discovering her deceits.

On the night of 25 August 1956, Freda Rumbold crept into the bedroom where her husband lay sleeping; she was carrying Albert's shotgun, loaded with cartridges borrowed from a friend. Then she simply blasted Albert's head to a pulp. Freda left her husband's body where it lay on the bed, locked the bedroom door and pinned a hastily scribbled sign on it: 'Please do not enter.' To the neighbours and Albert's employers, Freda explained that he had been obliged to go away for a few days. When the rapidly decomposing corpse began to smell, Mrs Rumbold stuffed a towel soaked in eau-de-Cologne under the door. But such a charade could not go on indefinitely. Soon Albert's relatives started asking awkward questions, and when they got only vague, evasive answers they called in the police, who also had some awkward questions to ask.

According to Freda it happened like this. There had been a quarrel, during the course of which Albert had grabbed his 12-bore and threatened to kill her. Freda had tried to wrestle the gun from him and, well, you can guess the rest. Unfortunately for an already barely believable story, the gun was a single-shot weapon; *two* shots had been 'accidentally' fired that night.

At her trial, Freda Rumbold was convicted and sentenced to death, though this was later commuted to life imprisonment.

S

SABEIKOV, Heidemarie *see* DARTSCH, Sylvia

SACH, Amelia, and WALTERS, Annie The following story unfolded before Mr Justice Darling at the Old Bailey on 15 January 1903. In the dock stood Annie Walters, fifty-four years of age and claiming to be a nurse; and Amelia Sach, twenty-nine, also described as a 'nurse'.

During the latter part of 1902 Amelia Sach was carrying on the business of a private nursing home in which she played the roles of midwife and nurse. The 'home' was pleasantly situated in a house in London's East Finchley, to which clients were enticed by means of newspaper advertisements: 'Accouchement, before and during skilled nursing; home comforts; baby can remain.' That is the important phrase. *Baby can remain*.

It emerged at the trial that a set pattern had been developed by Sach and her accomplice to maximize the profit from their 'nursing' skills.

For example, in August 1902 a woman named Galley – unmarried and pregnant – contracted to pay Amelia Sach six guineas for a two-week stay at Claymore House, and thenceforth a guinea a week for as long as she remained confined.

Clearly aware of the situation, and prepared to take full advantage of it, Sach struck a bargain with the hapless Miss Galley whereby the latter handed over £25 in cash and the former promised to have the Galley offspring adopted.

On 15 November a boy was born to Miss Galley at eight o'clock in the morning; it was the last she ever saw of her son. That evening, Annie Walters arrived at the 'nursing home' to carry the infant back to her own lodging in Danbury Street, Islington. Walters had been observed buying a bottle of chlorodyne some days before, and it seems certain that the Galley baby, who died mysteriously at Danbury Street three days after its arrival, met its end as a result of chlorodyne poisoning.

It may be in the nature of baby-farmers to take risks; or it may be that Annie Walters was particularly stupid. Whichever was the case she seemed quite oblivious of the fact that she lodged in the same house as a policeman; certainly it did not restrict her illegal and immoral activities. So when Walters left home on the morning of the baby's death carrying a small corpse with her, the constable followed her to South Kensington railway station, where she was arrested, and charged with child murder.

When Sach was taken into custody at the Claymore House Nursing Home she denied any acquaintance with Walters or knowledge of the death of the infant. A post-mortem held on the body of the baby revealed death from asphyxia caused by morphine (a principal constituent of chlorodyne).

The court was treated to accounts of several similar incidents in the careers of these baby-farmers, and expressed its odium for the pair by sentencing them both to death. Annie Walters and Amelia Sach were hanged on the morning of 3 February 1903 – the first to be executed on the scaffold of London's Holloway Prison.

SAINSBURY, Pamela   Pamela and Paul Sainsbury met in 1982, while Pamela was holidaying with her parents in Paul's home town of Sidmouth, Devon. She was from a stable middle-class family, had left school with a clutch of qualifications and a strong ambition to work in a laboratory. Sainsbury, by contrast, was a builder by occupation, a fanatical body-builder, and had a history of violence. After an unremarkable courtship, Pamela gave up her job in London and moved to Sidmouth to live with Paul. Although the relationship had already developed an undercurrent of brutality, it was in 1986, after the birth of their second child that the partnership began to disintegrate dramatically. Sainsbury, who had always had a cruel streak, now began to abuse his wife unmercifully – she was beaten just for using words which his ill-bred and uneducated mind couldn't understand – 'posh words' he called them. The relationship became characterized by extreme sadism and acts of violent sexual degradation. It was common practice, for example, for Pamela to be forced to strip naked and, with a collar and chain around her neck, eat on all fours out of a dog's bowl.

On the night she killed him, 29 September 1990, Pamela and Paul Sainsbury had been to Carina's night-club, where they had first met. As they were leaving, Pamela casually passed the time of evening with a fellow reveller; a man. This was enough to provoke an outburst of such jealous fury from Paul that, when they reached home, Pamela was subjected to a beating so savage that, after two hours, Sainsbury fell exhausted on to the bed, literally too tired to hurt her any more.

She had thought of escaping so many times before, thought of running away, being free from the pain, free from the misery. But like so many others in her predicament – women, and men too – Pamela Sainsbury had become so spiritually broken, so dehumanized, that she was too terrified even to save herself. But tonight was different. As she looked down at the snoring monster, seeming now so helpless, a terrible resolve seized her. Pamela Sainsbury *would* be free. As though in a trance, she crept past the room where her two young children slept, down to Paul's toolbox where she found a nylon cord. Back in the bedroom, Pamela tied one end of the cord around the bed-post, passed the other round Sainsbury's neck, and pulled; pulled so hard and so long that the cord scarred her hands. 'She did not want to kill him, but she could not stop pulling. She was on automatic pilot . . . It was as if eight years of anger had come out in an instant'; that is how Helena Kennedy, Pamela's defence counsel, later described that dreadful act.

When it was all over Pamela Sainsbury walked to the calendar hanging on the kitchen wall; beside that day's date she drew an asterisk and wrote down the time, followed by the words 'This is the first day of the rest of my life.' Then she bundled Paul Sainsbury's body into the wardrobe and slept peacefully for the first time in years.

Three days later, Pamela cut the body up with a knife and saw, parcelling the pieces into five plastic bin-bags. These grisly remains were pushed in a wheelbarrow, at night, to a field near Pamela's home and thrown over the hedge. The severed head Pamela kept for a while, wrapped in a bag in the garden shed. It seems a strange sort of souvenir, but, you see, Pamela Sainsbury was so unsure of herself that she needed reminding now and again that the brute she had freed herself from really was dead! Eventually the head was thrown out with the rubbish.

Pamela's confidence returned slowly, and she began living a more normal life; to anybody who cared to ask where Paul was, she replied that he had left her – they weren't surprised and nobody missed him. Then in June 1991 Pamela Sainsbury confided in a girlfriend that she had murdered Paul. Prudently, the friend called the police.

It was not until December 1991 that Pamela Sainsbury, then thirty years old, faced her trial at Plymouth Crown Court. As the litany of horrors that had been her life for eight years was related to the court, the question on everybody's lips was *'Why didn't she leave him?'* Because, her counsel answered, 'She was in total fear for her life.' Pamela was represented by Helena Kennedy QC, a familiar figure in trials such as this, an outspoken legal reformer, and a vice-president of the Haldane Society of Socialist Lawyers. Ms Kennedy added: 'She was afraid that if she went to her parents they would be subjected to terror as well. Sainsbury had threatened to burn down their home.' Explaining Pamela's state of mind when she killed, counsel told the jury: 'She described a sadistic domination and a psychological torture so that she was unable to feel anything within herself. She says she felt like an eggshell. There probably can be few cases as bad as this in documenting one human being's abuse of another.'

The jury accepted Pamela Sainsbury's plea of not guilty of murder but guilty of manslaughter on the grounds of diminished responsibility. She also pleaded guilty to concealing a body. Exercising the greatest leniency in sentencing her to two years probation, Mr Justice Auld told Pamela: 'All the evidence shows that for many years you suffered regular and increasing violence and other forms of extreme sadism and sexual degradation at his hands. His domination of you mentally and physically was such that you lost even the nerve to run away from him.'

SCHREUDER, Frances Bradshaw   The notion that money is, indeed, the root of all manner of evils would have been enthusiastically supported by Mr Franklin J. Bradshaw, late of Salt Lake City, Utah. Having made a lot of money (over $60 million) from his own hard work, and believing in hanging on to what he had, Bradshaw was frequently heard advising that if it was money they wanted then the rest of the family should follow his example.

Youngest daughter Frances, however, having already failed twice to marry into money, and left with a family to rear on her own, was unprepared for so monotonous and time-consuming a route to the riches to which she felt entitled. Fortunately, her teenage son Marc was as unscrupulous as she herself, and in him Frances found a willing weapon. Although she had for some time been receiving welcome, if modest, hand-outs from Mrs Bradshaw, Frances had already openly declared that 'this family can't keep going much longer; not unless somebody kills my father'. And on 23 July 1978, Marc was dispatched with a Smith and Wesson .357 magnum to take care of the job.

After a protracted investigation, Marc Schreuder stood his trial in 1982, where he freely admitted killing his grandfather, for the simple reason that his mother had asked him to as a favour. So it came about, in 1983, that Frances Schreuder, who had never handled a gun in her life, was tried, convicted and sentenced to life imprisonment for conspiracy to murder her father. The worthless Marc escaped with a token five years.

SCIERRI, Antoinette   Antoinette Scierri had gone to live in the little village of Saint-Gilles, between Nîmes and Arles, in 1920. After an eclectic career – including a term of imprisonment for forgery – she settled down with a man named Joseph Rossignol and had begun to attract a good reputation as a thoughtful and diligent nurse.

Madame Drouard, an elderly, bedridden spinster had been one apparently successful recipient of Scierri's care, and her condition improved rapidly on the nourishing fare provided by the nurse. Then in December 1924, the old lady died suddenly of what was certified as heart failure.

By Christmas, Antoinette Scierri had become a regular home visitor to the Lachapelle household, where both husband and wife were suffering ill health. It was not to be a protracted sickness – on Christmas night Madame Lachapelle died of 'ptomaine poisoning' (an archaic name for food poisoning), and two days later the doctor certified the same cause of death for her husband.

It was some days after the holiday that Rossignol took sick with severe stomach pains. It was, in retrospect, a remarkable coincidence that his iliness followed closely on a domestic fracas in the course of which Joseph had physically abused his lover. Two days later 'ptomaine poisoning' had claimed his life too.

The next patient to die was old Marie Martin, after quaffing a cup of Scierri's coffee. Then Madame Gouan-Criquet passed away within forty-eight hours of receiving the nurse's ministrations. Due in large part to Monsieur Gouan-Criquet's outspoken suspicions – he had himself narrowly survived nurse Scierri's treatment – the doctor refused to issue a death certificate. The ensuing investigation revealed a bottle of pyralion under the latest victim's bed, casting doubt enough to have the bodies of four previous patients and Joseph Rossignol exhumed for autopsy.

The consequence of the post-mortem examinations was that Antoinette Scierri was arrested on five charges of murder by pyralion poisoning. At first she admitted responsibility for all but Madame Gouan-Criquet's death. During her trial at the Assize of Nîmes in 1929, Scierri attempted to push the blame on to a friend, Rosalie Gire, who had occasionally helped the nurse in her duties. Shrewdly, Gire had already offered her services as a prosecution witness and secured her own acquittal.

Antoinette Scierri was convicted of murder and sentenced to death – a sentence which was commuted to life imprisonment.

SCOTLAND, June The headline read almost like a music-hall gag – 'Wife beat husband to death with a rolling pin'. But for June Scotland it had been no joke, more like a nightmare from which the only way out was to strike back at the source of her seemingly endless ordeal. By 1987, Mrs Scotland had endured twenty-two years of psychological cruelty from her drunken, dictatorial husband Thomas. She later said: 'He was a pig. He used to mentally torture me, and the children dreaded him coming in at night. I just felt totally dominated. I was just like a zombie.' But it wasn't only the mental cruelty, Thomas Scotland also meted out physical violence, not only to his wife but to their three children. The problem was nobody could believe it. Scotland had one of those Jekyll and Hyde personalities, sociable and amusing at work, but an evil tyrant at home, throwing food at his wife if it was not to his liking. Worse still, by far, was Scotland's sexual abuse of his daughter, which started when she was eleven years old, and which, in 1987, was the direct cause of her attempting suicide.

There is always an incredulous public reaction to stories such as this, a horrified 'Why didn't you get out; why didn't you leave him?' The answer is that it is not always as easy as it sounds. In June Scotland's case she simply didn't have the nerve; her spirit had been utterly crushed: 'I knew the kind of person he was; that he would come and get me; it just seemed impossible to get away from him.' Mrs Scotland had, in her own words, become a 'zombie'. Of course, in similar circumstances some women do leave – an increasing number now that there is a more reliable self-help support network – and there are some that endure the torment for the whole of their lives. A few, very few, kill.

By August 1987, June Scotland had taken enough. There is rarely any special reason why one day is chosen over another, nothing planned, no truly dramatic event, just an unspoken realisation that it has to stop now. Later, Dr Nigel Eastman, a consultant forensic psychiatrist at London's St George's Hospital, attempted to explain what was going through Mrs Scotland's head. He said that her daughter's unsuccessful suicide attempt acted as a 'watershed': 'To Mrs Scotland it meant that not only was her husband controlling her and the family, he was on the point of destroying it.' Finally, she summoned the courage to tell Thomas Scotland she was leaving him. Predictably, perhaps, he laughed; and reminded her that she was his 'possession'. 'She believed the only thing to do to escape was to kill either her husband or herself,' Dr

Eastman continued. 'She felt abnormally helpless and hopeless. At the same time there was enough left in her to find a solution in terms of removing the cause of her helplessness in a total way.'

On that fateful evening in August, Mrs Scotland and the daughter whom she had taken into her confidence put their desperate plan into operation. June Scotland had already bought a stock of travel-sickness pills and now crushed up fifty of them, along with half a dozen Valium tablets, and sprinkled them on Thomas Scotland's Chinese stir-fry supper. If she had hoped the drugs would kill him, June Scotland was to be disappointed. Scotland complained of feeling very ill, as well he might, and went off to bed ordering his wife to call the doctor. She did not do so. Instead, June Scotland took a heavy rolling pin from the kitchen and bludgeoned her husband to death as he lay unconscious. Afterwards she and her daughter had a drink before trussing the body up in a tarpaulin and putting it in the outside tool-shed. Two days later, under cover of darkness, the two women put Thomas Scotland into a shallow grave at the end of the garden.

As far as the neighbours knew, Scotland had been called abroad on business – to Saudi Arabia; even his two sons had no inkling of the truth of their father's sudden disappearance from their lives.

The lie was lived for almost four years, during which time the neighbours probably began to think that Thomas Scotland had simply left home. And then, on Easter Sunday 1991, one of those neighbours decided to replace a broken fence at the foot of his garden; it was the fence which also ran along the end of Mrs Scotland's garden – just where the late Thomas Scotland's earthly remains had been laid to rest. It seemed that even from beyond the grave Scotland had returned to haunt his family.

Mrs June Scotland and her twenty-three-year-old daughter appeared before Mr Justice Garland at Luton Crown Court in March 1992. Mrs Scotland faced a charge of murder, which she denied, and both women admitted a charge of preventing lawful Christian burial. It was not that Mrs Scotland denied killing her husband, she denied *murdering* him. Her defence counsel, the redoubtable Ms Helena Kennedy QC, explained to the court: 'The idea that this was some well-planned thing was clearly not the reality . . . We are not talking about murder – the mark of Cain – we are talking about manslaughter. . . She was someone who for many years was abused and subjected to the most terrible, terrible behaviour . . . eventually her psyche surrendered.' In other words, 'she was suffering from mental impairment – diminished responsibility.'

After hearing the evidence of the three psychiatrists, the jury agreed. In sentencing Mrs Scotland to two years' probation for manslaughter, Mr Justice Garland told her: 'No good whatsoever would be served by seeking to punish you further.' Mrs Scotland's daughter was given the same sentence after the judge said: 'When you were eighteen you found yourself in a situation which must have been impossible, aimost an intolerable burden on you. For three and a half years you were burdened with that dark and terrible secret.'

SHERMAN, Lydia The 'Queen Poisoner', as she was christened at her trial, was one of the greediest and most successful poisoners to emerge from the criminal records of nineteenth-century America. Always for profit, Lydia Sherman killed, according to her own detailed confession, at least eleven people, though there could, she added as an afterthought, have been a dozen or fifteen more.

In the early 1860s, Lydia had married a policeman named Edward Struck, and she had already borne him six children. It was obviously enough for Mrs Struck, who decided to put a stop to childbirth by the simple expedient of poisoning her husband; to earn a little money out of the venture she also insured his life for a modest sum. It seemed to work well enough, with the chemist accepting without question her alleged intention to kill rats, so Lydia first insured and then poisoned all six of her children. Thus was she rich and free both at the same time. It can only be added, as a compliment to her skill as an actress, that never once was the slightest suspicion cast on this tragic widow.

In 1868 Lydia was married to Dennis Hurlbrut, a moderately rich, elderly (some said senile) farmer from New Haven, Connecticut. By 1870, the widow Hurlbrut had squandered her way through the late Dennis's estate, and was looking for more. In April, Lydia became housekeeper to wealthy Nelson Sherman of Derby, Connecticut, and when he had agreed to marry her, showed gratitude first by poisoning his baby with arsenic, and then his fourteen-year-old daughter Addie. Nelson Sherman himself, grief-stricken over the loss of his beloved children, succumbed to a poisoned hot chocolate drink on 12 May 1871.

This time, the local doctor became suspicious and called in a second opinion, and then a third. Which was three too many for Lydia, who had fled to New York at the first hint of trouble. Proved correct in his diagnosis of arsenic poisoning by the exhumation of the Sherman children, Dr Beardsley made his findings known to the police who lost no time in ordering Mrs Sherman's extradition back to Connecticut to face trial.

Lydia Sherman was convicted of second-degree murder, which reflected the mainly circumstantial nature of the evidence. She was sentenced to life and died in prison on 16 May 1878.

SMART, Pamela   Pamela and Greg Smart were just six days away from their first wedding anniversary. They had first met at a party, drawn together by their mutual fondness for heavy metal rock music and in particular the band Van Halen. Pamela was twenty-two, a media studies consultant for the local high schools, and Greg, two years older, was an aspiring insurance salesman. After their marriage they had bought a modest but comfortable home on a street with the inappropriately tranquil name of Misty Morning Drive, in Derry, New Hampshire. Here they slotted into the anticipated lifestyle of young middle-class America. Or so it seemed.

On the dark evening of 1 May 1989, Greg Smart let himself into the house to await his wife's return. He got no further than the hallway before an assassin jumped out from the shadows to confront him. The house had been very obviously ransacked, and police concluded that this had been a case of burglary going tragically wrong; only much later, when more information had become available did detectives become suspicious of the fact that there were no signs of forced entry, nor was anything of great value missing.

It had been Pamela who found her husband's body and alerted neighbours. After some preliminary histrionics, Pam calmed down to such an extent that in the days and weeks after Greg's death everybody remarked how *unnaturally* complacent she seemed. Pamela herself attributed it to some 'inner strength' conveyed to her by Greg's spirit. Weird, but people have different ways of coping with grief, and Pam was just allowed to get on with things the way that suited her best. Then she began to do strange things; she began to interfere in the police investigation, constantly telephoning the station, pestering to know the latest news of the inquiry.

Six weeks after the killing, the murder team were tipped off that a group of high-school kids were boasting about being involved in the Greg Smart incident. Finally, three youths were taken into custody, questioned, and charged with Greg's murder. They were Vance 'JR' Lattime, who supplied and drove the getaway car, Patrick 'Pete' Randall, who is supposed to have taken his father's gun for the killing, and William 'Bill' Flynn, just sixteen years old and accused of the shooting. All three were put on trial in January 1990, found guilty and sentenced to terms of life imprisonment.

But this was far from the end of the story. The same

grapevine of rumour and gossip which had exposed Lattime, Randall and Flynn was humming again, with the information that Pam Smart had been having a tempestuous affair with young Bill Flynn in the months before the murder. Much of this information was later given on oath by Cecilia Pierce, a girlfriend of Pam's who had been terrorized into silence. By now there was enough evidence to bring Pamela Smart to trial, and the most powerful of that evidence would come from the three convicted youths who had already plea-bargained their sentences in exchange for their testimony against Pam.

'Pete' Randall described how Pamela Smart had worked out the plan for her own husband's murder, instructing the boys on how to proceed, and leaving the back door of the house open for them. On two points she had been emphatic: they were not to harm her dog (called Halen after the band), and they were not to stain her new white leather sofa with blood.

Vance Lattime was not present during the murder, but waiting outside in the car for Flynn and Randall. He had, however, been in on all Pam's briefings. In her turn, according to Lattime's evidence, Pam had consulted them on how she ought to behave when she came home and 'found' Greg's body – should she scream, should she run out into the street, should she knock up the neighbours? They told her to act 'normal', whatever that means. Although the plan had always been to shoot Greg, Randall also took along a butcher's knife with which he confronted Greg first, demanding he take off his gold wedding ring. Greg Smart refused, and when asked why, replied: 'My wife would kill me.' It was when Randall lost his nerve and could not use the knife that Flynn drew out the gun.

When Bill Flynn entered the witness box he described, between bouts of sobbing, how the murder had taken place:

He [Greg] was yelling and trying to get back out of the house . . . Pete jumped up from where he was and shut the door. . . Greg was saying 'What's going on?' I told him to get down on his knees . . . he was kneeling there, it was obvious we weren't going to cut his throat . . . we couldn't bring ourselves to do it. I motioned to Pete like this [touches his breast pocket where the gun was hidden]; I took the gun out of my pocket, cocked the hammer back and pointed the gun at his head. I stood there for what seemed like a hundred years, then said 'God forgive me' . . . I pulled the trigger.

Flynn went on to describe the plans for after the murder, when Pam got the insurance money and was intending, so she said, to buy a house nearer to where he lived with his parents: 'So we could be together.'

The story that emerged was one of total infatuation on the part of Bill Flynn, and total domination on the part of Pamela Smart. What was in doubt was whether Pam had been the prime mover in the dreadful plot, or whether Flynn had been obsessed enough to dream up the plan to rid himself of his rival for Pam's affections. In his testimony, Bill was emphatic that he would never have killed Greg if Pam hadn't told him to.

But what of Pamela Smart? After all, it is easy to forget that this is her trial; that of her lover and his side-kicks is over, and sentences already passed.

Next into the witness box was Pam's close friend and confidante Cecilia Pierce. Cecilia was the first person let into the secret of Pam and Bill's romance, although at the time she didn't take it too seriously. It was also Cecilia who was the first to be consulted on the matter of Greg's untimely death – it was either that, Pam said, or divorce. The problem with divorce was that 'Greg would take the dog. Greg would take the house. She would have no money and nowhere to live.' When the three boys were arrested, Cecilia went immediately to the police, who arranged that her next meeting with Pam would be recorded via a miniature microphone concealed in her clothing.

In that conversation, Pamela Smart was reassuring her friend that just because she knew about Pam's plans, knew about her decision to have Greg killed, it didn't make her an accessory: 'I mean they're not going to believe Bill and Pete on the witness stand against you – they're on trial for murder.' Pam ended with the suggestion that: 'If you tell the fucking truth, you're probably going to get arrested. And even if you're not arrested, you're going to have to send Bill, Pete, JR and me to the fucking slammer for the rest of our life . . .'

Now came the point in the trial the media had been waiting for; Pamela Smart was about to take the stand in her own defence. During the months since her husband's murder, she had shown so little emotion that the press had nicknamed her 'The Ice Princess'. What everybody wanted to know was whether she would break under cross-examination.

Pam Smart admitted her attraction to Bill Flynn, fifteen years old at the time, although she was 'trying to fight her feelings'. Then on 24 March they were sexually intimate, and although she claimed under oath that she tried to break off the romance and remain faithful to her husband, 'Bill became obsessive and threatened to commit suicide.' What Pam emphasized now, as she had all along, was that she had not even been aware of the plot to kill Greg – let alone planned it. Of the night of the killing she said:

I walked up the steps, put the key in the lock and pushed the door open. I turned on the light and saw Greg. It all happened in less than a second. I remember seeing things near him, like a candlestick and a pillow. The first thing I thought was to go and get help. I called Greg's name; when he didn't give any answer I ran . . . It all happened so quickly. I didn't know what was going on, but I thought someone was in the house still . . . I ran next door and started banging on the door. No one would help me. It seemed it was taking for ever. I was ringing the door-bell and screaming 'Someone call the police, someone help

me.' It seemed they didn't come fast enough . . . so I ran to
the next door, and then the next one . . .

Then Pamela was asked about meetings with Bill Flynn
subsequent to the murder. She said that at first he acted like
everyone else, asking if she was all right, if there was anything
he could do to help, and so on. Then as time passed, Bill began
to ask a lot of questions about the police inquiry – whether they
were getting anywhere, whether they had any suspects. This is
the stage at which Pam, so she claimed, began to wonder if Bill
had had anything to do with Greg's death. Then Bill and his
cronies were arrested.

Asked if, in hindsight, she could now think of any reason
why Bill Flynn would have wanted to murder Greg, Pam
reluctantly admitted that it had crossed her mind it might be to
clear the way for their relationship. But the most damaging
block in this wall of evidence against her was the secret tape-
recording of Pam's conversation with Cecilia Pierce in which
she claimed she knew about the murder before it happened. So
why hadn't she told the police? Simple, Pam didn't want
anybody to know about her affair with Bill Flynn; or so she
said. If things were getting confusing for the jury, then they
seemed no less confusing for Pam Smart. She did not make a
good witness, having difficulty explaining herself, and when
she did, giving the unfortunate impression of a greedy and self-
centred woman who was quite capable of conspiring in the
death of her husband rather than lose out financially in the
divorce court.

And that is the impression that the jury must have formed,
because when they returned from their ten-hour deliberation
they announced verdicts of guilty on each of the three charges
– conspiracy to murder, accomplice to first-degree murder, and
tampering with a witness (in advising Cecilia not to go to the
police). It was unnecessary to do more than sentence Pamela
Smart on the conviction of being an accomplice to murder,

because it carries a mandatory sentence of life imprisonment without possibility of parole.

SMITH, Madeleine Madeleine Smith was born in Glasgow, the eldest daughter of James Smith, architect of that city, and a man of considerable wealth and influence. Smith kept a town house at India Street and a country home at Row, to which the family retreated during the summer months. In 1855, the Smiths comprised James and his wife, daughters Madeleine, aged nineteen, Bessie, aged seventeen, two sons, sixteen and fourteen, and little Janet, aged twelve; they kept two servants, Charlotte McLean and Christina Haggart.

Madeleine had been sent to boarding school in London and returned home in 1853 a 'finished' young lady – well bred, well read, and with an above average aptitude for music. Madeleine was also a singularly vivacious and attractive young woman and, on the streets of her native city, what was quaintly termed a 'head-turner'. Certainly she turned the head of Pierre L'Angelier.

But then, young L'Angelier had a head for turning, as they might have said. He had been born in Jersey in 1827 of French extraction, and at the time Madeleine crossed his path he was a humble clerk with the firm of Huggins and Company. Despite his modest circumstances, Pierre affected the manner of the dandy, and with his flowing whiskers and coiffed hair was, in his 'continental' way, considered attractive by the opposite sex. Indeed, it was his passionate hope one day to marry into social and financial security. By the slightly devious intervention of Robert Baird, a mutual friend of his and Madeleine's, L'Angelier contrived to meet the young lady in question by 'chance' in the street.

And it would seem that Madeleine was as attracted to Pierre L'Angelier as he was to her, and this 'casual' meeting in the street continued until gossip reached the ears of Mrs Smith who, rightly or wrongly, wanted better for her daughter than a poorly paid warehouse clerk. So the blossoming romance went underground, and Madeleine and Pierre continued their courting by the surreptitious exchange of letters.

In April Mr Smith intervened and, on the face of it, made Madeleine 'see sense'. At any rate, a letter dated 18 April leads us to believe as much:

> My dear Pierre,
>   I think you will agree with me in what I intend proposing, viz. that for the present the correspondence had better stop. I know your good feeling will not take this unkind . . .
>
> Madeleine

At about the same time Madeleine wrote a letter to Miss Mary Perry, a sort of confidante of L'Angelier's:

> Dearest Miss Perry,
>   Many kind thanks for all your kindness to me. Pierre will tell you I have bid him adieu. Papa would not give his consent so I am duty bound to obey him. Comfort dear Pierre; it is a heavy blow to us both.
>
> Mimi [a pet name used by L'Angelier]

It is, in hindsight, a pity that Miss Perry chose not to intervene to calm the situation down, for L'Angelier himself clearly had not the slightest intention of giving up graciously – or at all. His response is typically self-pitying and recriminatory by turns:

> Show my letters to anyone, Madeleine, I don't care who, and if any find that I mislead you I will free you from all blame. I warned you repeatedly not to be rash in your engagement and vows to me but you persisted in that false and deceitful flirtation, playing with affections which you knew to be pure and undivided and knowing at the same

time that at a word from your father you would break all
your engagement.

Then, no doubt to boost his sense of self-importance, unlucky
Pierre threatened to exile himself to Peru. And very effective it
was; in no time the secret affair was resumed. Furthermore,
Madeleine was now so caught up in the romance that her
father's anger at discovering the continuance of the amour
merely served to harden Madeleine's resolve.

Madeleine had not been unaided in conducting her postal
love affair; the family servant, Christina Haggart, had been
acting as courier – collecting Pierre's letters to her young
mistress from the post office, and taking hers to L'Angelier's
lodgings in Franklin Place. On more daring occasions, it was
Miss Haggart who let Pierre into the Smiths' house to keep his
secret assignations with Madeleine in the laundry.

If L'Angelier had been completely overwhelmed by his own
drama, then he had been as successful in carrying Madeleine
with him; by December the third she was addressing her letters
to 'My Own Darling Husband', and signing them 'Mimi
L'Angelier'. She was also actively encouraging Pierre to elope
with her. This, quite understandably, did not at all fit in with his
plans – he still had his eye firmly set on the family fortune. In
a quite heartless letter, L'Angelier began to get menacing:

My Dearest and Beloved Wife Mimi,
  Unless Huggins helps me I cannot see how I shall be
able to marry you for years. What misery to have such a
future in one's mind. Do speak to your father, open your
heart to him and try to win his friendship. Mimi, dearest,
you must take a bold step to be my wife. I entreat you, pet,
by the love you have for me, Mimi, do speak to your
mother – tell her it is the last time you ever shall speak of
me to her. You are right, Mimi, you cannot be the wife of
anyone else than me. I never, never can be happy until you

are my own, my dear, fond wife. Oh, Mimi, be bold for once, do not fear them – tell them you are my wife before God. Do not let them leave you without being married, for I cannot answer what would happen. My conscience reproaches me of a sin that marriage can only efface.

In the meantime, James Smith had moved his family to Blythswood Square, and in their next-door neighbour – a certain Mr Minnoch – thought he had found the ideal suitor for Madeleine. It is known that L'Angelier met Madeleine inside the new house at least once, and that they used her semi-basement bedroom window as a place not only to leave their letters, but to hold secret conversations. For Madeleine, the despair at her situation becomes apparent in a letter dated 23 January 1857:

My dear Pierre,

I was so very sorry that I could not see you tonight. I had expected an hour's chat with you; but we must just hope for better the next time . . . Dear darling, pray for our happiness. I weep now, Pierre, to think of our fate. If we could only get married, and all would be well. But alas, alas, I see no chance of happiness for me. I must speak with you. Yes, I must again be pressed to your loving bosom, be kissed by you, my only love, my dearest darling husband. Why were we fated to be so unhappy? Why were we made to be kept separate? My heart is too full to write more. Oh, pardon, forgive me . . . I am your ever true, and devoted,

Mimi L'Angelier

Things were looking increasingly desperate to Pierre as well, and out of frustration he went so far as to return some of Madeleine's letters – the consequence of which must have been very different from his expectations:

This may astonish you; but you have more than once returned me my letters, and my mind was made up that I should not stand the same thing again. Altogether, I think, owing to coolness and indifference (nothing else), that we had better, for the future, consider ourselves strangers.

I trust to your honour as a gentleman that you will not reveal anything that may have passed between us. I shall feel obliged by your bringing me my letters and the likeness [photograph] on Thursday evening at seven .

. . . I did once love you truly and fondly, but for some time back I have lost much of that love. There is no other reason for my conduct, and I think it but fair to let you know this. Adieu.

As might have been expected, Pierre L'Angelier behaved in neither an honourable nor a gentlemanly fashion. Not only did he flatly refuse to surrender Madeleine's letters, but held out the threat that he may well be inclined to show them to her father.

Madeleine made two more appeals for the return of her letters, and the depth of her despair is apparent in every line:

Monday night

Pierre,

I have just had your note. Pierre, for the love you once had for me, do nothing till I see you. For God's sake do not bring your once-loved Mimi to an open shame . . . Pierre, write to no one – to papa or any other. Oh! do not till I see you on Wednesday night. Pierre, be not harsh to me. I am the most guilty, miserable wretch on the face of the earth .

. .

Tuesday morning
I am ill. God knows what I have suffered. My punishment is

more than I can bear. Do nothing till I see you. For the love of heaven do nothing. I am mad. I am ill.

Tuesday evening

Pierre,

For the love you once had for me, do not denounce me to my P . . . if he should read my letters to you he will put me from him – he will hate me as a guilty wretch.

For God's love forgive me, and betray me not. For the love you once had for me do not bring down my father's wrath on me. I shall be ruined. Who would trust me? Shame will be my lot. Despise me, hate me, but make me not the public scandal. Forget me for ever. Blot out all remembrance of me.

Oh, for God's sake, for the love of Heaven, hear me. I grow mad. I have been ill, very ill, all day. I have had what has given me a false spirit. I had resource to what I should not have taken, but my brain is on fire. I feel as if death would indeed be sweet. Denounce me not. Pierre, Pierre, think of our once happy days. Pardon me if you can; pray for me as the most wretched, guilty, miserable creature on the earth.

Pierre L'Angelier never returned Madeleine's love letters.

L'Angelier died on 23 March 1857, at his lodgings in Franklin Place; he had been poisoned with arsenic. On 31 March, Madeleine Smith was arrested and charged with his murder.

Madeleine's trial opened in Edinburgh on Tuesday 30 June 1857, where she faced three charges of administering poison to Pierre L'Angelier, resulting in his death.

Evidence established that Miss Smith, on the pretence of killing rats, had purchased considerable quantities of arsenic; a previous attempt to send the family's house-boy on an errand for prussic acid had failed when the chemist refused to serve the youth. The three occasions on which arsenic had been purchased coincided, the court was told, with three occasions on which Pierre L'Angelier had been taken violently ill. They also coincided with three occasions on which he had visited Madeleine at their private rendezvous outside her bedroom window at Blythswood Square and had been given a warming cup of cocoa. The last date had been 22 March, after which assignation, L'Angelier had returned to his lodgings so painfully ill that the landlady, Mrs Jenkins, summoned a doctor. The doctor arrived, felt the pulse, lifted L'Angelier's head, and said he was dead.

However, this evidence was in no way assisted by the post-mortem results. The arsenic bought by Madeleine Smith had been mixed with soot and indigo. It was a simple precaution to avoid the naturally white powdered arsenic being mistaken for a more innocuous substance. When L'Angelier's stomach was opened up for examination, no traces of either soot or indigo were found – just arsenic. In fact, Madeleine's able defence attorney, Mr John Inglis, drew a sufficiently convincing picture of his client's innocence that the jury, after a deliberation just short of half an hour, found the case against her Not Proven.

It is a matter for conjecture whether, deprived of that convenient Scottish alternative, the jury would have found her Guilty or Not Guilty; but as it was, Madeleine Smith left the court a free woman.

SNYDER, Ruth, and GRAY, Henry Judd   The neighbours found Albert Snyder lying on the bed of his Queen's Village, Long Island home, his head and face battered beyond recognition. It was the morning of 20 March 1927, and they had been alerted to the tragedy by ten-year-old Lorraine Snyder, who had woken up to find her mother, Ruth, bound and gagged, lying outside the bedroom door. When Ruth Snyder had been released from her bondage she claimed that she and Albert had been asleep when an intruder – with a moustache and looking like an Italian – had knocked her unconscious, dragged her out of bed and tied her up. Certainly there was some superficial evidence of a robbery attempt, a few drawers had been ransacked and some cooking pots and crockery had been thrown about in the kitchen, but there was no sign that the intruder had forced an entry. That was not all. Mrs Snyder had told the police that some valuable jewellery was missing, presumably stolen; why, then, was it found underneath her mattress? By now the doctor had made his examination of Snyder's corpse, and what had at first looked like a simple bludgeoning was now revealed as a carefully calculated murder. In addition to the head wounds, a length of wire had been tied tightly round the victim's neck, and chloroform-soaked wads had been forced into his nostrils and his mouth.

It was clear that Mrs Snyder would have more than a bit of explaining to do; and when detectives pieced together the torn scraps of a letter to Ruth from a person signing themselves 'Judd' she decided to co-operate. Or at least she decided to talk. 'Judd' was Henry Judd Gray, a quiet thirty-five-year-old salesman with whom Ruth Snyder was having an affair. Gray was questioned, and he too admitted the liaison, but denied any part in Albert Snyder's murder. Playing a tough game, detectives told Ruth that Gray had confessed and blamed her for the killing. The ruse worked, sort of. Ruth now made a statement in which she admitted to conspiring with Judd Gray in the murder of her husband, but stressed she played no physically active part in the crime herself. Gray disagreed, he insisted that they had carried out the murder together at Ruth's insistence. He added, rather pathetically: 'She had this power over me.'

Both Ruth Snyder and Judd Gray were charged jointly on counts of first-degree murder. From all the evidence it would seem that poor Judd had been right about his mistress; she had schemed and cajoled and finally manoeuvred the unfortunate fellow into a position where he would have done anything for her. Not that this cut much ice with the jury, and both Snyder and Gray were found guilty as charged. In January 1928 they were judicially executed in the electric chair at Sing Sing.

There is an interesting postscript to the executions. A reporter named Thomas Howard working with the *Daily News,* smuggled a camera into the execution chamber strapped to his ankle. Just as the surge of electricity hit Ruth's body Howard activated the shutter by remote cable and immortalized the final moment of her life. It remains one of the most powerful images in the history of crime.

SOLIS, Magdalena and Eleazor, and **HERNANDEZ, Cayetano and Santos**   The Solis siblings began in a modest enough way of business, Magdalena plying her trade as a prostitute around the industrial city of Monterrey, her homosexual brother Eleazor occupying himself as her pimp. And it might have continued so until the twin ravages of age and disease robbed them of professional credibility. But in 1962 they were approached with a proposition so bizarre that it would defy the talents of a novelist to invent. Two brothers named Cayetano and Santos Hernandez had set up some kind of sex cult in Yerba Buena, and desperately needed a god and goddess – did Eleazor and Magdalena want the job? Of course they did, it was a whole lot more attractive than life on the streets of Monterrey.

The Hernandez brothers had been using the cult in order to squeeze money out of the gullible local farmers and, as an added bonus, had persuaded them that submitting to sexual molestation by the priests (themselves) was essential to the purging of demons. With the recruitment of the Solises, activities were expanded, and Magdalena satisfied the lesbian tendencies of the priestesses, while Eleazor and Cayetano Hernandez indulged their homosexual appetites with the farmers. It is in the nature of events that, sooner or later, all good things come to an end, and it was only a matter of time before the peasants tired of giving body, soul and their meagre income to the cult.

This was the point at which Magdalena introduced the idea of revitalizing interest with a couple of human sacrifices, and ordered two men stoned to death and their blood collected for a kind of unholy communion. The venture proved to be such a success that blood sacrifice became a regular feature of cult life. Indeed, Magdalena offered the ultimate sacrifice and gave her lesbian lover up to be beaten to a pulp, accompanied by another luckless member who had his heart cut out.

Unknown to the celebrants, these last two ritual murders had been observed by a teenage boy who took his horrifying tale as fast as his legs would carry him to officer Martinez, the local policeman. Martinez followed the lad back to Yerba Buena to investigate, and they themselves were hacked to death by devotees.

A few missing peasants were one thing, but when a policeman disappeared the authorities wanted to know why, and an armed police squad was sent in to root out the reason why officer Martinez deserted in such a peremptory fashion. During the battle that followed, members of the cult were routed, and after the shooting of Santos Hernandez they surrendered.

On 13 June 1963 – eleven days after their arrest – Magdalena and Eleazor Solis together with twelve members of the cult were tried on charges of multiple murder, convicted and given the maximum sentence of thirty years in the state prison. Cayetano Hernandez, founder of the cult, had been murdered by a disaffected follower after the killing of officer Martinez.

SPENCER, Brenda There are many motives for murder, almost as many as there are murderers to commit them; but there can be few more fatuous excuses for taking two lives than that offered by Brenda Spencer.

On Monday morning, 29 January 1979, sixteen-year-old

high-school student Brenda Spencer took up her position outside the Cleveland Elementary School and waited for the principal to open the gate. As he did so, and as the children were milling around, Brenda opened fire with a .22 semi-automatic rifle. The twenty- minute shooting spree left principal Burton Wragg and the school caretaker dead and nine children between the ages of six and twelve wounded. Then Brenda ran back home to wait for the police.

Brenda Spencer lived with her divorced father and had always been a problem child. This was partly a reaction to her parents' separation and partly because she just was. Even before her mid-teens she had been involved with drugs and petty theft, and was unhealthily addicted to violent films. For some years Brenda had owned a BB gun which she used to kill birds and break windows. Then at Christmas 1978, Brenda's father bought her a proper gun as a present – it was the gun she used to shoot up the Cleveland Elementary.

And now the outside of the house was swarming with heavily armed police and media reporters. At last Brenda was getting the attention she had craved for so long; she was famous. For two hours Brenda talked to negotiators and pressmen on the telephone. Why, they all wanted to know, did she do such a thing? Brenda explained: 'I just started shooting, that's it. I just did it for the fun of it. I just don't like Mondays . . . I did it because it's a way to cheer the day up. Nobody likes Mondays . . .'

Later in 1979, the Irish punk rock band, The Boomtown Rats, immortalized Brenda Spencer with their hit song 'I Don't Like Mondays'. Despite the fact that many American radio stations refused to play the song 'for reasons of good taste', it was actually an insightful and thought-provoking depiction of the school shooting ... and broke the record for longest stay at the number one spot in the pop charts in both the UK and the US.

Brenda Spencer was put on trial in Santa Ana, California and convicted on two charges of murder, for which she received two twenty-five-to-life terms, and one charge of assault with a deadly weapon, for which she was sentenced to a concurrent forty-eight-year term.

To date, the now middle-aged Brenda Spencer has been refused parole on three occasions, largely because she has refused to accept any blame for the shooting rampage. Her explanations range from the semi-plausible claim that she was too drunk at the time to know what she was doing, to the totally incredible suggestion that all her victims were actually shot by the police, who then framed her.

STEINHEIL, Jeanne-Marguerite It was one of the most extraordinary crimes of its time, involving as it did those ingredients of passion and intrigue that made the French assize courts so beloved of sensation seekers.

Jeanne-Marguerite Japy was born in 1869 to a successful businessman of Beaucourt and his wife. She grew into an attractive, coquettish young woman with more than her share of admirers. However, when it came to taking a husband, Jeanne-Marguerite chose Adolphe Steinheil, a painter with little talent and fewer prospects. But that was to reckon without the new Madame Steinheil, for it became her habit to insist that each of her lovers – and they were many and high-placed – purchase one of Adolphe's mediocre canvases. Soon there were enough Steinheils hanging on the walls of Paris's fashionable residences for his to have become quite a celebrated name in his chosen art. Eventually, Jeanne-Marguerite aimed for the top and dragged the bewildered Adolphe with her. She became mistress of no less a public figure than the President of France himself, Monsieur Felix Fauré'. Fauré had paid his dues by commissiomng a portrait of himself by Steinheil, and had been so pleased with the result that the painter was knighted.

There is one episode which is worth repeating, though it has nothing to do with the incidents which later brought shame to the Steinheil name. On the afternoon of 16 February 1899, the president's servants ran into their master's bed-chamber to investigate the loud sounds of distress that emanated from that direction. There they found Jeanne-Marguerite with not a stitch of clothing about her, screaming hysterically. On the floor beside the bed lay President Fauré, dead. It transpired that, during a particularly energetic bout of love-making, the unfortunate man had suffered a heart attack. It is not recorded whether he died with a smile on his face.

Tragedy struck the Steinheil household in 1908. On the morning of 1 June the servant was alerted by a cry from Madame's bedroom, and scampering up the stairs as fast as his legs would carry him, discovered Madame tied to the bed and the master dead on the floor, a rope around his neck. In another bedroom lay the body of Jeanne-Marguerite's mother, Madame Japy; she too had been strangled. Madame Steinheil told detectives from the Sûréte that three men and a red-haired woman had burst into her room in the early hours demanding money; she refused, and for her obstinacy one of the men knocked her unconscious. When she came round, Jeanne-Marguerite found herself lashed to the bedframe. A subsequent inventory revealed that cash and jewellery to the value of 6,000 francs were missing. Although a bevy of likely suspects was rounded up and Madame Steinheil obligingly identified them as her attackers, they all had watertight alibis. Meanwhile, the description of the missing jewellery which had been circulated to the Paris jewellers and hock-shops was beginning to produce results. A jewellery repairer had been given some items that fitted the description, and had been asked to alter them. They had been left by a Mademoiselle Mariette Wolff; the same Mariette Wolff who was in service as Madame Steinheil's maid.

Although the circumstantial evidence pointing to Jeanne-Marguerite was convincing, there was nothing tangible to link her to the murders. It was thought at one stage that the two victims might have been poisoned before the killer had rigged the scene of the crime to look like strangulation, but when the bodies were exhumed, neither corpse bore any trace of poison. The trial was confusing and inconclusive, though one bizarre touch was provided by a man named Jean Lefèvre, who had apparently quite fallen for Jeanne-Marguerite in her time of adversity. In the middle of the trial, Lefèvre leapt from his seat and protested loudly that he had been one of the murderers – the woman with red hair.

It was but a brief diversion, and as the process ground to a halt it was clear that the prosecution case was too weak to persuade a jury beyond reasonable doubt. Madame Steinheil was acquitted and left her native shores for England, where she married into the aristocracy. She died in 1954 – as Lady Abinger.

T

TARNOWSKA, Countess Maria Born in St Petersburg, Russia, in 1878, her rather extraordinary names (for a Russian) – Maria Nicolaievna O'Rourk – were the consequence of having a Russian noblewoman for a mother and an Irish soldier of fortune (who had ended up commanding a military unit for Peter the Great) as a father. From an early age Maria exuded sensuality, and was sexually provocative beyond her tender years, attracting an entourage of young cavalry officers from her father's camp.

At the age of seventeen, decidedly against her father's wishes, Maria became involved with the notorious libertine Count Vassili Tarnowsky; in fact, they eloped, and Maria bore the Count a son. That was before he tired of her company and went back to his seemingly endless string of mistresses. Left to her own devices Maria retaliated by taking a succession of lovers – most of them her husband's friends, one of them his teenage brother Peter. When she left Peter he hanged himself. Not that Maria paid it much mind, by this time she was involved with Captain Alexis Bozevsky, a member of the Tsar's personal guard and, like her husband, a legendary womanizer. When she tired of Bozevsky, Maria contrived for Tarnowsky to find them in bed together, sure in the belief that the insanely jealous Count would kill Bozevsky; he did.

Next on Maria's casualty list was Dr Dmitri Stahl, a family friend, who insinuated himself into her boudoir by the simple expedient of drugging her with cocaine, to which she later became hopelessly addicted. When Maria had bled the doctor dry of any wealth he may have had, she ditched him, causing the unhappy fellow to put a bullet into his own brain. In May 1903 Maria took up with a married lawyer named Donat Prilukoff. Prilukoff had originally been hired to help Maria get her hands on Tarnowsky's estate if he was imprisoned for the killing of Captain Bozevsky; instead, Tarnowsky was awarded a verdict of justifiable homicide, and rather than dismiss the lawyer, Maria took him on as a lover. And very useful he was too; as soon as Maria had squandered his own modest wealth, Prilukoff started to embezzle his firm.

Not long after, and still with the dog-like Prilukoff following on, Maria entrapped a wealthy Polish count named Karamowsky. While this ill-assorted trio were in Warsaw at the Count's expense, he introduced Maria to Dr Nicolai Naumoff. And in Naumoff Maria found the perfect partner for her sado-sexual fantasies; on one occasion, it is said, she carved her initials in his arm for the pleasure of watching the blood flow. And other things too exotic for such a book as this. These were the kind of bedgames which later earned Maria the sobriquet 'The Russian Vampire'. Perhaps it is understandable that Count Karamowsky took a dim view of being usurped by Naumoff, and in a moment of pique he withdrew the rather generous allowance he had bestowed on Maria. It was the worst thing he could possibly have done; Maria did not take kindly to being deprived of money.

On the pretence that she would marry him, Maria persuaded Karamowsky to take out a large insurance policy on his life. And then set about planning his decease. This was to be achieved with help from the faithful Naumoff and the devoted

Prilukoff. First Maria told Naumoff that the Count had forcibly raped her, and insisted the doctor avenge her honour by shooting him; obediently Dr Naumoff agreed. Then, with a promise that when the Count was out of the way they would spend eternity together, Prilukoff was dispatched on a similar errand.

On 6 September 1907, Nicolai Naumoff burst into the Italian villa which Karamowsky was leasing and fired six shots into the Count's body. Prilukoff, who had wind of Naumoff's attempt on the Count's life decided to do a bit of double-crossing himself and put the police on Naumoff's trail; the idea being that with both Karamowsky and Naumoff out of the way Maria would be his.

The fact was, Naumoff, Prilukoff and Maria Tarnowska were all in custody in a very short time, and after some legal wrangling appeared before a court in Venice on 4 March 1910. The trial was one of the decade's great spectacles, and press representatives flocked to the city from all corners of the globe – everybody wanted a glimpse of the woman they were calling 'The Sphinx in Crêpe', the 'Wax Madonna', the *femme fatale* who had been responsible for the death of so many men. And they were not disappointed; a columnist for the *Mail* of London reported that 'Only Guy de Maupassant, or Gabriele D'Annunzio, could describe the peculiar power of those weird black eyes . . . those inscrutable eyes seem to read one's very soul.'

Naumoff, visibly cracking under the strain, collapsed weeping in the dock, blaming Maria's 'evil spell' for his predicament; Prilukoff made a similar excuse. The trial, after all the fuss, was quite short; Maria Tarnowska was sentenced to eight years and four months' imprisonment, Prilukoff to ten years; and, rather inexplicably considering his finger had been on the trigger, Naumoff was given just three years and four months. Perhaps the judge felt he had already suffered enough at the hands of 'The Vampire'.

Maria was confined in Trani Prison where she adapted fairly well, penning morbid verses for publication in French magazines. It is said that she received more than fifty offers of marriage during her time inside. Maria Tarnowska was released in August 1912 and died in obscurity eleven years later, her health permanently damaged by her cocaine habit.

TERRELL, Bobbie Sue Dudley   Bobbie Sue was night-nurse supervisor at the North Horizon Health Care Center in Saint Petersburg, Florida. During a thirteen-day period in November 1984, twelve elderly patients died at the hospital, an attempt was made to set the building on fire, there was a miscellany of vandalism and Bobbie Sue Terrell herself, so she claimed, was stabbed by a prowler.

Following an intensive inquiry by the Florida state authorities, Terrell was dismissed from her job and entered hospital as a patient for medical and psychiatric treatment. Meanwhile, the police had launched a full-scale investigation into the mysterious deaths at North Horizon. During the course of these inquiries, detectives discovered that Ms Terrell had been dismissed from a similar hospital post in Illinois after a self-inflicted stab wound aroused fears concerning her mental stability. They also learned that a large supply of insulin had gone missing from a locked cabinet at around the time that ninety-four-year-old Mrs Anna Larsen had been overdosed with the drug, but thankfully not fatally. Exhumations were ordered for nine of the dozen patients who had died in November, and autopsies confirmed that at least two of them had been murdered.

After a Grand Jury hearing, Terrell was charged on four counts of first-degree murder and one of attempted murder. In detail, these related to the strangulation or asphyxiation, on 13 November 1984, of Mrs Aggie Marsh, aged ninety-seven; the injection with overdoses of insulin of Mrs Leathy McKnight, eighty-five, and seventy-nine-year-old Mrs Mary Carter on 23 and 26 November respectively; and the murder by either asphyxiation or the injection of an unknown lethal substance of Mrs Stella Bradham, also on 26 November. The attempted murder charge related to the case of Mrs Larsen.

As the result of a plea-bargaining arrangement entered into to take account of Bobbie Sue Terrell's history of mental instability and complications arising from the fact that many of the witnesses were elderly and in frail health, she pleaded guilty to second-degree murder, and in February 1988 was sentenced to sixty-five years' imprisonment.

THOMAS, Sarah Harriet   Though she was reputed to be wealthy – and many reclusive old people are, with more or less reason – Miss Jefferies was known to have been endowed with an exceptionally mean and grasping nature, which, frustrating though it must have been to her servant, was hardly grounds for bloody murder.

At the time of the occurrence, which was in the early part of the year 1849, Miss Jefferies was residing at 6 Trenchard Street, Bristol. It had been on the fifth of February that Sarah Harriet Jones – by all reports a presentable, even pretty, young woman, if of simple birth – was taken on as an all-purpose servant. In no time at all neighbours began to hear the mistress/servant sounds with which they had become familiar through many changes of domestic staff; that is, the shouting and raving of Miss Jefferies and the terrified sobbing of Sarah Thomas.

There followed an unexpected day of silence; a succession of days, on which not even the shutters of No. 6 were opened. And they remained closed until the police were eventually summoned to investigate the unaccustomed lack of activity. The sight that met them on entering Miss Jefferies' house was shocking in the extreme; the lady of the house lay twisted in a puddle of congealed blood on the floor, her head a bloody pulp from the severe battering that it had suffered. The body of her small dog was found pushed into the water closet, its throat slashed across.

Missing from the house was Sarah Thomas, upon whose head suspicion immediately fell. The unfortunate girl was eventually found hiding in the coal cellar of her parents' house at Pensford, surrounded by the money and jewellery which she had stolen from her late employer's home.

Brought to trial, Sarah Thomas related the most heart-rending account of the cruelty of her mistress, of the constant fear of further ill-usage, and finally the hatred, the blind rage that had caused her to destroy the single source of all her misery.

Found guilty, and despite a petition signed by 3,500 Bristol women, Sarah Thomas was condemned to the gallows; but it was to be one of the most difficult and harrowing executions of hangman Calcraft's long career. On the fatal day, the prisoner refused absolutely to co-operate in her own death, and it took half a dozen burly warders to drag the struggling, screaming victim to her fate.

THOMPSON, Edith, and BYWATERS, Frederick   Edith Graydon was born on Christmas Day 1893, and brought up in Manor Park, near Ilford. At school she proved both intelligent and charming, if a little deceitful, and on leaving obtained a respectable post first as secretary and later as manageress to a wholesale milliners in the City of London. It was while travelling up to work each morning on the train that she first met Percy Thompson, a shipping clerk. They were married on 15 January 1915, when she was twenty-two and he was twenty-six. In July 1920 the Thompsons bought their own terraced house at 41 Kensington Gardens, Ilford.

The Thompsons settled down to the sort of respectable and unexciting existence typical of couples of their age and station, and Edith was left to satisfy the more frivolous and romantic aspects of her nature by harmlessly flirting with Percy's men friends and retreating into her own colourful imagination, fuelled by a voracious appetite for romantic novels. What is clear is that married life in general, and Percy Thompson in particular, was a great disappointment to her.

In June 1921 the Thompsons spent their summer holiday at Shanklin on the Isle of Wight. Avis Graydon, Edith's younger sister, was invited along and in order to even up the numbers Percy extended an invitation to a young friend of the Graydon family, Freddie Bywaters. Bywaters was just eighteen, and two years earlier he had gone into the Merchant Navy. He had just returned from a trip to Australia when he joined the holiday party. For Edith Thompson it was a perfect holiday. She was free of all the normal restraints and could join in with the youngsters swimming, playing tennis and having a generally good time. But it was more than that, because dashing young Freddie, with his tales of foreign parts, had turned his attentions from the younger Avis towards Edith.

The thought of a secret lover must have seemed like a dream come true to Edith. The mutual attraction must have been fairly obvious, but all that Percy Thompson noticed was that his wife seemed happier and that Freddie seemed a pleasant young fellow. He needed little persuading to take Bywaters on as a lodger at Kensington Gardens.

Such close proximity created the right climate for Edith's affair to go further, and it was only a matter of time before even Percy Thompson began to notice what was going on in his own house.

The inevitable happened on Monday 1 August; according to Edith's later evidence in court:

I had some trouble with my husband that day. I think it originated over a pin. But eventually it was brought to a head by my sister not appearing at tea when she said she would. I wanted to wait for her, but my husband objected, and said a lot of things to me about my family that I resented. He then struck me several times, and eventually threw me across the room. Bywaters was in the garden ... He came into the room and stopped my husband. Later on that day there was a discussion about a separation . . . I wanted a separation and Bywaters entreated my husband to separate from me. But he said what he usually said, that he would not.

Freddie Bywaters was, not unnaturally, asked to find alternative accommodation.

The separation of the two lovers did nothing to dampen the ardour of their affair. They met whenever possible, snatched lunchtime meetings in restaurants, and more regularly when Edith went to see her family on Fridays and Bywaters would be there on the pretext of visiting Avis. Bywaters was also away at sea on the SS *Morea* five times in the next year for periods of between six weeks and two months. The progress of their relationship was charted through a succession of rambling love letters. Edith wrote more than eighty in just over a year and Bywaters was little less prolific. But for all their secrecy, Percy Thompson was sporadically aware that something was still going on. After one of his sea voyages, Freddie Bywaters determined to have it out with Percy. This is how Bywaters recalled the events of 5 November:

I had taken Mrs Thompson out previously. Apparently he [Percy Thompson] had been waiting at the station for her and he had seen the two of us together. He made a statement to Mrs Thompson – 'He is not a man or else he would ask my permission to take you out' – and she reported that statement to me the following day. In consequence of that I went and saw Mr Thompson . . . I said: 'Why don't you come to an amicable agreement? Either have a separation or you can get a divorce.' And he hummed and hawed about it. He said: 'Yes – No – I don't see it concerns you.'

I said: 'You are making Edie's life a hell. You know she isn't happy with you.' He replied: 'Well, I've got her, and I will keep her.'

When Bywaters went to sea again, Edith didn't take long to resume writing to him. It may be wondered why Mrs Thompson didn't just leave her husband for Freddie Bywaters. After all, she had the security of her own job earning a good wage. But in that very different age any hint of scandal would have been sufficient to get her dismissed and thus lose any chance of gaining such respectable, well-paid employment in the future. Already, Percy had caused some fuss at her place of employment when he learned that Bywaters had been sending letters there. Edith Thompson might have been romantic, but she didn't much fancy the privations of poverty.

Besides, one suspects she quite liked the idea of having two men fighting over her. In early 1922, a predictable complication of her affair had to be dealt with. Although in 1922 to procure an abortion was an illegal act with serious consequences, Mrs Thompson was sufficiently afraid of motherhood to risk both the dangerous medical measures and the possibility of imprisonment if discovered.

Throughout this period Edith was growing increasingly concerned over Bywaters' continued devotion to her during his prolonged trips at sea; and so she began to weave the fantasy which would eventually put a noose around her neck.

You must do something this time . . . opportunities come and go by – they have to – because I'm helpless and I think and think and think . . . It would be so easy darlint – if I had things – I do hope I shall . . . Have enclosed cuttings of Dr Wallis's case. It might prove interesting. [The letter contained two newspaper cuttings, one headed 'Mystery of Curate's Death', the other 'Poisoned Chocolates for

University Chief. Deadly Powder posted to Oxford
Chancellor. Ground Glass in Box.']
(Letter from Mrs Thompson to Bywaters, 10 February
1922)

He puts great stress on the fact of the tea tasting bitter, 'as
if something had been put in it' he says. Now I think
whatever else I try it in again will still taste bitter – he will
recognize it and be more suspicious still . . . I wish we had
not got electric light – it would be so easy. I'm going to try
the glass again occasionally – when it is safe. I've got an
electric light globe this time.
(Letter from Mrs Thompson to Bywaters, 1 April 1922)

I used the 'light bulb' three times but the third time – he
found a piece – so I've given up – until you come home.
(Letter from Mrs Thompson to Bywaters, 24 April 1922)

None of this actually occurred, as Percy Thompson's perfect
health and later medical evidence was to indicate. Its intention
seems to have been understood by Bywaters, who pandered to
her little fiction but avoided anything which resembled action.

On 23 September 1922, Bywaters arrived back in Tilbury; he
was resolved to settle matters once and for all. He would 'have
it out' with Percy Thompson and be done with it. Over the next
ten days the lovers met several times.

On 3 October, after tea with Freddie at Fuller's, Mrs
Thompson went off to meet her husband at Aldersgate Street
Station. They had arranged to go with some friends to the
theatre. Meanwhile, Freddie Bywaters went to visit the
Graydons for the evening. He left them at about 11.00 p.m.

At midnight the Thompsons arrived back at Ilford, and as
they walked along Belgrave Road, on their way to Kensington
Gardens, Freddie Bywaters rushed up from behind pushing Mrs
Thompson aside and confronting her husband. Edith cried out,

'Oh, don't! Oh, don't!' as Bywaters and Percy Thompson struggled.

This is how Freddie described the incident:

> I pushed Mrs Thompson with my right hand, like that. With my left I held Thompson and caught him by the back of his coat and pushed him along the street, swinging him round . . . I said to him: 'Why don't you get a divorce or separation, you cad?' . . .
> He said: 'I know that's what you want. But I'm not going to give it to you. It would make it too pleasant for both of you.' I said:
> 'You take a delight in making Edie's life hell.' Then he said: 'I've got her – I'll keep her – and I'll shoot you' . . . going at the same time like that with his right hand – as if to draw a gun from his pocket. As he said that he pushed me in the chest with his left fist, and I said: 'Oh, will you?' and drew a knife and put it in his arm . . . I had the knife in my left hand. All the time struggling, I thought he was going to kill me . . . and I tried to stop him.

Bywaters ran off down Seymour Gardens, eventually arriving back at his mother's house in Norwood by taxi at three in the morning.

Percy Thompson had received four superficial cuts beneath the ribs on his left side. There were two on his chin and two deeper ones on his lower law. He had a stab wound on his right forearm and there were two stab wounds in the back of his neck, one of which had severed the carotid artery and caused the death some minutes later. Meanwhile, Mrs Thompson had hurried over to her husband: 'He fell against me and said "O-er" . . . I helped him along by the side of the wall, and I think he slid down the wall on to the pavement . . . I went to get a doctor.' The doctor arrived a little later, followed at 1.00 a.m. by Police Sergeant Mew.

On the following evening Freddie Bywaters was arrested, and Edith Thompson was taken into custody later that night when she made a statement admitting that Bywaters had been Percy Thompson's attacker. That evening Bywaters was informed that Mrs Thompson would be charged with her husband's murder. 'Why her? Mrs Thompson was not aware of my movements,' he claimed. He then made a full confession.

A week after the crime police discovered in Bywaters' sea chest aboard the SS *Morea* at Tilbury a large cache of letters that Mrs Thompson had written to him. They made interesting reading. The charges of conspiring to murder, attempting to murder and inciting to murder were added to the basic charge against Mrs Thompson.

When the trial of Edith Thompson and Frederick Bywaters opened at the Old Bailey on 6 December 1922, large crowds had collected outside the courtroom to witness the spectacle. Sir Henry Curtis- Bennett, defending Mrs Thompson, immediately asked the judge that the bundle of sixty-two letters that the prosecution wished to use be declared inadmissible. This was refused and Curtis-Bennett had to fall back on an agreement that had been reached with the prosecution that only limited extracts would be read out. This had the advantage of excluding references to Mrs Thompson's attempts at self-abortion which, it was felt, would set the jury implacably against her. The disadvantage, however, was that editing out the gossipy and inconsequential bulk of the letters failed to reveal their fantastic and highly romanticized character. The references to poisoning seemed far more sinister in this bare context.

The second disaster for the defence was Mrs Thompson's insistence on going into the witness box. She was sure that the jury would understand the tragedy of her 'great love' but in the shaken and pallid state she presented to the world during the trial she was often confused and made to appear to lie under cross-examination. Freddie Bywaters was already reconciled to his fate, and sought only to exonerate his lover from any blame for his actions.

The greatest disadvantage that Edith Thompson faced, however, was the stifling tone of moral rectitude with which the prosecution attempted to envelop the trial, an attitude which the judge seemed to endorse. The love affair was painted as a sordid, secretive piece of adultery leading inevitably to a grubby crime committed by two deceitful and amoral people. Curtis-Bennett tried his eloquent best to counteract this impression, but in his summing-up to the jury, Mr Justice Shearman adopted the tones of an Old Testament prophet:

> The charge really is – I am not saying whether it is proved – a common or ordinary charge of a wife and an adulterer murdering the husband . . . You are told this is a case of great love. Take one of the letters as a test – 'He has the right by law to all that you have a right to by nature and by love.' If that means anything, it means that the love of a husband for his wife is something improper because marriage is acknowledged by law, and that the love of a woman for her lover, illicit and clandestine, is something great and noble. I am certain that you, like any other right-minded person, will be filled with disgust at such a notion.

The jury retired on 11 December; it took them just over two hours to reach a verdict of guilty against both defendants.

While some sections of public opinion were smugly satisfied by the verdict, others were horrified. To many, Edith Thompson had been sentenced to hang for adultery. It was also fifteen years since a woman had been hanged and it seemed now a primitive act of vengeance. A petition for a reprieve was raised, and collected several thousand signatures. Three days before the sentence was to be carried out Freddie Bywaters made a final statement on his mistress's behalf, claiming all responsibility for the killing himself.

The Home Secretary was unmoved. At 9.00 a.m. on 9 January 1923, Edith Thompson was carried, barely conscious, from her cell in Holloway Prison and hanged by the executioner John Ellis. At the same moment Frederick Bywaters was hanged in Pentonville Prison by Thomas Pierrepoint.

Most modern observers would agree that two murders resulted from the tragic love affair between Freddie Bywaters and Edith Thompson: the fatal stabbing of Percy Thompson in the darkness of Belgrave Road, and the judicial hanging of Edith Thompson in the crisp morning air at Holloway Prison. There were also two murderers, young Freddie Bywaters and the English judicial system.

THORNTON, Sara By the early summer of 1989 Sara Thornton thought she had suffered enough. After almost a year of physical and mental abuse at the hands of the violent alcoholic she had married, thirty-six-year-old Mrs Thornton snapped, finally sick of the death threats against herself and her eleven-year-old daughter Louise. On the night of 14 June, ex-policeman Malcolm Thornton, drunk as ever, provoked the fight which would end with his wife driving a kitchen knife six inches into his stomach; or at least that is the way Sara remembered it.

Sara Thornton's trial was as predictable as her story was tragic. Her defence of diminished responsibility failed, and she was, correctly according to her conviction for murder, sentenced to life imprisonment. At the time it was a low-key affair, scarcely covered by the newspapers and ignored completely by the other media; it was just, as they call them, a 'domestic'. However, thanks to a startling turn-about on the part of the press, the world was to hear a lot more of Sara Thornton – brutal killer reinvented as avenging angel.

Much of the credit for this transformation must go to a man named George Delf, who had visited Sara in prison and fallen in love with her. Delf subsequently masterminded the Free Sara Thornton campaign, and by a judicious manipulation of the available resources – women's pressure groups, the media, local politicians and so on – turned a previously unglamorous case into a national *cause célèbre,* attracting widespread support for Sara's appeal. Having failed in the attempt to establish diminished responsibility at trial, the defence team fought on a revised plea of provocation at appeal in 1991. However, it had already been agreed in evidence that Sara was not reacting to actual physical danger; in other words at the *time he was killed* Malcolm Thornton was not beating her up; indeed, he was lying drunk on the sofa. Besides which, the usual defence of 'hot-blooded' killing was effectively destroyed by testimony that just before using it, Sara Thornton had gone out and sharpened the knife. Police who had been called to the scene found Malcolm Thornton still alive and Sara doing a spot of housework; they recorded her telling them: 'Let him die . . . I sharpened the knife so I could kill him. Do you want to know what he's done to me in the past?'

With the rejection of Sara's appeal the vanguard of the women's rights movements increased their pressure, and from a case pivoting upon justice and mercy the campaign now sought to attack on grounds of women's rights to have available the defence of what has become known as 'battered woman syndrome'; a controversy which continues to bedevil the British legal system.

Meanwhile, Sara Thornton remained in Bullwood Hall prison, Essex. In August 1993 she had her plea to the then Home Secretary, Michael Howard, turned down. Mr Howard refused to refer the case back to the Court of Appeal on the (perfectly correct) grounds that: 'I would not normally consider it right to do so unless there were new evidence or other considerations of substance which had not been before the courts and which appeared to cast doubt on the safety of the conviction.' At present the campaign to secure Sara's release continues, albeit at a quieter level now that the appeal process has been exhausted.

But that is only one part of an increasingly complex story; because a number of investigators have begun to reassemble the portrait of a rather different Sara Thornton, a character some way distant from the battered woman fighting for safety and sanity. One of the first to voice his misgivings was Richard Pendry in an article in the *Spectator* of 1 August 1992. In his very perceptive analysis of the case, Pendry suggests that the campaign for Sara Thornton's release 'has more to do with feminism than justice', and stresses the evidence that was given at her original trial and which has conveniently been forgotten by the Free Sara Thornton campaign. Notable among these allegations is the report that Malcolm had been seriously considering divorce, and indeed had told Sara of his plans on the day he was killed. It was also known that Sara feared losing out in any divorce settlement, to the extent that four days before the murder, she is reported to have told a colleague that she was unprepared to be the loser and would kill Malcolm. As if this were not damaging enough, Sara, according to Richard Pendry, 'hand-fed him tranquillizers hidden in pieces of chicken while he was in the bath, then phoned the doctor to say he was suicidal and had taken an overdose'.

In the wake of the Home Secretary's adverse decision, the tabloids were having a field day interviewing anybody who might have a bad word to say about Sara Thornton – and there seemed to be no shortage of candidates, particularly in her home town of Atherstone, Warwickshire. The landlady of one pub in which Sara regularly drank (and by all accounts was regularly asked to leave) is reported as saying: 'Her favourite trick was to strip off. She'd suddenly throw off her clothes and parade around naked . . . She could turn very nasty when she was drunk.'

Whether anybody will ever get to the truth of the 'real' Sara Thornton is debatable. The veteran of one protest hunger strike, Sara has vowed to continue her fight for freedom based on her allegations of frequent beatings. Others close to the Thorntons, however, have emphatically denied that Malcolm was violent, claiming that Sara invented the story to evade justice.

On Friday 29 May, 1996, Sara Thornton was found not guilty of murder by a jury at Oxford Crown Court. They found her guilty of manslaughter but did not indicate whether it was on grounds of provocation or diminished responsibility or a combination of both. As she had already served over five years in custody she walked free from the court.

TIERNEY, Nora Patricia   It happened in the leafy north London suburb of St John's Wood on 12 August 1949. Many of the splendid houses and villas of the district had fallen victim to the activities of the Luftwaffe during the recent conflict, but Elsworthy Road on the north side of Primrose Hill looked quiet and green in the summer sun. When she left home to go to the shops, Mrs Basil Ward said goodbye to her three-year-old daughter Marion and left her playing in front of the house with her six-year-old companion Stephanie Tierney. When Mrs Ward returned she found Stephanie alone. 'Where's Marion?' she asked, a hint of anxiety in her voice. 'She went off to play by herself,' Stephanie told her. It was the beginning of every parent's worst nightmare. By dark a full-scale police search was combing the neighbourhood and beyond for the missing child.

It was not until three days later that police found Marion Ward; her head had been smashed with a heavy instrument, and her body had been left in a bombed-out house close to where Stephanie lived with her parents John and Nora Tierney. By the side of the body was an imprint of a woman's shoe.

A routine visit by detectives showed Nora Tierney to be a dowdy, rather limp-looking woman, older than her twenty-nine years. She could not help, she said; she hadn't seen Mrs Ward's daughter at all that day. Even so, Scotland Yard's Chief Inspector James Jamieson had what he could only describe as a 'feeling'; that kind of instinct born of experience that proves so invaluable to long-serving detectives. He asked to look at Mrs

Tierney's wardrobe and found some shoes, one of which later proved a perfect match for the impression left beside the victim. Next Jamieson asked to see the woman's fingernails. Already clearly upset by the way the interview was going, Mrs Tierney broke down and wept. 'It was my husband,' she sobbed. 'He did it. I saw him.' Apparently the Tierneys had been in the bomb-damaged house looking for electrical fittings and flex – it was not uncommon in those post-war years for ruins to be cannibalized for useful materials. Suddenly James Tierney had appeared with little Marion struggling in his arms, and he started beating her head with a hammer. Although she tried to stop the attack it was too late, and Mrs Tierney fled after her husband, leaving the motionless infant sprawled on the rubble where the police found her. According to Nora Tierney, James had begged her to take the blame for the killing because 'they hang men, they won't hang a woman'.

Mrs Tierney did not attempt to explain why her husband, not known as a violent man, had suddenly turned child-killer. Not that it mattered, because in no time the police had proved to their satisfaction that James Tierney was nowhere near Elsworthy Road at the time of the child's disappearance. Which just left Mrs Tierney, and she was immediately taken into custody. In October 1949 she appeared at London's Central Criminal Court – the famous 'Old Bailey'. Inspector Jamieson had persisted with his examination of Nora Tierney's fingernails, and was rewarded by finding, in the scrapings taken from under them, fibres which matched a woollen jumper worn by little Marion Ward the day she died.

There was no attempt by the prosecution to suggest a motive for this senseless crime, and one has not emerged since. Mrs Tierney was found guilty but insane, and spent the rest of her days in the Broadmoor Criminal Lunatic Asylum.

TILFORD, Lizzie Lizzie had arrived in Canada in 1928. A big, capable, energetic woman, a chorister, Guide leader,

Salvationist and, incongruously, fortune-teller; she had brought with her William Walker, her second husband, and their four children. They were looking for a new start away from the English coal mines where Walker had worked, and set up a farm in Woodstock, Ontario. But Walker shortly fell ill, went blind and died – apparently of a brain tumour – on 19 February 1929.

It was not long before Tyrrell Tilford became aware of the conspicuous Lizzie at choir practice. They were married on 10 November 1930, a quiet ceremony since Tilford's family declined the invitation. There was something about this voluminous woman, old enough to be Tyrrell's mother, which turned them against her. So when Tyrrell built a home for Lizzie and her children on Cronyn Street, he began to keep a little distance from his parents. Until, that is, the night of Friday 29 March 1935, when old James Tyrrell opened the door to the sight of his son doubled up, black in the face, gasping: 'I'm going to die, Dad. I'm full of arsenic.'

The story he told was that Lizzie and her two sons had been dosing his food with arsenic, giving him capsules of the poison, pouring it on to his tongue. Bill Blake, a friend of Lizzie's, who was always hanging around the house, had said: 'My God, he's had enough poison to kill twenty people!'

The doctor, however, found nothing much amiss, and the following night Lizzie came to the Tilfords' house to nurse her husband, fending off his accusations – 'You've killed two, Lizzie – but you'll kill no more!' – and sending his parents off to bed. In the morning the couple were gone. Tyrrell Tilford, carried home like a baby in the arms of his wife, died in his bed at 5 a.m. on Sunday 31 March.

Despite the suspicious circumstances, cause of death was recorded as 'influenza and a weak heart', and Tyrrell was buried without a post-mortem. But his parents, getting no response from the local police, took their suspicions to the provincial attorney-general in Toronto. An exhumation was ordered; Professor Joselyn Rogers of the University of Toronto was shortly able to report the discovery of the fatal dose of two grains of arsenic in Tilford's stomach.

The witnesses at the subsequent inquest fell neatly into two categories – those who were under Lizzie Tilford's influence, and those who were not. The evidence of the latter, that on 20 March two ounces of arsenic had been delivered to the Tilford home, on Lizzie's instruction, was enough to commit her to trial. Sentenced to death, she spent her last remaining hours knitting baby bootees for sale at a charity bazaar, before being hanged at Oxford County Jail on the morning of 17 December.

Whether or not Lizzie Tilford killed her other husbands we will never know. When William Walker's body was exhumed in June 1935 no trace of poison was found; but it was remembered how, in 1929, Lizzie had passed on a 'folk remedy' to a friend with a troublesome husband with the words 'That will fix him. You'll soon be rid of him.'

TINNING, Marybeth Rose The first of Marybeth's children to die was baby Jennifer, in January 1972. She had been born with meningitis and lived for just nine days. Fifteen days after Jennifer's death, when two-year-old Joseph stopped breathing Mrs Tinning rushed him from their home in Schenectady, in New York state, to the local hospital; she claimed at the time that her son had suffered a 'seizure'. The boy was kept in hospital for ten days receiving treatment for a suspected viral infection and sent home as soon as he had recovered. Later the same day, Joseph was back in the clinic, but this time he was dead on arrival. According to the hospital records it was a tragedy, but one for which there was a perfectly sound explanation – little Joe had suffered cardio-respiratory arrest.

In March, Marybeth Tinning's four-year-old daughter Barbara was admitted to hospital, where she died shortly after arrival; death was certified as due to Reye's syndrome. In November the following year, 1973, Marybeth gave birth to baby Timothy, whom she returned to the hospital nineteen days later where he was found to be dead. Timothy's death was assumed to be due to cot-death syndrome.

Baby Nathan was born on 30 March 1975, and three weeks later he too was in a clinic after having difficulties breathing and secreting blood from his nose and mouth. It was thought at the time he was suffering from pneumonia. After extensive treatment Nathan Tinning was returned to his parents, but by September was dead. The death certificate blamed 'acute pulmonary oedema'. Mary Frances, born in October 1978, underwent her first emergency treatment in January 1979, and her second attack, on 20 February, proved fatal. Mary was assumed to be a cot-death victim.

In 1978 the Tinnings applied to adopt a child. It might be thought that even though there was no reason for the hospital to suspect that Marybeth's children had died of other than natural, if distressing, causes, it was surely to some extent the responsibility of the adoption agency to question seriously the Tinnings' suitability to adopt, given their alarming level of 'bad luck'. As it was, the agency even went so far as to offer the suggestion that the deaths could have resulted from a genetic disorder. However far-fetched that may be, it did not help little Jonathan Tinning who was born after Michael's adoption in November 1979. He died on 20 February 1980, after having difficulty with his breathing. Almost a year later to the day it was Michael's turn to be rushed to a doctor, where he was found to be already dead.

Tami Lynne, Marybeth's ninth child arrived in August 1985, and survived for four months before being found dead in her crib with blood on the pillow. Initially another cot death was suspected, but clearly such persistent 'misfortune' could not go forever unremarked. The result was that an inquiry was set up, the conclusion of which was that little Tami Lynne had been suffocated.

Marybeth Tinning was interviewed by the police and

confessed to the murder of Tami Lynne, Timothy and Nathan. She also admitted trying to poison her husband Joseph. In the end Mrs Tinning was charged only with the killing of her daughter Tami Lynne. On 17 July 1987, she was convicted at trial and sentenced to twenty-years-to-life.

TOPPAN, Jane Jane was born Nora Kelley in 1854 in Boston, Massachusetts. After her mother died and her father was committed to an insane asylum, five-year-old Nora was adopted by Mr and Mrs Abner Toppan of Lowell, Massachusetts, in 1859.

The Toppans changed the girl's name to Jane and provided her with the benefits of a good education and a secure home life. It was a broken engagement which later caused Jane to withdraw into herself, and during this time she became convinced that she could see into the future; so bleak were her visions that Jane twice attempted suicide.

At the age of twenty-six, Jane suddenly decided to take up nursing, and immediately enrolled as a student in a Cambridge, Massachusetts, hospital. She was well liked by the staff and by her fellow trainees, though some might have wondered about her morbid fascination with the activities of the post-mortem room.

One day a patient who had been in Jane's care unexpectedly died. Then another. No official accusations were ever made against Nurse Toppan, but she was dismissed without the usual certificate of proficiency. Unbowed, Jane simply forged her own.

Between 1880 and 1901, Jane Toppan served as a private nurse in many New England homes – and what did it matter if a large number of her patients died? Illnesses, particularly at the turn of the last century, were frequently fatal.

On 7 July 1901, Jane was among a group of mourners in the small cemetery in Cataumet. Inside the coffin was the late Mrs Mattie Davis, one of Jane's patients; it was touching, everybody thought, how the nurse was so loyally devoted even to the last. The unfortunate woman's family were so impressed that they begged Jane to stay on and look after the rest of them who had also unaccountably fallen sick.

Mrs Annie Goodman, the deceased's married daughter, was so sick that on 29 July 1901, it was necessary to summon a doctor. When he arrived a few hours later, Mrs Goodman was already dead.

Next to suffer was Captain Alden Davis. The regular funerals were proving depressing, and it was with gratitude that he accepted Jane's soothing nightcap. Next morning, Captain Davis was found dead in his bed. 'A stroke,' Jane explained to the sole surviving daughter, Mary Gibbs. Mrs Gibbs succumbed to Jane's ministrations after only a few days. Thus the whole of the Davis family had been wiped out in just six weeks. Jane simply packed her bags and left.

When Captain Gibbs returned from sea and found his wife dead, he was informed by his distraught cousin Beulah Jacobs that Nurse Toppan had refused to allow an autopsy. 'Such practices,' she had told the doctor, 'are against the religious beliefs of the family.' Gibbs wasted no time in sharing his suspicions with Detective John H. Whitney, and the result was that Mary Gibbs' body was exhumed and autopsied. Mrs Gibbs had been murdered with an overdose of morphine.

In the time it took for Detective Whitney to catch up with her, Jane Toppan had already murdered her foster sister, Mrs Edna Bannister, and moved on to nurse the Nichols family in Amherst, New Hampshire. On the night of 29 October 1901, Detective Whitney stood at the door in the rain and asked: 'Jane Toppan, the nurse?' 'Yes.' 'You are wanted in Massachusetts for questioning in connection with the deaths of Mrs Henry Goodman and Mrs Irving Gibbs.'

Police throughout New England began to disinter dozens of bodies – former patients of Nurse Toppan. Autopsies proved that all had died of morphine and atropine poisoning. Then Jane was identified as the woman making purchases at Benjamin Waters' pharmacy; a check of his poisons register confirmed frequent large prescriptions for morphine.

Meanwhile, from her cell Jane was embarking on her manic confession:

> Yes, I killed all of them. I might have killed George Nichols and his sister that night if the detective hadn't taken me away. I fooled them all – I fooled the stupid doctors and the ignorant relatives; I have been fooling them for years and years . . . I use morphia and atropia, the latter to hide the effects of the former.
>
> I want to be known as the greatest criminal that ever lived. That is my ambition.

Jane then began an inventory of her victims, but by the time she reached thirty-one she became a trifle confused; it was so annoying not being able to remember, she observed – because there were at least seventy altogether. Not counting the hospital deaths at the beginning, as they were only 'practice murders'.

On 25 June 1902, Jane Toppan was put on trial. Dr Stedman, the psychiatrist, gave evidence that 'Jane Toppan is suffering from a form of insanity that can never be cured.' At which, with an indignant cry, Jane shouted: 'The alienist lies. I am not crazy, and all of you know it.'

Even so, Jane Toppan was confined to the Taunton State Asylum for the Criminally Insane. She lived a long and healthy life until, on 17 August 1938, she died of old age at eighty-four.

TREVIS, Tina Constance Richards was a kind-hearted woman. Even as it became less and less popular to feed the potentially disease-spreading flocks of pigeons that infest every British town, she was regularly seen throwing crusts to the birds around her home in the Newton section of Birmingham. She was so common a sight, in fact, that the locals nicknamed her 'the Bird Lady'. All the more shocking, therefore, when eighty-two-year-old Constance was found savagely beaten and stabbed to death in her home in October 2002.

Constance's maisonette flat had clearly been burgled, and police initially suspected a man or youth to have been the killer – women are less prone to both violent attacks on others and, indeed, burglary in general. Of course, this is not always true, as we saw in the case of Rosella Rousseau (page 232) and the numerous fingerprints found on Constance's possessions proved to be those of Tina Trevis, a thirty-five-year-old mother-of-two, who had been caught burglarising Mrs Richards' home just six months before.

Scene-of-crime officers (known as the SOCO) easily reconstructed the events of the squalid murder. Mrs Richards had discovered the inept burglar and recognised her as her former persecutor. Tina beat her unconscious with a heavy, ornamental set of bellows then, to stop her from identifying her, took a kitchen knife and deliberately stabbed the defenceless old lady through the heart.

Trevis pleaded not guilty, claiming to have simply found the corpse while robbing the flat, and to have then run away. The lack of evidence that anyone else had been in the flat convinced the jury otherwise, however, and Trevis was found guilty and sentenced to life imprisonment for murder, plus a further eighteen months for burglary.

Why did a mature mother of two stoop to burglary and murder? In the case of Rosella Rousseau, the risk of poverty and starvation in 1900s Paris was a motivating factor, and a similar cause can be found in the Trevis case. She and her family were not starving, but Tina Trevis was hungry in another way: she was a crack cocaine addict.

TURNER, Lise Jane   Like Minnie Dean almost a hundred years before her (see page 103), Lise Turner was also tried in the High Court at Christchurch, New Zealand. It was in

November 1984, and Mrs Turner, like Minnie, was charged with the murders of three children. The difference was that two of them were Lise Turner's own. She also faced three counts of the attempted murder of other babies.

On 11 January 1980, Turner's eleven-week-old daughter Megan was rushed to hospital by her mother, but found to be dead on arrival. A post-mortem failed to establish any serious disorder and death was attributed to cot-death syndrome. Cheney Louise, Turner's second child, was born on 31 January 1982; she died after vomiting blood on 15 March.

With such a record it is surprising that Mrs Turner was entrusted with the care of any more babies, but in October four-month-old Catherine Packer was left by her mother while she went shopping. When she returned, Mrs Packer found the baby bleeding from the mouth and vomiting. Thankfully little Catherine Packer appeared to make a full recovery. However, the attacks recurred periodically over the next six months (in fact whenever Lise Turner was around) and on 1 April 1983, Catherine was again found unconscious with blood trickling from her nostrils. Emergency treatment again saved the child's life. This time, after Mrs Packer had visited Catherine in hospital in company with Lise Turner and the child had cowered into the corner of her cot screaming as she recognized Turner, the woman was never again let near the child and Catherine regained her health.

It was a pity that Mrs Hall did not know Mrs Packer; if she had five-week-old Katrina Hall might not have been found 'sick' after Lise Turner's offer to babysit. She recovered; Michael Clark Tinnion was not so lucky. Michael had been left by his mother in Turner's charge on 28 May 1984, and when Mrs Tinnion returned her eight-month-old son was dead, a sticky fluid dribbling out of his nose and mouth. This time there was no difficulty in establishing the cause of death – asphyxia, and with Lise Turner's past record of disasters it was not long before she was up against some very searching questions. And that is how Mrs Turner found herself facing three counts of murder and three of attempted murder.

At her trial the prosecution alleged that Turner had caused the deaths (and near deaths) by smothering the infants' faces. Lise Turner did not give evidence on her own behalf, though her attorney advanced a plea of diminished responsibility. The verdict, nevertheless, was a well-deserved 'guilty'. Lise Turner did not share Minnie Dean's fate; the habitual baby-killer was sentenced to life imprisonment for murder and further terms of imprisonment on each count of attempted murder.

V

VELGO, Marie Havlick   Just read this note:

> I hereby agree to pay you the sum of 5,000 kronen for services, the nature of which are known to us both. In the event of my death, this obligation will be met through a clause in my will. You are bound to talk to nobody about this agreement, to show it to nobody, or to make claims of any third person. This debt may not be collected by litigation or by force. In the event of your death, your wife and son will inherit your claim. The above sum may be paid in monthly instalments or as a lump sum. Upon a full payment this note is to be returned. In the event of my divorce, this note becomes null and void.
>
> (Signed) Marie Havlick Velgo

It is a contract; a contract to kill.

Of all the reasons which motivate a man to take a wife, professional advancement is by no means a rarity; and of the many motives open to a woman taking a husband, financial advancement must be among the top five. Which is how Marie Havlick, an attractive twenty-one-year-old, and a somewhat older circuit court judge named Jan Velgo came to marry and take up residence in a luxurious flat in the Czechoslovakian city of Brno. And things might have turned out mutually beneficial had the judge not compounded the cynicism of marrying just to improve his chances of being appointed to the Supreme Court with the foolishness of letting his wife hear that he planned to divorce her as soon as the appointment was confirmed. Marie was furious – not so much at the prospect of losing a husband as at losing a life of luxury.

Marie Velgo consulted with her trusty maid; the maid came up with a name. Marie consulted the petty crook named Wenzel Cerny; Cerny came up with a solution. He would murder Judge Velgo. What followed next veered close to farce. When Jan Velgo let himself into their apartment on the evening of 16 March 1936, he had no sooner closed the door behind him than out popped the crooked Wenzel and cracked him over the skull, drawing blood and knocking the judge unconscious. Wenzel Cerny dragged his victim to the bathroom, dumped him in the tub and turned on the water tap, holding his victim's head under till he drowned. The next part wasn't in the script. Marie, who unknown to Cerny had been hiding in a cupboard, sneaked out of her hidey-hole, crept up behind the luckless Wenzel and shot him. Now came the ingenious part of her plot – Marie Velgo pressed the pistol into the prostrate Wenzel's hand with the intention of creating the impression that, in a moment of remorse over drowning the judge, he had shot himself. Unfortunately, the noise of the various struggles going on over their heads had already persuaded the Velgos' downstairs neighbours to call the police. As it was, Marie had only enough time to secrete herself in a wardrobe before a number of burly representatives of the Brno force shouldered down the front door. Inside the flat they found Judge Jan Velgo dead in the bath, Wenzel Cerny lying in a pool of his own blood but still alive, and Marie Velgo in the wardrobe protesting that Cerny had attacked her.

But Wenzel Cerny was rather smarter than Marie had given

him credit for – otherwise she would never have given him that written contract. The wily assassin had prudently hidden the document in the lining of his jacket, where detectives found it. Cerny was sentenced to life imprisonment for the murder of Jan Velgo.

Mrs Velgo was tried once, fluttered her eyelashes at the jury, and was acquitted. It only worked once though; in October 1937 she was tried for conspiracy, found guilty and sentenced to twelve years.

VIDAL, Ginette   As far as I can discover, the following brief case is the only one of its kind in recent criminal history. There have been other instances of what might be called 'murder by request', but never murder as part of a 'marriage' contract.

When Ginette Vidal moved into an apartment block in the Paris suburb of Montfermeil in the early part of 1972, she was forty-one years old, dowdy, overweight and married. But this did not deter her new neighbour, Gérard Osselin, from forming a deep and passionate attachment to her; which was the more surprising because the personable Monsieur Osselin was more than ten years her junior and married to an attractive young woman named Mireille. Madame Vidal responded enthusiastically, and in no time the couple had deserted their respective families and set up home together in Clichy-sur-Bois. But not before Ginette had laid down the ground rules. There was to be no, absolutely no, infidelity; this was going to be a partnership for life. We do not know with what misgivings, but Gérard Osselin agreed, and signed the contract which Ginette had drawn up. It stated that if either she or Gérard should prove unfaithful the other would have the right to kill them. Osselin might already have been tiring of the oppressive relationship anyway; regretting his impetuosity perhaps; missing his wife. At any rate, in November 1972 he was secretly visiting Mireille at their old Montfermeil apartment. Ginette may have suspected something like this would happen when she drew up the contract, but when she found a note in his wife's handwriting, Gérard's betrayal was unquestionable. So she shot him, twice, just as the contract said she could. Ginette Vidal then spent three days in their apartment with the rapidly decomposing corpse of Gérard Osselin – talking to it, cooking meals for it, caressing it . . . Things came to an end when Mireille Osselin became suspicious because Gérard had not kept an appointment with her. She alerted the police, and the police paid a visit to the flat in Clichy. There they found Ginette and her lover. How long she would have continued to sleep with Gérard's body or try to spoon soup between its putrefying lips is anybody's guess.

One thing was certain, as far as Ginette was concerned she had been perfectly within her rights when she shot Gérard. 'Look, look,' she was screaming at the horrified gendarmes, 'I have a paper.' It is true that as far as Ginette Vidal was concerned this contract was a legal document; it is equally true that as far as the law was concerned it was not. Which left Ginette charged with murder, of which she was proved guilty and imprisoned for ten years.

W

WADDINGHAM, Dorothea Nancy   Dorothea Waddingham
had almost as insalubrious an entry into this world as she was
to have a departure from it. She was born to a poor family who
eked out an existence in the village of Hucknall, seven miles
north of Nottingham. After a brief and undistinguished spell at
the village school Dorothy (as she was known) spent a brief and
undistinguished spell in a local factory. When she was in her
early twenties she exchanged the drudgery of the factory for
that of the workhouse infirmary at Burton-on-Trent, where she
was taken on as a ward maid.

It was while she was at Burton that Thomas Willoughby
Leech came into her life. Leech was considerably older than
Dorothy – in fact, almost twice her age – and neither wealthy
nor physically fit; he was indeed very poor, and a chronic
invalid. Nevertheless, for reasons that may for all we know
have been connected with love, the couple married and set up
their first home under the roof of one of Leech's sisters, at
Church Gresley, not far from Burton. During their eight years
of marriage Dorothy bore three children – Edwin, Alan, and
little Mary who was still a baby when tragedy finally struck the
sickly Thomas Leech in the form of throat cancer, to which he
succumbed. As a fmal act of unwitting generosity Thomas had

provided his widow with a new partner. Ronald Sullivan was near to Dorothy's age, and when his marriage had collapsed and his family split up, his friend Tom Leech invited him to share his home, which was by now in Haydn Road, in Sherwood, Nottingham.

Now, there is a great deal of difference between a ward maid and a nurse; but for Dorothy it was but a short stretch of the imagination. Rudimentary understanding of nursing care she may have picked up, but despite her own extravagant claims, and despite the fact that she has subsequently become notorious as 'Nurse' Waddingham, she was no more entitled to that distinction than the next ward maid. Not that it prevented her from turning the Haydn Road house into a nursing home.

Following her husband's death, Dorothea Waddingham – now Nurse Waddingham – took a smaller house in Devon Drive, accompanied by Sullivan and the three children. Before long there was another mouth to feed in the person of baby Ronald, and it was as much as the new 'nursing home' could manage to keep those mouths satisfied.

On the afternoon of 5 January 1935, Dorothy was away from the house, so it was Ronald Sullivan who opened the door to Miss Blagg, dynamic secretary ('hon.') of the County Nursing Association. The Waddingham home had come to the favourable notice of the Association, it seems – which probably meant that they were cheap and not too particular – and Miss Blagg wondered if it might be the suitable accommodation she sought for elderly Mrs Louisa Baguley and her paralytic daughter Ada; the former 'delightful old lady' was nearing ninety, the latter somewhere around fifty.

The Baguleys were a courageous couple in their own modest way; Ada had since early womanhood suffered with what is known medically as progressive disseminated sclerosis, and popularly as 'creeping paralysis'. She had become worse as the disease had progressed over the past twenty years, and was now unable to walk or to employ her arms and hands to any very useful degree. Mr Baguley had died six years previously, and despite her own great age and frailty, her mother now devoted her time to caring for Ada the best she could. But she was beginning to realize that her best was no longer adequate, and far from being able to sustain the pressure imposed by an invalid's needs, she was feeling the want of care and attention herself.

And so a bargain was struck, pending the approval of Nurse Waddingham; and after visiting the two ladies at their present home in Burton Joyce, Dorothea accepted the rather paltry offer of thirty shillings a week each, and made ready the ground-floor back room. On 12 January Mrs Baguley and Ada took up residence.

During the following six weeks the two lady 'patients' settled in comfortably to their new surroundings; and Miss Blagg was delighted to have found so pleasant a refuge for her charges. This too was the impression of Ada's cousin Lawrence, who was subsequently called upon to testify in court as to the great peace of mind now enjoyed by his elderly aunt and cousin.

At the end of February the house went into brief mourning for the passing of Nurse Waddingham's other patient at the time, who had died on the twenty-sixth.

Now Dorothea Waddingham was beginning to have second thoughts about the income from the Baguleys; she was frequently to be heard grumbling about the miserable reward for the huge burden of two infirm patients: 'They would have to pay five guineas for no better treatment in hospital; which is really the proper place for them.' In hindsight, it is a pity the ladies had not been put in a five-guinea hospital, for they would certainly have had better 'treatment' than that which they were about to receive at Devon Drive. But money was not as plentiful as it might have been, and all that stood between the Baguleys and the dreaded workhouse were Ada's nest-eggs. These comprised a £500 Conversion Loan, about £120 in the bank, and a further £1,000 inherited from her father, of which the interest went to Mrs Baguley during her lifetime. Whatever remained after her death, Ada had willed to Fred Gilbert. Gilbert, although a cousin, was also Ada's fiancé, and but for the devastating effect of her illness they might have been married long before. As it was, the closeness of even their friendship had been put under considerable strain over the years, and by now Fred's visits had all but stopped. In despair, and probably out of pique, Ada made a new will; very much at variance with the advice of her solicitor, Mr Lane. Ada proposed to settle upon Nurse Waddingham the whole of her property in return for an undertaking to look after her and her mother for the rest of their lives. As a compromise, Lane persuaded the petulant Ada Baguley that instead of handing over her property, she should simply make her will in favour of Waddingham and Sullivan, in consideration of their caring for her mother and herself during their lives. The document was signed on 4 May.

A week later old Mrs Baguley died and was laid to rest beneath the earth of Caunton churchyard. Among the mourners, Ronald Sullivan and Ada Baguley and, reunited in sorrow, Fred Gilbert. Fred Gilbert, after all this time; Fred pushing Ada in her wheelchair to the church! In fact, nothing of the old romance seemed to develop, but it may have given Sullivan pause to think on the future of his recently promised inheritance.

Back at Devon Drive, life for Ada, now that her greatest companion had passed away, was a succession of unremarkable days. One rare excitement was the visit of Mrs Briggs, a friend of the Baguley family for as long as anybody could remember. It was 10 September, and Mrs Briggs' unexpected arrival found Ada in the garden snoozing in the last of the late summer sun. They chatted over tea, and ate some of the chocolate drops that Mrs Briggs had brought from her little shop in Alfred Street – The Black Boy Chocolate Shop. At four o'clock, after fond farewells and promises of future visits, Ada's guest left. At two o'clock the following morning Ada Baguley slipped into a coma; at nine, Sullivan phoned and left a message for Dr Manfield to attend urgently. At midday Manfield arrived. Ada was dead.

With the medical certificate reading 'Death through cerebral haemorrhage due to cardio-vascular degeneration', Nurse Waddingham wasted no time in arranging for Ada's body to be cremated. Which would not be remarkable now; but in 1936 less than 1 per cent of deaths received cremation, and those that did were unusual enough to be noticed. But there were other reasons why Miss Baguley's disposal attracted the attention of Dr Cyril Banks. Banks was the Crematorium referee, and in that capacity had received an extraordinary letter requesting: 'It is my desire to be cremated at my death. And it is my wish to remain with Nurse [Waddingham] until I die. It is my final wish that my relatives shall not know of my death.' The note purported to have been signed by Ada, but had been written by Ronald Sullivan. And it had been addressed from 32 Devon Drive, a house which, in his capacity as Medical Officer of Health for Nottingham, Dr Banks had reason to know was not, as it advertised, a 'registered' nursing home and was in contravention of the law in describing itself as such.

It was as well that Cyril Banks had his misgivings; for poor Ada Baguley had not died of cerebral haemorrhage at all. That became clear when the Nottingham city analyst performed his post-mortem examination; after ten days' careful investigation Dr W.W. Taylor found 2.59 grains of morphine in the stomach, 0.37 grains in the spleen and kidneys, 0.14 grains in a portion of the liver, and 0.092 grains in the heart. A convincingly lethal dose of 3.192 grains. Given the speed with which the body tissues break down morphine, the celebrated Home Office analyst, Dr Roche Lynch, was able to state that the original ingestion must have been a very much greater dose than that found.

Clearly Ada Baguley had died from acute morphine poisoning; which gave rise, not surprisingly, to misgivings about the cause of her mother's sudden death. On 30 September, Mrs Baguley's body was exhumed from the churchyard and taken to Leenside mortuary, where Dr Roche Lynch was to perform the post-mortem. Casting aside the medical jargon, the conclusion was dramatically simple – Mrs Louisa Baguley had died of an excessive dose of morphine!

Somebody would have some questions to answer.

On 14 February 1936, Dorothea Waddingham and Ronald Sullivan were put on trial before Mr Justice Goddard (later Lord Chief Justice). In an unusual switch from his familiar role as defender, Mr Norman Birkett QC led for the Crown. On 26 February, Mr Justice Goddard instructed the jury to formally acquit Ronald Sullivan, against whom there was no evidence of complicity to murder. The following day he passed sentence of death on Dorothea Waddingham in accordance with the verdict of the jury; she was removed to Winson Green Prison, Birmingham.

Despite the recommendation to mercy, the Home Office could find no grounds on which to interfere with the course of justice, and on the morning of 16 April 1936, Nurse Waddingham walked to the gallows.

WAGNER, Waltraud, et al. In Austria's most sensational trial since the end of the Second World War, four nursing assistants at Vienna's largest hospital, the Lainz, stood accused of the murder of at least forty-two patients between 1988 and 1989. Waltraud Wagner, said to be the dominant force behind the 'death squad', Maria Gruber, Irene Leidolf and Stefanija Mayer sat in the dock of the Vienna District Court before Presiding Judge Herr Peter Straub.

Like many of Vienna's grand buildings, what is now the Krankenhaus der Stadt Wien was erected during the glorious rule of the Hapsburgs, and is showing its age. The Lainz, as it is called, stands in half a dozen acres of wooded parkland on the edge of the Vienna woods. But if the exterior of the hospital suggests one typical face of Vienna, then the interior shows quite another. It is still severe, but there is a prim, somewhat puritanical sense of efficiency and mannered orderliness about the wards which, while neither warm nor cheerful, is at least reassuring.

Although the four nursing auxiliaries were charged with responsibility for only forty-two deaths taking place over two years, it is generally believed that the true figure could be in hundreds over as many as six years.

The frightening fact is, this horrifying crime might never have come to light at all had it not been for the incautious boasting of the killers themselves. It had become a harmless routine for four of the female staff from the Lainz's night shift to get together in a bar, drink a couple of bottles of wine and exchange a bit of gossip. On one such evening a doctor attached to the Lainz also happened to be unwinding after a long shift at the hospital. What he overheard from the next table turned his blood cold. Speaking with that braggartly loudness which drink so often bestows upon the naturally arrogant, nursing auxiliary Waltraud Wagner was boasting about killing patients. The incident in the bar was reported to the hospital authorities and to the police. A closer watch was ordered on the activities in D ward when a study of the hospital records revealed that a considerably higher proportion of patients who died had done so during the night-shift. It was not until the end of February that any proof of misconduct was forthcoming. One of the doctors, noticing that a patient was responding adversely to treatment, confronted Waltraud Wagner directly: had she, perhaps mistakenly, given this patient unprescribed injections of insulin? No, Waltraud most emphatically had not. An answer which rang very false indeed when the post-mortem on the woman who died shortly afterwards showed abnormally high levels of insulin.

All the defendants had made confessions at the time of their arrest, though claiming the most altruistic of motives – to end the interminable misery and suffering of their patients. Waltraud Wagner, thirty-two years old at the opening of the trial, had confessed to starting her career as an 'angel of death' in 1983 (when she was just twenty-four); at that time it was an infrequent activity, though by her own admission in 1989 it had reached a rate of one killing a week.

The methods used to 'release' these patients to 'a place of peace' were overdoses of drugs and the fearful 'oral hygiene treatment', where one nurse held the patient's head back and mouth open, while another nurse poured water down the victim's throat until they literally drowned.

As the trial opened in February 1991, state attorney Ernst Kloyber began to describe a series of murders which, he said, represented only the tip of the iceberg: 'How big the iceberg really is we will never know.' Recalling the awful recent past when Adolf Hider and his Nazis had annexed Austria, Herr Kloyber said: 'It is a small step from killing the terminally ill to the killing of insolent, burdensome patients, and from there to that which was known under the Third Reich as "euthanasia". It is a door which must never be opened again.'

The process occupied the whole of the month of March, and on the twenty-eighth judge Herr Peter Straub summed up the long and complicated case for the benefit of the jury, concluding: 'Despite the defendants' previous good records, in each case above all was the horrifying brutality of some of their actions, the helplessness of their victims, and the gross abuse of the trust that had been placed in them.'

The result of the jury's lengthy deliberations was that Waltraud Wagner was convicted of fifteen counts of murder, seventeen of attempted murder, and two of aggravated assault; she was sentenced to life imprisonment. Twenty-nine-year-old Irene Leidolf was sentenced to life imprisonment; Stefanija

Mayer, aged fifty- two, received twenty years; and Maria Gruber, twenty-nine, fifteen years.

WARDLAW SISTERS Killer couples occur quite frequendy in the annals of true crime, even within a single family – brothers, sisters, cousins; but to find three in a family is a rarity, and three elderly sisters borders on the unique.

The Wardlaws were all born around the middle of the nineteenth century, and during their early years developed quite separately. Virginia in particular distinguished herself at Wellesley College, almost an unheard-of achievement in those days when a woman's place was most decidedly thought to be keeping house; she subsequently became a highly regarded educationist. Sisters Caroline and Mary married and became, respectively, Caroline Wardlaw Martin and Mary Wardlaw Snead. In 1900 Caroline and Mary left their husbands and joined Virginia; from this point onwards, apart from 'business' trips, the sisters were inseparable.

The first profitable fatality in the family was that of Mary's son John Snead. When he died in a fire the sisters found themselves collecting $12,000 insurance. Then it was Caroline's turn. She effected a 'reconciliation' with her husband, Colonel John Martin, and moved to New York with their daughter Oscey. There, within a very short time Martin died (it is now thought of poisoning) and Caroline was $10,000 the richer. With Oscey in tow, she rejoined her sisters in Tennessee, their wall of respectability unassailable now that Virginia was head of Soule College.

Perhaps it was just the habit of mourning they had got into, but the Wardlaw sisters now took to wearing oniy black, and were known locally as the 'Black Sisters'. Maybe they thought that at the rate they were disposing of the family they might as well be prepared.

Not long after Caroline's return they were in mourning again. This time Oscey was the victim, found drowned in her bath; but not before a hefty insurance had been taken out on her life. It was one insurance claim too many, and in 1913 all three of the Wardlaw sisters were arrested, charged with Oscey's murder and put on trial. Mary was acquitted, Caroline was found guilty but insane, and Virginia was found guilty and sent to prison where she starved herself to death.

WARMUS, Carolyn Carolyn Warmus was a glamorous blonde, intelligent and charming, a vivacious twenty-six-year-old who liked to 'dress to kill', as the saying goes. She had friends, a bachelor's degree from the University of Michigan and a master's from Columbia, and a good career as a teacher. But that, it seems, was not enough. She was driven by an impulse to destroy.

In 1983 she had attempted to sabotage the engagement of an ex-lover with another woman, forcibly entering their apartment and sending the prospective bride a disturbing letter threatening, 'Now I am back from vacation you can start worrying all over again.' The police warned her off. Three years later she was employing a private investigator to check the fidelity of her current lover – a business arrangement which slid effortlessly into a sexual relationship. Carolyn Warmus was skating on thin ice.

She started an affair with Paul Solomon in the summer of 1987, and dreamed that one day they would be wed. The only problem was that Solomon was married already. Carolyn's first instinct was to attempt to sabotage the marriage by hiring a private detective to prove that Betty Jeanne Solomon was cheating on her husband. She told another investigator that a woman named 'Jeanne or Betty Jeanne' was attempting foul play against her family. And then, at the beginning of 1989, she persuaded her original detective friend to sell her a .25-calibre Beretta pistol.

At midnight on 15 January 1989 Paul Solomon phoned the police from his apartment in Westchester County, outside New York. He had arrived home to find his wife lying dead in a pool of her own blood. She had been shot, nine times, in the head and chest, and the empty cases of the .25-calibre murder weapon were lying on the floor around the body.

Solomon and Warmus backed up each other's statements to the police: they had been at a Yonkers Holiday Inn together that evening, had had a few drinks, and enjoyed a further intimate hour in Carolyn's car before parting at 11.30 p.m. The police had little to go on, but kept the couple under surveillance. It was to be another six months before the dark side of Carolyn Warmus' nature revealed itself.

Paul Solomon was travelling on vacation to Puerto Rico with another female teacher, with whom he was having an affair. Warmus followed the pair and, once again, the sabotage began. Messages delivered by bribed employees at the hotel; an anonymous phone call to the woman's room-mate in New York; calls to the woman's family, in which Warmus impersonated a police officer.

The revelation, in November 1989, that a private investigator had sold a Beretta to Warmus, was the cherry on the icing of the police case against her, and on 1 February 1990 she was indicted for second-degree murder. The first trial floundered on a technicality, the second on a hung jury. At the third trial the new exhibit of a glove 'similar' to one owned by Warmus and discovered near the body – but subsequently somehow lost – swayed the jury in favour of a guilty verdict. On 26 June 1992 Carolyn Warmus, having been found guilty of murder in the second degree and of possession of an illegal weapon, was sentenced to twenty-five-years-to-life in prison.

WEBER, Jeanne   Jeanne Weber occupied a squalid apartment in one of the many slums that housed the impoverished wrecks of turn-of-the-last-century Paris; its only distinction was of being in the inappropriately named Passage de la Goutte d'Or. Jeanne had given birth to three children, of whom only seven-year-old Marcel still survived.

In spite of her dubious record with children, Jeanne Weber was entrusted by her sister-in-law with the care of her eighteen-month-old daughter Georgette; it was the morning of 2 March 1905, and by evening the baby was dead. Despite the blue marks around the child's throat, a doctor certified the death as due to 'convulsions', a catch-all which was given to account for many infant fatalities of the time.

Unbelievably, within a fortnight Jeanne's brother and sister-in-law had left another of their children, two-year-old Suzanne, at the run-down apartment. When they returned to reclaim the child some hours later, she was dying; and before their eyes the unlucky infant joined her sister as a victim of 'convulsions'.

In hindsight it is remarkable that anybody would let Jeanne Weber within a mile of their children, but on 25 March Jeanne was to be found looking after another sister-in-law's offspring, Germaine; she was seven months old and, as things turned out, she would get no older. The doctor attributed Germaine's death to 'diphtheria'. It was just three days later, ironically on the very day that Germaine's tiny coffin was consigned to the earth, that Jeanne's remaining child, young Marcel, died. Cause of death? The same as Germaine's – 'diphtheria', and like her too, he was found with red marks around his neck.

The Webers were a large family, and on 5 April Jeanne Weber was baby-sitting one-year-old Maurice while his mother, another of Jeanne's sisters-in-law, went to the shops. When she returned, the boy was blue in the face, convulsed and foaming at the mouth. The victim's life was saved only by prompt attention from the doctors at the Hôpital Bretonneau, and this time the child's mother was smart enough to talk to the police.

Madame Weber appeared before the Seine Assizes at the end of January 1906, where, largely due to the sympathetic evidence given by the government pathologist in charge of the exhumations and post-mortems, Jeanne was acquitted. But her reputation had not gone unscarred, and Jeanne Weber moved out of the city to the village of Chambon. Here she became first the housekeeper and then the mistress of a man named Bavouzet. Part of the attraction was no doubt Monsieur's three small children. The first fatality was nine-year-old Auguste from 'convulsions'. The second tragedy – for Jeanne at least – was that Auguste's sister was rummaging in Madame's handbag when she found a bundle of press cuttings covering the trial in Paris and showing a picture of Jeanne Weber titled 'L'Ogresse de la Goutte d'Or'. This discovery resulted in Jeanne finding herself under arrest again, and arraigned on a second murder charge.

Again, it was Dr Thoinot who spoke up in Jeanne's defence, and she was acquitted for a second time.

In 1908, the spectre of 'L'Ogresse' appeared again before an astonished French public. Jeanne Weber was now living with a lime-burner named Emile Bouchery, and they lodged at the inn kept by a couple named Poirot. The Poirots had two small children, and one night in May while Bouchery was away at work, Jeanne asked if seven-year-old Marcel might sleep in her room as she became anxious being alone at night.

In the dark of night, the inn was rent with screaming, and when an alarmed Monsieur Poirot burst into the Boucherys' room there was Marcel, his face discoloured and bloody, dead. Pacing the room was a highly agitated and incoherent Jeanne Weber, her hands and clothes smeared with the child's blood.

This final act had clearly loosened completely Madame Weber's already limited grip on sanity, and she was certified and committed to an insane asylum where she died two years later, in 1910, as the result of injuries sustained trying to strangle herself.

WEBER, Simone Simone Weber married for the first time to Jacques Thuot, with whom she had five children. It was not the happiest of marriages, and the couple divorced in 1978. Simone was not getting any younger or any wealthier, in fact she was downright hard-up. There was not a lot she could do about the ravages of time, but she could materially increase her portion by marrying again.

This she did with a man she met through the medium of a newspaper lonely-hearts column. Marcel Fixart was all of eighty years old when he married Simone Weber in 1980. Or rather, he didn't *actually* marry Simone. She chose instead to go through the ceremony with a man named Georges Hesling who borrowed Fixart's name for the occasion. In fact, it is rather unlikely that Monsieur Fixart even knew he was married; besides, three weeks after the 'wedding' he died, and Madame Fixart became the sole owner of his house at Rosieres-aux-Salines, and the sole beneficiary of his will.

In December 1981 Simone Weber, now more financially secure, set about replacing the romance in her life. She became the latest in a long succession of women who had fallen for an apparently charming, gentle man named Bernard Hettier.

Despite a number of harmless indiscretions on Bernard's part, the ship of love kept a fairly steady keel until 1983, when Bernard Hettier's ardour began to cool. Not so Simone's. It may be no coincidence that on such occasions as they met, Bernard began to suffer bouts of illness – stomach pains and faintness. More precisely it was after Simone had fixed him a drink, or some food. In fact, the poor man became so concerned after blacking out at the wheel of his car that he underwent a thorough medical examination.

Then, in late June 1985, Bernard Hettier disappeared. It was his daughter Patricia who first raised doubts about his safety when he failed to keep one of their regular appointments. Besides, Patricia had thought for about a month that Bernard was looking unwell. Worried, she went to the police who told her politely but firmly:

'Your father is fifty-three years old; he is free to do whatever he chooses, even to disappear.'

Then Hettier's sisters, Georgette and Monique, joined in the clamour for police action, and at the same time, like a pair of Miss Marples, embarked on their own inquiries. When asked, Simone calmly explained that, as far as she knew, Bernard was alive and well and on holiday. At their insistence she escorted the two sisters around the flat at 158 rue de Strasbourg which, although neither of them was in permanent residence, was owned by Simone and her sister Madeleine; it had proved a useful venue for her romantic trysts with Bernard. The Hettier sisters later claimed that the atmosphere in the place had been 'damp', especially in the kitchen, and they couldn't fail to notice that while the rest of the apartment was untidy and grubby through lack of use, the kitchen had obviously recently been scrubbed clean.

Enquiries revealed that Bernard Hettier had not returned to work after the weekend of 22–23 June, but they had received a call from a man claiming to be Bernard's friend to say that there had been a few problems with a holiday cottage they owned in the Vosges, and Bernard would be back in a few days.

It was at this stage that the police were obliged to agree that the evidence assembled by the Hettier family did put Bernard's disappearance in a suspicious light. For a start, his Renault car was missing, and so were a number of papers relating to his financial affairs; but he had taken none of his clothes, money or his cheque book, and a quick call through to his bank established that Hettier had not used his cash dispenser card.

On 9 July 1985 the police were sufficiently puzzled to call in the examining magistrate, in this case Judge Gilbert Thiel. Thiel, a notoriously thorough and tenacious man would, over the coming years, develop the case of Simone Weber into a personal crusade for justice. Among the list of useful witnesses that Judge Thiel interviewed as part of his investigation were Monsieur and Madame Haag. An elderly couple with little else to do with their time but gossip and keep tabs on the comings and goings of their neighbours, the Haags occupied the apartment below the Weber sisters' flat at rue de Strasbourg. On the evening of 22 June, the last day on which Bernard Hettier was seen alive, the Haags saw Simone Weber enter the building and manipulate a man who appeared to be drunk up the stairs to her flat. Later that same night the couple were awakened by a continuous mechanical sound that they thought might be a vacuum cleaner. Keeping vigil behind the lace curtains on the following Tuesday morning, Madame Haag was able to monitor Simone Weber as she carried no fewer than fourteen black plastic rubbish sacks followed by a brown suitcase down into the boot of her car.

Simone Weber. Again. Judge Thiel had been hearing that name a lot during his inquiry, and he was going to hear it a great many more times before his job was complete. He was going to hear it from the pharmacist who provided the then Madame Fixart with the deadly poison digitalis on a forged prescription; it had been just before Monsieur Fixart unexpectedly passed away. And most terrible of all, Judge Thiel was going to hear Simone Weber's name from the manager of the hire-shop where she conducted some business around the time of Bernard Hettier's disappearance. Simone had hired a concrete-cutter, a sort of older brother in the chain-saw family which would shear through concrete and steel as easily as a hot knife cuts butter. It wasn't for the manager to question Madame's need for such a piece of machinery, nor was he too perturbed when some days later she returned to say the cutter had been stolen from the back of her car; after all, Madame had volunteered the price of a new one.

Yes, Simone Weber was beginning to look as though she might be the pivot of this strange case, and Judge Thiel was prudent enough to see just what information Madame Weber herself could give without arousing her suspicions. And that is how the police came to be listening in to Simone's telephone calls to her sister Madeleine, and making notes on the increasingly urgent requirement to 'find a new school for Bernadette quickly'. Then a further conversation with an estate agent based in Cannes was intercepted. It transpired that Simone, using a false address and the name Chevalier, had been renting a garage down in Cannes. An official investigation was made by the local police, who discovered 'Bernadette' in her present 'school', because stored in the garage was an elderly Renault 4L – Bernard Hettier's elderly Renault 4L. In the back of the car was a concrete-cutter. No wonder Bernadette needed a new school! It was obvious that both Simone and Madeleine had some serious questions to answer.

It was on 15 September, about a week after Simone Weber was arrested, that an angler fishing on one of the Marne's tributaries at Poincy hauled from the river a waterlogged brown suitcase. It contained a male torso, the head and limbs cleanly removed, and a block of concrete. The human remains, although they could not be proved to be Hettier's, did share certain physical similarities with the missing man. The suitcase and the weight, however, were very significant. The former was identified as having belonged to Bernard Hettier and the latter bore a blue paint stain chemically identical with four samples of paint removed from around Simone Weber's house at Rosieres. Scientific evidence was also forthcoming from the 'stolen' concrete-cutter. Analysis of minute traces that remained between the saw's teeth proved to be human body tissue.

While all this activity had been going on in the world outside, Madame Weber languished in Nancy's Charles-III Prison. She made regular appeals for freedom from custody, and they were as regularly dismissed. The trial eventually opened in January 1991 and lasted for six weeks. The huge weight of evidence so skilfully assembled by Judge Thiel and the prosecutors was paraded before the court like the car of the juggernaut, though when the process ended, Simone stood convicted only of the *unpremeditated* murder of Bernard Hettier. The sentence passed by the president of the court was twenty years' imprisonment.

Perhaps it was only the cynical who came away from the proceedings with the feeling that it was not the sentence itself that was Simone Weber's real punishment, but rather, as one reporter suggested, to fade out of the spotlight on which she had become so reliant, now just an anonymous number inside the grey walls of Charles-III.

WEBSTER, Kate Shortly before seven on the morning of 5 March 1879 Henry Wheatley, a coal porter, was driving his horse and cart along the banks of the Thames. Near Barnes Bridge he spotted a wooden box lying half in and half out of the water. Overcome by curiosity Wheatley dismounted and dragged the box to dry ground. It was made of plain deal, had a hinged lid, and was secured with a cord, which he cut; the box lid fell back revealing a mass of mutilated flesh.

A horrified Henry Wheatley reported his find at the Barnes police station and Dr James Adams, the police surgeon, was summoned. As had been feared from the start, the flesh was identified as human; pieced together it formed almost the entire body of a woman. The head and a few lesser parts were missing, and most of the rest, judging by its parchment-like complexion and lack of decomposition, had been recently boiled.

Identification of the remains was impossible, and it was not until the box was recognized by young Robert Porter on 23 March that a connection was made with Mrs Julia Thomas who was known to be missing. This disappearance had caused no alarm at the time because the old lady was something of an eccentric who never resided for very long in one place. Since the death of her second husband in 1873 Mrs Thomas had lived alone at various addresses, the last being 2 Vine Cottages, Richmond. She was anxious to appear prosperous and genteel, and flaunted an extravagant wardrobe and fondness for jewellery. Excitable and vexatious, Mrs Thomas was reputedly a tartar to her servants, and none stayed with her for long.

It was strange, then, that in February 1879 this fussy, particular and over-cautious widow should have offered employment to one Kate Webster, without demanding references, and on the chance suggestion of a friend. That friend can have had only the slightest acquaintance with Webster, for she was a savage of a woman, an accomplished liar with a passionate temper, quick of wit and strong of body, whose life had been a chain of petty offences.

All Kate Webster's 'professional' instincts must have been aroused by Mrs Thomas, with her ostentation of wealth. Whether she took the job with the intent to commit a crime we will never know; perhaps she genuinely desired to lead an honest life of toil. But the atmosphere at Vine Cottages, strained from the start, quickly became explosive. On the one hand Mrs Thomas, prim, tactless and fault-finding; on the other Kate, rugged, clumsy, vicious and resentful. The servant shortly became rude and defiant, and her mistress grew increasingly alarmed and doubtful – in fact, she gave Kate notice to quit on Friday 28 February. Kate successfully negotiated a few more days, and Monday of the following week was agreed upon.

On Sunday 2 March 1879, Kate Webster returned late in the afternoon after a long session in the public house; she found Mrs Thomas dressed for church and most peeved at being kept waiting. Webster, inflamed with drink, flew into a terrible rage, showering the foulest language upon the horrified Mrs Thomas. When they eventually arrived at the Hill Street Presbyterian Hall, Mrs Thomas was pale, agitated and almost paralysed with fear. Nevertheless, after the Sacrament she returned home to spend that final night under the same roof as the appalling Kate Webster.

'We had an argument, which ripened into a quarrel, and I threw her from the top of the stairs to the ground floor. To stop her screaming I caught her by the throat, and in the struggle she choked.' This is how Kate later explained the death of Mrs

Thomas. From the evidence of a next-door neighbour, Mrs Ives, who had heard through the wall a solitary noise 'like the fall of a heavy chair', it seems more probable that Webster struck the old lady down with a single blow to the head. We can be more positive about what followed.

Kate laid Mrs Thomas, possibly still alive, at full length on the kitchen table. She cut off the head with a razor, and dismembered the rest with a meat saw and carving knife. The entrails were chopped up and burned, while the flesh was placed in the copper with water and boiled up to prevent identification. This work, including cleaning away the blood and tidying the dreadful mess in the kitchen, took all of Sunday night and until eleven the following morning.

Most of the body went into the box later found at Barnes. The head was put in a black handbag, while the odd bits left over, including a foot, were dumped on a manure heap at Crop Hill allotments in Twickenham. On the return journey, Kate looked in at the Hole in the Wall pub in Park Road, Richmond, where according to the proprietress, Mrs Hayhoe, she offered for sale two jars of fat, which she declared to be 'the best dripping'.

After more arcane housework that night, Kate Webster awoke to the crucial day in her plan, Tuesday 4 March. She dressed herself in one of her late mistress's silk gowns, put on her gold jewellery, and went to visit the Porters, a family living at Hammersmith who Kate had not seen for some years. She had been *longing* to see them again, she announced – to tell them her good news. Since last she had seen them, Kate had married a Mr Thomas, who was now dead, and her aunt had left her a nice house in Richmond which she was keen to sell. Perhaps Mr Porter could recommend a broker for the furniture? When she returned to Richmond, Kate was accompanied by Mr Porter and young Robert, who was to help her with 'a task'.

At first Kate carried the black handbag which had rested at her feet throughout afternoon tea; then, when she tired, it was entrusted to Robert, who later said he found it strangely heavy for so small an article. The party rested at the Oxford and Cambridge Arms by Hammersmith Bridge, at which point 'Mrs Thomas' as Webster was now calling herself, told the Porters she must take the handbag to a friend living in Barnes. She left abruptly, returning just twenty minutes later without the bag – exit the head of Julia Thomas.

Mr Porter left them at Hammersmith station and Robert and Kate travelled on to Richmond. There was a box, Kate told the youth, a box that had to be delivered to a friend who lived over the other side of Richmond Bridge; they could manage it together. So off they set, down Mount Ararat Road, lugging the dead weight awkwardly between them, the cords chaffing Robert's hands. Half-way across the bridge they rested on a seat in the recess to one side of the centre arch. This was where Kate had to meet her friend. Perhaps Robert would run back and wait for her? It was dark and lonely on the bridge, so the boy went back only as far as the next recess, from where he heard a loud splash in the water below. Suddenly Kate reappeared – she had seen her friend and handed over the box.

The disposal of the body accomplished, Kate next turned her attention to the furniture. Porter had kindly introduced 'Mrs Thomas' to his friend John Church, who agreed to make the necessary arrangements. It was on Tuesday 18 March, while the furniture was being loaded into the van, that Miss Ives popped out to ask Kate the whereabouts of her absent neighbour Mrs Thomas. Taken aback, Kate's powers of deceit momentarily deserted her. 'I don't know,' she blustered, 'I don't know.' Unnerved, Kate Webster panicked and fled to her home across the sea in Ireland. In doing so she left such a trail of clues that the police had no difficulty whatever in tracing her and bringing her back to justice.

After many ingenious attempts to implicate both Porter and John Church, Kate Webster finally confessed to her dreadful crime and was tried, convicted, and eventually hanged at Wandsworth Prison on Monday 30 June 1879.

WHALE, Ann *see* **PLEDGE, Sarah**

WILEY, Brenda Children killing members of their own family, particularly parents, seems, in criminological terms at least, to have reached almost epidemic proportions in the United States. Around California it has even been given an official name – 'West-Coast Syndrome' – and there are any number of examples to choose from. Ricky Kyle shot his millionaire father in 1983; Michael Miller eliminated his mother Marguerite in the same year, and only days later Eric Washington bludgeoned and strangled his mother to death in Long Beach. In the middle-class Los Angeles suburb of Grenada Hills, Thomas Tober executed his mother and his sister; and when Gerald and Vera Woodman drove into the garage of their Brentwood, California, home, they were shot dead by their sons Stewart and Neil. But it is not only on the West Coast that families are being decimated. Steven Benson killed his mother, sister and brother with a bomb in order to inherit the family fortune; military school cadet Harry de la Roche didn't want to go back to college so he shot his parents and two brothers in their beds; and Ronald 'Butch' DeFeo massacred his whole family in the celebrated Amityville horror.

But the one noticeable feature about all the cases listed above is that the slayings were committed by men. So do daughters not kill their parents? The answer is yes they do, though much less frequently; Brenda Wiley was one of those who did. It all started with much the same sort of trouble that most families with a teenage daughter face at some time or another – boyfriend trouble. At the time, in the summer of 1990, Brenda was fifteen years old, and like many fifteen-year-olds was obsessively in love. The object of these affections was eighteen-year-old Keith Santana. In fact, he was not a young man whom the Wileys took any exception to; until they caught the pair in bed together after Brenda sneaked Keith into the house in the middle of the night. It will come as no surprise to most parents that Mark and Bonnie Wiley were a lot less than happy. The boyfriend was thrown out of the house and Brenda was forbidden to see him again. Nor will it come as any surprise that Brenda and Keith continued to meet secretly; until Mark Wiley found out and Brenda was grounded. It happens all the time; kids get over it, everybody settles back in an uneasy truce until the next time. But with Brenda Wiley it was different; Brenda *really* resented it.

On 8 November 1990 Brenda and her fourteen-year-old brother Keith were in the house and Mrs Wiley was outside. Keith, as is the wont of younger brothers, was taunting his sister over some trifle as he had many times before. This time it cost him his life. Brenda suddenly snapped and smashed a bottle down on the lad's head, following up with a frenzied attack with a kitchen knife. When her mother came back into the house, Brenda savaged her too, crushing her skull and stabbing her thirty times. After making some attempt to clean the walls and floors of blood, Brenda invited her boyfriend over and confessed. It was all for him, she said, all for the love of him.

Later Brenda also confessed to the police, adding that it had been her intention to kill her father as well. Fortunately, the day she went berserk he was out at his job. Predictably, when it came to her trial, Brenda Wiley's attorney tried to persuade the court that at the time of the killings Brenda was temporarily insane, and it was alleged that she had twice tried to commit suicide. Equally predictably the state prosecutor claimed that Brenda was not insane, just very wicked; and that was the line the jury bought. They may have been confirmed in this opinion by the testimony of Brenda's boyfriend. According to his sworn evidence, Brenda had called him up a few days before the killings and asked him to help her kill her parents; he refused.

Brenda Wiley is now serving a term of life imprisonment with no possibility of parole for thirty years.

WILLIAMS, Margaret   Although the crime of which Mrs Williams was convicted took place in Austria, it is its only connection with that normally most peaceful of countries. For the rest, it was as English as they come.

In the spring of 1949 Montague Cyril Williams was on home leave from his Army posting in Klagenfeldt. While he was in England, Williams took up with a young woman and shortly afterwards they married. Now some marriages are said to be made in heaven, others in hell; for Cyril and Margaret Williams, marriage was made in the gin bottle. In short, Margaret only agreed to marry him because she was drunk, and by the time she came to her senses it was too late. So a bargain was struck in this loveless liaison; Cyril would not pester his wife for sex until she felt more passionately towards him. There have been more peculiar bases for a relationship, and but for the recurring interference of the demon drink the Williamses may well have grown together. As it was, they were no sooner back home at the Klagenfeldt Army base, than Mr and Mrs Williams were quarrelling. On 2 July 1949 the couple were downing drinks at the Grand Hotel in Anneheim; later that day, after they had returned to camp, they fell to fighting. Margaret stormed out of the house and joined some friends in a few more drinks. Cyril rounded up a couple of service pals and went in pursuit; between them they physically dragged Mrs Williams back to camp, where Cyril beat her up some more. It may have been the drink, it may have been the beatings, probably it was both, but Margaret Williams had had enough. Unfortunately, at just that time when the voice in her head told her that this would be the last time he ever hit her, Margaret's hand reached out and found itself closing round the knife on the table. Despite her efforts to get help to him, Cyril Williams bled to death from a perforated heart.

Margaret Williams stood trial back in England on 15 September 1949 at the Old Bailey. In truth, she should never have been convicted of murder; even Mr Justice Streatfield hinted that the jury might like to consider manslaughter, or possibly self-defence. But, in British law at least, the verdict of the jury is sacrosanct. And because they opted for a verdict of guilty of murder, the judge had no alternative but to pass the only sentence available to him – death. Thankfully, the Home Secretary commuted Margaret Williams' sentence to life imprisonment – which was almost certainly better than life with Cyril.

WILLIAMSON, Stella Old Stella Williamson was past seventy when she was taken into hospital, and when she was discharged back into the small cominunity of Gallitzin, Pennsylvania, she had suffered the amputation of one of her legs. Such major surgery is difficult enough to adjust to for the young, but at her age poor Stella simply couldn't cope, and within a few years she passed away with what good grace and dignity she could. To be honest, nobody paid it much attention. Stella Williamson had always been a very private person, almost reclusive, speaking to few and rarely venturing out save to the local church on Sunday. The fact that she was now resting beneath six feet of soil in God's little acre would hardly be noticed.

That was until they found the letter; an envelope marked 'to be opened in the event of my death' which had been discovered among Stella's papers during the search for her will. As a result of the contents, representatives from the local sheriff's office made a search of Stella's loft and found, just as the letter said they would, an old trunk. Inside the trunk were the promised five bundles wrapped in crumbling yellowed newspaper with dates between 1923 and 1933; and inside each of the bundles was the dried out body of an infant, their ages ranging from newly born to eight months old. That the woman who was believed by all to be a confirmed spinster should have given birth to five children was shock enough; but that she should have killed them and kept their remains with her through the years was almost beyond belief. But there they were, and more than fifty years on there was not much anybody could do about it.

The story created a sensation when it broke in 1980, but whether any more will ever be learned about the secret life of Stella Williamson we must wait and see.

WILSON, Mary Elizabeth There was hardly a good thing to be said about Mrs Wilson, not least because of the cruel way in which, having inflicted the excruciatingly painful death of poisoning with phosphorus on her husband of forty-four years, she went on to dispose of a lover and two further husbands.

At the time of her trial for the two latter murders, Mary Wilson was sixty-six years old, plump, arrogant and grasping; and with most of the least endearing characteristics of her working-class upbringing – notably the inclination to seek recreation in heavy drinking.

Mary's first husband had been John Knowles, a labourer, and the son of the household to whom she was in service. Displaying an early greed for everything, Mrs Knowles took John George Russell, a chimney sweep who lodged with them at Windy Nook, as a lover. By 1957 both were dead, both certified as the victims of 'natural causes'; both leaving their worldly goods to Mary – all £46 of it!

During the summer of 1957, Mary met Oliver James Leonard; she was sixty-four at the time and he was seventy-five, a retired estate agent. As with her previous 'attachments', it was money to which Mrs Wilson was attracted, a fact that she made no secret of when enquiring of Leonard's landlady: 'Has the old bugger any money?' Apparently he had – or at least sufficient to satisfy Mary Knowles. In a trice, she was Mrs Leonard, the marriage being solemnized in September 1957 at Jarrow Register Office; almost as quickly, Oliver Leonard fell ill. Thirteen days after the wedding Mrs Russell, a neighbour, was called in during the night and found Leonard in such a poor state that she was constrained to comment that she believed he might be dying. 'I think so too,' Mrs Leonard replied, 'I've called you because you will be handy if he does.' By the following morning Oliver Leonard was, indeed, dead, and after a cursory examination the doctor accounted for his sudden demise as due to myocardial degeneration and chronic nephritis. His wife had bettered her lot by £50.

The next death to occur by the widow Leonard's hand was that of Ernest Wilson. Wilson, like Oliver Leonard, had also reached his seventy-fifth year; like Leonard, he was fated not to reach his seventy-sixth. Mrs Leonard saw the immediate advantage of marriage when Ernest confided that in addition to being provident enough to have a fully paid-up insurance policy on his life, he also had £100 invested with the Co-op. No sooner had Mary moved into the rather squalid bungalow which Wilson rented from the council, than the old man suddenly died – of what the doctor diagnosed as 'cardiac muscular failure'.

It was only now that Mrs Wilson's 'jokes' – in poor taste even at the time – began to be seen in a decidedly sinister light. She had, for example, joshed with the undertaker that as she had put so much business his way, perhaps she was entitled to 'trade' price. Then at the modest reception after her marriage to Wilson, Mary had told the caterer: 'Save the left-over cakes – they will come in handy for the funeral,' adding later, 'Better not save them, I might give him a bit longer to live.'

Little surprise, then, that Mary Wilson came to the attention of the police; no surprise that the bodies of Messrs Leonard and Wilson were exhumed for post-mortem examination. The conclusion reached by pathologists Dr William Stewart and Dr David Price was that both men had died of phosphorus poisoning.

Mary Wilson was defended at her trial by Miss Rose Heilbron QC, who pointed out to the court that at that time phosphorus poisoning was relatively little known to forensic medicine – indeed, Dr Stewart had never seen a case previously and that as the rate of oxidization of phosphorus was then unknown, there was no reliable method of assessing how much of the poison had been ingested. It was advanced that both victims might have been taking sex-stimulant pills, one of whose ingredients was phosphorus. Miss Heilbron had also been wise enough to secure for the defence an expert medical witness of no less standing than Professor Francis Camps, later to become one of Britain's most celebrated forensic pathologists. Whilst Camps had not examined the two bodies in question, he was familiar with several instances of phosphorus poisoning, and stated that, in his opinion, this was not necessarily the direct cause of death in the cases of Leonard and Wilson.

Mary Wilson did not give evidence on her own behalf, which prompted Mr Justice Hinchcliffe to remark, rightly or wrongly, 'Has she helped us all she could?' As to the preposterous notion of sex-stimulant pills, his lordship suggested that it should be given 'as much weight as it deserves'.

Found guilty as charged, Mrs Wilson was sentenced to death, though in the event, her advanced years earned her the clemency she had done nothing to deserve. She served just four and a half years of a life sentence before dying in Holloway Prison, aged seventy.

It only remains to add that when the bodies of John Knowles and John George Russell were exhumed for pathological examination, they were found to contain appreciable traces of phosphorus.

WISE, Martha Hasel   The devil has been blamed for many things, and has become the scapegoat for many a brutal killer. Listen to this: 'It was the devil who told me to do it. He came to me when I was in the kitchen baking bread. He came to me while I was working in the fields. He followed me everywhere.' The speaker is Martha Hasel Wise, and at the time she was blaming Satan for her own misdeeds she was forty years of age and in police custody.

Martha was born in 1885, had married somewhere along the line, been widowed, and was living in poverty with her mother on a broken-down farm in Medina, Ohio. Then she fell in love. It was 1924, and to look at Martha you would have found it difficult not to agree with her mother that romance with the much younger Walter Johns was indeed 'capricious'. We do not know what Mr Johns thought about it, but he seems to have had no strong objections to such talk; but Martha was peeved as hell. In fact, on New Year's Eve 1924 she poisoned the old lady.

By now, Martha's 'cradle-robbing' had become something of a family joke, especially among the Geinkes – her aunt, uncle and cousins. In February 1925, Lily and Fred Geinke died suddenly; Martha had slipped arsenic into their coffee. Then she thought she might as well get rid of the whole damn family and have done with it, so out came the poison bottle again. This time Martha misiudged her doses, or the robustness of her victims, and although the remainder of the Geinke family were very ill indeed, they all lived to tell the tale. And it was to the police they told it.

Of course nobody really believed Martha's story about being followed around by the devil, and even when Walter Johns loyally tried to give it some credence by telling the court that during their love-making Martha barked like a dog, it served to make Martha look more comic than demonic.

At the end of her trial, Martha Wise, the woman they were calling 'America's Borgia', was convicted of first-degree murder and sentenced to life imprisonment.

WOOD, Catherine *see* **GRAHAM, Gwendolyn**

WOODWARD, Louise   It is a sad fact that, for all the talk of what Winston Churchill called 'the special relationship' between Britain and the United States, it doesn't take much to reveal the subsurface dislikes and irritations that lie between the two nations. The case of Louise Woodward is a good example. Throughout the teenager's odyssey through the labyrinthine US legal system, UK opinion polls were of the overall opinion that she was guiltless, while US polls on the same subject invariably leaned towards guilty . . . and a lot of bad blood and bile was spouted by tabloids and the opinionated on both sides of the Atlantic.

In November 1996, Louise Woodward from Elton in Cheshire successfully interviewed for the job of live-in-nanny for the Eappens, a well-to-do family in Boston, Massachusetts. Unfortunately, there were problems from the start. The 18-year-old, new to the US, wanted to stay up late and sample the Bostonian nightlife. The Eappens, on the other hand, told her that they wanted her back home no later than 11 p.m. Things got bad enough for Sunil and Deborah Eappen to draw up a set of their expectations from a nanny – the prime one being the 'safety and well-being' of their two children, baby Matthew and toddler Brendan.

On 4 February 1997, Louise Woodward called the emergency services and said that Matthew Eappen was having difficulty breathing. Rushed to hospital and put on a life-support machine, the eight-month-old baby died six days later. The autopsy showed that he had suffered a skull fracture and brain injuries. It was also noted that he had a month-old, untreated wrist fracture that had presumably gone unnoticed by both Louise and the Eappens.

The police arrested Louise and later claimed that the teenager made a verbal confession, stating that, because he would not stop crying, she had shaken Matthew and thrown him onto a pile of towels shortly before his breathing had become erratic; a confession Louise later vehemently denied ever making.

Whoever was telling the truth over the confession, it came as a shock to many when the Massachusetts State Prosecutor pressed a charge of first-degree murder against Woodward (implying, of course, that she had deliberately murdered the baby). In another shock, Louise was denied bail and sent to a maximum-security prison for women to await her trial – harsh treatment that infuriated the British press.

The trial was held the following October. Two doctors who had examined Matthew – surgeon Joseph Medsen and pathologist Gerard Feigin – gave evidence that, in their professional opinion, Matthew's skull fracture might have been sustained days or even weeks before the claimed 'shaking incident'. Feigin also stated that he had found no evidence that the baby had been shaken at all.

The defence then called the respected forensics expert Barry Scheck, who suggested that Matthew might have suffered from a genetic disorder that caused his skull to be over-prone to fracturing. Alternatively, he added, the two-year-old Brendan – the only other person in the Eappen house that night apart from Louise – might have caused the fracture.

At this stage it became clear to many just why the prosecution was pushing for the arguably overzealous charge of 'first-degree murder'. Under Massachusetts law, a charge of 'murder-one' cannot be reduced to manslaughter – the defendant is either deemed guilty or not guilty, the charge cannot be reduced. Given the evidence, manslaughter was the natural choice for the jury if they believed the 'shaking incident' story, but would they choose to find not guilty if denied this option? The prosecution was clearly going 'for all or nothing', and they won the gamble. Louise Woodward was found guilty of deliberately murdering Matthew Eappen, and was sentenced to life imprisonment – a minimum fifteen years in jail before getting even the possibility of winning a parole.

As it turned out, she served only 279 days in prison. Even the day after the verdict, a jury member admitted to the press that none of the jury members 'thought she tried to murder him'. An appeal was the obvious next step for Woodward and her supporters.

As it turned out, Judge Hiller Zobel, who had passed the life sentence on Louise, was one of those who had his doubts about the murder-one verdict. At an appeal hearing a few weeks later, he reduced the charge to manslaughter and, since Woodward had already spent the minimum term in jail for manslaughter (ironically because the prosecution had blocked bail before the trial) ordered her immediate release. She was forced to remain in Massachusetts pending the prosecution's appeal of the appeal verdict, but when this was quashed, she was allowed to return home to the UK. She is reported to have taken a law degree at a London university.

Did Louise Woodward kill – deliberately or otherwise – Matthew Eappen? She continues to deny the accusation and the Eappens continue to insist that she did. The gulf between the two viewpoints seems as wide and cold as the Atlantic itself.

WUORNOS, Aileen The first victim of the woman they labelled 'America's First Female Serial Killer' was fifty-one-year-old Richard Mallory, and his decomposed body was found in woods in December 1989. Mallory had been repeatedly shot with a small calibre gun. During the first few months of the following year five more bodies turned up in similar circumstances.

In June 1990, sixty-five-year-old missionary Peter Siems left his home in Jupiter, Florida, and headed along the Interstate 95 coast road through Daytona Beach; his body has never been found. However, on 4 July his grey Pontiac was involved in an accident, and witnesses running to the scene saw the two female occupants of the car flee from the wreck and disappear over the fields; from their descriptions police artists were able to compile a pair of likenesses which were broadcast nation-wide. It was not long before detectives came up with the names of twenty-seven-year-old Tyria J. Moore, and her lesbian lover Aileen 'Lee' Wuornos. In order to save her own skin, Ty Moore turned state's evidence and provided the police with enough information to enable undercover officers to stake out the bars and clubs around Daytona Beach in the hope of locating Aileen Wuornos – at a seedy bikers' bar which called itself the Last Resort, they got lucky.

The trial of Aileen Wuornos, by now dubbed by the media the 'Damsel of Death', opened at Deland, Florida, on 12 January 1992. Although she had made a videotape confession to seven killings, there was only one charge on the indictment – the first-degree murder of Richard Mallory. According to State Prosecutor John Tanner, Aileen had been plying her trade on the roadside when she was picked up by Mallory and driven along Interstate 4 to Daytona Beach, where Mallory pulled the car off the road into some woodland where they had sex before Aileen shot Mallory dead and hid his body. Aileen never denied any of this. What she claimed, however, was that the killing was self-defence. According to Aileen's story, Mallory tied her to the steering wheel, raped and sodomized her, and threatened to kill her if she kept struggling. She just managed to pull her gun from her purse as Mallory lunged forward at her. She insisted that Mallory was drunk and had been smoking marijuana. According to Aileen's attorney: 'What happened was bondage, rape, sodomy and degradation.'

It was a defence that attracted a measure of ridicule from the prosecution: 'She was a predatory prostitute,' John Tanner told the court. 'She killed out of greed. No longer satisfied with the ten, twenty, thirty dollars, she wanted it all. It wasn't enough to control his body, she wanted the ultimate – his car, his property, his life.'

This scenario was to a great extent supported by the evidence of Tyria Moore, who said in her testimony that on the evening of 30 November Aileen had come home the worse for drink, driving a new car. Later she announced she had just killed a man. Moore said: 'I didn't believe her.' Cross-examined, Ty Moore was adamant that her partner made no mention of being raped or beaten, nor seemed particularly upset about anything. Tanner's implication was clear: here was a cold-blooded, emotionless killer who, far from suffering the trauma of 'rape, sodomy and degradation' had simply shot one of her clients for his car and the contents of his wallet.

It was clearly the explanation favoured by the jury who, on 27 January, after a ninety-five-minute retirement, found Aileen Wuornos guilty as charged. As she was led from the dock, Wuornos turned on the jury, screaming: 'Scumbags of America!' before being hustled out. Two days later Judge Blount sentenced Aileen Wuornos to death. In May 1992, she was tried and convicted of three more of her seven admitted killings. After Judge Thomas Sawaya sentenced Wuornos to death she yelled: 'Thank you, I'll go to heaven now, and you will rot in hell.'

The Wuornos story spawned two movies, an opera and several books before she was executed by lethal injection on 9 October 2002. Shortly after her death, an anonymous joker posted a message on a website that was hosting an online discussion about the Wuornos execution. Signed Satan, it simply read: 'Umm . . . Could you guys take her back?'

Z

ZWANZIGER, Anna Maria Born Anna Shoenleben in Buremberg, Germany, in 1760, she was courted by and eventually married a lawyer named Zwanziger. By the time he collapsed and died, Zwanziger had drunk his way through every last pfennig of his earnings and their savings as well, leaving the widow nothing but debts and a bleak future as a domestic servant. After too many years of thankless, back-breaking, soul-destroying drudgery, the once beautiful, once vivacious Anna Maria had become a twisted, spiteful harridan, old before her years.

She was in service at the time to a judge named Glaser who, though he had not yet altered his will, had nevertheless separated from his wife and was about to disinherit her. With the cunning born of hatred Anna Maria sought, and at least temporarily achieved, a reconciliation between Judge Glaser and his estranged wife. Within weeks the unfortunate woman was dead, and before anyone could say 'poison', the widow Zwanziger had movèd on. Moved into the service of a middle-aged judge named Grohmann. Although she proved a loyal and devoted servant, Anna Maria was not fated to share in her master's fortune, for he announced his forthcoming marriage, and the piqued domestic found no alternative but to dispose of her employer forthwith; and just for the fun of it she poisoned a few of her fellow servants as well.

Frau Zwanziger's luck nearly ran out when she tried to poison the already ailing wife of her next employer, another judge, named Gebhard. Although his wife complained to judge Gebhard that the housekeeper was trying to poison her, he dismissed the accusation as nonsense and Frau Gebhard shortly perished; she was followed into her grave by the Gebhards' baby. Even then it was not until the judge himself began to suffer uncommonly bad stomach upsets, which seemed to be connected with the strange sediment in the bottom of his brandy glass, that he parcelled up a number of suspect comestibles and sent them to the apothecary for analysis. The contents of the salt cellar alone proved to be almost pure arsenic, and when Frau Gebhard and her child were exhumed, they also contained uncommonly large quantities of the same poison.

Anna Maria Zwanziger was taken into custody in Bayreuth in October 1809. Of course, she denied all the accusations made against her, but when she was proved to be in possession of a number of incriminating packets of white arsenic the dour domestic broke down and confessed. She was put to the headsman's sword in 1811.

Alphabetical Index

STEINHEIL, Jeanne-Marguerite (France)

TARNOWSKA, Countess Maria (Russia)
TERRELL, Bobbie Sue Dudley (USA)
THOMAS, Sarah Harriet (England)
THOMPSON, Edith, and BYWATERS, Frederick (England)
THORNTON, Sara (England)
TIERNEY, Nora Patricia (England)
TILFORD, Lizzie (Canada)
TINNING, Marybeth Rose (USA)
TOPPAN, Jane (USA)
TREVIS, Tina (England)
TURNER, Lise Jane (New Zealand)

VELGO, Marie Havlick (Czechoslovakia)
VIDAL, Ginette (France)

WADDINGHAM, Dorothea Nancy (England)
WAGNER, Waltraud, *et al*. (Austria)
WARDLAW SISTERS (USA)
WARMUS, Carolyn (USA)
WEBER, Jeanne (France)
WEBER, Simone (France)
WEBSTER, Kate (England)
WHALE, Ann *see* PLEDGE, Sarah
WILEY, Brenda (USA)
WILLIAMS, Margaret (Austria)
WILLIAMSON, Stella (USA)
WILSON, Mary Elizabeth (England)
WISE, Martha Hasel (USA)
WOOD, Catherine *see* GRAHAM, Gwendolyn
WOODWARD, Louise (USA)
WUORNOS, Aileen (USA)

ZWANZIGER, Anna Maria (Germany)

Geographical Index

(by location of murders)

Australia
GRILLS, Caroline (1947–53)
LEE, Jean (1949)
MILLER, Charlotte (1980)
MITCHELL, Pauline, and HEADLEY, Peter (1981)
MOORE, Helen Patricia (1980)
RENDALL, Martha (1907–9)

Austria
ANGELS OF DEATH
MAREK, Martha (1932–7)
WAGNER, Waltraud *et al.* (1988–9)
WILLIAMS, Margaret (1949)

Belgium
BECKER, Marie Alexandrine (1930s) GODFRIDA, Sister
  (1978)

Canada
DICK, Evelyn (1946)
HARPER, Katie (1959)
TILFORD, Lizzie (1935)

Channel Islands
DE LA MARE, Gertrude (1935)

Czechoslovakia
VELGO, Marie Havlick (1936)

England
AHLUWALIA, Kiranjit (1989)
ALLEN, Margaret (1948)
ALLITT, Beverley (1991)
ANSELL, Mary (1899)
ARDEN, Alice (1550)
BARBER, Susan (1981)
BARNEY, Elvira Dolores (1932)
BARTLETT, Adelaide (1885)
BATEMAN, Mary (1808)
BAXTER, Jeannie (1913)
BELL, Mary Flora (1968)
BLANDY, Mary (1751)
BRANCH, Elizabeth and Mary (1740)
BRYANT, Charlotte (1935)
BYRON, Kitty (1902)
CALVERT, Louie (1926)
CHANNEL, Mary (1703)
CHESHAM, Sarah (19th century)
CHRISTOFI, Styllou Pantopiou (1954)
CHUBB, Edith Daisy (1958)
CONROY, Teresa Miriam (1953)
COTTON, Mary Ann (1872)
COWE, Mary (1913)
DADDOW, Jean (1992)
DUFFY, Renee (1948)
DURKIN, Diana Jade (1984)
DYER, Amelia Elizabeth (1896)
EDMUNDS, Christiana (1871)
ELLIS, Ruth (1955)
FAHMY, Marie-Marguerite (1923)

BESSARABO, Hera *see* MYRTEL, Hera
BOMPARD, Gabrielle, and EYRAUD, Michel (1889)
BOUVIER, Léone (1952)
BRINVILLIERS, Marie Marguerite (1666–76)
CAILLAUX, Henriette (1914)
CHEVALLIER, Yvonne (1951)
DUBUISSON, Pauline (1952)
FAVRE-BULLE, Jeanne (1929)
JEGADO, Hélène (19th century)
LABBE, Denise (1954)
MYRTEL, Hera (1914)
NOZIÈRE, Violette (1934)
PAPIN, Christine and Lea (1933)
PIVAIN, Hugette, and MONTIGNY, Emile (1980)
ROUSSEAU, Rosella (1909)
SCIERRI, Antoinette (1924)
STEINHEIL, Jeanne-Marguerite (1908)
VIDAL, Ginette (1972)
WEBER, Jeanne (1905–8)
WEBER, Simone (1985)

Germany
BRUHNE, Vera (1960)
DARTSCH, Sylvia, and SABEIKOV, Heidemarie (1971)
DRYLAND, Christine (1992)
GOTTFRIED, Gesina Margaretha (19th century)
LEHMANN, Christa (1954)
RICHTER, Ursula (1972)
SABEIKOV, Heidemarie *see* DARTSCH, Sylvia
ZWANZIGER, Anna Maria (18th century)

Hungary
ANGEL MAKERS OF NAGYREV (1914–29)

India
FULLAM, Augusta Fairfield (1911)

HARTSON, Dorothy (1978)

United States
ADAMS, Millicent (1962)
ANARGEROS, Sophie (1950)
ARCHER-GILLIGAN, Amy (1913–17)
ARMISTEAD, Norma Jean (1975)
ARRINGTON, Marie Dean (1968)
BANISZEWSKI, Gertrude Wright (1965)
BARFIELD, Velma (1969–78)
BEAR, Suzan and Michael *see* CARSON, Susan and James
BECK, Martha, and FERNANDEZ, Raymond (1949)
BOLTON, Mildred (1936)
BORDEN, Lizzie (1892)
BRENNAN, Inez (1948–9)
BRODERICK, Elizabeth (1989)
CARSON, Susan and James (1981–3)
CLARK, Lorraine (1954)
CRANE, Cheryl (1958)
CRIMMINS, Alice (1965)
DOSS, Nannie (1920s–1954)
DOWNS, Elizabeth Diane (1983)
FALLING, Christine (1980–2)
FERRARA, Florence (1942)
GBUREK, Tillie *see* KLIMEK, Tillie
GIBBS, Janie Lou (1966–7)
GRAHAM, Barbara (1953)
GRAHAM, Gwendolyn Gail, and WOOD, Catherine (1987)
GUNNESS, Belle (1900–8)
HAHN, Anna Marie (1930s)
HILLEY, Audrey Marie (1975–8)
HOUSDEN, Nina (1947)
JONES, Genene (1981)
JUDD, Winnie Ruth (1931)
KLIMEK, Tillie (1914–21)
LYLES, Anjette (1958)
PUENTE, Dorothea (1982–8)

Note

Although 'Killer Couples' is more properly a separate study, examples have been included where either the female partner plays the dominant role (as in the case of Ruth Snyder and Henry Judd Gray), or where she plays a vital active role (as in the case of Myra Hindley and Ian Brady).